Innovations and Issues in Education

Planning for Competence

Innovations and Issues in Education

Joseph F. Callahan

Leonard H. Clark

Jersey City State College

Macmillan Publishing Co., Inc.
New York

Collier Macmillan Publishers
London

To Jane E. Callahan *and* Maria A. Clark

Copyright © 1977, Macmillan Publishing Co., Inc.

Printed in the United States of America

All rights reserved. No part of this book may be reproduced or transmitted in any form or by any means, electronic or mechanical, including photocopying, recording, or any information storage and retrieval system, without permission in writing from the Publisher.

Macmillan Publishing Co., Inc.
866 Third Avenue, New York, New York 10022

Collier Macmillan Canada, Ltd.

ISBN 0–02–318050–1

Printing: 1 2 3 4 5 6 7 8   Year: 7 8 9 0 1 2 3

Preface

The definitions of *innovations* and of *issues* for the purposes of this volume are indeed very general. It is not intended that these words generate great discussion but that they will serve to focus the readers' attention upon novel factors pertaining to education. If the traditional classroom with its single teacher and twenty-five students is looked upon as routine, anything that differs from that pattern may be accepted as novel.

The graduating of young citizens who are prepared to play a role in a democratic society and to grapple with crucial social issues is the thrust of Modules 6, 7, 8, and 12. Decades of debate, of criticism, and of change have brought the schools to a serious point of decision in the denouement of the twentieth century. Whether new teachers will be able to adapt to the massive forces impinging upon the school will determine not only the future of traditional efforts but also whether or not the school as an institution shall survive.

Scattered throughout this text are references to various novel factors that have been tried. Do not be disconcerted by the passing references in each module to topics that are treated in greater detail in other modules. The references, even though slightly repetitious, were retained to provide some ongoing review as you study, serving to test your recall of specific features described in depth elsewhere.

J. F. C.
L. H. C.

Contents

To the Student   1

1 **Process of Change**   3
Team Teaching / Differentiated Staffing / Flexible Modular Scheduling

2 **Individual Differences**   33
Individualized Instruction / Nongrading / Continuous Progress / Independent Study / Sequential Units

3 **Institutional Innovations**   55
Interaction Analysis / Behavioral Objectives / School Consortiums / Open Schools / Alternative Education / Student Governance / Teachers' Governance

4 **Computer Technology Innovations**   77
Gaming and Simulation / Programmed Instruction / Computer-assisted Instruction

5 **School System Innovations**   103
Accountability / Performance Contracts / Alternative Schools / Educational Vouchers

6 **Crucial Social Issues**   131
Racism in American Education / Desegregating the Schools / Urban School System

7 **Crucial Educational Issues**   149
Traditionalism versus Modernism / Censorship / Race and Ethnic Re-

lations / Financing the Schools / Compulsory Attendance / Community School / Impact of Leisure / Role of Athletics

8 **Crucial Emerging Issues**   173
Student Power / Teacher Power / Role of the Courts / Sex Education / Religion and the Schools / Alternative Education

9 **Organizational Innovations**   193
Mini-Courses / School Within a School / Block-of-Time Scheduling / Career Education Concept

10 **Trends in Organizing for Instruction**   219
Comprehensive High School / Regional-Vocational-Technical Variation / Middle School / Tracking and Phasing

11 **Curriculum-Based Trends**   247
Structure of Discipline Movement / Discovery and Inquiry Method / Humanism and the Humanities

12 **Trends in Education for Democratic Living**   271
Extreme Instructional Viewpoints / Moderate Instructional Systems

Post Test Answer Key   299

To the Student

Welcome to an adventure in learning.

Now that you have begun to think seriously about a career in teaching, it is our guess that you will find adventures of this sort very helpful in planning to meet the challenges that await you in the classroom. It seems safe to predict that not only will you increase your background in educational theory and methodology as you work your way through these modules, but also you will improve your chances of becoming an effective teacher when the time arrives to put theory learned into practice.

Probably you have not encountered many books organized as this one, calling for such active participation on your part. From this point forward, you are expected to become a sensitive, self-motivated learner engaged in making frequent and sound judgments about your learning. You will be the one to control the rate of progress through the various modules and you will decide when you have mastered the knowledge presented in each. We have tried to help by (1) listing the objectives of each module, (2) providing a comprehensive set of questions to test your mastery at the end of each module, and (3) providing an answer key for your use in evaluating progress. Those with little time to spend on study can move through the various modules and finish quickly so long as they study attentively and demonstrate the mastery called for on each test. Slower-paced individuals, who wish to ponder and probe various areas and who decide to read extensively from the selected readings listed in each module, can establish a pace that suits their purposes.

It is not intended that any student will be able to prepare himself for a teaching career solely by completion of this kind of study program. Teaching is a human activity. It deals with people, with children, parents, and fellow professionals. It involves various kinds of knowledge, judgments, and decision making; it requires communications skills, human relations techniques, and a host of other attributes for the cultivation of which human interaction and professional expertise are necessary. But faithful and zealous use of this learning tool will add depth and meaning to your classroom sessions in education courses. Mastery of these modules will carry you beyond the initial steps of preparation so that you may place into context more of the campus lectures about education which you hear, and ask questions about schools and students that go beyond the layman's level of significance.

The sections of the book are called modules, for essentially they are self-contained units that have cognitive values by themselves. Each module contains a rationale, a list of objectives, a post test, an answer key, and a list of selected readings. The rationale attempts to establish the purpose of each module and, in some cases, the link with other aspects of pedagogical knowledge. The objectives inform you very specifically what you should know and be able to do as a consequence of your study of the module. The test and the key inform you of your progress toward module mastery. The general study plan recommended is as follows:

1. Read the rationale to acquaint yourself with the task you are addressing and, if possible, with how this module fits among the others that you will study.
2. Examine carefully the module objectives. Find out what will be expected of you upon completion of your study.
3. Read through the module, checking back from time to time to see how well you are mastering the objectives. Review what you do not understand.
4. Take the Post Test. Evaluate your success by using the answer key. Where your answer differs from that of the author, search out the sentence or paragraph in the text that confirms your answer or his.
5. If you score less than 85 per cent on any test, reread and retake the test until your mastery improves.
6. Try out your knowledge by exposing yourself to some of the suggested reading. Your progress should accelerate as you bring more and more knowledge to each book that you read.
7. Engage in interaction with fellow students, professors, and members of your family on the topics studied, whenever possible.
8. Enjoy the experience. The profession needs zealous seekers of knowledge who enjoy learning and who, in the process, develop a capacity for infecting other people with the same "felicitous virus."

Process of Change

Joseph F. Callahan

Jersey City State College

module1

Team Teaching / Differentiated Staffing / Flexible Scheduling

RATIONALE

It used to be possible in our country to forecast with considerable accuracy what the schools of the future would be like decades in advance. Experienced students of education, by examining courses and programs of study in vogue, had only to focus their attention on the improvement and expansion of what already existed and demonstrate how more of the same might be achieved in order to delineate, fairly clearly, the classroom of the future. In those days, the commonly accepted axiom was that approximately fifty years were required for an educational innovation to gain full acceptance.

Today, no one can safely predict what the classrooms will be like even a year or two in advance. So much change has happened in the world, in our country, and in our communities within the last decade that pedagogical prophecy has run onto lean times. Forecasters today must consider so many more variables and allow for so many more shades of difference than ever before that forecasts are made only reluctantly or on a very tentative basis.

When prophecy was easy, preparing to teach was not complicated either. Research scholars who had observed successful teachers in action in the classroom and had arrived at conclusions regarding the virtues, skills, and knowledge they possessed, designed sequences of courses for study in college that would yield these qualities for postulant teachers. With the advent of almost universal concern, however, about the schools and teaching, the attitudes of teachers and the format of teacher-preparation programs changed. Interest in changing with the times and retooling for a new age became more common. Certitude vanished about the best route to take toward the achievement of our national goals regarding society and education. The teacher-preparation programs became much broader-based so as to prepare the future teacher to develop more flexibility. Each new teacher, it was obvious, would need to be as able in all facets of teaching as were those who had preceded him. In addition, however, he would have to be more aware of current events and of the impact of these events on the students of the future in order to match strides with the times. Today, the novice in preparation must equip himself to fit comfortably upon graduation into the school structure as it functions in the present. At the same time he must also become knowledgeable enough about society's drift and shifting values so as to be capable of modifying his teaching behavior when the appropriate time arrives.

The modules in this section will focus upon several of the innovations which appear to be capturing the attention of schools and schoolmen today. All have been tried and appear to offer promise for the schools of tomorrow. Our attempt will be to present the theoretical basis for these innovations so that you can prepare yourself to render judgments concerning the promise each contains for you, for your potential teaching community, and for your prospective students.

OBJECTIVES

In this module we shall consider several concepts about innovations and change in general and then focus on three specific innovations which have significance: team teaching; differentiated staffing; flexible modular scheduling. Often these three will all be parts of the same school program, implemented either to solve problems faced by the school or to improve the teaching performance of school personnel and the learning opportunities for the students.

Your main goal in studying this module will be to discover how you might have to function if you are employed by a school using one, two, or all three of these innovations. Upon the completion of your study of this module you should be able to perform all of the following objectives.

Specific Behavioral Objectives

1. Write a definition of team teaching that contains at least five subelements distinctive of the concept.
2. Cite ten advantages of team teaching over conventional classroom teaching.
3. Cite a minimum of five potential difficulties built into the framework of the team teaching concept and looked upon as disadvantages.
4. Select appropriate answers in the twenty-question, multiple-choice post test with no more than three errors.
5. Cite at least five reasons why you should study about educational innovations.
6. Cite five statements concerning individual differences attributed to research scientists.
7. Explain the *form follows function* axiom as it pertains to education.
8. Define vertical school organization, and in one sentence explain how it has worked in the past.
9. Describe horizontal structure in the school, and cite three methods used to structure horizontally.
10. Draw a diagram illustrating the concept of differentiated staffing.
11. Define single salary scale; cite two benefits accruing to teachers because of its use, and at least one drawback.
12. Write a paragraph illustrating how teacher status can be enhanced through use of the differentiated staffing concept.
13. Define a module of time and indicate the number of modules in a seven hour day using a unit that you devise.
14. Define a Carnegie unit and write a paragraph describing how it came into being and universal acceptance.
15. Define and describe module stacking and module stringing.
16. Cite five advantages postulated by proponents of flexible modular scheduling.
17. Cite three disadvantages or difficulties inherent in the concept of modular scheduling that are readily apparent to you.

MODULE TEXT

Process of Change

Woven into the fabric of the great American experiment in universal education is the fundamental belief that any system devised by man is infinitely perfectable. No matter how good the system at its inception, and despite the excellence of its current products, improvements can be made and excellence can be refined.

As a consequence, as the history of education reveals, hundreds of attempts have been made to modify the teaching-learning process for the better. Some of these efforts were modest, evolutionary innovations, designed to change the attitudes of teachers gradually over the years. Other efforts were more revolutionary in tone and content, intended to effect more immediate and radical modification.

The Sputnik Era. One of the most startling happenings in recent history, the launching of Sputnik, the Russian spacecraft, in 1957, provoked some of the most revolutionary proposals. Whereas many previous events and proposals had led educators to tinker with and polish what already existed in order to transform the schools gradually, the spirit of the post-Sputnik era tended toward the revolutionary, aiming toward drastic changes, based on new principles. In some instances, the thrust was in the direction of throwing out prior philosophy and practices almost totally in order to begin the preparation for a "brand new world." Giant strides that had been made in communications, transportation, and electronics, and the rapid increase in the growth of accumulated knowledge all appeared to support the efforts of the apostles of change.

Most of the schools, however, in this postwar period, continued to operate in a business-as-usual fashion. The basic organizational pattern for most schools remained the grade, and for many the curriculum was essentially what it had been in less complicated times. School systems scheduled certain subjects for mastery in each grade and appointed a teacher to meet with groups of students five days a week in periods lasting forty-five to fifty minutes to accumulate the number of Carnegie units required for graduation. Study halls, library work, and outside assignments remained essentially as they had been.

Implementors of Change. Creative teachers, perennially, have attempted to adapt their classroom behavior to new knowledge as it has emerged. Generally, theirs has been a search for the most effective teaching-learning climate and, like true artists, they have experimented and modified.

More pedestrian practitioners, lacking the genius or the drive of the teacher-artists, have attempted to keep pace by developing into "band wagon" followers. These teachers have followed the progress of the experimenters in other districts and, being interested in the acclaim accorded the innovator, have adapted their efforts to the new designs.

Problems have resulted, as a consequence, because of the conflicts that have ensued within school families. Factions of experienced teachers have resisted change, opting instead for a perpetuation of everything that has previously met with success. Other factions, attempting to introduce new theories or add new methods to the traditional school structure, have met with less success perhaps than their projects merited because of the impediments that the established structure has placed in the path of innovative practices. Still other factions have attempted to transplant modifications which were meeting with success elsewhere, without attending to the necessary preparation of the community, the building, the staff, the finances, the faculty, and the learners, and as a result have caused severe disruption for pupils, staff, and community.

Complications Resulting from Change. Since the publicly supported school is a social institution, almost every change in society invites proposals for change in the educational process. Inevitably, the problems faced by society become the problems of the school, and in this present era society as never before is providing critical challenges to the entire educational enterprise. Parents of children attending the schools become active as pressure groups to induce change as well as to resist change; so do politicians, sociologists, and the students themselves.

As a consequence, schools established upon older guidelines, shaped by a select and virtually homogenous clientele with little relevance to the diverse learning population of this new era, are forced to contemplate modifications at a disconcerting rate. The introduction of some innovations was facilitated for a time by the postwar baby boom of the 1940s and 1950s. As new communities were established and as old neighborhoods swelled with new students, new buildings and additions to old structures were authorized. With the new construction came opportunities for departures from what had been and attempts to capture the essence of what might be.

The findings of the behavioral scientists, however, established the foundation for many of the changes that were proposed. Their research documented the belief that real differences did indeed exist among individuals relative to their ability to master cognitive learning. These differences affected mastery of the subject matter that was studied, as well as the interaction of student with teacher and with other students. A good method in one discipline was not necessarily good in another. As a matter of fact, a good method of teaching an introductory course might not be at all satisfactory for teaching an advanced course in that same subject. An important finding of the researchers was that not all children are equally ready for learning content at the same age, nor will they be affected positively by the same procedures. Pupils do not all learn in the same way and their rate of mastery depends upon their individual capacities. The conclusion of these scientists was that instruction must be geared to each child's individual cognitive level if it is to be meaningful to him.

Impacts of Change. Part of the difficulty faced by the groups agitating for or against change stemmed from the fact that, like the blind men describing the elephant, each one was focusing upon a different component of the school. Each group pushed for a goal or resisted action in the context of its own perspective and generalized concept of the school and its purpose.

Those involved as agents in the change process, however, must broaden their perspectives as they inquire and must delve in great detail into the ramifications of the effects of change on all components of the schooling process. They must recognize that modification affecting functions and aims, school organization, students, curriculum, school staff, materials and media in teaching, school building, or methods may affect all of the other components and must be examined for impact.

Form and Function Considerations. The aims and goals of education should be the foundation of all that affects the schools. All consideration of current activities and all proposals for change must be examined in light of the support they will lend toward fulfillment of the school's function and realization of the school's goals.

In the field of architecture, the axiom upon which building design is based is that *form follows function*. That is, the purpose that the building is to serve should determine the kind of structure it shall be. In education, this axiom translates as follows: All components of the educational enterprise should enable the school to perform the function intended for it and thus facilitate the satisfying of aims and the reaching of goals which the school purports to reach. Changes which inhibit fulfillment of function or achievement of aims and goals are either illusory gains or are ignobly conceived.

Supporters of today's schools view the function as remaining essentially the same as it has always been. To meet their demands and expectations, very little needs to be changed except a course here or there and an increase in the amount of quality teaching available. Critics of education, however, call into question the contemporary function of the schools. Some maintain that the function has changed so drastically in the last decade that the school as we have known it is as out of place in the twentieth century as is the stagecoach for long-distance travel. For these critics, nothing short of elimination of the public schools will suffice. In their stead should appear storefront schools, free schools, open schools, community schools, proprietary schools supported by voucher payments, schools without walls, and so on.

The agitation and debate resulting from the attacks of such critics should prove very helpful in the long run. Such criticism should focus attention on the fact that the expectations of many citizens are delusions; that no institution is capable of accommodating itself to so many diametrically opposed demands; that before intelligent growth can be expected in the future, serious consideration must be given to a reaffirmation of previously established functions, goals, and aims or to the substitution of new or more acceptable functions, goals, and aims.

Organization of School. Some confusion arises from the failure to differentiate between the vertical and horizontal aspects of school organization. The former is the classifying and moving of students upward from admission to a point of departure; the latter is the placement of students into groups at any point on the vertical continuum for the purpose of instruction.

VERTICAL ORGANIZATION. Historically, students have moved from one grade to the next annually as they have progressed through school. Upon having mastered the subject matter and the skills earmarked for the year, students have been promoted annually for twelve years until their efforts have culminated in graduation from high school.

To assist students in their progression through the grades, textbooks have been provided for each subject at each annual level. Teachers who have been trained and certified to guide students in the first six grades have become known as elementary teachers, and those who have chosen to work in the upper grades have been classified as secondary teachers. Teachers working in schools which contain kindergarten through grade eight levels generally have been required to have elementary certification.

HORIZONTAL ORGANIZATION. Horizontally, students have been grouped for instruction in every grade in a number of ways. If they remained in one room, with one teacher, with all students having reached approximately the same chronological age, they were said to have been in a self-contained classroom. Elementary teachers in rooms of this sort have taught all of the subjects to all of the students in that room.

In the upper grades, students each day have faced a series of teachers who each specialized in a subject. In this departmentalized school, secondary teachers have moved from class to class for units of time called periods and assumed responsibility for teaching their subject specialty to each class group.

In some schools, efforts have been made to group the children of each grade according to ability as an aid to more effective and efficient instruction. In these schools, tests are administered to ascertain the potential, over-all ability or the actual achievement of each child. Students with similar academic potential or achievement are placed in the same classes or groups. Such grouping is called *homogeneous*. If, instead, pupils are assigned to rooms or groups on no basis other than grade level, the grouping is called *heterogeneous*.

Curricular Change. In some schools students are grouped in classes for instruction in the separate subjects. This type of horizontal structure is characteristic of the *subject matter curriculum*. Other schools organize pupils on the basis of problems without regard for subject matter distinctions, in clusters known as *problem-centered groups*.

To describe the over-all organizational pattern of any school, consequently, it is necessary to include a reference to both its vertical and its horizontal aspects. A school may be graded and self-contained, graded and departmentalized, graded with ability grouping, or graded with heterogeneous grouping. The terms *non graded* or *continuous progress* (treated in Module 2) may be substituted in these pairs for graded if the vertical structure encourages upward mobility in other ways than at traditional annual intervals.

School Staff Changes. Other terms may be added to these pairs to describe more clearly the horizontal organization of a school. If, for example, changes are made in allocating teacher responsibility for pupil learning, the distinguishing term may be *team teaching*. If the difference consists of more flexible use of time and personnel, the distinguishing term may be *modular scheduling*. If the emphasis is upon the utilization of teaching staff and competent lay citizens for specialized purposes, the distinguishing term may be *differentiated staffing*. It should be remembered, however, that these terms all refer to *horizontal structuring* and that they are not mutually exclusive of the others in connotation.

Team Teaching

Team teaching takes place when two or more teachers jointly share the responsibility for directing and evaluating the learning of a common group of students. As an attempt to secure better instruction for a group, the team approach appears to hold much promise. Because, however, of the built-in hazards connected with shared responsibilities and modifications of teaching design, the promise may not always be realized.

The theoretical design for the teaching team encompasses such attributes as (1) role differentiation of team members, (2) common time for planning, (3) flexibility of schedule, (4) variations in the size of student groups, (5) multiple uses of building space, (6) capitalization on use of team talents and equipment resources, (7) continued professional growth of teaching personnel, (8) development of teaching specialists, (9) achievement of unity of educational purpose through a focus as a team on differences among students, (10) on-the-job training for inductees, (11) integration of learning in a meaningful fashion, and (12) removal of road blocks to the progress of students. Each of these concepts shall be treated separately later in this module.

The literature concerning team teaching describes (1) single subject teams, (2) interdisciplinary teams, (3) student group teams, (4) equal partner teams, (5) hierarchical teams, and (6) bogus teams. Each of these types of teams reflects the convictions of the educators involved in the innovation. Departures from the theoretical design may be necessitated by planning limitations, financial limitations, space limitation, or reluctance to accept all of the philosophical ramifications of the theory.

Much of the literature is devoted to debunking the theoretical design or to denigrating the accomplishments of some of the schools that claim to be using team teaching. For teachers involved in establishing teams, these discussions make profitable reading because they can contribute to the understandings necessary for the inception of an effective, efficiently operating team. We shall not digress in this module to consider the merits of the various claims; our mission is not to discuss the semantics involved, but to get at the essence of the concept.

Now let us examine each of the twelve attributes of team teaching in order to establish the broad parameters of the concept.

Role Differentiation. When we move away from the traditional concept of telling, assigning, reciting, and testing as the description of the teaching act, we find that there are many roles which a teacher is expected to fill in successfully discharging professional responsibilities. He must at times function as a

1. Diagnostician: able to analyze the conditions affecting the students' learning and to discern the cause for lack of success.
2. Decision maker: able to set goals, to state behavioral objectives, to plan and help implement change in the school and school system.
3. Prescription maker: able to design exercises aimed at strengthening or remedying weaknesses.
4. Cooperator: able to work with students, with staff colleagues, with teams, with parents, with administrators.

5. Strategist: able to plan the best route for each student through the broad curriculum and through special aspects of school life.
6. Manager: able to orchestrate the various resources that are brought to bear on the student's learning, including staff aides and assistants, media, materials, packages, and experiences.
7. Facilitator: able to use group dynamics, independent study, research, and a variety of field experiences to improve learning rate.
8. Guide: able to work with students in selecting the right experiences, in stimulating and motivating creativity, in employing empathy, warmth, and understanding.
9. Evaluator: able to judge the success of the teaching, to observe changes in behavior, to transmit self-evaluation skills as a part of the learning process.
10. Scholar: able to keep acquainted with the resources in the field, and capable of adapting them for the utilization of students.
11. Actor: able to present prepared material with dramatic flair and effect.
12. Technician: able to operate mechanical aides in instruction.

The team concept is predicated upon the thesis that many professional people have the capacity for assuming one or more of these roles but that few can live up to expectations in all of them simultaneously. Consequently, if students are not to be denied the assistance they need, groups of people with various strengths need to pool their resources to achieve maximum results.

Shared Responsibility. In the traditional classroom, decisions about how, when, and what to teach rest upon the judgment of a single teacher. The general guidelines for a course are outlined or detailed in the school's course of study guide. Frequently, the department to which a teacher belongs has a syllabus for each course, indicating the content that the department has approved as important. Generally, though, the responsibility for arranging the order of the specific topics is left to the teacher in the classroom as are the selection of appropriate teaching methods and the depth of coverage. If a teacher feels secure in his knowledge of one area and unsure in another, he may yield to the temptation to spend too much time on the former and not enough on the latter.

In the team operation, decisions of this sort are made at team conferences during the course planning. Since the team possesses the strengths of each member, the chances of skimping an area because of the deficiencies of a single individual teacher are considerably lessened. With time built into daily schedules for team meeting, planning for instruction and allocation of teaching responsibilities can be insured.

Flexibility of Schedule. When masses of children began presenting themselves to the schools, the administrative device invented to facilitate the efforts of teachers was the fixed schedule. Rooms were reserved for a particular group of students to meet with a particular teacher daily at a particular period of time. Each day was divided into a number of fixed periods and students and teachers moved on cue from one period to the next.

As can be easily imagined, the school officer, confronted with multitudes of students to distribute among teachers and with a limited number of classrooms available, became very much preoccupied with the numbers game. If, on opening day in September, every student had a classroom and desk to go to and every teacher had a room in which to meet his students, the mission of the scheduler was considered accomplished.

In the team operation, the mission is not considered finished at this point. Schedule modification becomes part of the daily planning session. The members of the team re-shuffle the group assigned to them whenever the need arises. Because they are involved with fewer students and teachers than the schedule officer, and are familiar with the needs and the strengtns within their group and the team intentions and goals for any day or unit of time, it is much simpler for them to bring students and teachers appropriately together. Consequently they are better able to match the achievement of goals with the facilities and teaching personnel available.

Class Size. For some purposes, the established size of the traditional class group, generally twenty-five to thirty-five, has proved inefficient. Some authors claim that it is always inefficient because it is too large to permit all students to engage in the interaction required for good learning and too small to justify the expenditure of teacher effort required for quality presentations. Yet the fixed nature of the grouping discourages or prevents variation in group size.

Teaming of the teaching staff permits flexible grouping. It enables teachers to meet all the students for whom the team is responsible at one time or in groups of differing sizes depending upon the learning goals proposed. In a five-teacher team, for example, one teacher can be excused from classroom responsibilities for a period of time to prepare a special presentation, while the remaining four share the responsibility for all students. When the presentation is ready, all students belonging to the team can be collected for the performance. The presenter is then able to pour all of his creative talent into a single production for a large audience, instead of repeating with dwindling enthusiasm the same presentation for each of five classes in the daily schedule in a regular program. Under other circumstances, this teacher preparing for a future class would not have been able to find the time for preparation and could not have focused upon the topic in any depth.

Follow-up teaching and learning can be scheduled by the team through yet another kind of appropriate grouping. The team can arrange clusters of compatible students, who are enthusiastic or who are reluctant to talk, who are very much interested or only vaguely concerned, and place them with teachers who have demonstrated strength with the reluctant learners, or with the highly motivated students. The flexibility provided by the team presence also permits the clustering for instruction of groups as large or as small as the need demands.

School Space. Classrooms of uniform size have been the accepted school pattern for many years. School planners and architects have traditionally begun their task of school construction with decisions about the number of standard classrooms needed to accommodate the expected student population. The standard classroom of 660 square feet had evolved to accommodate thirty-five pupils in five rows of seven desks each. The resulting "egg-crate" structure featured several floors of identically shaped rooms, corridors of identical dimensions, and identical teaching spaces.

The space needs of working team members are different from the needs of teachers in traditional classrooms. Because of the way the teams function, not all rooms need to be the standard 660 square feet. Much smaller rooms will suffice for the meetings of small groups. For large groups, the need may be for rooms double or triple the size of the standard classroom.

Team Talents. In the traditional class, students are assigned to a teacher for a semester or a year. If the teacher is an exciting professional, those students may have an exciting year. If he is not, the students may have a very dull year. If he varies his methods, if he makes use of audio-visual equipment, if he is well organized, and if he relates well with students, the year usually results in considerable growth. If he is only some of these, the year is likely to be less successful than it might have been.

The team structure is designed to diminish the risk of unsuccessful years. All students will have exposure to the exciting teacher, to the teacher with sensitivity for students with problems, to the teacher capable of motivating the gifted to high levels of accomplishment.

Each team member can work in the area of his specific strength. Time can be reserved for the teacher with the most flair for the dramatic to present a topic to the entire student group at one time. Time, facilities, and support personnel can also be provided for the presentation preparation of supplemental instruction and material to accompany the large group session. Students who fare better in small discussion groups of ten to twelve can be scheduled to meet with those team members best equipped to interrelate with small groups of learners for this purpose.

Members of the team skilled in the technology can assume responsibility for the audio-visual equipment, thus relieving the teacher responsible for the lesson from the problems of procurement, operation, and return of the equipment.

Teacher Growth. The exigencies of the daily school schedule generally keep teachers immobilized in their own classrooms. Rarely do they have or exercise the opportunity of observing their fellow teachers in action. Team teaching, on the other hand, throws teachers together in so many intertwining ways that it is very difficult to avoid observing the performance of others. This type of professional association fosters teacher growth. In the first place, the fact that one's efforts are under the constant scrutiny of fellow professionals is an incentive for meticulous planning and flawless execution. Novices in their early years of teaching especially benefit by the sharing of responsibilities. They are permitted to function in areas of specific strengths and, hence, are spared from the pressure, at the outset of their careers, to display excellence in all facets of the teaching act. In the team planning sessions, growth is possible for all members. Master teachers lacking in organization can learn by observation of those team members who are strong in organization. Older teachers long away from the college campus can be attuned to the attitudes and movements of the younger generation by the newer members of the profession.

Advancement of Specialists. Most school systems operate with a single salary guide as a basis of payment for services rendered under contract. Single salary means that all teachers, no matter at what grade level or in what subject, are treated alike. Once entered on the guide, annual increments are forthcoming to all at an identical rate until the maximum allowed by the guide is reached. Advances in salary beyond the maximum are not possible in this plan except by special provision.

Historically, teachers who have aspired to a larger salary than that permitted by the maximum on the salary guide have had to prepare themselves for certification as administrators and, when the opportunity presented itself, abandon the classroom for the principal's office. A bright promise contained in the team concept provides for an end to this process by opening up new lines of advancement. Teams based on an hierarchical organization provide for coordinators, or captains, or master teachers to receive financial increases almost equivalent to those attached to administrative offices. Successful, effective teachers who wish to continue their effective teaching need no longer abandon the classroom to engage in activities for which they may not be especially equipped. Consequently, administration in the future can be reserved for those with appropriate skills and interests and no longer need constitute the only route of advancement.

Unity and Individuality. A perennial problem that teachers have sought to solve is the segmentation and compartmentalization that characterizes the typical school. Knowledge has been divided into segments called subjects, and subjects have been arranged on a continuum from easiest for beginners to hardest for the most senior. Not much success has rewarded the effort that has been expended on interrelating the knowledge in each of the various subjects taught in any one year. Frequently, history teachers, for example, do not even know what the English teachers in the adjacent classes are doing.

The interdisciplinary team seems to be a means for solving this problem. When the focus of the course is on problem solving, each team member contributes and functions as consultant when the proposals touch upon his area of specialization. When the reading of literature is coordinated or integrated with the study of history, the fiction read to satisfy the requirements in one class can support the historical inquiry in another. Skills in writing and speaking that are learned under one teacher can be utilized and practiced under the supervision of another. Similarly, mathematics teachers and science teachers can rely upon each other to prepare for the specific emphasis each intends to pursue and to supply follow-up with practice exercises to clinch the skill learning sought.

Getting help for students is also simplified. When a student is having difficulty in all subjects, an organized plan can be devised by the team to make maximum use of the assistance available. Provisions can be built into the plan for highly specialized input from particular members of the team when particular scholarship or knowledge of references is required. Personnel with specific skills then can be scheduled to function in the areas of their greatest strength so that the right material is taught by the most skilled practitioner at the strategic time.

Orientation. New teachers are generally expected to perform creditably all of the functions and to display all of the skills possessed by long-term veterans. Working alone in their isolated classrooms, new teachers have needed many years of trial and error to achieve the expertise required by their position.

As a new teacher member of the team, the introduction to teaching need not be so "cold turkey." There are a multitude of time-consuming things that need to be and can be done by a new teacher while he is becoming oriented to his new surroundings, becoming familiar with his students, and in general assuming new status as a professional. In the planning sessions, the new teacher, fresh from the college campus, can contribute generously concerning new research developments in the field. Operationally, he can perform in those areas in which he is strong. When additional maturation and further experience are needed, the new teacher member of the team can lengthen his apprenticeship by observing master teachers in action and then performing while master teachers supervise. When competence and confidence dictate, full teaching membership on the team can be granted.

Removing Road Blocks. Some students have failed to prosper in typical class-rooms because of personality conflicts with their teachers. For any one of a multitude of reasons, these students have become alienated from their teachers but, nevertheless, they have been doomed to spend an entire semester or even a year with them.

The exposure of these students to several teachers instead of to just one diminishes the extent of the catastrophic results of such conflicts. Not only are several teachers, instead of one, responsible for the evaluation of student progress, but also the team members share their guidance function and cooperate in helping students to cope with the realities of this situation. Team discussions about problems inform all team members about potential reasons for lack of pupils' success and about potential solutions to personality problems. When several members of a team are focusing upon the problems of a single child and when all members of the team are united in efforts to eliminate the problems, the difficulty caused by outside interference is diminished. The barrier to learning, erected by the personality conflict between one teacher and one student, is not so crucial nor insurmountable if instruction can be continued by other team members who enjoy a good relationship with the student.

Types of Teams. SINGLE-SUBJECT TEAMS. In single-subject teams, two or more teachers agree to teach the same subject at a particular grade level to the same group in a common period. If two teachers constitute the team, the student group might number fifty to sixty. If more than two teachers team, the student group grows in size by approximately the number of students each teacher might face if working alone. A four-teacher team might include 100 to 150 students each period.

Some single-subject teams are designed to work at more than one grade level. In an attempt to allow for individual differences and to work toward the nongraded ideal, these teams form student groups that spread over two or more years in grade placement. Such a group provides a large enough pool of students to make it possible to divide into smaller groups those who can profit from specialized instruction, advanced work, or remedial instruction. In this fashion, it will be possible to prevent capable students from uselessly marking time while waiting to be promoted to the next grade. It will also be possible to avoid the dooming of slower students to the continued bewilderment that accompanies being moved on before they are academically ready.

The flexibility provided by the team encourages great variation in the sizes of the groupings. In graded classrooms, each teacher is responsible for his twenty-five to thirty-five students for the year, no matter what. When instant reshuffling is possible, however, one teacher can siphon off the top ten to fifteen students for activities appropriate to their development, while another selects the five to ten who need the most help, and the two remaining teachers share or divide the remaining sixty to eighty students in accordance with the plan for the day.

INTERDISCIPLINARY TEAMS. In interdisciplinary teams, teachers of different subjects agree to assume responsibility for the same large group of students and are given a block of time in which to work with them. Thus the block of time for a mathematics, English, social studies, and science team might extend to four periods daily, and the student group might number 120 or more students.

Teams of this sort have also been known to work with groups of students of several ages or from several grades. Scheduling of meeting times, places, and membership of groups is thus placed in the hands of the professionals responsible for determining the purpose of the meeting.

The advantage of this type of scheduling is the locating of administrative power closer to the source of the need. The teachers who know the students and who are aware of the goals for a day or a unit determine how the students shall be clustered. This system enables a mathematics teacher, for example, by planning with his teammates, to select from the total 120 students the three or five students who appear to be having the same type of difficulty. As a small cluster, these students can be given additional instruction on the material that has been impeding their progress while the other teachers assume responsibility for the remaining students. On subsequent days, the other teachers on the team are given the opportunity to select and meet with their neediest students.

STUDENT GROUPS. In some situations, a team of five to seven teachers assumes full academic responsibility for the entire school day for a group of students. This team can function almost as a separate entity, providing guidance for all students, and calling upon other resources in the school only at scheduled times for specialized purposes.

With no special bells to control their movements, with no particular rooms assigned for any particular student to occupy regularly, with all members of the team ministering to the same group of students and, hence, knowledgeable of the strengths and weaknesses of each student, this kind of team is free to focus on learning and social and psychological goals, and to devise activities and experiences accordingly. Field trips, movies, and guest speakers can be scheduled without affecting the rest of the school. Community study and projects can be fitted in without disrupting other classes. Basic skills can be planned and focused upon, in anticipation of their being needed by all members of the team, so that prerequisites are satisfied before advanced work is started.

HIERARCHICAL TEAMS. In many of the teams of the types we have discussed, the teachers are equal partners, sharing the responsibility for all aspects of the teaching. Some teams, however, emphasizing the professional nature of the teaching act, are hierarchical—made up of teachers, aides, clerks, and assistants. Job descriptions delineate the distinctions between the roles of the various members of this kind of team, and each member is paid in accordance with the role he plays.

In these hierarchical teams, one professional teacher is designated (appointed or elected) team leader and functions as the administrator-in-charge. The remaining teachers perform professional duties as agreed upon by the team.

Aides perform such chores as operating and servicing audio-visual equipment, preparing transparencies, and reviewing test papers. Generally, aides are called upon to perform most of those tasks which, while necessary for the success of the teaching act, do not require pedagogical training and experience.

Clerks file, type, make appointments, take notes and, in general, relieve teachers of responsibilities for those chores which do not require advanced schooling or training.

Assistants are those who lack either the desire or the academic credentials to qualify as professional teachers. Some are expert in their field and serve on call when their available time coincides with the needs of the school. Others function on a part-time basis doing tasks for which their training, knowledge, and experience particularly equip them.

In theory, the hierarchical team is designed to resolve the largest number of impediments to effective teaching, including the following:

1. Remove clerical drudgery from the professional act of teaching.
2. Permit highly paid, highly trained, highly qualified teachers to focus upon the activities that are germane to their areas of expertise.
3. Provide the personnel necessary for supervision when groups are subdivided for accomplishment of particular goals.
4. Provides a mechanism for introducing competent nonprofessionals into the school when their knowledge and experience can be of use.
5. Place accountability for the progress of the group on the shoulders of the supervisor of the team. Theoretically, the person who takes an active daily role in the planning for a particular group should accept accountability more readily than the supervisor from the central office who only periodically visits while classes are in session.
6. Provide an avenue for financial and status promotion for professionals who wish to remain in the classroom.
7. Establish an atmosphere for growth and development of new teachers.
8. Make maximum use of the materials and resources accumulated by effective teachers over the years, and serve to motivate beginners to augment the collection to meet their current needs.

Bogus Teams. This category is inserted only to keep the record straight. Many teachers erroneously formulate negative attitudes toward team teaching after being exposed to the behavior of a so-called team in action. Counterfeit groups that are attracted by the band wagon praise but know little about successful teaming are prone to apply the name to any act of cooperation between teachers.

Harm is done only when inquirers are led to conclude incorrectly about the theory of team teaching from their exposure to a performance which does not actually satisfy the definition.

Purpose of Team Teaching. The goal of team teaching is improvement of instruction through a better utilization of personnel. As the teaching act is viewed, it becomes evident that time and a multiplicity of necessary chores are natural enemies of the classroom teacher. Although he is expected and no doubt would like to perform at the peak of his potential on each of the 180 days in which school is in session, he does not have the time to prepare for a polished performance day after day. Apart from the nonprofessional obligations of his job that impinge upon his time for preparation, there are the requirements of research, the impossibility of appearing fresh to the same student audience for the entire school year, and countless acts of judgment that must be made about countless items, such as aspects of the subject to highlight daily.

The provision of additional skilled personnel to free the teacher to concentrate upon his professional role reduces the teacher's task to the realm of the manageable. In addition, the establishment of a common time during the day for a planning meeting not only simplifies the selection of subject matter but also illuminates possibilities for successful cooperative efforts. In group planning, the collective effort often can yield success where one teacher alone might face only a discouragingly huge problem. The presence of several professionally competent teachers insures that one teacher does not assume total responsibility for every lesson. Thus, with a longer time for preparation, with aides to do some of the research and prepare some of the materials, the task of conducting attractive and motivating lessons becomes an invigorating challenge rather than a sporadic accident.

An important by-product of the team activity is the insurance that planning actually takes place. For the teacher in the usual classroom, it has been known that the pressure to prepare an examination, to evaluate homework papers, to meet an administrative deadline, even to solve some problem dealing with the household plumbing, has interfered with the planning for daily lessons which is expected of effective teachers. However, the presence in the daily schedule of a time when all personnel are expected to devote their attention to planning, diminishes the risk of slackness considerably.

The team concept also introduces the element of variety into the daily school routine. Historically, the propensity of teachers has been to overuse the lecture method of presentation. With the team focusing upon large groups, with each member of the team assigned to a role appropriate for the accomplishment of the goal being pursued, with technological equipment and aides available, the chances for differentiated approaches are enhanced.

The use of variable size groupings is the feature most generally associated with team teaching. When students are collected into large groups—any size group larger than standard class—only a minimum of active interaction can be expected. The assumption is that this type of teaching activity capitalizes upon staff competencies that emphasize teacher presentation and require a low level of pupil activity. The feature of economy of effort is at work with large groups. All students are exposed to the same outstanding teacher at the same time for the same fresh performance. They are saved from the last period of the day performance and also from being excluded from great classes because the great teacher is not on their schedule. Small groupings of five to fourteen students regularly follow large group presentations. Student-teacher interaction, involvement of the student in the learning process, and individualization of learning are goals of the small groups. The small size of the group is conducive to the development of reasoning and inquiry skills and logical and effective expression of ideas.

Advantages of Team Teaching. Team teaching seems to have the following advantages over ordinary organization:

1. Team operations appear to contribute to the flexibility of teachers. Away from the enforced isolation of a single classroom, forced to interact with teachers of the same or different subjects, and exposed to the successes or

failures of peers in the act of instruction, slipping into a teaching rut and developing reactionary attitudes becomes less likely.

2. Behavior problems become easier to resolve. Not only does the team involve the supervisory presence of observers when large groups of students are collected for instruction, but it also insures the presence of several different kinds of people, each of whom may have established a relationship with the potential problem student. Theoretically, confrontations should be considerably minimized.

3. Instruction for students need not suffer the interruption generally associated with the utilization of a substitute teacher. Teacher absences can be absorbed by the team by a quick reshuffle of responsibilities.

Disadvantages of Team Teaching. It has been claimed that several of the following militate against the success of the team endeavor:

1. The frequency and intensity of contact of the team members lead to complex problems of human relations.
2. The problem of status pyramiding of teachers under a team chairman may work against a healthy climate.
3. Inherent in the flexibility is the fact that much time and effort must be spent on the complexities of scheduling and planning.
4. Mechanical aspects of evaluation may be more difficult.
5. Questions provoked during large group lectures or demonstrations must be deferred until later for a response.
6. Opportunities for pupil leadership may be lost because of the complexities of the program and size of group.
7. Noise may be a problem in a large group or when several small groups are working in one room.
8. Instruction may tend to become more lecture-type and formal.
9. Interaction between the superior teachers and the learners (especially in the hierarchical plan) may be minimal and the contacts the learners have with teachers may be limited to those of lesser competence.
10. It is very difficult to find teachers with the special competencies and high qualifications necessary for team leaders and senior teachers.
11. It will probably cost more since the team leader and senior teacher will be paid more, secretarial help is usually provided, and new buildings with adjustable space will be needed.

Conclusion. The team concept can offer nothing more than the promise of a better education for the students of today and tomorrow.

Even this promise will fade unless teachers and school staffs (1) know how to utilize the team to facilitate the planning and organization of instruction; (2) understand the purposes and processes of team operation; (3) help each child get the opportunity to learn what he needs to learn in a way he is able to learn it.

Differentiated Staffing

In the section devoted to team teaching, we have discussed the complexity of the teacher's role, the single salary guide, the need for promotion opportunities for teachers who choose to remain in the classroom, and the specialized talents needed by various members of a team if effective teaching is to result. All of these concepts have also been offered as part of the rationale for experimenting with differentiation in staffing.

In addition, other considerations have been proposed, such as (1) shortage of certified personnel for many schools; (2) attracting top-quality candidates into the profession; (3) growth in status of teaching as a profession; (4) rising costs of education; and (5) need for additional personnel in classrooms.

History of Concept. In the late 1960s, when this innovation was receiving the most attention, serious shortages of certified teachers existed in many communities. School systems faced with large student enrollments and large numbers of teacher vacancies were actively engaged in recruiting eligible candidates willing to commit themselves to teaching. One source that was tapped to fill the need consisted of graduates of liberal arts colleges who lacked only the professional preparation for certification. By devising emergency, temporary, and other substandard certificates, bonafide graduates were invited into the field and permitted to teach while completing their professional training on a part-time basis. Another source consisted of college students, drafted from college classrooms, who contracted to teach while they worked part time to finish their undergraduate programs. Housewives, businessmen, foreign visitors, and others of all descriptions were also invited into the school to meet the emergency.

Under these circumstances of scarcity, the single salary guide became an impediment to progress. Introduced earlier to stabilize faculties in school systems and to stop the flow of teachers from elementary school classrooms to high-paying teaching positions in the high school, the guide began to constrict the recruitment efforts of employers. It inhibited personnel officers from bidding freely to secure the services of people whom they sought. To arrange higher salaries to attract excellent prospective candidates, they had to show cause why the guide should be violated or change the guide so that all teachers would benefit.

Quality Loss. Very capable undergraduate students chose to prepare for careers in fields other than teaching because the financial rewards elsewhere were much higher than could be found in the teaching professions. Boards of education, desirous of securing the services of talented students, found themselves unable to remain competitive. The increase in size of the teaching staffs in most districts had exacted such heavy financial commitments that the quest for quality had to be deferred. Quantity was established as the first priority in order to staff the new classrooms constructed to meet the influx of new students.

Status Loss. School systems were further stymied by the inflexibility of the single salary schedule. Despite his brilliance, dedication, contribution to the field, and personal success, an individual who selected teaching as a career could not achieve any more tangible benefits than the most pedestrian member of the staff.

In order to encourage and reward superior teaching, some districts introduced a merit system variation to their salary guides. According to this plan, teachers whose superior knowledge, skill, dedication, or scholarly contributions met the criteria approved by the superintendent and board of education were granted bonuses in addition to their annual increments. These bonuses in many instances became a part of the salary guide, moved the recipient into a new pay category, and in some districts, were granted annually from that time forward. Some districts introduced several levels of merit. After achieving tenure in the system, a teacher could be examined and be granted a merit increase every three years until he had achieved the third award for excellence.

Often, this recognition was only financial. To avoid the generating of hostilities between the successful and the nonsuccessful applicants for merit rewards and to minimize the overtones of failure and inferiority surrounding those who were not judged to be meritorious, no great fanfare accompanied the awards. The psychological aspects of reward for merit residing in the recognition by one's peers and the public acclaim of the community at large were, perforce, reserved for the meritorious in other professions.

Personnel Need. Many effective teachers clamored for personnel assistance rather than increased salaries as their greatest need. In their teaching, they felt that they knew what to do and how to do it but that because of the constrictions of time and scheduling, they fell far short of their goals. Alone, in a classroom with thirty or more students with differing needs, many teachers were unable to achieve the success they desired. Realizing that increasing the number of teachers on any staff so that teacher responsibilities could be reduced might not be economically feasible in an era of rising costs, this group of teachers proposed the hiring of aides, technicians, clerks, and other laymen to perform the specialized chores for which professional training is not required. As noncertified personnel, these workers would not qualify for placement upon the teachers' salary guide. Consequently, a new compensations system and requirements for employment could be devised for them.

The thrust of this differentiated staffing proposal was toward making the compensation of personnel commensurate with the degree of responsibility each carried, with the degree of preparation and education required, and with the length of the working year. One theory underlying the proposal, that it is spendthrifty to pay high-salaried teachers located at the upper levels of the pay scale to perform chores that can be performed just as well by lower-salaried persons, had considerable appeal to various groups. Boards of education seemed to be attracted by the money-saving features it offered: improve production by adding several members to the staff for the same amount it would cost to add only one certified teacher.

The elimination of these boring, nonchallenging, and distasteful aspects appealed to the teacher group. The paper grading, the test administration and marking, the supervision of playgrounds, lunchrooms, and bus lines, the proctoring of hallways and lavatories between classes, the typing and duplication of materials, and the collecting of lunch money, textbook fines, and library fines, although necessary in the school daily routine, never captured the professional imagination. Actually, these chores constituted the excuse for many teachers for failing to achieve the teaching excellence expected of them.

Differentiated staffing promised to solve a great many difficulties. It would introduce professional status to a school faculty and secure for the certified individual the psychological rewards which those at the upper level in other professions received as a matter of course. Financial recognition would cease to be a major problem. Since each school would have only limited numbers of professionals at the upper level, pay raises would not cause the great financial drain that across-the-board increments had brought about.

Further, citizens in every community could accept the concept of rewarding the meritorious, for it agreed with their beliefs about professional performance. They tended to resist increments for broad categories of people because in their opinion some did not deserve an increase. They found themselves unable to commend with a pay increase those whose contribution they applauded without also increasing the salary of those whose input was suspect.

In support of the concept, also, it was not difficult to find in every community several kinds of people capable of making valuable contributions to the school but unable or unwilling to accept full-time employment. Such people might be mothers with small children who could not leave the home for extended periods of time, or highly skilled women whose careers had been interrupted by the transfer of their spouses to new locations. Some school districts found authors, newspaper and magazine editors, and former college professors who enjoyed evaluating student compositions and working on a part-time basis with students and teachers. Other districts found trained laboratory personnel, reading specialists, and actuaries, interested in children and willing to accept the modified salary offered.

The models of differentiated staffing that began appearing all provided for the very important component of promotion that had previously been missing in the teaching profession. Ambitious teachers could begin while young at the bottom of the ladder and, by accumulating experience and additional college training, could progress upward while retaining original interest in classroom teaching.

The redeployment of personnel which became possible with differentiated staffing would make maximum use of the talents, interests, and commitments of the different types of people in the profession. It purported to allow them to do the things that they did well while not forcing them to perform functions ill-suited to their talents. In addition, it appeared to afford considerably more autonomy to teachers in determining their own professional development and to supply the motivation for continuation of growth in service.

Model Plan. Figure 1-1, adapted from a schema reported by John Rand and Fenwick English, illustrates how any faculty might be divided to achieve the benefits of differentiation.[1]

This model provides for four categories of teachers plus paraprofessional personnel. Let us examine those positions in some detail.

CATEGORY IV: THE CURRICULUM ASSOCIATE. The curriculum associate category represents the highest level of teacher specialist. It provides a niche for those very highly qualified people who in years past would have been moved up and away from the classroom. The qualifier for this position assumes responsibility for teaching and curriculum development on a professional level beyond that expected of the usual classroom teacher. Typical duties include demonstration and consultation in areas of particular competence, research in areas of specialized knowledge, planning for programs that require system-wide coordination, performance in experimental and innovative teaching situations, inservice training programs for intern and probationary teachers, evaluation of other categories of teachers, and service in special decision-making committees of the school or school system.

[1] John Rand and Fenwick English, "Towards a Differentiated Teaching Staff," *Phi Delta Kappan,* **49:**266 (Jan. 1968).

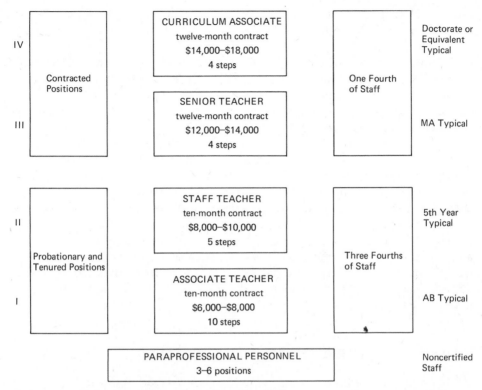

Figure 1-1 *Model for a Differentiated Teaching Staff.*

CATEGORY III: THE SENIOR TEACHER. The senior teacher category includes those professionals who have demonstrated their mastery of their profession. While not as responsible for the leadership expected of the Category IV people, senior teachers share the same kinds of duties in the same general areas and spend more of their time in direct contact with students in the classroom.

CATEGORY II: THE STAFF TEACHER. Teachers become eligible for promotion to the staff teacher category upon completion of a fifth year of college preparation and upon achievement of tenure in the district. They are responsible for general classroom teaching, for service on school committees, for engaging in curriculum research, and in specialized teaching activities previously associated with the regular classroom teacher.

CATEGORY I: THE ASSOCIATE TEACHER. All newly certificated members of the staff are eligible for membership as probationary teachers. They are expected to perform full-time classroom teaching service while working toward tenured status, and are provided opportunities to grow in skill while on the job through inservice opportunities. Under the supervision of the senior teacher and with the guidance, instruction, and motivation of curriculum specialists, associate teachers perfect skills in planning lessons, developing instructional materials, and evaluating teaching efforts.

PARAPROFESSIONAL PERSONNEL. The paraprofessional category encompasses not only the skilled professionals serving on a part-time basis, but also the clerks and aides who facilitate the activities of the professional personnel. This category includes technicians, who manage and operate the learning resource equipment, provide technical skill in the preparation of teaching materials desired by the teacher, supervise laboratory equipment rooms, or type, duplicate, or file for teachers.

Ideally, one fourth of the total staff would be made up of tenured faculty in the top two categories. The higher than usual salaries attached to these positions would be made possible by the lower than usual salaries at the lower levels. The remaining categories of tenured, probationary, and paraprofessional personnel would constitute the remaining three fourths of the staff.

Although some team-teaching plans may use a hierarchy similar to the Rand and English model for their team and although most differentiated staffing plans utilize team teaching, the terms are not synonymous. If equal-partner teams function, for example, there may be no differences in salary, none in status and authority, and no provision regarding tenure or probationary positions. Differentiated staffs, on the other hand, may not necessarily meet all the criteria for team teaching. Surrounding one professional teacher with a number of nonprofessional aides could achieve differentiated status. Such an arrangement, however, would lack the interplay of trained professionals working together to make joint decisions and also lack the mutual stimulation provided by the joint teaching that lies at the heart of the team concept.

Flexible Modular Scheduling

The Ubiquitous Carnegie Unit. The secondary schools with which we are all familiar have organized students and teachers according to a pattern that was standardized around the turn of the last century. In the 1870s colleges and universities were troubled about the diversity of curricula in the high schools whose graduates were presenting themselves for admission for further study. Stimulated by agitation for some standardization of quality in secondary education, the National Education Association in 1892 appointed a committee to study the problem. In 1909, as a result of the committee report, a standardized unit of instruction, known ever since as the Carnegie unit, was established. This measure of learning became the unit that was accumulated to satisfy requirements for graduation from the secondary school and for eligibility for admission to college.

Simply stated, a Carnegie unit is the amount of credit granted to a student for devoting one period a day for the thirty-six weeks of the school year to instruction in a given subject. For one unit, each class period must last approximately fifty minutes and meet five times weekly. A class that meets only half so often or for only one semester would therefore fulfill only one half of a Carnegie unit. Usually, sixteen units are required for graduation.

Since the establishment of the Carnegie unit as the norm, there has been opposition to the fact that time spent in class has been used as the criterion instead of knowledge mastered. In the past half century, many proposals have been made to establish new criteria. Of late, the push has been in the direction of more flexible use of time that focuses on the attainment of instructional objectives. Thus, instead of approving a student's promotion because he has spent so many standardized periods a year in a classroom, the emphasis would be placed upon the mastery of basic concepts, skills, and attitudes. The performance criteria for promotion would reflect the individual teacher's expectations for each particular course and disregard the number of minutes spent in instruction by the student.

New Modules. Instead of the conventional fifty minutes prescribed by the Carnegie unit as the standard period, each school would establish as its base the smallest unit of time that teachers and students could use profitably. These units would be known as modules. If, for example, a school decided that fifteen minutes was the smallest unit of time that could be used profitably, the basic building-block unit would become the fifteen-minute module. The schedule of such a school then would consist of modules used as separate short periods or combined in multiples of fifteen-minute units to form longer periods. If the day were six and a half hours long, it would consist of twenty-six modules; if seven hours long, twenty-eight modules. A school using modules of twenty minutes in a seven-hour day would operate on a schedule of twenty-one modules daily.

Single fifteen-minute module periods might be used for homeroom purposes, for giving directions, for filling out forms, for regrouping according to a pre-arranged plan for attendance at an all-school function. Such short periods might also be desirable for brief drill sessions in some subjects when progress requires frequent drill. Theoretically, this mini-sized period was intended to eliminate the necessity for padding or busy work that sometimes accompanied the standard fifty-minute period. In the traditional schedule, governed by the school bell, the regular fifty-minute period constituted the standard module. To collect students for twenty minutes required the use of a full period. Teachers were thus forced to manufacture things for students to do for the thirty to thirty-five minutes that remained.

Longer sessions are made possible by stacking modules, that is, by combining several fifteen-minute modules into a block of time. Depending upon the system of scheduling used by a school, it would be possible for groups to gather for two modules (thirty minutes), three modules (forty-five minutes), four modules (sixty minutes), and so on. The length of the period would depend upon the purpose for which the group was meeting. If, to accomplish its goals, a group needed to spend an extended time together, for example, to view a film ninety minutes long, exclusive of introduction and discussion, a minimum of seven modules would have to be stacked (six fifteen-minute modules for the movie plus at least one module for introduction and discussion). A twenty-minute film would require only two modules.

Scheduling. In the philosophy of the flexible modular schedule, not all classes need to meet daily or for the same amount of time. Neither do all units or all courses require the same number of meetings. Some types of subject matter appear to necessitate long periods for maximum results, but other subjects are better served by several short meetings. Laboratory classes, for instance, require time for research work. Practice sessions in language laboratories and typing classes, however, may be more efficient if provided in several short time periods. Theoretically, the flexible modular schedule makes it possible to distribute time more efficiently. The standard Carnegie unit number of minutes will be disregarded as too long for some purposes and too short for other purposes.

In planning their work for a week or a unit, teachers in some schools using modular scheduling are required to specify their goals and objectives and to request the allotment of modules that will facilitate their quest. They are expected to indicate in advance on what days their work can be accomplished in single-module sessions and on what days a block of several modules will be required.

When team teaching is used, large groups of students (75 to 200) can be scheduled at the team's request once or twice a week. On other days, these students are scheduled into small discussion groups (five to fifteen) for two or three days so that they can investigate, question, discuss, or evaluate their understanding of the concepts presented in the large group. In addition, it is also possible for each student to be scheduled for independent study in the library, for research in the resource center, for special projects in the laboratory or in the fine arts center.

Some schools by using a computer have been able to supply a new schedule for students, based upon faculty plans and objectives each week. In these schools, failures to complete intended projects can be rectified by modifying requests for period lengths in ensuing weeks.

Other schools, lacking in technological facilities, have established patterns for stringing modules throughout the unit or year. Here, the student pattern may include two extended sessions a week and three days of single or double modules. The pattern once established often becomes as regular and binding as was the conventional schedule, but because of the variations in length of periods, it may permit more flexibility through careful planning.

The schedule for one school that has used the modular design successfully is arranged around thirty-minute time modules.[2] Teachers are assigned forty to fifty-five modules of student contact time in a seventy-module week as well as ten to twelve modules a week for clinics. Students report to teachers on a voluntary basis individually or in small groups for the clinic sessions which replace the traditional study hall. Course work, advanced or remedial, can be the focus of the clinic, as can personal guidance sessions or consultation on independent study projects. The flexibility in this plan stems from the fact that every day is not exactly like every other day as in the traditional schedule. Foreign language classes, for example, meet for sixty minutes (two modules) on Monday and Wednesday and for thirty minutes (one module) on Tuesday, Thursday, and Friday. Eventually, students are permitted to delay reporting to school until their first classes meet and to leave when their last classes are finished. They are also permitted to take final examinations in each class when they are ready, at any time during the year.

Advantages of Flexible Scheduling. Proponents of flexible modular scheduling prefer it for the following reasons:

1. It gives more control to the teacher over the parameters of instruction: length of meetings, frequency of meetings, and size of meeting groups.
2. It enables teachers to focus on instructional activities and objectives in their planning instead of upon the arbitrary rigidities of a fixed daily schedule.
3. It enriches school programs by providing more opportunities for more students to participate in electives without being constrained by schedule limitations. Able students are freed to avail themselves of more of the

---

[2] John W. Allan, "Computer Builds Modules Around Student Requests," *American Education: Foundations and Superstructure*, Weldon, Bechner and Wayne Dumas (eds.). (Scranton, Pa.: Intext, Inc., 1970), p. 485.

school's offerings when the requirements pertaining to frequency and length of periods are modified.

4. Students can assume more responsibility for their own learning and instruction, can engage in independent study, and can make profitable use of the library and resource centers provided.
5. More effective use can be made of school facilities. Activities currently scheduled as extracurricular can be absorbed into the school day.
6. School traffic problems, such as crowded corridors, crowded cafeterias, and overloaded bus schedules, may be reduced. Students move at differing times instead of simultaneously with the bell as in the traditional schedule.
7. Team teaching can be encouraged because of the common planning and conference time which becomes possible.
8. Teacher-pupil conferences during the school day are more easily arranged. Freeing a student for a module is much easier than freeing him for an entire period.
9. It is more possible to attend to individual differences among students. Because of the schedule's flexibility, students can be grouped according to need or according to different criteria for each class session, and each individual can proceed at a rate geared more closely to his individual abilities.

Disadvantages of Flexible Scheduling. Despite the attractiveness of the benefits contemplated as possible with a flexible modular schedule, the following built-in difficulties are inherent in the plan:

1. The flexible modular schedule can be very difficult to implement. Because of the many choices and possible combinations of courses, modules, students, teachers, and room spaces, it may be necessary to use a computer to achieve optimum results.
2. The schedule may rigidify after the first few weeks of school and become no more flexible than the schedule it replaced.
3. It may appear confusing, complex, and not worth the bother when presented to a faculty.
4. It involves much anticipation of teaching sequences and much planning of the kinds of modules that will be needed to achieve the objectives desired. It requires decisions about length of the basic module, about stringing patterns, about the optimal amount of independent study possible, about the team teaching patterns possible, and the numbers of contact modules that may be formed without resulting in faculty overload.

Conclusion. Schools using independent study, variable-size groupings, and other approaches to individualized instruction need a flexible system of scheduling. Usually, modular scheduling increases the amount of unscheduled time for both students and teachers and hence places a greater burden for appropriate utilization of time upon each. Teachers can use the unscheduled time for team planning, conferences with students doing independent study, tutoring those in need of remedial assistance, and researching for future classes. Students are found to use their unstructured time for working in an open laboratory, study in the library, study in the research center, conferences with teacher or counselor, relaxing in the student lounge, auditing noncredit courses, researching an independent study project, or perhaps off campus, serving as teacher assistant, tutor, or resource center aide.

Although much of the promised strength of modular scheduling lies in the use of this unscheduled time, most of the potential weakness resides there also. Vandalism, theft, discipline problems, and general time wasting must be acknowledged as problems to resolve when a school attempts this innovation. In addition, there is the unfavorable attitude about the "indolent country club atmosphere in the school" which sometimes arises in the community when citizens observe students socializing or leaving the school grounds at unusual hours. Schools that have faced and solved the problems and have moved generally in the direction of greater freedom and more responsibility for their high school students, however, appear to indicate "they have no desire to go back to the traditional form" of scheduling.[3]

SUGGESTED READING

Alexander, William M., Ed. *The Changing Secondary School Curriculum.* New York: Holt, Rinehart & Winston, Inc., 1967.

Beggs, David W., III, Ed. *Team Teaching: Bold New Venture.* Indianapolis: Unified College Press, Inc., 1964.

Cooper, James W. Ed. *Differentiated Staffing.* Philadelphia: W. B. Saunders Company, 1972.

Davis, Harold S., and Ellsworth Tompkins. *How to Organize an Effective Team Teaching Program.* Englewood Cliffs, N.J.: Prentice-Hall, Inc., 1966.

Dempsey, Richard A., and Rodney P. Smith, Jr. *Differentiated Staffing.* Englewood Cliffs, N.J.: Prentice-Hall, Inc., 1972.

Florida State Department of Education. *Flexible Scheduling: A Vehicle for Change.* Tallahassee, Fla.: The Department, 1972.

Heidenreich, Richard R., Ed. *Improvement in Curriculum.* Arlington, Va.: College Readings, Inc., 1972.

Hillson, Maurie, and Ronald T. Hyman. *Change and Innovation in Elementary and Secondary Organization.* New York: Holt, Rinehart & Winston, Inc., 1971.

Rollins, Sidney P. *Developing Nongraded Schools.* Itasca, Ill.: F. E. Peacock Publishers, Inc., 1968.

Shaplin, Judson T., and Henry F. Olds, Jr., Eds. *Team Teaching.* New York: Harper & Row Publishers, 1964.

Swenson, Gardner, and Donald Keys. *Providing for Flexibility in Scheduling and Instruction.* Englewood Cliffs, N.J.: Prentice-Hall, Inc., 1966.

POST TEST

Select the best answer to complete each statement and put the correct letter in the space provided.

_____ **1.** Anticipating the changes that will be made in any school system is
   a. just as easy as it has always been since the schools are fundamentally the same as they always were.

---

[3] Unruh and Alexander, *Innovation in Secondary Education* (New York: Holt, Rinehart & Winston, Inc., 1970), p. 120.

    b. easier than it used to be because people know more theory now.

    c. harder than it used to be because there are more people to consider.

    d. harder than it used to be because of the changes happening in society that will affect the purpose of the schools.

_____ **2.** In a sentence or two, distinguish between the vertical organization and horizontal organization of a school.

_____ **3.** Unrest in a community regarding the schools is generally caused by

    a. malicious activists and provocateurs who wish to cause trouble.

    b. unmotivated teachers who resist change.

    c. social movements which modify our beliefs about the school and learners.

    d. the rapid rise of the middle class with its accompanying financial benefits to the socially mobile.

_____ **4.** Teachers in training can prepare for a professional career best by

    a. following the successful programs established in the past for preparation.

    b. ignoring the efforts of training programs and focusing upon contemporary social changes.

    c. learning more about the subject they intend to teach.

    d. adding an inquiry into innovations to their quest of skills and knowledge previously needed.

_____ **5.** Common time scheduled in the school day for teacher planning is

    a. an unnecessary frill.

    b. an expensive item that may be dropped if finances are tight.

    c. an absolute necessity for the success of team teaching.

    d. a fringe benefit insisted upon by teachers' associations.

_____ **6.** Innovations take so long to become established practices because

    a. administrators and boards of education are unwilling to finance them.

    b. established teachers are reluctant to change.

    c. faculty leaders are not energetic enough in researching the theory.

    d. convincing results of the merits of the innovation take time to collect.

_____ **7.** Many new practices fail to blossom because

    a. teachers are not fully knowledgeable of the theory upon which the new practices are based.

    b. communities have not been adequately prepared for the change.

    c. new ideas are introduced into old organizations that are not flexible enough to accommodate the changes made.

    d. band wagon actions have prompted replication of experiments successful elsewhere without considering fundamental local differences.

    e. all of the above.

_____ **8.** Audio-visual aids will be used more by a team than by a teacher in a regular class because

  a. a school budget has been prepared for procurement.
  b. such aids provide a good method for gaining the attention of a large group.
  c. such aids constitute a good public relations gimmick for the innovation.
  d. the differentiation of roles assigns the responsibility for procuring and operating to a specially trained team member.

_____ **9.** Team teaching will attract and retain ambitious teachers because it

  a. provides a method for promotion and salary increment by its hierarchical organization.
  b. permits the acquisition of power by the aggressive.
  c. rewards those participating by getting better public relations coverage.
  d. enables organizers to challenge the autocracy of the administration.

_____**10.** Knowledge about individual differences

  a. is the result of recent research of behavioral scientists.
  b. has been available for a long time but only now is receiving the recognition which it merits.
  c. should not modify greatly our approach to the education of the masses.
  d. has been implemented adequately by teachers since little red schoolhouse days.

_____**11.** New teachers should find it easier in a team situation to become oriented to teaching because they

  a. are permitted to prolong their period of dependency.
  b. can become part of an influential clique which has status on the faculty.
  c. are provided opportunities to see experienced teachers in action and are made privy to planning for teaching.
  d. can use their youth in relating to the younger students.

_____**12.** Homogeneous grouping is an example of

  a. vertical organization.
  b. horizontal organization.
  c. modular scheduling.
  d. differentiated staffing.

_____**13.** The purest form of the philosophy of team teaching is operating if two or more teachers

  a. pool classes for occasional large group sessions.
  b. agree to alternate in giving lectures to pooled large sessions.
  c. plan to adjust their curriculum so that each is covering material that is supportive of the efforts of the others.
  d. assume responsibility for planning the content, for presenting the activities, and for grouping for instruction all the pupils in the unit for which they are responsible.

_____14. The strength of differentiated staffing lies in the fact that it
    a. may help to lure more people of talent into teaching.

    b. provides appropriate roles for several kinds of people with specialized training and skills.
    c. tends to diminish the mechanical and routine aspects of teaching for which a teacher is responsible.
    d. is designed to increase the staff and increase the pay of established teachers while not increasing the cost of education.
    e. does all of the above.

_____15. With regard to the use of teachers, team teaching can best be described as
    a. reducing the number of teachers needed in a given school.
    b. redeployment of teachers and reallocation of teacher responsibilities.
    c. eliminating the need for costly and time-consuming inservice training of teachers.
    d. providing built-in backup personnel, thereby eliminating the need for substitute teachers.

_____16. A module of time is a unit used to
    a. measure the length of a classroom project.
    b. define the number of class hours in one Carnegie credit.
    c. establish the smallest utilizable period in a school day.
    d. measure the required years for tenure.

_____17. Flexible scheduling permits
    a. teachers to arrange length of classes to coincide with the goals of lesson plans.
    b. students to see teachers for conference during the school day.
    c. the use of unstructured time during the day for work on approved projects.
    d. the elimination of busy work associated with partial use of a full regular period.
    e. all of the above.

_____18. In flexible scheduling
    a. teachers meet the same students every day at the same time.
    b. more sessions are held daily because the class time for each has been reduced.
    c. modules may be stacked to provide an extended time for any class period.
    d. planning for daily lessons remains the same as in the traditional program.

_____19. A team that features a senior teacher and a beginning teacher among its members is generally
    a. single subject team.   **d.** hierarchical team.
    b. interdisciplinary team.   **e.** bogus team.
    c. student group team.

_____**20.** Twenty-five students in each classroom is

    a. the optimum size of a class because the teacher can get to know each student well.

    b. the ideal grouping which teaching teams strive to obtain for their clusters.

    c. too small for efficient instruction and too large for effective instruction.

    d. too large since the one-on-one ratio is endorsed as best for learning.

Individual Differences

Raymond L. Klein

The University of Arizona

module 2

Individualized Instruction / Nongrading / Continuous Progress / Independent Study / Sequential Units

RATIONALE

Innovations have been introduced during the past two decades at a relatively high rate. It sometimes has seemed that every new issue of educational journals and the mass media carries a story about something new that is supposed to solve all or at least some of the problems facing those persons engaged in the educational process today. Since the event of Sputnik in the late 1950s, sums of money in excess of one billion dollars have been spent by federal, state, and local agencies for innovations. It is somewhat disheartening then to discover that the problems that faced educators in 1955 are still with us and, furthermore, additional problems have been added to the already overburdened classroom teacher. One problem with innovations is that in some cases they were never implemented because of lack of funds, because of inertia, or lack of leadership for implementation. Some teachers who have been teaching a number of years turn a cynical eye toward any innovation. They see them as nothing more than a rehash of something done twenty or more years ago, with a new title, and accompanied by money that has to be spent since it has been appropriated.

This module will consider some innovations that the reader may find new and refreshing; the historian may question the newness and the experienced teacher may question the viability. Each reader is free to accept that which appears to be the way to go for him or her. The first subject is that of individual differences. Upon the completion of your study of this module you should be able to perform all of the following objectives.

Specific Behavioral Objectives

1. Write a short statement about the importance of the I.Q. with 100 per cent accuracy.
2. List seven kinds of motivation with 100 per cent accuracy.
3. List four of five teaching acts for individualized instruction.
4. List seven strategies for individualizing instruction with 90 per cent accuracy.
5. Write definitions of seven strategies for individualizing instruction with 100 per cent accuracy.
6. Analyze a continuous progress proposal for feasibility with 60 per cent chance of success.
7. List points of comparison of a regular school program with a continuous progress program, providing five or more points of comparison.
8. Define sequential units with 100 per cent accuracy.
9. List all the steps in developing a sequence.
10. Explain each step in developing a sequential unit with 100 per cent accuracy.
11. List five individual differences of students in a classroom with 100 per cent accuracy.

12. Describe three types of organization for independent study with 100 per cent accuracy.

MODULE TEXT

Individual Differences

Intelligence. Of all differences in individuals, intelligence is one of the most important to be considered by the teacher. Intelligence is a very general term and connotes a wide range of abilities including problem solving, concept building, quantitative manipulation, number concepts, vocabulary, and the like. The score on an intelligence test can be converted to an intelligence quotient (I.Q.) which purports to measure the native ability of a student, or to other statistical representations such as stanines which indicate a student's relative standing in the population.

Over the years, great importance has been attached to the student's I.Q., and much controversy has been generated about the use to which it could be put. If the original inventors of the intelligence test and I.Q. concept, however, had viewed it as an index of academic potential rather than as one of intellectual potential, there would probably be less controversy today about the meaning and value of any given I.Q. score.

For many years, schools have sought to group students in one way or another so that special programs might be provided for them. Gifted students have been divided into various kinds of high-level groups. On some occasions they were separated on the basis of their I.Q., with a score of 130 being used to separate the gifted from the high average. On other occasions, those students constituting the top 5 per cent of the population were considered the group which merited the title of superior or most highly qualified.

Logically, it would seem quite simple to group by using this device—high I.Q. means superior achievement; low I.Q. means less adequate achievement. It also would seem to be simple to give tests to all students and derive a finite number with which the teacher could work. As in most things concerned with learning by the youth of America, factors affecting intelligence and related to the use of I.Q. for purposes of facilitating learning are such that a new look must be taken at the use of the I.Q. measure. The innovation germane to this issue is that intelligence tests must be used more carefully than in the past. New tests are being developed, but a serious question has been raised about older tests that emphasize verbal ability. The social group used for standardization of verbal ability on the older tests was usually middle-class white. Subsequent study in recent years has raised the question of the degree of racial bias such a test has built into it when the test is used to measure a student with a different language or an entirely different environment from that of the middle-class white. It has been well established that both heredity and environment determine the intelligence of the individual. So the problem that is with us is which environment shall be the norm? The Black ghetto? The Cuban ghetto? The Northeast coastal city? The small town of the great plains? Fishing villages of the Northwest? Pueblos of the Southwest? The modern teacher must use the intelligence test with considerable caution—it must fit the student being tested if it is to give a true measure of the student's scholastic aptitude. Since not even identical twins have the same I.Q., it is incumbent upon the teacher to be aware of the differences in intelligence as they influence the teacher's judgment in making educational decisions affecting each learner.

Achievement Level. By the time the pupil has arrived in the seventh grade, he will be capable of working at a particular level of skill and knowledge in various areas. If the student is given some kind of general achievement test, the resulting test scores will indicate that he is at the 6.6 grade level in arithmetic, 7.8 grade level in science, and so on. The norms established by the test maker, derived during the experimental period, enable the teacher to determine whether the student has achieved above or below that expected of the "average" student of that age at that point in the year. Ideally, a student entering the seventh grade should receive a complete evaluation of his achievement. Then by using known strategies of instruction, one could design a program that would meet his personal requirements, the state's requirements, and requirements set by the district. Through the process of giving credit for required courses by examination, for instance, the pupil could be guided into those educational experiences appropriate for his achievement level.

A term often used for describing the point in a pupil's educational career when he is able to attack successfully the next unit of study is *readiness*. Readiness is a key to successful teaching and learning. Unless a pupil can do all the arithmetic functions, he will usually not do well in algebra. Yet some people are ready for and do well in algebra in the seventh grade. Others are nowhere near ready in the tenth grade. It is axiomatic that a student engaged in a course beyond his academic capabilities will not be successful enough to maintain interest. The pupil's achievement level is of primary importance to the teacher in determining what should be the next sequence, the next learning packet, the next unit, and so on, if the pupil is to continue to make progress toward personal and societal goals.

In the past, considerable attention has been given to cognitive skills and abilities. Many schools still have valedictorians, and colleges and universities still place great emphasis upon the *grade point* which supposedly reflects a cognitive evaluation. While affective skills were implied in the Seven Cardinal Principles of Education of the early twentieth century, little attention has been given to their development.[1] Control of one's emotions does not appear to have a high priority value in our schools, as evidenced by pupils' behavior at football and basketball games. It is well known that a primary reason for the firing of employees is not inability to do the work, but rather inability to get along with fellow employees and the employer. Perhaps strong unions may be able to inhibit future dismissals, but union action will not rectify the weakness evidenced. Failure in the affective domain is also evidenced in the home. To meet the evident need, innovative programs of both full semester and short course varieties have been devised to develop the affective skills of the high school graduate.

---

[1] The following Seven Cardinal Principles describing the areas of life activity that should be of concern to education were agreed on by a special committee of the National Education Association in 1912: health, command of fundamental processes, worthy home membership, vocation, civic education, worthy use of leisure, and ethical character.

It is expecting the impossible to insist that the classroom teacher do all things for all pupils. But the teacher, if cognizant of the importance of the affective domain, can plan activities that provide educational experiences at the proper level of achievement in the student's area of learning.

A relatively new aspect of achievement is that of *visual literacy*. Just as an illiterate person cannot read the printed word, some pupils because of inadequate environmental experiences cannot "read" a picture or a scene being viewed live or recorded. Such a person is considered to be a functional visual illiterate and lives at a disadvantage in our visual world. Without proper visual learnings, such a person would have difficulty operating a car on a freeway, purchasing hard and soft goods, walking about on the deserts of the Southwest, or living successfully in one of our large cosmopolitan areas. If the school accepts as the general purpose of education the preparing of youths to live successfully in our world, then additional attention needs to be paid to the visual literacy concept.

Motivation. Certainly one of the more perplexing puzzles in education is what makes some students work hard and long to learn knowledge which they may never use while others will not stir themselves to learn knowledge that may be most essential to their survival in our society. The concept of motivation is exceedingly complicated—much broader than the scope of this module. The following are some of the factors that are presently receiving innovative attention.

Authority figure approval still is a powerfully motivating force. If father or mother or teacher says "study," many high school youths *will* study. Casual observance would seem to show that the number is decreasing and that students now are asking *why* something must be learned.

Peer approval may at times be so dominating that it supersedes other types of motivation. Certainly peer approval has been an important factor in the drug scene. Interscholastic sports and other group activities provide an incentive for students who are most responsive to the accolades of their classmates.

Competition, the desire to win, or to be number one can be powerful forces. While some educators decry competition in the classroom, others recognize that healthy competition, properly controlled, can be of benefit to some pupils.

Self-concept has assumed new importance in recent years. Pupils from an environment pervaded by a sense of futility about bettering one's situation will make little effort. Such pupils lack confidence and self-assurance of being successful in even minor tasks. Teachers are working diligently to develop a self-pride and a feeling of well-being with one's self for all of our youth. Some efforts at developing pride in one's race have been successful as shown by the "Black is beautiful" slogans.

Ease of learning for other students may be just what the doctor ordered. However, if something is too easy, many soon lose interest.

Life goals may provide the motivation for the long haul. New requirements are being added each year to the list for high school graduation by many states. Although a pupil may not be particularly interested in the subject matter of the requirement, to attain his life goals may require achieving a high school diploma. So the pupil learns the material. However, more and more of the curriculum of the schools is being changed so that the subject matter is more directly related to the goals of the pupils. Courses in bachelor survival, car driving, Western literature, family living, and woodworking for girls are popular, and students approach the work zestfully since they see a direct need for these skills in the near future in marriage or in operating a household.

Rewards may be what some pupils respond to more than any other type of motivation. Rewards can be material things such as money, an automobile, jewelry, grades, candy, or even nonmaterial gains such as release from class or from assigned work.

In years past, educational philosophers favored rewards of a spiritual nature. "The joy of learning," "the pleasure of excellence," "the delight in knowing" were the kinds of rewards held out to all students. "Learning for the sake of learning" was the accepted procedure. Of late, though, some important use has been made of rewards of the material kind and significant gains have been recorded as a consequence. Programs, sponsored by private enterprise companies called *performance contractors,* have featured awards of redeemable green stamps, tokens, and increased leisure time for work done well and on time. Students have been encouraged to apply themselves to their lessons in order to earn stamps or tokens which could be redeemed for cameras, cokes, or candy. Free time, TV periods, or play time could also be purchased with accumulated awards.

So the teacher of the future will have to decide which type of motivation will be most effective with which student and, finally, whether or not the attainment of the behavioral objectives justifies use of a particular type of motivation.

Reading. More attention is probably given to reading than to any other subject in the elementary schools. Yet by the time the pupils begin secondary education in the seventh grade, there may be a six-grade spread in grade-level achievement in reading, as measured on a standardized test. High schools and colleges are heavily oriented toward the use of printed matter as part of instruction. Reading is also important after schooling has been left behind, almost as a survivor skill as in decoding the instruction manuals of a life preserver or a fire extinguisher. In the state of Arizona, a student cannot graduate from high school unless he or she reads English (American style) at the ninth-grade level or better. Such a requirement presents a difficult task to a Mexican-American who has not been long in this country.

Throughout the United States, schools are instituting remedial courses in reading under various headings. Sometimes they are called "speed reading," or "six-week reading," or even just "reading." Such courses meet the needs of those pupils who for one reason or another are two or more grade levels below the norm.

Race and Ethnic Background. A recent newspaper article about stealing passports stated that the United States passport is the most desired because any person of any country of the world could be a United States citizen. Certainly our population contains many more races than most countries and more naturalized citizens and their descendants than any other country.

A student's cultural background can so dominate his thinking that a statement accepted in stride by members of one group may be highly offensive to members of another group. The modern teacher needs to develop a sensitivity or social awareness that was little contemplated previously, and to accomplish this task many have attended workshops focusing on just that topic.

Courses have been developed especially to meet the demands of minority groups, such as the courses in Black history. Other courses have been developed to provide outlets for interests in ethnic activities, such as Chinese cooking, Yoga, soul food, and French cuisine.

We Americans have always had an interest in other lands, which we have tried to cultivate through the study of foreign languages, geography, and other social studies. Except for those periods of war when hysteria prevented it, millions of students each year study many and varied languages. A program new in the 1960s that is meeting with some success because it goes beyond mere instruction in another language is the *bilingual* program. In such a program there is instruction in the language to be learned as well as in the language that is native to the pupil. Thus, a Mexican-American would study science, mathematics, and other subjects in both Spanish and English. There is also specific instruction in Spanish and English as separate subjects. Emphasis throughout the program is on pride in one's heritage. Students now entering high school after some years in such a program are reported to be superior achievers in comparison to those completing a regular elementary school program.

Individual Differences Matrix. As you can see, educators have invented a multitude of provisions for individual differences. A teacher might use a matrix such as the one in Figure 2-1 to keep track of his own provisions for individual differences in a mass teaching situation of the type found in most schools. In the *Unit of Learning* column, he lists units by name or by number of individual learning packet (to be described later in this module.)

Individualized Instruction

American schools are essentially a mass education enterprise. They have to be that way to handle millions of students within somewhat meager budgets. So the immediate problem for the high school teacher, confronted with five sections of English with a total of 180 students, is prescribing the educational experiences that the pupils need at any particular time. No matter what method of individualized instruction is used, it will cost the teacher more effort and more time and the school district more money than the often followed but never recommended practice of using a single textbook for all students in the course. The educational practices to be described herein are all being done now in schools about the country.

Teaching Atmosphere. No matter what one plans to do, it is especially important when considering individualizing instruction to create a relationship be-

Student's Name	I.Q.	Achievement Level	Motivating Factors Operating	Reading Level	Unit of Learning	Ethnic Background	Evaluation
1.							
2.							

Figure 2-1 *Instructional Components.*

tween students and teacher that is conducive to instruction. Teachers must create an atmosphere in which the pupils of the class feel that they are accepted and that what they have to offer will be considered. Pupils discern quickly whether or not a teacher really means it when he or she asks, "Any questions?" or "Is there anybody who does not understand?" A good teaching atmosphere is determined by the relationship between student and teacher and by the attitudes of both toward learning.

In summary, attitudes that particularly influence the atmosphere of the classroom are

1. Positive attitudes toward all persons involved in the instructional process. Students will build their concept of self from the attitude of the teacher and other persons of importance to them. The teacher needs to have a helping positive attitude that oozes confidence in the success of the student in whatever the pupil attempts. If the teacher has the positive attitude of expecting good work, pupils will probably have a similar feeling toward their work and develop acceptance and status in the class group through good work.

2. Attitudes of acceptance of differences. While a certain degree of conformity is necessary in an organized society, differences in value systems, hobbies, ethnic backgrounds, dress, and hairstyle are what make the United States such a unique place in which to live. The teacher who accepts differences can go on to encourage each individual to accept and cherish his own uniqueness and individuality within the framework of group mores, laws, and regulations.

3. Favorable attitudes by both teacher and pupil toward learning. A young child's zest for learning sometimes changes or is diminished by the time he enters the secondary school because of the poor attitudes by which he is surrounded. After leaving high school, sadly enough, some adults stop having any interest in learning anything new. Others go on and never stop, as witness the attendance of golden-agers at seminars on government, classes in handicrafts and painting, square dancing, and the like. In large measure, a pupil's attitude toward learning reflects that of his peers and of his social status. If teachers and classmates place nonlearning activities, such as spectator sports, above learning something new, an indifferent attitude toward knowledge is soon learned. A teacher, however, who is constantly expanding his configuration of experience, seeking new skills and new knowledge, and who demonstrates that he is widely read about contemporary affairs affecting teenagers and the adult world, may help build an attitude of respect for learning in the students with whom he interacts.

4. Receptive attitudes toward pupils' contributions to class activities. Sometimes a student will relate a discovery to the teacher and the class. The teacher needs to nurture any desire of the pupil to seek to understand the unknown. It is through the process of discovery and by relating his discovery to previous learning that a pupil can gain increased control over a field of knowledge. By welcoming pupils' contributions the teacher can cause the students to become more involved in the learning activities of the classroom. Just knowing that the teacher will welcome whatever a pupil has to bring to the discussion creates a wholesome pupil-teacher attitude that is

conducive to a healthy classroom atmosphere. In prescribing individualized instructions, it is especially important that a teacher be receptive to that which a student is discovering for himself and wants to share with someone.

Teaching in Five Acts. Individualized instruction can be divided into five acts.

ACT I—LISTEN. For many teachers who are normally verbal and want to do most of the talking, listening becomes a real challenge. Yet listening can be an important way to gather data for diagnostic purposes. For example, it is through listening that one can determine the speaking vocabulary available for a unit of learning being studied. To comprehend the subject matter, a student needs to have the vocabulary of that field of knowledge. Listening can provide one way of gathering data for diagnostic purposes.

ACT II—OBSERVE. In the affective domain, the only way teachers have of determining the extent of skills is to observe overt behavior. One needs to train oneself to really see what is going on between students. Practiced observers perceive that how a student acts reflects his concept of self. The teacher needs to watch for such blocks to learning as apathy, depression, cultural shock, and the like.

ACT III—DIAGNOSE. An exceedingly difficult task is determining the why of students' learning problems. For example, in some cases, students have done poorly on assignments that involve a considerable amount of reading, both from the chalkboard and from printed matter. These students have shown up under teacher diagnosis to have had problems of poor eyesight. Prescription: Make sure the student sits near the blackboard and also that he puts himself under the care of an ophthalmologist. For the student who reveals that he does not hear well enough or often enough all that is said, the prescription may be similar. Simply provide the opportunity for him to sit near the place from which the sound will come and advise the student to see a doctor.

In such cases, part of the success of the treatment involves the relationship existing between student and teacher and the diplomatic skills possessed by the teacher. Students often know what's wrong with them but are reluctant to face facts. Many students refuse to take steps to remedy bad situations because they fear that their actions will make them conspicuous. Rather than let their peers know that any malady exists, afflicted students may affect a haughty or bored exterior, or resort to disruptive behavior. If teachers have established the proper emotional climate in the classroom, their efforts may be welcomed when they address themselves to traumatic topics of this sort. Effective teachers are sensitive of students' feelings when they discuss the problem discovered. They are also very creative in designing classroom strategies which do not accentuate the overt actions of the afflicted student.

Some of the educational problems not related to the external sense organs are not so obvious. Since teachers are not trained to be medical or psychiatric diagnosticians, it is not expected that their performances will be of a sophisticated nature when they deal with problems of the psyche. Their strength lies in their interest in their students. As they interact with troubled students, they keep themselves alert for cues. The routine nuances of the psychological well-being of adolescents they have learned about from experience. By friendly counsel and encouragement, and with gentle tact and solicitous concern, teachers strive to help young students level out somewhat the undulating pattern of normal emotional life.

However, students who reveal signs of serious difficulty or who appear to be struggling with problems larger than the routine variety must be treated with special attention. Effective teachers gather data and help as much as possible. Their main effort is directed toward either getting professional help through the school for the troubled student or alerting the student and the home to the necessity for action.

ACT IV—PRESCRIBE. Because of the difficulty of diagnosing the exact point of distress a student may be experiencing, the teacher may have to review or reteach somewhat more than is really necessary. Without the ability to determine precisely the point of difficulty in the learning pattern, he may have to adopt a shotgun approach. For example, instead of trying to solve the exact problem causing a student's poor performance in reading, a teacher may assign the student to an entire course in remedial reading. On the other hand, if the course of study has been organized into learning packets, so that the teacher can take individual differences into consideration, the student would need only that program or packet that pertains to the problem.

ACT V—EVALUATE. It is necessary to determine whether the diagnosis and prescription were successful or not. Evaluation may take various forms and may include observation, a performance test, a written test, an electronic response, an oral demonstration of achieving objectives, or other methods. When an evaluation proves that the objectives have not been achieved, then additional remedial steps should be taken after another diagnosis.

Individualized Innovations. Seven types of innovations that focus upon the individual will now be explained.

STUDENT CONTRACTS. The concept of a *contract* in teaching is nothing new, but the amalgamation of the contract concept with behavioral objectives and modern technology is new. Also new is the creation of Contract Learning Centers such as in the Hollis Junior High School in Greenville, South Carolina. Essential to any contract agreement between the student and the teacher is the matter of diagnosis that may involve some or all of the individual differences previously delineated. After the diagnosis is complete, the teacher and student reach agreement upon the level of competence to be achieved as stated in behavioral objectives and upon the anticipated time period required to complete the task. These agreements then become a contract between student and teacher. The student knows the task to be accomplished and when it is to be done. He has assurance, in addition, because of the diagnosis that preceded his meeting, that the task is within his capability.

TEAM TEACHING. Team teaching has been with us for some time now but many still consider it an innovation. As originally conceived and as properly practiced, a team consists of three or more teachers who work cooperatively with a fairly large group of students. Emphasis is on planning the activities, with each teacher assuming responsibility for the area of the course of study in which he has greater knowledge. Depending upon the size of the school, multiple sections of the same course can be scheduled simultaneously for two or more periods of the day. The team can then regroup students to individualize instruction. Or, the team member who is particularly adept at large group presentations may present material to all of the classes. With this method, guests also can be scheduled to talk to and discuss material presented to the entire group. Arranging for such guests is not very feasible in the standard school where five sections of a class are scattered throughout the day in traditional scheduling. The advantage of team teaching, as far as individualization goes, is that it provides a vehicle for small group and individual study.

PROGRAMMED INSTRUCTION. Programmed learning, based on the notion of operant conditioning, has come into its own and is being used by an ever-increasing number of schools. The two basic considerations in this kind of learning are the dividing of the knowledge to be gained into a large number of small steps and the reinforcing of each step for which the presentation of an appropriate stimulus evokes a correct response. By making each successive step as small as possible, the frequency of reinforcement can be raised to a maximum while the possibly aversive consequences of being wrong are reduced to a minimum. Teaching machines have been devised to supply the mechanical help needed so that the teacher can attend to a classroom of students independently following a variety of programs. The device makes it possible to present carefully designed material in which the solution of one problem can depend upon the answer to the preceding problem and in which each student must meet with constant success in order to progress.

Some of the programs are of the textbook variety, which some students have found to be effective and which others have found to be quite dull. Generally, the format used has been that of frames for the presentation of knowledge and instruction, and correct responses to questions posed have been presented in the margin of the page or following the information presented. Students are informed to cover the answer column while they study the explanation and read the question requiring a response. After students decide upon the answer, they are urged to check for accuracy and to continue to the next frame or, if in error, to reread and restudy until the particular frame is mastered. Presently, there are more than 3,500 programmed texts available to the schools. If the student does not like programmed textbooks, there are 500 machine-based multimedia programs to choose from.

A computer-assisted instruction (CAI) program that warrants mention is Westinghouse Electric Corp.'s Learning PLAN (Program for Learning in Accordance with Needs). This program uses instructional materials available in a school, 4,500 cognitive behavioral objectives, and the input of students' records to produce computerized, personalized plans for 30,000 students. Another programmed system that is considered successful is called IPI or Individually Prescribed Instruction. It uses teacher aides as monitors, and in 1972 was under contract for 100,000 pupils in mathematics, English, language arts, and science.[2]

INSTRUCTIONAL OR LEARNING PACKETS. The instructional package is a device that the average classroom teacher can use to bring instruction to each student at the right time and at the correct level. The usual alphabet game has been played by designers in the naming or identifying of their instruction packages: LAP stands for Learning Activity Packages; ARPAC for Arizona Packet; IM for Instructional Module; TLU for Teaching-Learning Units; HIP for Hartford Instructional Packet. Whatever the title, the packets are designed to be virtually self-teaching and include information, directions, and instructions for the pupil to follow. Charts and supplementary readings may be provided in the packet, or students may be referred to the library where materials are on reserve.

---

[2] Phil C. Lange, "What's the Score On: Programmed Instruction?" *Today's Education* (New York: The Journal of the National Education Association, Feb. 1972), p. 59.

There are usually seven components of an instructional package. Different originators, though, have their personal preferences, so some packages may not include all of the following components:

1. Packets concentrate on single concepts. The packet could be concerned with just a part of the whole, something that the student could master in a portion of a regular class period. It is up to the teacher to match the content of the package with the state of educational development of the student. Taking into consideration all of the individual differences that were discussed previously, the teacher makes an educational judgment about the suitability of the packet for any one student. Making such a value judgment is much more challenging and demanding than the stereotyped use of the textbook in teaching. Students and teachers alike are actively engaged in decision making about appropriateness of material and the quality of mastery. Properly used, instructional packets can cause teaching to become a satisfying and rewarding way of life.

2. Behavioral objectives are used as the terminal goals of the packet. Again, it is up to the teacher working with the pupil to make a contract of those objectives that the student is willing to accept and a length of time to reach the terminal behavior. It is important that the pupil accept the objectives of the packet as attainable and proper.

3. The pupils progress at their own rate, using whatever learning style is most efficient for them. Keeping the class at the same place in the textbook has always meant that some students would finish quickly while others who work more slowly might require five or more times as long to learn the material. Packets allow all students to pace themselves. Individual packets also solve the problem of being up one day and down the next. If it is a good day, then the student will speed right along in the packet. By setting one's own pace, the pressure is off the slower student, and the quick learner can zip along without hindrance from the rest of the class. Because of a student's background, some parts of a unit of teaching may be easier for him than are others. The packet takes care of these problems very nicely.

4. Many activities and teaching strategies are incorporated into the packet. The packet offers one way that instruction can be sequenced (to be discussed later) by varying the type of activities. Thus, students may be asked to just list characteristics of some form of plant life, or to use raw data to construct a graph or chart. Media of various types can also be incorporated so that, for example, pupils might view a synchronized silde-tape presentation. Even more sophistication is possible with the new video cassette that could easily be part of an instructional package. Methods of instruction in the packet may range all the way from a didactic presentation to discovery.

5. Enrichment activities are suggested. Many students will want to pursue an idea in considerable depth and breadth. Packets direct attention to readings available in the local library and also in university or regional libraries for further exploration of fields of study.

6. Evaluation techniques or the application of criteria to attainment of the behavioral objectives are used both before and after the student completes the packet. Such evaluative measures range from simple oral questioning before beginning the packet to requests for demonstrable proof upon com-

pletion that the objectives have been achieved. A packet on silver making for a metal overlay project, for example, may set forth at the outset the criteria that will be used to judge the bracelet, ring, or other artifact that the pupil is to make. For some academic areas, the evaluation might include the administration of a standardized test to ensure that the pupil has met state requirements for graduation or advancement.

7. If a pupil does not satisfactorily attain the objectives, he may be required to repeat the packet. When mastery of the subject matter in the packet is an objective, then the pupil should do the work over and over again until the process or material is overlearned. Ideally, there should be more than one matching packet so that a packet with the same concept but with different activities can be issued to the student.

In practice, the use of packets has worked well, but procuring the packets always is a problem. Some good ones are available commercially. Some school districts are keeping teachers on the payroll during the summer to develop packets for the next year. Teachers must exercise caution in the use of packets, lest they turn themselves into clerks who merely keep track of who has what packet, for how long, and scores attained. Whenever possible, the clerical work should be done by the pupils.

MODULAR SCHEDULING. Modular scheduling makes possible individualized instruction in a large school designed for mass instruction. It gets its name from the use of a block of time that is called a *module*. Periods are scheduled using one or more blocks of time to form each class period. Thus period one might be two modules; period two, one module; period three, four modules; period four, three modules; and lunch hour, three modules. A common period of time for a module is twenty minutes. A computer will greatly facilitate the scheduling and is probably essential for schools in which enrollments are in the thousands.

Using the modular schedule makes possible several things in a large school. For above-average students, it facilitates their taking more courses since no one is frozen into a daily course mold. For students who have difficulty in one or more subjects, it facilitates their receiving extra attention or remedial assistance from the teacher.

TUTORIAL METHODS. Tutoring can bring the instruction down to a one to one level by using humans or tape recorders/players. In the Dallas Independent School District, the tutoring program is administered by educators, but the tutoring is done by students. To be eligible to serve as a tutor, a student must attain a prescribed grade average. By 1973, the Dallas system had achieved such status that students were lining up to become part of the program. In addition to the help provided for the tutored student, tutors get to know the subject better, all students get to know each other better, and some new student interests develop.[3]

Another type of tutoring is done by the tape recorder. Vocabulary lists, arithmetic problems, science explanations and instructions can be recorded so that the student can use them at his own pace. With modular scheduling, students are able to come into the laboratory, draw the necessary laboratory equipment along with tape recorder and tape, and proceed to do the lesson. Significantly, the course in science can be structured so that after a certain minimum number of experiments

[3] Wanda Vassallo, "Learning by Tutoring," *American Education* (April 1973), pp. 25–28.

are completed, the tape-tutor provides experiments to meet the needs and interests of the student who wants enrichment activities. Of course, the tape could also be used to present factual material, supplementing a textbook but in such a way that it is more easily understood by the pupils. Students might even make a tape, explaining sections with which other students are experiencing difficulty.

ELECTRONIC EVALUATION. Electronic evaluation may solve some of the ever-occurring problems of teaching—how to find time to grade papers, enter grades in the record book, report grades, and obtain complete information about a student. Computers have been used for more than fifteen years to score standardized examinations, but now a computer service has made it possible to record scores and give readouts of a student's programs. When students are tested at learning centers, the raw score becomes part of the student's record in the computer which is programmed to provide a three-part analysis. The computer can provide in less than two minutes a raw score analysis, subject by subject and skill by skill, a comparison of the student's performance with national norms, and an individual study program, based upon the pupil's past scores, present requirements, and future goals.

When a computer is used for computer-assisted instruction, each response of the student is recorded by the computer. The computer can then give a readout showing the student's strengths and weaknesses for that unit of instruction. Additional information about the student can be stored in the computer so that, by entering the proper code, a teacher can be given an immediate readout that shows the student's age, address, educational progress, life goals, test scores, and any other information placed in the records about the student. Reporting to parents is also greatly simplified since the computer can be programmed to supply upon request printouts of reports all addressed. As of 1974, computers were used more by administrations for grade reporting and record-keeping than by the teachers.

Nongrading

In an attempt to solve some of the problems posed by critics of the schools, educators have sought to do away with the lock-step organization common to many high schools. In most schools, students are organized into grades, and promotion in some cases has been by age and by time (social promotion) rather than by achievement. The average and superior students have to achieve a grade in a subject to receive credit for it and hence be promoted to the next year, sophomore, junior, or senior. Three or more decades ago, a plan was evolved that would do away with grades and allow students to advance according to their accomplishments. Schools operating on such a plan are called nongraded, ungraded, or gradeless schools. In these schools students often work in small groups or as individuals. Such schools are characterized by an organization that has no retention or grade failure, but rather stresses individualized instruction to allow students to progress at their own rate and allows adjustments in programs to fit intrapersonal and interpersonal variability.

More schools on the elementary than the high school level are nongraded. Nongraded primary units have been fairly common for years. One of the best known nongraded high schools in the 1960s was the Melbourne High School in Florida, where subjects were designed for students in five phases of learning dimensions:

1. Special assistance in small classes.
2. Basic skills emphasis.
3. Average ability level subject matter.
4. Subject matter for study in depth.
5. Challenging courses for the superior student working at a level above high school achievement levels.[4]

If one really desires to do away with grade designations, the logistics of the problem do not seem to present any obstacle. With modern computers available for record-keeping, it would seem a simple matter to keep track of any number of students as they complete various packets, courses, or units of work. But change comes hard—in some cases, that which was called nongraded was in fact merely a kind of grouping or semidepartmentalization of instruction. One researcher, John Goodlad, visited many so-called nongraded schools and found none that was truly nongraded.[5]

There seems to be some evidence to show that nongrading can be beneficial. A 1966 study of sixty-two seniors at the Melbourne, Florida High School showed the experimental group outperformed matched pairs at significant levels in English, mathematics, science, and attitudes toward school. However, a 1967 study in which a Nevada nongraded school was compared with a traditional high school found a significant difference in only one of sixty-three hypotheses tested. That one was a gain for the nongraded school students in mathematics reasoning.[6]

Continuous Progress

The term *continuous progress* should be self-explanatory. Continuous progress describes a type of organization that permits a student to increase his achievement level in those areas deemed worthy of study without regard to course designations, grade designations, and other types of inhibitors that might stand in the way of progress. To operate within the full meaning of the term, a secondary school student, for instance, would begin his secondary education after completing the sixth grade and continue until either the required years of attendance set by the state or district had been met, the units required for graduation or admittance to college had been acquired, or his needs had been met. Continuous progress could mean that each student in a school might be working on something entirely different in any one class period.

Obviously, in a continuous progress program there has to be a great deal of individualized instruction. If all subjects are made a part of the program, logistics of the situation can cause a problem. There must be, though, enough material to take care of the largest number of students working in any subject laboratory at any one time. Should all of the students whom a teacher faces on any one day opt to engage in the same activity on a given day, it would become necessary for that

[4] From B. Frank Brown, *The Ungraded High School* (Englewood Cliffs, N.J.: Prentice-Hall, Inc., 1963), p. 50.

[5] Ronald F. Malan and M. David Merrill, "Acronyms Anonymous: Toward A Framework for the Empirical Validation of Methods of Individualizing Instruction," *Educational Technology* (Dec. 1971), p. 32.

[6] Bob F. Steers, "Nongradedness: Relevant Research for Decision Making," *Educational Leadership* (May 1972), p. 710.

teacher to provide 180 copies of the individualized guide. Generally, though, not all students will want the same thing on the same day. Realistically, a continuous progress program could survive if there existed thirty to fifty packets on any of the units of study focused upon for each teacher.

Each teacher must keep daily records of the progress of each student. Although one of the objectives of this kind of program is the cultivation of responsibility by each student for his own progress, for planning purposes and certification purposes each teacher must also have an accounting.

Where continuous progress has been most successful, aides and assistants have been available to serve in several capacities. Some have served primarily as clerks, recording pupil progress or serving as librarians for the subject laboratory. Others, with more specialized qualifications, have devoted their time to writing new packets and adding appropriate materials to the learning center files.

Costs for increased space for learning center facilities, for materials, and for personnel make this type of program more expensive than the conventional program in the average school. As a consequence, the implementation of the continuous progress concept may take long to materialize since few school districts are ready to so tax their financial resources.

Another problem created by the continuous progress program concerns school facilities. With the typical class group sitting, more or less controlled, in front of the teacher, there are a minimum of accoustical problems. Change the size from thirty to sixty, permit each student to work on a different lesson, to talk, to discuss, to operate sound projectors, to use tape recorders, and the learning environment is radically changed. When sounds from the teacher giving directions, and sounds from students experimenting or from students working with different packets are added, the feasibility of carrying on as usual may be severely diminished. Accompany all that with the normal tendencies of teenagers to emit noise when in visual contact, and hope may cease to exist. Instead of planning buildings for large group instruction for all classes, new arrangements are necessary with large spaces for many task-oriented individuals to work. More attention needs to be paid in a continuous-program school to the control of visual and auditory stimuli so that there are quiet areas, soundproof areas, and visual barriers.

With more emphasis on individual effort and on the discovery process, resources need to be made more easily available, possibly from a central instructional resource center and subcenters for those subjects requiring special equipment, such as science, home economics, industrial arts, and others. Such centers need to be properly staffed, probably with a combination media specialist-librarian and clerks.

Independent Study

In the broadest sense independent study is what the pupil does when he learns. Input may be from the visual and aural stimuli received by the pupil, but since only the pupil can learn (that is, since nobody can learn for him), whenever a student learns, independent study is involved. Independent study usually means something in addition to private and solitary application of student to a learning task. A more limiting definition is that independent study is the endeavor of an individual, with the guidance of a teacher, to investigate an area of interest with the responsibility for completion of the task resting with the pupil. We will describe some of the newer types of organization and problems of independent study.

One type of organization is the independent study section or seminar, scheduled to meet regularly as a class and with a teacher-director as leader. There is the danger that such a procedure might become just another class, but it does provide a home base for the pupils enrolled. In a social studies class, for example, a specific topic might be selected for students to pursue individually. Such methodology provides an opportunity for the pupils to attain depth and breadth on a topic. The advantages of such a class organization for independent study are that there are some assurances that the curriculum usually included in regents' exams or board tests would be covered and that some leader is available daily for counsel. In this first type of organization, considerable structuring by the teacher is acceptable and expected.

In another type of organization there is also a section scheduled for independent study. In a seminar arrangement, students select an area of knowledge for investigation with the guidance of the teacher assigned and cooperatively work out the objectives and agree on the time to be devoted to the study. In this variety of independent study plan, each student pursues that which is of most interest to him and consults the teacher when help is needed. The absence of structure is apparent.

In the freest kind of organizations, participating students are scheduled for an independent study period. The pupil is thus free to contact any teacher in the school to work out an independent study program with a teacher of his choice and then for control purposes, file the topic, details, and contract with an administrative officer. This kind of organization puts the maximum amount of responsibility upon the student and requires a great deal of student initiative and dedication if he is to begin and continue until the task is completed.

In this form of independent study, a student follows these procedures:

1. With the guidance of the teacher, determine goals, investigative procedures, and estimate of the amount of time required to complete study of the area of interest.
2. Confer with the teacher on an "as needed" basis. Teacher will help the student maintain proper direction, give encouragement, discuss ideas with possible challenges, and help keep the student motivated for completion of task.
3. Student may share his findings with the independent study group or with another class.
4. Informal discussions with other students in the program on a one-to-one basis may help the student clarify or reinforce ideas gathered from study.
5. Study of the area of interest may be on or off campus. The student may work in a classroom equipped for the specialty work, in an instructional resource center, in a hospital laboratory, or in the law court of a municipal judge.

Evaluation of the independent study could be a real chore for a teacher if responsible for large numbers of students, or if the system or the teacher-director insists upon pencil and paper mastery tests. When computers are available, all the school districts in a region on a time-sharing basis could develop a test question bank about areas of interest commonly studied, and thus reduce the problem to the pushing of a computer button. Such an operation would avoid tests getting out. Other kinds of evaluation include oral reports, final projects evaluated with predetermined criteria, conferences, papers, and scrutiny by the teacher-student team of the degree to which the preset goals were achieved.

Independent study appears to be the answer for some schools to some of the problems that have faced education for a long time. Why then isn't independent study more widely used? In a survey reported by John Casey,[7] the reasons listed were need for additional personnel, no demand from teachers or students, limited library and AV facilities, schedule problems, presence of other pressing problems, regular classes handle such study, the curriculum has no room for independent study, and not needed since 50 per cent of students do not go on to college. The last reason points up a misconception that independent study is only for the superior or college-bound students. Some schools have not found this to be true. The program in some cases has provided the kind of subject matter sought by potential dropouts and the average student seeking more than the standard academic curriculum offers.

Sequential Units

Some educational psychology theory maintains that in learning the student goes from the known to the unknown. Other theory maintains that if we are to get beyond the simple regurgitation of facts, it is necessary to structure the educational experiences so that mental processes of a higher level than simple recall will happen in the mind of the pupil. It is generally accepted that for these processes to happen the instructional operation must be a planned one. The term for that type of instruction which may involve units or topics is *sequential*.

The Kleinway Sequencing Procedure. Based upon the *Taxonomy of Educational Objectives* of Bloom and others, the following planned procedure is offered as an illustration of a sequential operation:

1. Select the idea, topic, or area of study and determine the terminal goals. State the goals in the form and terms of behavioral objectives.
2. Determine the entry level of achievement. It is up to the teacher to use judgment at this point to decide whether or not the student has the level of ability and prior experience for successful achievement in areas pertaining to the established goals.
3. Select sensory experiences to stimulate and provide for simple recall level. Students at this point can give facts, definitions, and symbols.
4. Let students prepare summaries, lists, and categories.
5. Develop opportunities for students to respond to demonstrate comprehension. Encourage the use of graphs and raw data from which students can draw inferences and make interpretations.
6. Provide situations and practice problems in which students can apply what they have just learned.

[7] John P. Casey, "Independent Study for All Pupils," *Clearing House,* **46**:173–174 (Nov. 1971).

7. Give students a whole to break into its component parts. In social studies, an analysis might be made of the causes of the Vietnam War; or in English, a novel or a play might be examined to determine the component parts of the plot.

8. Provide choices of activities wherein pupils demonstrate their ability to build, to construct, to design, and hence to synthesize. In English this might be the writing of an original short story on a topic of their choosing or an adaptation of a classic story in which incidents are changed which then modify and necessitate a new ending. In social studies, it might be writing or constructing a basic document for the rule of a fictitious country or the writing of new laws for cities, states, or the country that are deemed needed for the present time.

9. Apply the criterion or criteria of completion of task. Have the terminal goals been reached? If the pupil is deficient in meeting one or more criteria expressed as behavioral objectives, then the teacher needs to follow the advice given in Number 10.

10. Diagnose and apply remedial instruction, repeating steps 3 through 9 with new subject matter to avoid boredom.

It might be noted that the Kleinway procedure incorporates the following processes: (1) concept formation; (2) intellectual synthesis; (3) early sensory experiences; (4) taxonomy of cognition; (5) principle formation; (6) application of criteria, and (7) diagnosis and reteaching.

SUGGESTED READING

Alcorn, Marvin, et al. *Better Teaching in Secondary Schools,* 3rd Ed. New York: Holt, Rinehart & Winston, Inc., 1970.

Brown, B. Frank. *The Ungraded High School.* Englewood Cliffs, N.J.: Prentice-Hall, Inc., 1963.

————, *New Directions for the Comprehensive High School.* West Nyack, N.Y.: Parker Publishing Company, 1972.

Carl, Dorothy L. "Independent Study Isn't New." *NASSP Bulletin,* **54** (Sept. 1970), 1–8.

Gagne, Robert M. *The Conditions of Learning.* New York: Holt, Rinehart & Winston, Inc., 1965.

Gronlund, Norman E. *Individualizing Classroom Instruction.* New York: Macmillan Publishing Co., Inc., 1974.

Herd, Arthur A. "Successful Practices in Individualized Instruction." *NASSP Bulletin,* **55** (Dec. 1971), 75–82.

Hillson, Maurie, and Joseph Bongo. *Continuous-Progress Education.* Chicago: Science Research Associates, Inc., 1973.

Klingstedt, Joe Lars. "Developing Instructional Modules for Individualized Learning." *Educational Technology,* **11** (Oct. 1971), 34.

McLouglin, William P. "Individualization of Instruction vs Nongrading." *Phi Delta Kappan,* **53** (Feb. 1972), 378–81.

Noar, Gertrude. *Individualized Instruction: Every Child a Winner.* New York: John Wiley & Sons, Inc., 1972.

Popham, W. James. *Criterion-Referenced Measurement*. Englewood Cliffs, N.J.: Educational Technology Publications, 1973.

Ringis, R. Herbert. "What Is 'An Instruction,'" *Journal of Secondary Education,* **49** (May 1971), 96–236.

Sharp, Billy B. "Contract Learning and Humanistic Education." *Educational Technology,* **11** (June 1971), 28–30.

POST TEST

1. Cite five ways of providing for individual differences.

_____

_____

_____

_____

_____

2. Explain briefly how some schools use the I.Q.

_____

_____

_____

3. What are four of the teaching acts used in individualized instruction?

_____

_____

_____

4. Name six of the strategies for individualizing instruction.

_____

_____

5. Write a short paragraph describing how a regular school's program differs from the program of a school that has a continuous progress program.

_____

_____

_____

_____

_____

_____

_____

_____

6. Write a definition or a description of a sequential unit.

_____

_____

_____

_____

7. List the steps for developing a Kleinway sequential unit. Explain what you will do in each step.

_____

_____

_____

_____

_____

_____

_____

_____

_____

_____

_____

_____

8. Define modular scheduling and mention how it is used to provide for individual differences.

_____

_____

_____

_____

_____

_____

9. What are the components of an instructional package?

_____

_____

_____

_____

_____

10. Describe the characteristics of a nongraded school.

_____

_____

11. Describe three types of individual study organizations.

_____

_____

_____

_____

_____

_____

_____

Institutional Innovations

Raymond L. Klein

The University of Arizona

module 3

Interaction Analysis / Behavioral Objectives / School Consortiums / Open Schools / Alternative Education / Student Governance / Teachers' Governance

RATIONALE

The variety of innovations being introduced in the schools throughout the country for the purposes of improving instruction and enriching the learning experiences of students results from a number of causes. In some cases, the concept and the components of the new program are the result of efforts by experienced teachers to upgrade the quality of learning in the traditional classroom. In other cases, the new design has little relation to what has been considered standard in the past, but sets out to achieve the goal of improvement in the product by changing the process radically or by postulating a whole series of new and different goals.

Established teachers, already deeply committed to a school system, have accustomed themselves to the adaptation process over the years of their teaching experience. Many aspects of innovations designed as integral parts of radical programs have frequently attracted the professional eye of the conscientious teacher and have been adapted and installed out of context to do a job that needs to be done.

As teachers in training now, your career steps may place you in a situation in which the new is commonplace. The school that will employ you in the future may already have introduced all of the innovations treated in this module and may expect you to arrive fully equipped to pick up the tempo of the drums to which that faculty is marching. It could be, though, that you, too, will be expected to live through one or many years of adaptation before the old is laid aside. As you study this module, strive to capture the vivifying spirit behind each of the innovations discussed. Learn how to apply analysis to your teaching so that you can avoid the monotony inherently possible in the lecture method, and learn how to devise objectives that make it possible for your students to know what is expected of them. Wrestle with the pros and cons of the other issues, such as the open school and the alternative school, consortia, and student governance to determine the aspects of each that can be absorbed into your philosophy of education. No matter what the pace of your professional career, you will be expected to know much more about each of these innovations than can be accommodated in the small space allotted to this module.

Specific Behavioral Objectives

Upon completion of your study of this module, you should be able to perform all of the following objectives:

1. Write a definition of interaction analysis with 100 per cent accuracy.
2. Name the leading exponent of the interaction analysis system.
3. Contrast direct and indirect influence of teacher behavior and give six differences.
4. List the categories of interaction analysis with 90 per cent accuracy.

5. Given a list of categories of interaction analysis, describe and define each category with 100 per cent accuracy.
6. Given a class, tab the behaviors in the matrix in a thirty-minute presentation.
7. Given a tabulated matrix, interpret it with 100 per cent accuracy.
8. Write a definition of behavioral objectives with 100 per cent accuracy.
9. Apply three criteria to written statements to determine their quality as behavioral objectives with 100 per cent accuracy.
10. List the differences between an open school and an alternative school.
11. From past experience, contrast an alternative school with a regular school.
12. Cite some examples of alternative schools in the United States.
13. List three guiding principles for writing regulations for length of hair and for mustaches.
14. Given the type of student governance problems, cite at least one court case with the court's finding decided for the problem.
15. Given the name of a court case about student governance, write a summarizing sentence about the decision of the court.
16. Describe the difference between tenure and continuing contracts.

MODULE TEXT

Interaction Analysis

In any classroom there is constant action and interaction going on between students and teachers, teacher and students, and among the students themselves.

Attempts have been made to analyze the verbal behavior component of this interaction between students and teachers to determine the extent of the relationship in classes of high achievers as compared to classes of low achievers. Varied teacher behaviors, the researchers found, elicit different responses from the students. The very method used in asking a question, even to the wording of the question, it seems, can condition the response of the student in a number of ways.

If a narrow recitation type of question is asked, the response might well be a single word, phrase, or sentence. If the teacher poses a broader question, the pupil may initiate ideas or make a contribution that of itself raises a question, so that other students are stimulated to participate.

Various systems of analysis which classify pupil and teacher talk have been evolved. The earliest and the one well established by research is that of Ned Flanders, called the Flanders System of Interaction Analysis. Not only does it categorize the verbal behavior occurring in the classroom, but it also enables the observer and the teacher to summarize, analyze, and draw inferences from the data collected by means of application of the system.

Essentially, in devising their systems, researchers compared classrooms in which they found teacher behavior patterns that were different from each other. These they identified as integrative or dominative, authoritarian or democratic, teacher-centered or student-centered, preclusive or inclusive, direct influence or indirect influence. The characteristics of the patterns are contrasted in the chart below:

Democratic Pattern (*Indirect influence*)	*Autocratic Pattern* (*Direct Influence*)
Determines policies by group discussion.	Policies determined by teacher.
Praises and encourages in an objective manner.	Gives praise or criticism in a personal way.
Takes part in group activities.	Remains aloof from group participation.
Uses questions to stimulate pupil participation.	Gives orders and directions to students sometimes like army sergeant.
Directs goal-centered activities with alternatives of action.	Selects techniques and activities and presents one at a time.
Accepts and clarifies ideas of pupils and is supportive of ideas.	Lectures much, presents own ideas or knowledge by didactic method.

Generally speaking, the researchers concluded that the democratic pattern or indirect influence type of teacher behavior produced the more favorable results. They recognized, however, that teaching effectiveness could mean different things to the different judges. Supervisors and principals, for example, might apply one set of criteria while pupils might apply another. And so they caution that the conclusion should not be made from their findings that indirect influence is to be preferred all of the time or that it is used by superior teachers all of the time.

Statements of some basic research findings, listed here, provide the basis for the interaction analysis procedure.

1. When students perceive a teacher's behavior as democratic, they do more assigned and extra school work.
2. Teachers adapt to the situation and vary democratic and autocratic behavior.
3. Psychologically different students have different reactions to the same teacher behavior pattern.
4. In a study using ten-year-old children, aggression (hostility) was eight to thirty times greater in the autocratic situation.
5. There is some evidence that older pupils react differently to an autocratic situation than do younger pupils five to seven years old.
6. When teacher behavior is observed over a fairly long period of time, the indirect (democratic) rather than the direct (autocratic) behavior pattern develops desirable pupils' attitudes and superior work patterns.

Categories of the Interaction System. The Flanders system of categorizing teacher behavior uses ten categories. Teacher behavior is classified as either direct influence with three categories, or indirect with four categories. Student behavior uses two categories and the remaining category is used to record silence or confusion in the classroom. Flanders has defined the two kinds of influence as follows:

Direct influence consists of the teacher's stating of own opinion or ideas, directing the pupil's action, criticizing pupil behavior, or justifying the teacher's authority or use of that authority.

Indirect influence consists of the teacher's soliciting the opinions or ideas of the pupils, applying or enlarging on those opinions or ideas, praising or encouraging the participation of pupils, or clarifying and accepting their feelings.[1]

INDIRECT TEACHER BEHAVIOR. Category *1* is characterized by acceptance of feeling. Evidence of this teacher behavior is that the teacher accepts the feelings of the pupils and does not punish them for how they feel. He believes and shows by his behavior that youths have a right to have feelings and may reveal without penalty their convictions about past, present, or future events. The teacher's overt behavior and statement that he knows how youths feel will be reassurance that the feelings expressed are accepted without penalty.

Category *2* is characterized by praise or encouragement. If praise is given without being warranted, then praise will cease to have any effect. But if judiciously applied, even if it is just a word or two, praise will cause good rapport and increase motivation on the part of the student. On Flanders' interaction analysis, it will get the teacher a good mark. Encouragement is verbal or nonverbal communication that supports the student in what he is doing. It might include statements such as, "That is correct" or "Very good—tell me more."

Category *3* involves accepting ideas. Like category one, this category includes the concept of acceptance. Instead of feelings, however, Category *3* deals with the acceptance of students' specific ideas. A teacher may show acceptance by paraphrasing a student's statement, saying, "That's a good point. Would anyone like to comment on the effects of what Jack proposes?" Also proper for this category is the summarizing by the teacher of what a student has said. A key factor will be whether the teacher's statement reflects the student's idea or is really an expansion, made up mostly of the teacher's commentary. If it is the latter, then it is classified as Category *5*.

Category *4* involves asking questions. Only questions that require an answer from the students are included in this category. If a rhetorical question is asked, it is classified in Category *5* since it is really lecturing. Similarly, questions used to maintain control of the class are not categorized as asking questions but rather as statements to be classified in Category *7*. Both recall type or the reflective thinking type are classified as asking questions. So whether a teacher asks, "What year was the Constitution ratified?" or "What were the causes of the United States entering World War I?" both are classified in Category *4*.

DIRECT TEACHER BEHAVIOR. Category *5* emphasizes the lecture approach. Lecture as used here has a somewhat broader connotation than the lecture method. Any form of verbal behavior used to present facts, ideas, opinion, information via chalkboard or projector is called a lecture. Usually in precollegiate schools, teacher lectures are interspersed with questions, illustrations, and students' questions and comments.

Category *6* involves giving directions. Sometimes there is a fine line between giving a direction and a command but, regardless of which it is, this type of action is classified in Category *6*.

---

[1] Edmund J. Amidon and John B. Hough, editors, *Interaction Analysis: Theory, Research, and Application* (Reading, Mass.: Addison-Wesley Publishing Inc., 1967), p. 109.

Category *7* concerns criticizing or justifying authority. Verbal criticism includes statements designed to change behavior which the teacher considers to be nonacceptable to that which is acceptable. Included in this category are "chewing someone out," reprimanding, or chastizing. Also included here are the teacher's defense of his actions and the extreme self-reference of the "do this for me" variety.

STUDENT BEHAVIOR. Category *8* involves student talk as response. Included in the category is the verbal response to what the teacher has said. Even though the teacher has initiated the contact, if the student responds, the classification is Category *8*.

Category *9* concerns student talk as initiation. Talk initiated by students falls in this category. Any comments in a discussion made by a student that are not directly solicited by the teacher are appropriate for this listing.

OTHER BEHAVIOR. Category *10* involves silence or confusion. Anything not included in the other categories falls here. Periods of silence, pauses, poor communication with resulting confusion all are to be classified as Category *10*.

Procedure for Categorizing Teacher-Pupil Interaction. The first step in mastering the technique is to overlearn the various categories and to have practice observation sessions. After the observer knows the categories extremely well, he is ready to record the verbal behavior in the classroom. Using a regular class session or the tape recording of such a session, every three seconds the observer writes down the appropriate category number for the verbal behavior going on in the classroom. The numbers are recorded in a sequence in a column beginning and ending with *10*. A typical recording session might result in a column of numbers that looks like this:

10
6
10
8
1
7
2
4
3
3
1
9
9
6
10

Categorizing is an extremely complex operation. Perhaps a few suggestions might help develop consistency in classifying teacher behavior.

1. Spend about five or ten minutes orienting yourself to the classroom situation whether it is live or on tape.
2. Stop classifying when the activity changes. Draw a line under the recorded numbers making a note of the change.

3. At all times make notes about the type of activity being observed.
4. When uncertain about the category to use to classify a behavior, use the number farthest from *5*. Thus if in doubt about a *3* or *4*, use a *3*. Similarly if in doubt about an *8* or *9*, use *9*. This procedure applies for all categories except *10*, which is never chosen if an alternate category is under consideration.
5. If a teacher is consistently direct or indirect in his behavior, do not classify anything as the opposite type of behavior unless there is a clear indication that the teacher has moved in that direction. There often is a danger here that the observer will not move into the opposite category early enough or at all.
6. The observer must remove himself from the influence of his own biases or the teacher intent and be most concerned with the effect the behavior has upon the students. Even though the teacher intends to try to increase pupil participation, if his action does not elicit the desired pupil behavior, it should be categorized as a *7* or *5* instead of one of the direct categories.
7. At the three-second interval, all behavior that happens is to be categorized. There may be two or three categories recorded for the interval but if no change in behavior occurs, then the same category number is used that was used for the previous classification.
8. A *10* is recorded for silence longer than three seconds. Short pauses are usually ignored.

A device called a matrix is used to convert the raw data into a form that can be used for interpretation of the classroom behavior. The column of figures is tabulated into the squares of the matrix to represent pairs of numbers. A beginning of a column of classifications might appear as follows:

$$
\begin{array}{c}
10 \\
10 \\
6 \\
6 \\
2 \\
4 \\
8 \\
3 \\
9 \\
9 \\
9 \\
10
\end{array}
$$

These numbers are entered into the matrix in sequence pairs in such a way that each number is entered twice—once as the first number in a pair and once as a second number in a pair. The rows of the matrix represent the first number in the pair, and the columns, the second number in the pair. For example, the first sequence pair, *10–10* would be tallied in the cell that is located at the intersection of Row *10*–Column *10*. The next pair is entered in cell *10–6*, the cell at the intersection of Row *10* and Column *6*, the third pair *6–6* into the cell located at the intersection of Row *6* and Column *6*. It is for this reason that a *10* is entered as the first number and the last, and was chosen since it is assumed that each recording began and ended with silence. The numbers in the example cited were part of a recording session. The full matrix for the example is shown in Figure 3-1.

Examination of the matrix table shows that in this class the teacher talked 54 per cent of the time and students talked 45 per cent of the time. With only two tallies in column 10, only 1 per cent of the time was spent in silence or confusion.

Use of the Matrix. If one were to shade columns 4 and 5 both horizontally and vertically, the shaded area would form what has been called the *content cross,* because the tallies in these squares indicate that the teacher is verbalizing heavily by lecture, presenting ideas and information, and questioning about material that he has presented. Heavy tallies in *6–6, 6–7, 7–6,* and *7–7* indicate use of criticism, heavy use of authority, and often show a discipline problem. Heavy concentration in *8–8, 8–9, 9–8,* and *9–9* indicates that there is much student talk that has been stimulated by the classroom situation. If *10–8* and *10–9* were heavily tabulated, then it would indicate that the student discussion was followed by silence or confusion.

Although the best use of interaction analysis would be for teachers to listen to and criticize their own tapes, administrators could use it for performance recertification. Teachers who did not reach the arbitrary standard set, such as teacher talk no more than 60 per cent and student talk no less than 30 per cent, would not be recommended for recertification.

Additional findings from matrix data research note that little difference in the use of Category *1* has been found between direct and indirect influence

						Second						
		1	2	3	4	5	6	7	8	9	10	Total
	1	10										
	2		25		1		1					
	3			4					4	1		
	4		2		3				1			
	5					20						
First	6		1				6					
	7							4				
	8			1	6				25	15		
	9	3			5				16	15	1	
	10						1				1	
	Total	13	28	5	15	20	8	4	46	31	2	172
	Col.%	8	16	3	9	12	5	2	27	18	1	

Teacher talk
Columns 1–7 = 93
or 54%

Student talk
Columns 8–9 = 77
or 45%

Figure 3-1   *An Interaction Analysis Matrix.*

teachers, and both kinds of teachers seem to use the same amount of praise as indicated by Category *2*. Also, in Category *3,* acceptance of ideas, direct teachers use this about 2 per cent and indirect teachers do this about 9 per cent of the time. In Category *4,* responses vary 8 to 15 per cent, and in Category *5,* from 25 to 50 per cent. There is a variance by subject, with science or mathematics teachers using lecture about 50 per cent of the time, and in social studies, the teacher is likely to lecture about 30 per cent of the time.

The kinds of questions can be ascertained by examining the number of tallies in cells *4–8* and *8–4* of the matrix. If there is a concentration in cell *4–8,* it indicates that the teacher-questions are followed immediately by student response, and shows that the teacher has asked many direct questions that solicit a small range of student responses. If the *8–4* cell is loaded but there are few tallies in other *8* cells, then it may be that the teacher is responding to the students' questions with another question. A *4–10* tally would indicate that periods of silence follow the teacher's questions. If the heavy *4–10* cell is accompanied by heavy tallies in *10–8* or *10–9* cells, then the teacher has probably asked the type of questions requiring time to think through. A teacher with heavy tallies in the *4–5* and *4–6* cells may not be giving the students time to answer his questions; if the *5–4* cell is heavy, questions are being asked during lecturing. If the *5–7* cell is heavy, the teacher is probably trying to maintain control while lecturing by using criticism of one kind or another.

The matrices can be a real aid to a teacher for self-evaluation. All that is necessary is to tape record a class session, play it back, and categorize the verbal behavior. By keeping matrices over a period of time, the teacher can work to develop teaching behavior in those areas in which he may desire to effect change.

BEHAVIORAL OBJECTIVES

To use or not to use behavioral objectives is a moot question. Those who would not, argue that teaching by behavioral objectives is bad because the specificity of the objectives puts the instruction in the category of training rather than in education. Those who would use behavioral objectives say that teachers must have a specific idea where they are going in order to be effective. Some educators would draw a fine line between the terms *behavioral objectives, instructional objectives,* and *performance objectives.* The three terms will be used interchangeably in this module.

Behavioral objectives are statements about the specific behavior to be demonstrated by a student after he has completed and as a result of having completed the learning assignment. You will note that in the treatment of innovations in Module 2, again and again reference was made to such behavioral objectives. New educational materials, such as costly multimedia kits, often include behavioral objectives in statements of what is termed performance objectives. From the standpoint of students, the advantage of these objectives lies in being informed of the specific details of that which they are expected to learn. Unfortunately, we have no hard research data that either supports or contests the use of objectives of this sort.

Any study designed to determine a significant difference between two methods of instruction in which one uses performance objectives and another does not would be biased in favor of the former. The reason is that the criterion tests used in situations in which behavioral objectives are specified usually reflect the objectives listed. Thus, although one student might prepare himself by study to respond to specific questions about which he has been alerted, the other student would be forced to prepare himself in general to respond to questions of any sort. For purposes of illustration, suppose we were to give two students with equal skill two pieces of silver: a 3x6-inch piece of sheet silver of 20 gauge, a 12-inch length of 18-gauge silver wire, and also a turquoise gem stone, elliptically shaped, typed cabochon. From the materials one student might make a bracelet. The second student might produce a large bolo tie clasp. If we compare the products of these students and choose as our criterion of success the attributes of a bracelet, the second student would lose out. Obviously, he had no intention of making a bracelet, so comparing his product to a bracelet and failing him would make no sense. Of course, other criteria of workmanship and design could have been used, but without prior publication of these criteria, it is not proper to use them as evaluative criteria. If the students had knowledge of the criteria prior to beginning, there would have been a greater chance that the criteria would have been met. Similarly in the teaching situation, once the criteria for comparing teaching strategies are known, there is fair certainty that the strategies will be biased to satisfy criteria.

Please note that we do not insist that performance objectives have to be used in all instruction. Rather, we believe that being able to utilize them is a skill that will profit the neophyte teacher when evaluating the performance objectives that accompany textbooks and media, and also when submitting proposals for grants.

When writing behavioral objectives:

First, develop a thorough knowledge of the subject matter. If it helps you to acquire overlearning of the area of knowledge you are concerned with, outline a part of it.

Second, make a list of some of the behaviors you would expect pupils to exhibit after completing the unit, module, packet, or program.

Remember that a performance objective is a statement of certain specific behaviors to be demonstrated by a student after the completion of a unit of instruction, a packet, or a program. The statement should stipulate clearly and concisely under what conditions and to what extent the student will be able to perform as requested in order to demonstrate attainment of the objective.

The term *behavior* has sometimes been misinterpreted in a narrow sense to mean a mechanistic dehumanizing type of performance. This is a misunderstanding. The intention is rather to describe overt behavior that demonstrates or reveals cognitive and affective learnings that have occurred. It should be noted that there are three criteria to be applied to establishing goals that are called behavioral objectives:

1. There must be a precise statement of how attainment of the objective is to be measured.
2. There must be a statement of the given conditions.
3. There must be a precise action verb used to designate the specific kind of behavior that is to be observed by the teacher.

In past years it has not been unusual to read such objectives as, "To appreciate fine music" or "To know the causes of the Civil War." Such statements were, of course, vague and provided little direction to the learning of the class. When did student or teacher know how or when appreciation was achieved or knowledge mastered? Performance objectives are quite specific, on the other hand, even to the point of giving the kinds of conditions under which the goals are to be realized. The kinds of conditions described might include the materials and surroundings to which the student is to be exposed during the process of evaluation and also the materials and experiences of the instructional period. These conditions are called the *situation*. An example of a situation statement might be, "After viewing a filmstrip depicting ten causes of the Civil War and without any additional materials. . . ." Since additional materials are excluded, the requirement of stating the testing situation has been met.

Another example of a situation specified as part of a performance objective follows: "Given a map of the Battle of Gettysburg with color code keys for the combatants and symbols for the lines of attack, withdrawal, and siege, the student will be able to contrast three battle actions of the Confederacy with three of the Union." Here the situation statement describes the material available to the student in learning along with the testing situation. To check if you have correctly stated the situation statement, ask yourself whether one of your better students or a colleague could create the test condition that you intended.

Since the only way one can determine if a pupil has learned all or part of the unit of instruction is by the pupil's overt behavior, the objective has to have a behavioral term or action verb. Typical verbs are *state, group, name, demonstrate, identify, list, construct, design, write, contrast, classify, match, remove, analyze*. The criteria for a behavioral term are that it denotes action and that it is measurable.

The last part of a performance objective is a statement of the acceptable or minimum level of performance. In the previous example, students must be able to contrast three actions of the combatants. Acceptable levels may be stated in the number or percentage of correct responses to a teacher-constructed test that constitute the acceptable level. A pupil may have to list a certain number of things, facts, or conditions. Sometimes the criterion is 100 per cent learning; for example, students might be expected to list all of the elements in table sugar.

Performance objectives are difficult to write correctly, and the process is qui[te] time-consuming. Fortunately, depositories of objectives have been compiled t[hat] can be of great help. One file in Los Angeles has thousands of performance[ob]jectives for particular subjects and grade levels.[2] Another featuring measures i[n the] affective domain is at the University of Colorado, under the leadership of G[ene] Glass.[3]

We reiterate it is not our position that all instruction in the classroom[be] described in performance objectives. It may well be that there are some [that] are not easily definable, yet are of great importance. These probably wo[uld consti]tute a relatively small portion of the total goals of the school year. [A] teacher's objectives should be clear, concise, and measurable statem[ents of what] is to be learned.

---

[2] Instructional Objectives Exchange, Box 24095, Los Angeles, Calif. 90[
[3] Laboratory of Educational Research, University of Colorado, Boulder.

School Consortiums

Rising costs, decreasing enrollments, ever-increasing curricular demands, and new and continuing requests for more services have set the stage for a new arrangement between schools and districts. The arrangement has made it possible for relatively small or remote schools and districts to offer courses and services previously common to only fairly large, urban schools. Such arrangements have been called consortiums or shared services. A *consortium* is a formal partnership or association between two or more schools or school districts. It can be a legalized, formal arrangement or an agreement between two or more parties sealed with a handshake. The schools or districts work together cooperatively to provide the services or courses that neither could afford to offer alone. The next few paragraphs describe some representative consortium projects.

Some Examples. One of the problems facing the youth of today is that of obtaining career information for the making of vocational choices. A project called the Heart of Georgia Shared Services Project has provided pupil personnel services for students in seven Georgia districts. In North Dakota consortiums have been used to expand the curriculum. The Coteau Hills Resource Center at Ellendale, North Dakota, serves 143 schools in fifty-three districts, offers courses such as power mechanics and basic electronics, and provides needed books to schools in remote areas.[4] In the rural Southern Appalachian Mountain area, the Appalachia Educational Laboratory has taken the leadership in developing designs for *course sharing*. In some cases, courses taught by master teachers are transmitted to other schools by using media of various sorts, including mobile laboratories. The methods and procedures for instruction in a course have also been revised to meet the approval of all, and are then distributed to schools for self-instruction. One outstanding example of cooperating effort was in the development of a driver-education course. Fundamentals were taught by film with half of the behind-the-wheel work handled by simulators transported from school to school in trailers. Automobiles for the course also move from school to school. It is estimated that this can increase the number of students trained by 150 per cent and do the [5]

Open Schools

The philosophy behind open schools has been with us for hundreds of years. The surge of the open school probably got its greatest impetus when it developed in England in the years following World War II. This idea had spread to the United States and has been growing

The open school is more than just an organization of the building or physical

"... g up the Small School Districts," *American Education,* **6:**18–

... be obtained from The Research and Information Center, ...ry, Inc., Box 1348, Charleston, W.Va. 25325.

facilities. Rather, it is a general acceptance and implementation of a philosophy that makes the instructional process somewhat different from that in traditional schools. Some general distinguishing qualities of open schools are

1. There is a general informality about the school. Children move freely about the building and grounds and around the classroom. It sometimes seems that whatever the pupils want to bring to school they do; for example, some bring old things and animals of various species.
2. Teachers look upon each pupil as unique, and emphasize the total growth of the individual. Development as a person seems to be more important than the development of skill or knowledge.
3. Evaluation procedures are varied. Observation of the pupils over a long period of time plays a larger role, and formal testing procedures, a much smaller part in the evaluative process than in a regular school.
4. Teachers and administrators play a greater role in determining what the student will learn than they do in schools with structured, preset curriculums. Such is the case with the teacher who is selecting the learning experiences on a daily basis for the pupil with more attention to the needs and interests of the students.
5. In the elementary and junior high schools the teachers implement the theory that children learn by proceeding from the concrete to the abstract. There is great emphasis on realism and experiences with people and places.

Throughout the open school, there is an atmosphere of human warmth with closer relationships between instructor and student. The students seem to respond well and believe that the open school fills their personal needs better than a regular school.

One school that has utilized much of the philosophy of the open school is the John Dewey High School in Brooklyn, New York. In this school, the grade levels are gone; so are the Carnegie unit, five-period-a-week daily meetings, major and minor subjects, artificial restrictions upon college-bound and noncollege students, and lock-step learning. Attendance at the school is voluntary. A factor in the success of the school seems to be that new faculty members have to attend a summer institute for a program of orientation and preparation of materials.[6]

A certain degree of caution might be voiced about adopting the open school in this country. One must always be careful when transplanting a way of doing something from one culture to another. Although both the British and Americans speak English, the traditions and customs of each country are obviously quite different. In the English open schools, although there is informality, there is direction on the part of the instructors. The teaching is not laissez faire; rather, it follows the discipline of the task. Even if American students should be ready for open schools, it may well be that the faculty and administrators are not ready to implement the concept.

The band wagon syndrome is quite prevalent. Some schools that have changed appearance by removing desks and introducing casual furniture and old lounge chairs use the new open school vocabulary. But as in the past with so many so-

[6] Sol Levine, "The John Dewey High School Adventure," *Phi Delta Kappan,* **53:**108–109 (Oct. 1971).

called innovations, the changes made have been only surface deep and have little profound significance. Many of these ephemeral changes have not been thought through and are only minimally planned. There has been little or no faculty involvement to determine if the teachers want to be committed to the open school idea. Since it is possible that a fine idea may be unworkable in some districts or in some schools, it is wise practice that administrators, students, teachers, parents, and boards of education investigate thoroughly before moving too far toward open education.

Alternative Education

The open school is, in effect, a type of alternative education; it is an alternative to the regular school. But there are other methods of handling the problems facing education today that result in other ways for pupils to complete secondary education. Alternative schools represent another choice or even several other alternatives to the regular, highly structured school. In an alternative school, the curriculum might consist of studying cybernetics, keeping ahead of the building inspector, Zen gardens, raising goats, organizing food crops, and some structured courses not usually offered by the regular schools. The following list includes many characteristics commonly found in alternative schools. Not all alternative schools would have all of these characteristics, but most would have at least some of them.

1. There is an informal structure with no grades or grade levels.
2. The organization of the school is democratic or non-autocratic.
3. There is a minimum of formal requirements. Students take courses according to their interests and needs. No courses are required for graduation.
4. There is great concern with the whole of life experiences. Aesthetic, cognitive, and sensory experiences and value systems are viewed not as separate elements, but as integral parts of the whole person.
5. Some aspects of the activities of alternative schools take on a politically radical hue when compared to the middle-road political philosophy dominating the country.
6. Teachers are looked upon as managers of the learning environment rather than imparters of knowledge.
7. The community is often used as a learning laboratory.
8. Classes are conducted with a great deal of flexibility. In some schools, classes are quite small.

Recently, however, as a reaction, a number of alternative schools seem to be more traditional and old-fashioned than those they replaced.

Types of Alternative Schools. There have been alternatives to the regular high schools for a number of years. Many large cities of the United States have vocational schools, technical schools, schools of fine arts, and other specialized high schools. But most of the schools that are called alternative schools today go a step further. In the alternative schools of the past, there was still considerable structure in curriculum requirements and in organization of the school. The following are representative of the various types of the newer alternative schools:

CULTURE-ORIENTED. Such schools might enroll students of many cultures who study their own cultures, Chicano, Black, Chinese or German, and who also meet and work together in multicultural activities. Another such type of school is a monoculture school or a monoethnic school, such as one for Blacks only.

COMMUNITY SCHOOLS. Just as the name implies, the organization and curriculum of the true community schools is outside of the schools' walls. Although many districts have a community education program, they still operate a regular school. For a community school to qualify as an alternative school, its students must have the option of attending the community school instead of the regular school and upon satisfactory completion of the community school program, they must be granted a diploma.

HUMANISTIC SCHOOLS. In humanistic schools, emphasis is upon the development of the person. The school-without-walls is an attempt to design a program that enables a pupil to realize his capabilities, to develop a high self-concept, and to strive for a satisfactory relationship with the social world.

ENVIRONMENTAL SCHOOLS. This curriculum is centered upon the world about one, the environment, hence the name.

BASIC SKILLS. The schools of the basic skill type were organized to meet the need of those pupils who for one reason or another need strengthening in the area of basic skills.

CAREER EDUCATION. The program in this type school might be of a general nature that involves career exploration, or it might offer courses in specific vocational skill areas.

SPECIAL AREA SKILLS. Some educators will probably quarrel with the choice of placing college preparation schools in this category. But in the true sense of the word *skill,* students who excel at college prep work are high in scholastic aptitude and therefore develop scholastic skills. Also included here would be those schools having special programs in the fine arts—music, art, and photography.

Some Examples. A few examples of schools and their programs about the United States will illustrate the diversity of the alternative school movement. Berkeley, California offers students about twenty-five alternative schools each of which enrolls 50 to 600 students. These schools offer an extremely wide range of alternatives. For instance, the school called the Asian Component concentrates on Asian studies; Black House, on Black studies; Genesis, on Student governance; Model A, on college studies; and KARE, on basic skills.[7]

A Portland, Oregon alternative is called the "Personalized Education Program (PEP). Its dominating philosophy is that the school should be shaped to fit the students' needs. The staff developed a program for dropouts, called the Vocational Village, and a type of Job Corps, entitled the Residential Manpower Center (RMC). Although the administration of the schools is a responsibility of the Portland Board of Education, the instructional activities are in facilities other than regular school buildings. The Vocational Village is in a storefront business-warehouse, and RMC is in three separate buildings, formerly used for a junior college, a hotel, and a seminary, about twenty miles from Portland. Although some school districts have alternative schools within the regular school on the same grounds,

[7] Larry Wells, "Options in a Small District," *National Association of Secondary School Principals Bulletin,* **57:**55–60 (Sept. 1973).

Portland is having success with separate facilities for those pupils with special needs.[8]

The Cambridge Pilot School in Cambridge, Massachusetts offers an informal program, with diverse curricular offerings, that includes a wide range of personal and communicative styles. It is housed within its parent school and so provides an example of an alternative school-within-a-school. Efforts of the faculty and students have been evaluated annually, and the continuing success experienced has helped to diminish steadily the negative pressure applied earlier. The school is now accepted by more people as a respectable option for students' secondary education.[9]

Costs. One last comment concerns the cost of alternative schools. In some cases, attendance in an alternative school is determined by the economic status of the student, since some tuitions are as high as $600 a year. Other such schools are operated as part of the budget of the school district with only normal charges, similar to those paid by students in regular schools. If an alternative school does have a rather large tuition, it may not be available for the very student who might need it the most, the student of low socioeconomic status.

Student Governance

To delimit this topic of governance of students because of space limitations in this module, only the areas of appearance, communication, and search of lockers will be explored here. In past years, the guides for legal action have revolved around the principles of in *loco parentis* and the reasonableness of rules and regulations. Court decisions since 1960 have pretty well done away with the *loco parentis* concept wherein the teachers, administrators, and boards of education set regulations that in some cases were quite restricting. These decisions have supported reasonableness as the test of whether or not the action of a student could cause disruption of the activities of the school or interfere with the control of the student body.

Appearance. Many of the cases reaching the courts had to do with length of hair and the right to wear beards and mustaches. A majority of the cases between 1960 and 1971 were decided against the students. Of a total of sixty-nine cases in federal and state courts, thirty-eight were decided unfavorably to the students.[10] In such cases, issues other than hair, disruption of the school, and health and safety hazards were involved. The courts have held that the administrator should be allowed to exercise judgment in determining what is or what is not a disruption of the school. In such cases the courts accepted the testimony of educators that the

[8] Richard Boss, "Portland's Personalized Education Program," *Educational Leadership,* **29:**405–407 (Feb. 1972).

[9] Ray F. Shurtleff, "Administrative Problems? Cambridge Pilot School," *National Association of Secondary School Principals Bulletin,* **374:**76–82.

[10] Elwood M. Clayton and Gene S. Jacobsen, "An Analysis of Court Cases Concerned with Student Rights 1960–1971," *National Association of Secondary School Principals Bulletin,* **58:**49 (Feb. 1974).

wearing of long hair constituted a disruptive influence in the school.[11] The 1970s, however, have seen something of a shift in the courts' position.

The courts in recent years have held that the students' rights do not cease when they enter the school grounds. Rather, they have the same rights generally that an adult has under the United States Constitution. Some guiding principles have been given by the courts to the schools in this matter, such as that a regulation must not be vague or violate due process. A law or regulation violates due process if it is so vague and standardless that the persons involved are uncertain about the conduct covered. In *Meyers* v. *Arcata Union High School District,*[12] the principal was the sole judge of the hair style, and the court held that the rule being administered by a single official was a violation of the students' due process of law. In a Wisconsin case,[13] the court held that it would be impossible to comply with the school's regulation and follow the wishes of the parents outside of school, so the court stated that *loco parentis* would not apply. The court also held that the rule was arbitrary and that the administration had not shown the hair length involved to be disruptive. Hence, the court held the rule to be in violation of the due process guaranteed by the Fourteenth Amendment.

Communication. As used here, communication refers only to the areas of freedom of speech and the press. The wearing of buttons or armbands has been held by the courts to be a form of speech. The right of freedom of speech as guaranteed under the First Amendment must not be infringed upon by state or local officials. In one case that reached the federal court of appeals, a Mississippi high school principal forbade students to wear buttons proclaiming, "One Man One Vote" and with "SNCC" printed in the center. Significant in this decision was a statement by the judge that the school officials presented no evidence of any disturbance as a result of the display of the buttons. In the *Burnside* v. *Byars* case, the court stated that persons must have the right to communicate and that school officials cannot ignore expressions of feelings with which they do not wish to contend.[14]

The same court decided against the students in another case. However, in the case *Blackwell* v. *Issaquena County Board of Education,* evidence showed that a disturbance resulted from the wearing of similar buttons. Students wearing buttons attempted to pin buttons on other students, left class without permission, engaged in loud conversation in halls and corridors, and acted rudely toward school officials. The court held that the subsequent punishment was not only right but necessary and that the First Amendment guarantee of free speech does not give an absolute right to speak.[15]

A decision that is quoted much is one that was handed down by the United States Supreme Court in 1969. It had to do with a student's wearing an armband

[11] For a list of the litigation, see Michael W. LaMorte, "The Courts and the Governance of Student Conduct," *School and Society,* **100:**92 (Feb. 1972).

[12] *Meyers* v. *Arcata Union High School District* 269 Cal. App. 2d 549, 75 *California Reporter* 68 (1969).

[13] *Breen* v. *Kahl,* 419 F. 2d 1034 (7th Cir. 1969).

[14] *Burnside* v. *Byars,* 363 F. 2d 744, 749 (5th Cir. 1969).

[15] *Blackwell* v. *Issaquena County Board of Education,* 363 F. 2d 749, 753, 754 (5th Cir. 1966).

protesting the Vietnam War. The court held the wearing of the armband was like "pure speech." It was in this case that the phrase, "teacher and students do not shed their constitutional rights at the schoolhouse gate," was coined. This decision held that fear of a disturbance is not enough to overcome the constitutional right to freedom of expression.[16]

In a significant case about a publication called *Grass High,* a literary journal, the courts upheld the right of the students to write and to sell the publication on campus. However, in the writing of the decision, Judge Napoli clearly upheld the right of school authorities to regulate the right to free speech and free press when the exercise of the latter rights constitutes a threat to the satisfactory operation of the school. The court also made the statement, in effect, that school administrators may be criticized by the high school students provided such criticism is responsible.[17]

In another case involving an underground newspaper, what castigated school officials and was also deemed obscene language resulted in a decision rendered in favor of the school.[18] The court held that the First Amendment's rights have to be balanced against the duty and obligation of the state to educate the students in an orderly manner and to protect the rights of not just a few but of all the students. It further held that a student could be expelled for gross disrespect and contempt for officials of an educational institution.

Search of Lockers. Principals have always had the right to search school lockers. In recent years, with the drugs and narcotics problems related to thefts, there appear to be more searches. What the courts have done is to reaffirm the right of the principal to search the locker. In one case, the court even held that the officials not only had the right to search lockers but, when there was a suspicion that there might be something illegal in the lockers, it became a duty to search.[19] If misconduct is related to the contents of the locker and a search is needed to obtain evidence, such a search was held to be proper to maintain the discipline of the school.[20]

Teachers' Governance

In the case of governance of teachers, the matter of retaining or dismissing teachers is becoming increasingly sensitive because of decreasing enrollments and of accountability demands by boards of education. The matter of the safety of teachers is most critical, with assaults increasing alarmingly between 1964 and 1968.[21] Teachers bear the brunt of litigations against the school district in which students and parents charge negligence and assault. Let us look briefly at some of these developments and summarize the significance for teachers.

[16] *Tinker* v. *Des Moines Community School District,* 393 U.S. 503, 89 S. Ct. 733 (1969).
[17] *Scoville* v. *Board of Education of Joliet Township High School District* 204, 286 F. Supp. 988(N.D. Ill. 1968), revised 425 F. 2d 10 (7th Cir. 1970).
[18] *Schwartz* v. *Schuker,* 298 F. Supp. 238 (E. D. N. Y. 1969).
[19] *People* v. *Overton,* 249 N.E. (2d) 366 (1969).
[20] *In Re Donaldson,* 75 *California Reporter* 220 (1969).
[21] George Triezenberg, "Student Communication Rights," *National Association of Secondary School Principals Bulletin,* **53:**22 (April 1973).

Tenure and Continuing Contract. After teachers teach for a prescribed length of time, they may receive a permanent appointment that is renewed from year to year. Such an arrangement is called *tenure*. Teachers on tenure can be dismissed only under unusual circumstances or for grave offenses such as moral turpitude or a capital crime. Boards of education have dismissed tenured teachers when there was no money to pay them, or no students, or when there was proof of gross misconduct. In some states, what is called tenure is really *continuing contract*. While it is difficult to dismiss a tenured teacher, under continuing contract laws, the procedure is easier than under the tenure law. Under the continuing contract law, the board must set a date by which each teacher must be notified that he is not to receive a contract for next year. If a teacher is not informed by the notification date, then the teacher's present contract continues for the next school year. Renewal may be at the same or at an increased stipend. Whether a teacher is dismissed from a tenured position or from a continuing contract position, the procedure of due process in law, as guaranteed under the Constitution must be followed.

Liability. It used to be that only wealthy parents brought suit. With federally subsidized legal advisory offices available to the lower socioeconomic groups, this is no longer true. For adequate protection a teacher is advised to carry, by 1974 standards, about $250,000 of liability insurance. Many professional associations have such coverage as part of their dues structure. It is important for teachers to keep out of court. Many suits are filed that charge a teacher with negligence in performing a certain act. In a laboratory situation, for instance, the teacher must make sure that all safety precautions are taken. Similarly in other subjects, there must be instruction in safety of operation to avoid a charge of negligence.

Certification. Teacher certification laws are presently undergoing changes, partly as a result of the accountability movement. Arizona, for instance, inaugurated a new certification procedure, effective July 1, 1974, under the Performance Recertification Act. This law provides that every school district must evaluate each of its teachers and attest that each meets the standards for recertification. If a teacher does not meet the standards, a period of retraining is provided. At the end of the retraining period, the teacher is reevaluated. If, at this time, school district officials decide that they cannot or will not certify that the teacher is competent, the teacher loses his certificate to teach and, in effect, loses his means of livelihood.

Negotiations. A few states have passed legislation permitting or requiring teachers' associations to negotiate with school boards concerning salaries, fringe benefits, and teaching conditions. In past years, teachers have received only what boards of education have been willing to dole out. In 1974 wage and salary rates, a teacher with four or five years of training and ten years of service made less money than a transcontinental truck driver. This is not to denigrate truck drivers, but it does seem that teachers ought to fare at least as well. To improve their status, teachers have turned to the negotiation table.

Miscellaneous. Teachers for the most part have been easygoing and have done many things in the spirit of professionalism. For example, teachers have collected tickets at football games with little or no compensation; they have worked at carnivals to raise money for the Parent-Teacher Association or for the school principal's fund. They attend summer school at their own expense although business firms and the armed forces pay personnel to attend school; they purchase many materials at their own expense; and they attend conventions at their own expense. What was once done either pleasantly or grudgingly now becomes a matter of negotiation. It is only normal that teachers who are concerned with the most important resource of the future, children and young people, are interested in getting a fair share of the wealth. Such an interest is evident in the increased militancy of the teacher organizations.

SUGGESTED READING

Amidon-Hough, Eds. *Interaction Analysis: Theory, Research, Application.* Reading, Mass.: Addison-Wesley Publishing Co. Inc., 1967.

Bremer, John, and Michael Von Moschzisher. *The School Without Walls.* New York: Holt, Rinehart & Winston, Inc., 1971).

Clayton, Elwood M., and Gene S. Jacobsen. "An Analysis of Court Cases Concerned with Student Rights, 1960–1971." *NASSP Bulletin,* **58** (Feb. 1974), 49–53.

Dropkin, Stan, Ernest Schwarcz, and Harold Full. *Contemporary American Education: An Anthology of Issues, Problems, and Challenges.* New York: Macmillan Publishing Co., Inc., 1975.

Haubrich, Vernon, Ed. *Freedom, Bureaucracy, and Schooling.* Washington, D.C.: The Association for Supervision and Curriculum Development, NEA, 1971.

Hudgins, H. C. Jr. "Are Student Lockers Off Limits to Principals?" *NASSP Bulletin,* **54** (Sept. 1970), 101–104.

Johnson, T. Page. "The Constitution, the Courts and Long Hair." *NASSP Bulletin,* **57** (April 1973), 24–53.

Kembrough, Ralph B., and Michael Y. Nunnery. *Education Administration: An Introduction.* New York: Macmillan Publishing Co. Inc., 1975.

La Morte, Michael W. "The Courts and the Governance of Student Conduct" *School and Society,* **100** (Feb. 1972), 89–93.

National Association of Secondary Principals. "Alternatives in Public Education: Movement or Fad?" *NASSP Bulletin,* **57** (Sept. 1973), 1–126. [Twenty-two authors have contributed to the theme of alternatives in education.]

Phi Delta Kappan. "Community Education: A Special Issue." *Phi Delta Kappan* [Twenty-four authors and co-authors contributed to the theme of the issue.] **53** (March 1972).

Schlosser, Courtney D. *The Person in Education: A Humanistic Approach.* New York: Macmillan Publishing Co., Inc., 1976.

Weigand, James E., Ed. *Developing Teacher Competencies.* Englewood Cliffs, N.J.: Prentice-Hall, Inc., 1971).

POST TEST

1. Write a short paragraph description of interaction analysis.

_____

_____

_____

2. List the ten categories of the interaction analysis system.

_____

_____

_____

3. Write an explanation of the categories listed in your answer to question 2.

_____

_____

_____

_____

_____

_____

_____

_____

_____

_____

_____

_____

_____

_____

_____

4. Explain the meaning of a tab in the cells of *8–8, 8–9, 9–8, 4–5, 4–6, 5–7.*

_____

5. Analyze the following objectives according to the criteria for behavioral objectives:
   a. For a unit on World War II—to develop an appreciation for the massive supply problem of the allies.
   b. Given a map of Europe, pupils will be able to draw the route of General Patton's march from southern France to the Rhine River within five miles of the actual march.
   c. The simple sugar molecule is composed of six atoms of carbon, twelve atoms of hydrogen, and six atoms of oxygen.

_____

_____

_____

_____

6. List three types of alternative schools and give the location of an example of each one.

_____

_____

_____

_____

7. Can a school regulate the length of a student's hair? Cite a court case to support your answer. What was the court's decision?

_____

_____

_____

_____

_____

8. Can a principal search a student's locker without a search warrant? Cite a court case to support your answer. What was the court's decision?

_____

_____

_____

_____

_____

9. Can students legally publish and distribute a newspaper that degrades school officials and uses obscene words? Cite a court case to support your answer. What was the court's decision?

_____

10. Describe the intent of the performance contract law of Arizona.

_____

_____

_____

_____

Computer Technology Innovations

Ronald W. Hill

Fryeburg Academy

module 4

Gaming and Simulation / Programmed Instruction / Computer-Assisted Instruction

NEED FOR CRITICAL STUDY

Short of being an innovator in your own right, the first step in dealing with innovations is just what you are doing, reading about them. But do not be satisfied with what you find on these pages; if an innovation appeals to you, then look beyond these brief descriptions, examine the literature in depth, and most important, observe the innovation in action if possible.

You would be well advised to be critical, even skeptical, of what you read. Often, the persons who write about an innovation are those who have a vested interest in its success; for example, their incomes may derive from the innovation, or their professional reputations may depend on its success. But whether the bias stems from the enthusiasm of the reporter or from guile prompted by self-interest, the reader would be naive to ignore the possibility of extravagant claims or of conclusions lacking in documentation.

RATIONALE

Our purpose in this module is to describe three practices that are generally considered to be innovative, although their origins date back several years. There exists a unifying thread, albeit a delicate one, throughout these innovations, namely that in one way or another each involves a commitment to computer technology. In some instances, we shall see that this commitment is not fully recognized by some who are ostensibly experts in the implementing of these innovations.

Study Plan

Instructions to the reader for the study and mastery of this module are simply to read, study, and meditate; *read* the module throughout, take the post test at the end of the module; *study* those areas in which you were unable to correctly answer the question; finally, *meditate* about what you have read. You may wish to further examine some items from the list of suggested reading.

Specific Behavioral Objectives

Upon completion of your study of this module, you should be able to perform all of the following objectives:

1. Write a one-sentence definition for each of the following: (a) simulation gaming; (b) game theory; (c) programmed instruction; (d) computer-assisted instruction.

2. Write a one-sentence identification of each of the following: (a) John von Neumann, and (b) B. F. Skinner.
3. Cite two advantages of manual games over computer games.
4. Describe three classifications of business games.
5. Name five areas of education in which simulation gaming has been used as a teaching tool.
6. Name at least four problems associated with the administration and use of simulation games as a teaching method.
7. Identify the major constraint faced by the teacher using programmed instruction.
8. Cite four advantages of programmed instruction over traditional instruction.
9. Name four activities that may be used to maintain student interest while involved with programmed instruction.
10. Cite four types of computer-assisted instruction.
11. Cite the three disciplines that have the greatest utilization of computer-assisted instruction.

MODULE TEXT

Gaming and Simulation

Just as math is a word easily used by young school children, as well as laureates in mathematics, with two vastly different depths of meaning, *gaming and simulation* represent similar differences regarding depth of meaning. The analogy with mathematics is not accidental; gaming and simulation at their more sophisticated levels constitute a branch of mathematical endeavor with its own societies, journals, and body of literature. In addition to the difficulties that arise out of the range of sophistication, semantic confusion exists with regard to the use of the two words, gaming and simulation. And finally, the considerable interest exhibited by specialists in many fields, ranging from business and industry, through mathematics and military, and into social sciences and education, results in a potpourri of literature that is outstanding in its diversity, if not always in its scholarship.

Of these three problems, the semantic confusion is perhaps the most trivial but, at the same time, annoying. It is safe to say that any game is a simulation (including such well-known games as chess, bridge, and poker). The converse, however, is not strictly true, because a simulation does not necessarily require a winner whereas a game does. The distinction between gaming and simulation is seldom made clear in the literature, and for good reason: through usage, no clear distinction exists. A distinction appears to become evident in the computer simulation of a lunar landing; one would not ordinarily consider the possibility of a winner in such an exercise, the purpose being solely to simulate the process of a lunar landing. But even this exercise can be considered a one-person game of man against an indifferent universe. Small wonder that confusion exists over the definition of these terms. Let us say that the two words may be used synonymously, as they usually are, making a distinction only when the discussion concerns mathematical theory or computer simulation.

The problem concerning the interest by specialists across many fields vanishes if we look upon gaming and simulation as a tool just as mathematics is a tool. Certainly we would never concede confusion in mathematics because specialists in many different fields are using it. The advantage that mathematics enjoys as a discipline is that those who use mathematics do not take liberties with the structure of the discipline unless they are mathematicians, whereas the same cannot be said of the users of gaming and simulation.

The levels of sophistication can essentially be reduced to two, the mathematical and the nonmathematical, and we shall be primarily concerned with the latter.

In this module, we shall attempt to define gaming and simulation through its history, identify those aspects that are of particular interest to education, and finally, discuss various examples and uses for gaming and simulation.

Definition. Simulation techniques as used in classroom teaching have been described as a combination of role playing and problem solving. They derive from the war games and command post exercises used by the military forces of all nations. They can range from highly sophisticated scenarios, dependent upon complicated programming by computers, to the simplest kind of make-believe that children use when they "play house." Basically, in any simulation exercise, what happens is

1. The players are assigned parts in a fairly well-defined situation.
2. The players are confronted with a series of incidents in which they must take action or make decisions, according to the characters they are playing and the information they have at hand. As a rule, whatever actions and decisions a player takes plus the actions and decisions of the other players lead to further incidents that require of everyone more action and more decisions.

It should be noted that in these simulations the player is not free to act in any way he wishes. He must act or decide only within the bounds of the supposed realities of the situation, which may be changed at any minute by the actions or decisions of the other players, the umpire, or the computer that is scripting the simulation.[1]

Outside of classroom teaching, simulation and gaming have much broader connotations, as we shall see.

History. Perhaps the greatest tragedy in the growth of civilization is that man established a theoretical basis for physical phenomena before he was able to do the same for social phenomena. Possibly a civilization that understood the theory of social interaction would have been better able to cope with the technological results of physical knowledge. The development of equally successful theory for the social sciences might well usher in a new era of human understanding and cooperation.

An important contribution along these lines was made by the mathematician, John von Neumann, through his efforts beginning in 1928 and culminating in

---

[1] Leonard H. Clark, *Strategies and Tactics in Secondary School Teaching* (New York: Macmillan Publishing Co., Inc., 1968), p. 218.

1944 with the publication, with Morgenstern, of the classic work in this field, *Theory of Games and Economic Behavior*. To the few laymen who may have been aware of game theory in its early years, it was just an extension of the success that we had enjoyed in our wartime strategies; to mathematicians, it was another manifestation of the genius of von Neumann, who had tackled so many problems from computer design to quantum physics.

Game theory, although brilliant in its conception and logic, did not attain the success that had been anticipated. It has, however, become a part of the theoretical basis and support for several other disciplines that have enjoyed considerable success, such as operations research, systems analysis, and decision analysis.

During the 1950s, caught up in the optimistic promises for game theory to accomplish for the social sciences what mathematics had done for the physical sciences, researchers from the social sciences understandably began to look to game theory to answer some of their questions. And it is here that a significant split occurred between game theory, with its related disciplines, and gaming and simulation. The divergence grew out of the mathematically oriented research by the former and the nonmathematical research by the latter. Although the social scientists borrowed heavily from the vocabulary and prestige of game theory, they neglected to pursue the concomitant mathematics.

The result of this split was the rapid growth of games that simulated social and business phenomena but made little attempt to quantify results. The rationale for these games was that the players would learn, or get the feel for, a political, economic, or business process by experiencing it through simulation. Generally, the games would be prepared in such a way that the players would be called upon to make decisions based upon criteria made available to them.

By the early 1960s there was considerable controversy concerning the validity of gaming and simulation as a teaching tool. Hailed by some as the ultimate in teaching methodology and by others as little more than an interesting diversion, gaming has continued to grow with an ever-widening field of users. In the early 1960s there was no hard evidence to support either point of view; in the early 1970s there still existed a paucity of research validating the effectiveness of gaming and simulation as a teaching tool. Examples of the limited research will be discussed later.

Historically, then, gaming and simulation have their genesis in game theory, but began their independent, nonmathematical development in the mid 1950s. Their early applications were an outgrowth of efforts by the American Management Association to provide simulated business experiences for its executives and executive trainees. We shall now consider those aspects of gaming and simulation that are of particular interest to education.

Gaming and Simulation in Management and Business Training. We speak briefly here of gaming in business and industry training programs, and point out again that these early efforts represent the pioneering work in gaming and simulation.

MANAGEMENT AND BUSINESS TRAINING GAMES. In May 1957, the American Management Association demonstrated its Top Management Decision Simulation game to twenty corporation presidents, and declared it to be a major breakthrough in management education. This was the beginning of many such games, with a variety of corporations and business schools preparing their own games, while business games spread rapidly overseas as well. This plethora of games quickly raised questions of fadism; was involvement with simulation merely a status symbol? Was simulation just an interesting gimmick which, because of its newness, provided the ever-necessary motivation?

In the late 1950s and early 1960s there was an abundance of manual business games as opposed to computer business games. The latter of course enjoyed far more glamor and publicity, but they also required a much larger investment of time and money in the design as well as in the playing. The manual games further provided the convenience of being utilizable any time and place without regard to computer availability.

In addition to the distinction of being either manual- or computer-operated, games may also differ by being competitive or noncompetitive, team or individual, deterministic or random, and, of course, they vary in subject matter. The subject matter of business games may be classified as general management games, functional games, industry games, and bureaucracy games.

GENERAL MANAGEMENT GAMES. This type of game is usually designed as a team game and is characterized by competition and interaction. As the games become more involved, they tend to become predominantly deterministic and must be computer-scored. Determinism in games refers to game procedures and to plays that have been predetermined by the authors of the game, as opposed to the random plays that can easily be generated at various points during the game. General management games include all of the major business functions, such as making business loans, negotiating labor contracts, arranging mergers, and the like.

A typical game might consist of dividing the players into teams, each team representing one of several competing companies. All teams start out with the same financial base and with identical availability of resources (a reasonable variation, however, is to begin with widely differing financial bases). Players are given all necessary data about their companies and must make decisions concerning production, research and development, expansion, advertising, and investments. Decisions made by one team of players have an effect on other teams, of course. A computer is almost a necessity in games of this magnitude to allocate sales based upon fixed formulas that consider prices, advertising costs, and other variables. The play proceeds for certain time periods, with new decisions necessary for each period.

General management games are numerous, quite realistic, and are designed for top management, involving decisions of top-management caliber.

FUNCTIONAL GAMES. These games are aimed at certain functions of middle and lower management, such as marketing, production, inventory control, and transportation, and may take many different forms. Many of the specific management functions, lend themselves to computer simulation or, more specifically, to operations research techniques.

INDUSTRY GAMES. These games may be either of the general management type or functional. However, they are so-named because they are designed to reflect the problems that are unique to a particular industry, such as oil, gas, insurance, or aircraft manufacturing.

BUREAUCRACY GAMES. Games in this category tend to be very complicated and seek to introduce problems of organization and human relations. One of the most complicated is a detergent industry game that has been developed by the Carnegie Institute of Technology. The game is designed to be played over a period of one or two semesters, involves more than 200 decisions in each time period, and encompasses three companies, multiple products, marketing regions, and raw materials. In meeting an objective of these games, teams are made purposefully large so that authority must be delegated, thereby providing training in administrative skills.

Gaming and Simulation in Education. Our main concern in this module is directed toward the use of gaming and simulation in education and, in particular, in public education. It is difficult to conceive a use for gaming that is not in some way related to education. Even when games are designed exclusively for entertainment, education and training are inevitable outcomes.

Gaming and simulation have become useful and popular tools in the instruction of political science, sociology, psychology, anthropology, and education. We shall look at each of these areas and discuss examples of gaming in each.

POLITICAL SCIENCE. Games in this area may be considered to be outgrowths of war games of World War II vintage, such as those carried on by RAND. Military gaming techniques did not overlook the politics of war, a fact which can be quickly verified by examining records of war gaming activities by Japan, Germany, and the United States during World War II.

An important effort, and perhaps the first in political science, is that known as the Inter-Nation Simulation, (INS), which constitutes a generalized model of national and international politics. The players in this game act as national leaders and are called upon to make decisions concerning national defense, public opinion, revolutions, democratic values, elections, alliances, and war. INS, with its long history in a young field, has served repeatedly as a research tool as well as a teaching tool.

Another game, Technological, Economic, Military and Political Evaluation Routine, resulting in the interesting acronym TEMPER, has been developed for the United States Joint Chiefs of Staff. This game encompasses a wide range of disciplines and attempts to simulate interrelations of all nations in the world.

Scott and others have done extensive work with the simulation of political problems in a hypothetical, developing nation which they have called Simuland. The game's stated purpose is "to simulate the interplay among the active political elites of a hypothetical society in the process of economic development." This very interesting simulation, which was used primarily for teaching Peace Corps volunteers, is well described in the book, *Simulation and National Development,* by Scott and his colleagues.

SOCIOLOGY. The field of sociology is rich with examples of simulation games, one being Simulation of Society or SIMSOC which grew out of its author's dissatisfaction with orthodox teaching. The author, Gamson, reports success over several years of experience, but not without problems. Some of the problems encountered should be instructive to consider, and should be generally applicable to any simulation effort.

Gamson noted that this game, which can accommodate up to sixty players for ten sessions of play, presented him initially with technical problems that consumed an inordinate amount of time. These problems rapidly faded with experience, as did the problem of instructor participation; the recommendation is that the instructor should not participate, but instead leave the interpretive decisions that he might be called upon to make to be made by a selected group of players. Likewise, it was found that instructor intervention to change rules was quite demoralizing to the progress of the game. Another demoralizing problem that developed concerned the players' disregard for the rules of the game. The author indicated less difficulty with this problem when a sharp distinction was made between the rules of the game and the rules developed by the society itself. The game rules now take on the character of rules of nature; for example, one cannot reasonably elect to defy the law of gravity.

Certain other problems proved to be more permanent in nature, such as those of alienation and apathy. Typically, the society would quickly become dominated by those few who were willing to do the work, while the other students would gladly sit by and busy themselves with their personal interests and pursuits. This is somewhat reminiscent of science laboratory work; pairs of cooperating students in a chemistry laboratory often end up with a dominant student who figures out and performs the experiment while the other student watches. Tying grades to performance did not have the anticipated effect of increasing conflict; rather, it served to unite the class against the instructor, not viciously but rather as a socially expedient way to avoid "cutting each other's throats."

Gamson suggests that perhaps the greatest learning is that done by the person who develops the simulation, and that perhaps we should be concentrating on students as simulators rather than students as players.

The simulation game known as Homunculus is another example from the field of sociology. The game, as well as its name, is closely allied to the position espoused by the social theoretist, George C. Homans. This computer simulation, designed by Gullahorn and Gullahorn, is a model of elementary social behavior which has its theoretical roots in experimental psychology and classical economics.

Other sociological games that we shall mention briefly are Empire, which concerns eighteenth-century trade among the nations of Europe and the American colonies; the Hunting Game, which illustrates the necessity for cooperation between tribes while hunting game in Africa; and the Caribou Hunting Game, which again illustrates the need for cooperation in developing hunting strategies. These games are examples of some of those that are available for lower-grade levels.

PSYCHOLOGY. Little has been done with gaming and simulation in the field of psychology, quite probably because of the strong tradition in psychology for accurate experimentation and measurement attainable only through highly controlled efforts. Interestingly, though, gaming and simulation, as we have been discussing it, is rather closely related to role playing, a well-known psychological technique.

EDUCATION. Simulation games have enjoyed a certain success in schools of educational administration. The University Council of Educational Administration (UCEA) has developed a series of simulations for various purposes. Their most comprehensive is *Professional Negotiation in Education,* written by John J. Horvat. Other simulations have been prepared under the auspices of the UCEA in the areas of school-community relations and the politics of education.

GUIDANCE. School guidance programs usually have two major thrusts: students' personal problems, either school or home-related, and career guidance. Many of the problems of the first type develop in children who are classified as disadvantaged, a term which covers a wide range of circumstances. Games have been found to succeed with these students when other methods of teaching have not. One such game, known as Raid, has been used successfully with disadvantaged children from metropolitan areas. The game involves police, racketeers, and teams of students representing the populations in each of a few city blocks. Such games as these seem to have great potential for increasing student involvement and attention, while at the same time teaching that being a policeman can be difficult but rewarding work.

Several games have been developed to aid young people in becoming familiar with various occupations and professions. A game of particular importance in this area has been developed by Boocock and is known as the Life Career Game. The game is intended for young women of high school age, but may be used successfully by either younger or older girls. The Life Career Game instructs by taking the player through aspects of her life, education, job, marriage, and children. Through this trip, the player is able to experience success or failure and become much more confident and knowledgeable in making decisions concerning her own life.

Simulations of Technical Skills. Some of the most valuable simulations in terms of both money and human life are those of aircraft and space ships. Aircraft simulators are capable of simulating just about any type of inflight emergency and therefore allow pilots to safely practice these skills that are so important to the welfare of their passengers.

The whole nation must be aware of the sophisticated simulation that has been the hallmark of our successful space program. Practically nothing has been done during our many space flights that has not been previously tried as a simulation. We have all been properly apprised by the news commentators of the computer simulations that were done in Houston before instructing the astronauts of proper actions to compensate for damaged equipment.

Conclusion. Simulation gaming has apparently become an effective teaching tool although there still does not seem to be any conclusive research to substantiate this claim. Evidence supporting the effectiveness of this teaching methodology is subjective in nature and centers mostly upon the observation that students appear to be more highly motivated by this approach than by traditional approaches. In a report of research completed in the evaluation of two learning games, Boocock reported that ". . . there was no apparent relationship between rate of learning in the game and reported general academic performance." Boocock concluded, however, that "the experiment supports a basic tenet of the philosophy of educational gaming—that students can have fun and learn at the same time."[2]

Programmed Instruction

Programmed instruction may be defined as any form of instruction, be it textbook, machine, or computer, such that the student may learn by himself, proceeding through sequential tasks to a higher level of proficiency. We shall see later that the theoretical basis for programmed instruction lies within the framework of the behaviorist school of psychology and, therefore, all philosophical controversy that is visited upon that psychology is likewise visited upon programmed instruction.

---

[2] Sarane S. Boocock, "An Experimental Study of the Learning Effects of Two Games with Simulated Environments," in Sarane S. Boocock and E. O. Schild (eds.), *Simulation Games in Learning* (Beverly Hills, Calif.: Sage Publications, Inc., 1968), p. 130.

The threat of Orwellian outcomes that were predicted by the early critics of programmed instruction do not seem to have materialized by the mid-seventies, although a controversy is very much alive between behaviorists and those who view any form of programming as dehumanizing.

History. Although widely considered to be contemporary as well as innovative, programmed instruction had its beginning as long ago as 1924 when Sidney L. Pressey exhibited a teaching machine at a meeting of the American Psychological Association. Perhaps Pressey's consideration of himself first as a psychologist and second as an educator constitutes partial explanation of why programmed instruction went relatively unnoticed in educational circles for three decades.

The rationale for programmed instruction was given considerable impetus in 1954 with B. F. Skinner's article, "The Science of Learning and the Art of Teaching," in the *Harvard Education Review*. Skinner, a psychologist of the behaviorist school, was a pioneer in programmed instruction as a theoretician as well as a practitioner. The *modus operandi* of programmed instruction is well supported by learning theory and has rather profound implications for education.

One of the first programmed texts was developed by Norman Crowder in 1955 in his efforts to develop a method of training electronics engineers in trouble shooting. Crowder's programmed text introduced the concept of branching of which more will be said later.

Programmed instruction has come to mean programmed texts primarily, but also teaching machines of the noncomputer variety, and as such, programmed instruction remains quite stable in its technology and production.

Types of Programmed Instruction. TEACHING MACHINES. A teaching machine may be described as a mechanical device that is designed to present to the student a sequential program in small increments. The student in operating the machine is required to make an overt response and is then provided with immediate feedback as to the accuracy of his response. The machine itself can take many forms, ranging from the very simple to the very sophisticated and expensive. One type consists of a drum upon which the printed program is placed so that the student may see information and questions through a small window. He is required to write his responses in a similar window. After he has responded, the drum is rotated so that the answer appears, allowing the student to check the accuracy of his response and to go on to the next question. The drum, of course, may be electrically driven, and the responses may be printed so that the student may indicate his choice of response by pressing an appropriate electrically operated push button. Unless the right button is pushed the machine will not move forward. The many refinements that are possible do not affect the nature of the machine.

PROGRAMMED TEXTBOOKS. Although there are substantial differences among programmed textbooks, Homme and Glaser describe the typical programmed text as follows:

Its external appearance will not differ from an ordinary textbook, but its interior is quite different. Each page consists of n (usually 4 or 5) panels; the sequence of the panels is not from the top of the page to the bottom as in a conventional textbook; only one panel is 'read' or responded to before the student turns it. The student begins with the top panel on page 1, responds to it, turns to page 2 to get his answer confirmed on the top panel, goes to the top panel on page 3, responds to it, confirms his answer by turning the page, and so on, to the end of the unit or chapter, where he is instructed to return to page 1 and respond to the second panel on each page, and so on . . . .[3]

In general there are two types of programs: *linear* and *branched*. The linear program is a single sequential path in which the student responds to one question after another and the path is exactly the same for anyone who participates in the program. In the branched type of program, if the student should incorrectly respond to a bit of information or to a question he then would be routed into another branch of questions which give more information, more clues, and more explanation so that the student can be brought back to the primary path of information. In some branched programs, key questions are asked from time to time and if the student correctly responds to these questions, he may skip large segments of the program without loss of continuity. Branched programs are highly acclaimed as providing for individual differences among students. However, there are those who believe that all students should proceed through exactly the same experience (linear program) and that individual differences may be accommodated by treating time as a variable, so each student proceeds at his own pace.

COMPUTER-ASSISTED INSTRUCTION. This aspect of programmed instruction is of such magnitude and importance that it shall be discussed at length in another section of this module.

There is little difference between machines and programmed texts. The programmed textbook can do whatever the teaching machine can and can accomplish it without expensive hardware. One possible advantage of teaching machines is that cheating can be virtually eliminated. However, with well-designed programs, cheating should not be a problem in any event.

Psychological Basis. The art of teaching constitutes to a great extent the eliciting of desired behavior. Given that a teacher knows the desired behavior for his students, he then goes about using his expertise to elicit this behavior from them. He may smile encouragement, frown disapproval, shout his praise, or raise his voice in anger; he may nod or shake his head, he may give the student an "A" or an "F." In all of these cases, the teacher is doing what his conscience dictates to elicit desired behavior, and his actions constitute what are known as *contingencies of reinforcement,* both positive and negative. Skinner defined these as "the relations which prevail between behavior on the one hand and the consequences of that behavior on the other. . . ."[4]

Skinner's research in the psychology of learning involved extensive experimentation with animals wherein carefully designed schedules of reinforcement were observed to permit the shaping of behavior almost at will. The process of shaping behavior, or eliciting the desired response to a given stimulus, involves many reinforcements, and as the complexity of the desired behavior increases, so too does the number of necessary reinforcements. Skinner reported the recording of many millions of responses from a single organism and suggested that the only

[3] Lloyd E. Homme and Robert Glaser, "Relationships Between the Programmed Textbooks and Teaching Machines," in Eugene Galanter, ed., *Automatic Teaching: The State of the Art.* New York: John Wiley & Sons, Inc., 1959, p. 103.
[4] B. F. Skinner, "The Science of Learning and the Art of Teaching," *Harvard Educational Review* (Spring 1954), p. 86.

reasonable way to accommodate such a magnitude of responses is through the use of a machine.

Skinner's oft-quoted article of 1954 cited the results of his experiments as having rather important implications for education. He saw his practice of using machines to monitor responses of his animal subjects to be a reasonable and viable alternative, even a requisite, for the efficient programs of learning in the schools.

Although Skinner's work provided a respectable psychological basis for programmed instruction, his teachings are by no means universally accepted. There are many psychologists and philosophers who would argue the pitfalls of programmed instruction (PI) on the grounds that such activity is dehumanizing. Certainly it does not take much imagination to bridge the gap between the scholarly endeavors of Skinnerian psychologists and the fictional classic by George Orwell, *1984*. Perhaps we can take some comfort in the wisdom of the ancients in their teachings of moderation; there undoubtedly exists a middle ground of thought and action which can utilize the best of programmed instruction while not losing sight of individual human dignity.

Role of the Teacher. There are several different ways of using programmed instruction based upon the varying needs of the students, and it is important that the teacher be aware of these as well as how to proceed in implementing each use. The varied applications of PI are discussed elsewhere; however, a couple of these should be discussed here in terms of the teacher's role in the process of programmed instruction.

First, it should be pointed out that the general approach to programmed instruction, and therefore the teacher's role, is quite different between the first through fourth or fifth grades than it is with fifth or sixth grades and above. The reason for this is that in American schools classroom organization generally changes around the fifth or sixth grade from self-contained classrooms to some form of departmentalization.

Second, the teacher's role in programmed instruction differs considerably depending upon how widely it is used in the classroom. For example, if the teacher plans to use programmed instruction with all students, his role would be considerably different than if he were to use it for remediation or enrichment only.

FULL CLASSROOM INSTRUCTION. Let us first discuss the teacher's role as it relates to using programmed instruction with a whole class. If programmed instruction is introduced and used as envisioned by its proponents, the teacher becomes more free to spend time with individual students than if he were teaching the same material in the traditional fashion. This assumption is certainly reasonable in that the bulk of material normally presented in lecture format would now be presented by machine or programmed text. There are, however, some rather important restrictions upon the teacher's time that will become evident as we proceed. Perhaps the major constraint is one concerning motivation; unless a student is externally motivated to continue a program to reach a goal, the program itself quickly exhausts its ability to motivate continued participation. It behooves the teacher then to plan a variety of activities and experiences. In this respect, successful teaching with programmed instruction does not differ from successful teaching by any method in that the teacher must vary his activities and pace to maintain interest and motivate students. It is also of interest to note that in so doing the teacher is taking away from the time that he has available to spend with individual students. Let us explain; in its purest (yet not its noblest) form, programmed instruction should relieve the teacher entirely of any planning, thereby allowing the teacher to be free at all times for individual assistance. Of course, in its purest form, programmed instruction should also be so complete and self-explanatory that extra assistance from a teacher is unnecessary. Why then should we discuss the role of the teacher if one is unnecessary? The answer must be that perfection in PI, as in all other endeavors, is mercifully unattainable.

The activities and methods of varying them with programmed instruction to attain the desired level of interest among students are limited only by the imagination and versatility of the teacher. Certainly procedures involving the use of programmed instruction on certain days of the week, and then for perhaps only part of the period, should be considered. The use of programmed instruction could then be amply interspersed with discussion, audio-visual materials, lecture, and examination.

First Through Fifth Grade. The bulk of programmed instruction at the earlier elementary levels is in the area of reading, and in some cases serves as the sole method of teaching reading. In nearly all instances at these levels, students are allowed to proceed at their own pace without having to complete regular assignments. This aspect of programmed instruction has a certain appeal to the proponents of nongraded schools and open classrooms.

The teacher's role in programmed instruction at the lower elementary level is not as critical as it is at higher levels. Continued interest at the higher levels is quite dependent upon planning by the teacher, but at the primary level the program itself, coupled with competition, serves to motivate children to continue at their own rate.

Remediation and Enrichment. Although the use of programmed instruction for remediation and enrichment constitutes a wide range of student application, the teacher's role remains essentially the same for both. Additional attention that is so often necessary for the slow learner and desirable for the gifted can be made available through the careful selection of programmed instruction materials. In such situations, the teacher supplies the student with extra help, albeit in terms of programmed instruction rather than time. A relatively small amount of time is taken to brief the student who may then proceed at his own rate.

It is reasonable, and often convenient, to use the same programmed materials for both remediation and enrichment. An example of such practice might well be the use of a programmed text on the nature and use of vectors as a remedial tool for a twelfth-grade physics student, and also as an enrichment activity for an eleventh-grade chemistry student who has become interested in quantum physics while studying atoms.

Applications. In general, it would appear that programmed instruction does its greatest service to education in the areas of drill. Taken in small amounts on a regular basis, programmed instruction has been seen to drastically improve performance in arithmetic skills, for example.

Mathematics. Examples of successful use of programmed instruction in mathematics at the secondary level are numerous. Generally, these examples take the form of programmed texts and may involve large groups of from 50 to 100 students under the supervision of two or three teachers. Much of the literature indicates particular success with programmed instruction in the teaching of general mathematics, traditionally consisting of the lower-ability students with a high percentage of any school's disruptive students. The success of programmed instruction with this level student is attributed by its users to the fact that for the first time these students are able to work successfully at their own rates.

As an enrichment device in mathematics, programmed instruction has been used as a means of giving gifted students opportunities to take courses such as plane geometry in addition to the normal load. When such students have been able to successfully complete the final examination, they are then credited with the extra mathematics course during that year.

Research studies indicate that programmed instruction in mathematics has been as effective in both achievement and retention as traditional methods. One summary of controlled experiments indicated that although programmed instruction was found to be superior to conventional teaching methods in only a small number of experiments, many experiments indicated no statistical differences in either direction, and no experiments indicated that programmed instruction was significantly inferior to conventional methods.[5]

Reading. M. W. Sullivan has stated that programmed instruction has had its most dramatic success in the area of reading. The major programmed reading materials were tested and revised for a period of fifteen years prior to publication, resulting in good testing procedures, reliable standards, and programming content that is free of errors as well as conceptual defects. This should serve as a note of caution to would-be writers of programmed instruction: it is neither an easy nor a short task to write a PI text.

Reading is taught almost exclusively at the elementary level in self-contained classrooms and, therefore, has the advantage that there are no firm time restrictions as to when the child may read. The child is free to work at his own rate and is regularly given a test after completing approximately fifty frames in the programmed materials. (A frame is another word for panel, as described by Homme and Glaser on page 87.)

As indicated earlier, programmed reading has a definite appeal to those who support the concepts of nongraded schools and open classrooms. Unfortunately, in some instances, the purchase of a few programmed reading books for the primary classrooms is offered as *prima facie* evidence of meeting the criteria for nongradedness or openness. Whatever educational advantages may exist in the open classroom or nongraded school are soon rendered suspect with this band wagon approach. Aside from this caution, however, it should be stressed that programmed reading is particularly well adapted to the concept of the open classroom.

The areas of reading and mathematics constitute the bulk of programmed instruction in schools today. Programs exist, however, in many disciplines as well as those developed specifically for such institutions as the Job Corps.

Other Applications. Successful programs have been prepared in spelling, foreign languages, chemistry, physics, calculus, social sciences, and creative thinking, to name a few. Programmed instruction has met with success in programs for

---

[5] Leslie J. Briggs and David Angell, "Programmed Instruction in Science and Mathematics," *Review of Educational Research,* **34:**354–71 (June 1964).

culturally deprived as well as for special education students, including the mentally retarded. It is difficult to conceive of an area of knowledge wherein programmed instruction could not be used.

Perhaps the greatest single area of success with programmed instruction as a teaching technique has been in drill and practice during regular short intervals of time. We shall see that this success is similarly realized in yet another area of programmed instruction, computer-assisted instruction.

Computer-assisted Instruction

Computer-assisted instruction (CAI) is a form of programmed instruction which has enjoyed such success that it merits treatment as an educational innovation apart from programmed texts and mechanical teaching machines. Some authorities maintain that computers were originally programmed to assist in instruction because of the inadequacies of teaching machines, particularly their inability to adapt to individual differences among students. It is a virtual certainty, however, that computers would have been used in this capacity regardless of the success or failure of other forms of programmed instruction.

This section of the module is devoted to the history of CAI, and identifies the types or categories of CAI that have evolved during this brief history. Rather extensive consideration is given to the applications of CAI, and the section concludes with a discussion of the pros and cons of this innovation.

History. The history of programmed instruction, as described earlier, necessarily constitutes the history of CAI as well. Unique to CAI, however, are the first computer programs for instructional purposes which were developed in 1959 by International Business Machines (IBM) to teach stenotyping and binary arithmetic. In the relatively few years since then, hundreds of programs have been written for CAI. Such programs are proliferating at a startling rate; the University of Wisconsin–Milwaukee, which periodically compiles a comprehensive listing of computer programs in CAI, reports that there were fewer than 100 programs in 1967, 456 reported in 1968, and within another year the list had grown to 910 programs. These constitute what is known as *software* for CAI.

In 1966 IBM introduced the 1500 Instructional System, which is the first computer to be designed for instructional purposes exclusively. Computers, the machines necessary to utilize the software, are known as *hardware*.

Types of CAI. Computers may be used as an aid to instruction in several ways, both directly and indirectly. Possibly the most esoteric description of proposed uses of computers in education is that given by Leonard in his book, *Education and Ecstasy,* in which he describes his conception of educational utopia. There are many other uses of computers that are already operational.

Record Keeper and Retriever of Information. The functions of record keeping and information retrieval were the first uses of computers envisioned by business and industry as well as by education. Certainly education shares with big business all of the administrative record keeping that goes with personnel records, payroll, scheduling, inventories, and fiscal planning. In addition to these functions, computers are used in reporting pupil progress, processing tests, and reporting results. It is probably true that this record-keeping function is the most widespread and readily accepted use of computers in public education today. It represents the path whereby school officials enter the realm of computer technology, gradually becoming familiar and at ease with the capabilities and limitations of computers.

In early encounters with computers, it is quite typical for neophytes to credit the computer with errors as if it were endowed with its own vindictive personality; such explanations are offered only slightly in jest and are often presumed to constitute complete exoneration from any personal involvement in computer-related catastrophes. (If you should call to report an error in a computer-generated bill, you may well get the explanation, "We've been having some trouble with our computer.") Continued use of the computer in its record-keeping functions soon convinces one of its accuracy and reliability, and the user is then ready to examine it as a tool whose uses are limited only by the imagination and skills of the programmer.

LABORATORY COMPUTING DEVICE. The very name *computer* dictates that a primary function of such a machine is solving problems that involve computations. Again in business and industry, the computer has made available not only rapid calculations of the well-known arithmetic and algebraic variety, but has also made available the use of mathematical procedures that could only be dreamed of in the past because of time limitations. The speed of the computer has opened new avenues for statistical procedures that have contributed to rapid advancement in the physical and biological sciences as well as in the social sciences.

A very common use of CAI, with a wide range of sophistication, has been the use of computers in mathematics, physics, and chemistry classes and laboratories. This varies from simple use as a calculator to highly involved and complex computer programs.

TUTOR. So far in our discussion of types of CAI, our examples have involved the indirect assistance of record keeping on the one hand, and the direct assistance of computational capabilities on the other hand. These examples assist instruction, respectively, in much the same way that a file drawer assists by storing records and a pencil assists as a tool to help in computation. Let us examine now what is probably the heart of computer-assisted instruction, the use of a computer to actually instruct a student.

We shall label this aspect of CAI as its tutorial function. In its simpler forms, the computer may be programmed for drill and practice work in all disciplines. In more advanced forms of CAI, the computer may serve as the primary source of instruction for the capable and motivated student.

SIMULATION. The simulation aspect of the computer's use as an aid to instruction has many ramifications and was treated separately in this module under the heading of "Gaming and Simulation." A couple of examples here will suffice for this discussion. In the multitude of cases where bona fide instructional practice is prohibitively expensive or excessively dangerous to life and limb, computer simulation of real life experiences has been found to be attractive as well as effective. One such example of simulation has been in medical schools, where models of human bodies have been fitted with sensors that feed signals to a computer program. The student's diagnosis and subsequent action upon the model results in the computer assessment of the success of such action, a rapid "recovery" or the untimely "death of the patient." Another example of long-standing use is the aircraft simulator, commencing with the Link Trainer of World War II fame and advancing to today's highly technical models that are capable of simulating nearly any eventuality that could befall an aircraft. A "crash" in a simulator is not taken lightly by any pilot (nor by his examiner), but it certainly is easier to "live with" than the real thing. The lessons learned can be applied at a later date as opposed to the terminal nature of such lessons in life.

Applications. The four categories of CAI give some indication of the wide range of applications that may be available for use. We now consider the most prevalent applications of CAI currently in use.

ADMINISTRATIVE. The function of CAI that serves to keep records and retrieve information is primarily an administrative tool. The widespread use of computers for this function in public education can be attributed to the well-known success of computers in business and industry for the same purposes. Members of boards of education are aware of these uses, understand them, and are willing to vote for such services in their school systems. Typically, all but the largest school systems purchase computer services from organizations, such as banks and insurance companies, that sell these services in an effort to get greater utilization and financial return on the large investment that necessarily accompanies a computer installation. Regionalization provides another alternative whereby smaller towns may join with others to establish their own computer center and hire the qualified personnel required to operate such a center.

The administrative function of computer use, such as bookkeeping, payroll, personnel records, and scheduling, has served education well, not only in performing these tasks but in familiarizing the educational decision makers with the capabilities of modern computer technology. Perhaps an indication of how well computers may eventually be accepted and used by administrators is the fact that at least one college president, Dr. J. G. Kemeny of Dartmouth College, has a computer terminal available for use in his office.

DRILL AND PRACTICE. More in the spirit of CAI is the use of computers by students in the classroom. Quite commonly, computer programs are used for drill and practice problems in mathematics. Any athlete will attest to the importance of drill and practice in the attainment of the physical skills necessary for excellence in any sport. Drill and practice are no less important in the attainment of certain academic skills. The amount and success of drill and practice in, say, mathematics are largely dependent upon either availability of time for the teacher to work on drill with students or the degree to which students possess self-discipline so that they may conduct their own drill sessions.

The computer has been demonstrated to be a very effective substitute for a teacher in this rather mundane but often necessary chore. Suppes reported in 1966 that ten to fifteen minutes of drill in mathematics each day resulted in the advancement of 1.10 to 2.03 years among experimental classes, compared with 0.26 to 1.26 years in the control classes. Results such as these are impressive but warrant further study. An important factor in any study of this nature is that of motivation. Pragmatically, it makes little difference whether the computer is innately better at presenting drill work or the students were motivated by the computer program. It would be somewhat less than prudent, however, to make a massive commitment to computer technology on the basis of this report, only to find that interest and motivation rapidly decrease as familiarity with the hardware increases. Several investigators have warned of the defeating aspects of overexposure to programmed instruction materials. The concerned educator will not take such warnings lightly, but will plan varied activities so that student interest may be kept at an acceptably high level.

It should be instructive to the reader to be aware of the relative use of CAI in the various disciplines. Although not entirely accurate, possibly the most readily available measure of this use would be an accounting of the programs in each of several disciplines as a percentage of the total CAI programs available. This information is presented in Table 4-1.

MATHEMATICS. Quite understandably, programs in mathematics top the list with nearly one fourth of all available CAI programs being in that discipline. This is to be expected for the reason that computer technology was sired by mathematicians, and they seem to retain their status as legal guardians as the technology grows. The majority of the programs involve drill and practice, although many of these may also constitute tutorial programs wherein the student is introduced to new material and concepts. It is quite common to see programs of short duration used to develop a single concept, such as the use of scientific notation. Most of the programs appear to be designed so that the student spends only short periods of time each day at the computer even when the program represents many sequential lessons.

Table 4-1 CAI Programs by Subject Matter Shown As a Per cent of Total Programs Available*

	PERCENT OF TOTAL	EACH OF THE FOLLOWING CONSTITUTES LESS THAN 1% OF TOTAL
10% or more of total		Accounting
Mathematics	24	Anthropology
Computer-related	12	Art
5% to 10%		Astronomy
Health professions	8.7	Business
Physics	6.6	Communications
Foreign languages	5.7	Demography
Chemistry	5.0	Geography
3% to 5%		Geology
Psychology	4.9	History
General science	4.6	Home economics
Reading	3.4	International relations
Demonstrations and games	3.1	Library science
Biology	3.0	Management
1% to 3%		Music
Spelling	2.2	Philosophy
Statistics	2.1	Political science
Economics	2.0	Social science
Guidance and counseling	2.0	Speech pathology
Education	1.8	Other
English	1.4	
Engineering	1.1	

* Information derived from Helen A. Lekan, ed., *Index to Computer-Assisted Instruction*. (Milwaukee: University of Wisconsin, 1970).

The range of instructional level for CAI programs in mathematics varies from grade one at the elementary level to advanced college and university courses.

COMPUTER-RELATED TOPICS. As in mathematics, we would expect to see a high percentage of computer-related CAI programs available and the 12 per cent indicated in Table 4-1 does not disappoint us. Many of these programs are tutorial and relate to the learning of computer languages and programming techniques.

HEALTH PROFESSIONS. It is gratifying to note that the third largest area of CAI programs is in the health professions, and although it is not as easy to explain the interest in CAI in this area as in mathematics, the importance of this application is obvious.

The viability of computer technology as an aid to medical diagnosis has not gone unnoticed by the medical profession. Likewise, the great utility of computers in the simulation of disease and the subsequent simulated treatment as a training process has received wide attention in the profession. These two important applications of computer technology have made the profession quite aware of the technology and open to the consideration of additional uses.

Of course, CAI is a tool of educators, but the medical profession is somewhat unique in that its educators are also its practitioners. As practitioners, medical doctors are well aware of the technology; as educators they are eager to utilize the technology.

The bulk of the programs in this area are offered at the graduate school level (medical school) and are tutorial in nature. Visual displays are widely used as a part of these CAI programs since a doctor's ability to make accurate visual observations constitutes one of his greatest assets as a diagnostician.

PHYSICS. The relatively large number of programs available in physics can be attributed to the fact that teachers and professors of physics are generally well trained in mathematics and, like mathematicians, are eager to utilize the computer for laboratory problem solving as well as for instruction.

Although there is at least one complete, college-level, introductory physics course designed as a CAI program, most of the CAI offerings concern a single topic, tend to be about an hour in length, and are designed for the high school and college instructional level.

FOREIGN LANGUAGE. The use of CAI in the field of foreign languages seems most appropriate and we can only predict that the 5.7 per cent of CAI programs devoted to the area will rapidly increase. The study of languages, perhaps as much as any other endeavor, involves the use of drill and practice. That CAI meets this need extremely well is evidenced by the fact that nearly all of the CAI programs in foreign languages are designated as the drill and practice type.

CHEMISTRY. As in other areas of science, chemistry is yet another discipline whose members have applied its lessons to the memory banks of CAI. If we were to group all science areas together, we would encompass fully 19 per cent of all CAI programs, putting science areas second only to mathematics as an area of CAI programming.

OTHER. The reader's attention is directed to Table 4-1 for further reference to the various subject matters of CAI. We shall simply point out what appear to be anomalies in a teaching methodology that is most distinctive in its success at drill and practice; it is perhaps surprising to note that there are CAI programs in art, international relations, music, and philosophy, all of which would appear to be quite individualistic.

A Final Comment. There can be no doubt that CAI in its tutorial sense will increase as a teaching methodology. The present state of the methodology, loaded with programs from mathematics and science, will expand to include any and all other areas of intellectual endeavor. An expert in any discipline, when assisted by a competent computer programmer, can devise a CAI program that may result in the sharing of knowledge and expertise with an audience that could never be reached without the aid of the computer.

SUGGESTED READING

Gaming and Simulation

Abt, Clark C. *Serious Games.* New York: The Viking Press, Inc. 1970.

Boocock, Sarane S., and E. O. Schild, Eds. *Simulation Games in Learning.* Beverly Hills, Calif.: Sage Publications, Inc., 1968.

Herron, Lowell W. *Executive Action Simulation.* Englewood Cliffs, N.J.: Prentice-Hall, Inc., 1960.

Horvat, John J. *Professional Negotiation in Education—A Bargaining Game.* Columbus, Ohio: Charles E. Merrill Publishers, 1968.

Inbar, Michael, and Clarice S. Stoll. *Simulation and Gaming in Social Science.* New York: The Free Press, 1972.

Martin, Francis F. *Computer Modeling and Simulation.* New York: John Wiley and Sons, Inc., 1968.

Roser, John R., *Simulation and Society.* Boston: Allyn and Bacon, Inc., 1971.

Scott, Andrew M. and others, *Simulation and National Development.* New York: John Wiley & Sons, Inc., 1966.

Programmed Instruction

Calvin, Allen D., Ed. *Programmed Instruction.* Bloomington, Ind.: Indiana University Press, 1969.

Espich, James E., and Bill Williams. *Developing Programmed Instructional Materials.* Belmont, Calif.: Fearon Publishers, Inc., 1967.

Roucek, Joseph S., Ed. Programmed Teaching. New York: Philosophical Library, Inc., 1965.

Computer Assisted Instruction

Dyer, Charles A. *Preparing for Computer Assisted Instruction.* Englewood Cliffs, N.J.: Educational Technology Publications, Inc., 1972.

Holtzman, Wayne H., Ed. *Computer Assisted Instruction, Testing, and Guidance.* New York: Harper & Row, Publishers, 1970.

Le Kan, Helen A., Ed. *Index to Computer Assisted Instruction.* Milwaukee: University of Wisconsin, 1970.

Oettinger, A. G., and S. Marks. *Run, Computer, Run.* Cambridge, Mass.: Harvard Studies in Technology and Society, No. 1., Harvard University Press, 1969.

POST TEST

1. Define gaming and simulation.

_____

_____

_____

2. Define game theory.

_____

_____

_____

3. Who is generally credited with the development of game theory?

_____

4. Explain a split that occurred during the mid-1950s with regard to this discussion.

_____

_____

_____

5. With what words would you identify the two factions that evolved from this split?

_____

6. To which faction is our discussion primarily devoted?

_____

7. Make another attempt to define gaming and simulation in the sense that you identified in question 6.

_____

_____

8. What group is primarily responsible for the early growth of gaming and simulation?

_____

9. What are some advantages of manual games as opposed to computer games?

_____

_____

10. Describe the four classifications of business games.

_____

11. Name five areas of education in which simulation gaming has been used as a teaching tool.

_____

12. Gamson identified some common problems associated with simulation gaming. Name at least four of these problems.

_____

_____

_____

_____

13. There are those who feel that simulation gaming is little more than role playing.
   a. Briefly defend this point of view.
   b. Briefly contest this point of view.

_____

_____

_____

_____

_____

_____

_____

14. a. Is simulation gaming a learning method that you would enjoy as a student?
   b. Is it a teaching method that you would like to try as a teacher?

_____

_____

15. Define simulation gaming.

_____

_____

16. Define programmed instruction.

_____

_____

_____

17. What school of psychology provides the theoretical basis for programmed instruction?

_____

_____

18. Identify B. F. Skinner.

_____

_____

19. Describe a programmed textbook.

_____

_____

_____

_____

_____

_____

_____

_____

20. Describe the difference between *linear* and *branched* programs.

_____

_____

_____

21. What are *contingencies of reinforcement?*

_____

_____

22. Upon what grounds is programmed instruction sometimes condemned?

_____

_____

_____

23. How drastically does the teacher's role change when he uses programmed instruction?

_____

_____

_____

24. What is probably the major constraint that faces the teacher using programmed instruction?

_____

_____

25. What strikes you as being the greatest advantage of programmed instruction?

_____

26. What methods would you employ to maintain student interest?

_____

27. Name another advantage of programmed instruction.

_____

_____

_____

28. What are two areas that have used programmed instruction extensively?

_____

29. Define computer-assisted instruction (CAI).

_____

_____

30. Distinguish between *hardware* and *software* with regard to CAI.

_____

_____

31. Name four types of computer-assisted instruction.

_____

_____

_____

_____

32. What is probably the most common use of CAI in public education today?

_____

_____

33. Try to name the five or six disciplines that have the greatest number of CAI programs available.

_____

_____

_____

_____

_____

34. How can you explain the large number of programs available in some disciplines?

_____

_____

_____

35. What does research have to say about the effectiveness of simulation gaming?

_____

_____

School System Innovations

Roy E. Dwyer

Roger E. Johnson

University of Florida

module 5

Accountability / Performance Contracts / Alternative Schools / Educational Vouchers

RATIONALE

Accountability in education implies that teachers can be expected to produce tangible educational effects. Essential components of this concept are that these effects be clearly defined and that the necessary resources be made available. Forces in society not necessarily within the teaching profession have helped shape and implement the concept of accountability.

The development of more precise measurement of human behavior and the growing availability of means of processing data have given great impetus to production of accountability procedures. Stating objectives in operational terms and precise differentiation between *goals* and *objectives* (goals are long-range end results; objectives are short-range, specific targets) have given assurances of greater degrees of objectivity in many areas of behavior previously assessed only by personal, subjective evaluations. While the primary thrust in accountability has been in the cognitive domain, efforts in the affective and psychomotor domains will undoubtedly increase as techniques are redefined.

Psychometricians, teachers, administrators, educational observers and writers, and parents are concerned with accountability. None of these groups presents a united front either for or against the concept of accountability, although many teachers see current accountability practices as a threat to their over-all effectiveness, focusing too much attention on a relatively small area of the total development of children. Administrators, perhaps, tend to favor it more than the other groups, for accountability is an administrative device, not really an instructional one. Parents in general do not appear as yet to have joined into vocal for or against factions although there appears to be support for some kind of device to use in upgrading educational efforts in many communities.

Industry has contributed much to the concept of accountability. A prime reason for this is that industry is product-oriented. Accountability, too, is product-oriented. One method used by industry is the development of a charter of accountability. This system was originally developed by the Ground Systems Group of the Hughes Aircraft Company. A charter is an agreement by two individuals or groups, one in a subordinate and the other in a superordinate position. Provision is made for discussion and negotiation. The process is repeated by each divisional unit until the entire organization is covered by a series of charters. The purpose is that all parties will know their responsibilities.

Accountability in education can never be a replication of accountability in industry. "Nader's Raiders" can isolate a flaw in a product, pinpoint its cause, and demand retribution. In education, the relationship is quite difficult to establish. It may happen that a child spends a year or more in school, then is found to be quite deficient in such basic skills as reading and arithmetic. It is too often assumed in such cases that the child is mentally retarded or his teachers were inferior. Both assumptions, of course, are quite possible and may at times be true. But it is also true that in classrooms in which the instructor is competent, the materials and resources quite adequate, children do not learn. Direct and measurable cause and effect relationships in human behavior cannot be pinpointed to the degree possible in machine behavior.

Accountability in education may in time transcend the simplistic identification with industry. Professional accountability can be realized only when education is considered as being analogous to similar human endeavors, such as those in law and medicine. In both of those professions, accountability has long been an accepted commitment by the practitioner. Doctors and lawyers are held accountable for what they do but not necessarily for the results of their efforts. Note the difference between this and the auto manufacturer's accountability for what he makes or produces. A lawyer may skillfully present a case for his client, and even though he loses the case and his client is executed, the lawyer is paid and his reputation remains intact if he has performed well. In other words, he is judged by his adherence to a set of operations or behaviors, specified by his fellow professionals and accepted by the public he serves.

A doctor, like a lawyer, is accountable for what he does. His patient may die or recover. In either case, the doctor is paid so long as he observes ethical, established, and accepted behaviors. "The operation was a success, but the patient died," is more than a humorous cliché; it is factual. The doctor's accountability lies wholly in a specified set of behaviors and not in the outcome.

Can the legal-medical examples contribute to a model for educational accountability? If not, why not? A major problem lies in the difficulty in identifying and describing teaching procedures that can be applied with predictable success when used with a group of children. We have not yet zeroed in on the teaching act to the degree that we can isolate procedures from personality or from environmental factors. A second obstacle is the public's expectation of 100 per cent success. The common judgment is that all children must learn to read, and if all children do not learn to read, the schools have failed. No other profession has such an impossible task. We expect doctors and lawyers to "lose some and win some."

OBJECTIVES

In this module we shall consider concepts about four innovations in education: (1) educational accountability, (2) performance contracting, (3) alternative schools, and (4) educational vouchers. Actually, they are all parts of the same concept which is concerned with improving the teaching performance of professional personnel and improving the learning opportunities for the students.

Your goal in studying this module is to discover the various components of each of the innovations, to be able to discuss, knowingly, the advantages and disadvantages of each, and to be able to envision how you might have to function if you were employed by a school using any one of the four.

Specific Behavioral Objectives

Upon completion of your study of this module, you should be able to perform all of the following objectives:

1. Differentiate between goals and objectives by both precise definition and examples.
2. Write a brief statement (100 words) identifying the societal forces contributing to the development of educational accountability and explaining the impact of each.
3. List three differences between accountability in industry and education.
4. Compare by listing two differences in the concepts of accountability in law and medicine with those in education.
5. Write a brief description (fifty words) of each of the following concepts, especially pointing out their common and dissimilar aspects: a) educational accountability, b) performance contracting, c) alternative schools, and d) educational vouchers.
6. Identify two major problem areas that confront implementation of accountability programs.
7. List at least six conditions which should be in evidence if the teacher is to be held accountable.
8. Present two arguments for and two arguments against making school administrators accountable.
9. List four important conditions that must be in evidence if accountability is to be functional and meaningful.
10. Utilizing a study of the Texarkana and OEO projects in performance contracting, present two arguments in support of this technique, and two arguments against it.
11. Define alternative school, listing three underlying motives for its creation.
12. List five suggestions for change in the public school that are ascribed to observed characteristics of various successful alternative schools.
13. List two essential features of the *educational voucher* plan.
14. List two problems that might attend implementation of the educational voucher plan on a wide scale.
15. Correctly answer twenty of twenty-four items on a test.

MODULE TEXT

Accountability

Accountability in education means that someone, a public or private agent, will be held answerable for performing according to agreed-upon terms. After agreement has been reached upon objectives and decisions have been made about the input to achieve the objectives, a measuring instrument will be used to determine the degree to which the objectives have been met. Each member of the organization is expected to answer to someone for doing specific things according to specific plans and against certain timetables to accomplish tangible performance results.

Taxpayers in general have begun to show great concern not only about the rising cost of education to the point of voting down budgets, but also about the quality of education and the decline of standards. They register shock at the growing permissiveness among administrators, and the apparent lack of concern shown by parents of adolescent children.

Over the years, these citizens have evolved lists of assumptions which they have used as rule-of-thumb criteria for measuring the value of the schools. The fact that the assumptions are probably unwarranted does not appear to deter some critics from using them. It is assumed, for example, that[1]

1. There is clear-cut agreement upon what the authority structure of an educational system is or ought to be.
2. There exists a body of universally accepted doctrine for determining whether any school-related deed is good or bad.
3. More books in the library will result in more reading by students.
4. The more students read, the more they will learn.
5. Reduction in the size of class will be followed by the teacher's giving more attention to each student.
6. Increasing the amount of attention paid by the teacher to each child will result in more student learning.
7. A teacher who has a master's degree will know more about how to teach than a teacher with a bachelor's degree.
8. The performance of students as measured by tests is the direct and sole result of their experience in school.

To citizens who base their decisions upon simplistic assumptions of this sort, the acceptance and use of the principle of accountability would mean the closer positive correlation between academic achievement and community expenditure of funds, and the achievement of a higher quality of education through the exercise of professional responsibility for the product of education.

Some Background. Accountability has been around for a long time. Socrates wrote about it and urged that those appointed to positions of importance be voted on before taking office and scrutinized and evaluated by a board after holding office. The Bible (Gospel of St. Matthew) reminds us that men will be held accountable for everything they say on the day of judgment; Plutarch professed his belief that parents should evaluate the performance of those to whom they entrust their children. What is new about accountability is the degree to which the topic is being examined by both educators and lay persons in relation to intended learning outcomes. The thrust in this movement is toward the discovery of the causes of pupil failure so that they can be eliminated and all pupils presented with an opportunity for success. This represents a radical change in education. In previous years, the focus was generally upon the teaching act and the equipment and personnel required for defensible programs. Schools judged less than superior in quality by accrediting associations generally tried to get additional funds so that more materials and more personnel could be provided to enhance the teaching. Now, the focus is upon the learning of each child and the development of skills in each student rather than on what is presented by the teacher. Society is being urged to plan for all students to meet with success in learning, to provide the financial backing to permit it to happen, and then to continually assess to make sure it is happening. The one driving thought in these considerations appears to be that the

---

[1] Henry Dyer, *How to Achieve Accountability in the Public Schools* (Bloomington, Ind.: Phi Delta Kappa Educational Foundation, 1973), pp. 14–25.

educational process need not be as expensive as it is. The promise of accountability is that if everyone works effectively, education will cost much less, learning can be measured, and responsibility for successes and failures properly assigned.

Barro[2] identified at least four major strands of national agitation in education which appear to be tied into the accountability concept:

1. The new federally stimulated emphasis on evaluation of school systems and their programs.

In his 1970 Message to Congress on Education Reform, President Nixon stated:

In developing these new measurements, we will want to begin by comparing the actual effectiveness of schools in similar economic and geographic circumstances. . . . From these considerations we derive another new concept, accountability. School administrators and school teachers alike are responsible for their performance and it is in their interest as well as the interests of their pupils that they be held accountable.[3]

2. The growing tendency to look at educational enterprises in terms of cost effectiveness.

The late 1960s were marked by the clamor of voters for an accounting for the tax dollar. Many bond issues were defeated in an emphatic and resounding manner. By 1971, the Gallup Poll of public attitudes toward education revealed that Americans in general rated the financial crisis as the number one problem of local schools. The public wanted to know how effectively their educational dollar was being spent before they would agree to support new school programs. More than 50 per cent were opposed to the standard pay scale used for teachers. About 60 per cent felt that each teacher should be paid on the basis of the quality of his work, that tenure should be eliminated, and that a system should be introduced that would hold teachers and administrators more accountable for the progress of students.[4]

3. Increasing concentration on education for the disadvantaged as a priority area of responsibility for the schools.

The Elementary and Secondary Education Act (ESEA) of 1965 had provided approximately five billion dollars a year to compensatory programs, largely because of the shift in thinking which had taken place regarding the effects of the home environment, social class, and cultural milieu on the failure of the child in school. The requirement of the Act that schools evaluate the intended outcomes of the federally funded programs focused attention on student performance as a measure of educational success. By the 1970s the emphasis had changed from a

[2] Stephen M. Barro, "An Approach to Developing Accountability Measures for the Public School," *Phi Delta Kappan,* **52:**196–205 (Dec. 1970).

[3] Richard DeNovellis and Arthur Lewis, *Schools Become Accountable: A Pact Approach.* (Washington, D.C.: Association for Supervision and Curriculum Development, 1974), p. 77.

[4] Joe Huber, "Dangers in Misapplication," *National Association of Secondary School Principals Bulletin* (Sept. 1974), p. 14.

belief in responsibility for failure to a belief that if the child fails, "it is the teacher's fault."[5]

4. The movement to make school systems more directly responsive to their clientele and communities, either by establishing decentralized community control or by introducing consumer choice through a voucher scheme.

As city school systems had grown, their complexity had removed them from the sphere of influence of most citizens. The majority of voters had adopted the attitude that teachers were specialists who should be allowed to ply their own trade without interference. The political, social, and economic crosscurrents of recent years, however, which have accentuated self-determination, self-identity, and self-responsibility as admirable virtues, have modified the former permissive attitude. Today, active parents are demanding much more intimate involvement in what happens pertaining to their schools.

Under the accountability banner, these diverse programs for educational reform coalesce and reenforce one another. They add strength to the already powerful pressures for educational change.

The basic idea of accountability, that the professional educators who operate schools should be held responsible for educational outcomes, is a concept that few could quarrel with in the abstract. Almost no one is opposed to the doctrine that those employed by the public to provide a service should be answerable to the public. The problem arises, it seems, when attempts are made to put the principle into operation, for it encompasses a number of distinct though closely interwoven elements.

Unless, however, an over-all perspective is preserved so that inquirers can examine the educational process in an holistic way or can consider each facet of the process in its appropriate position of importance, the danger is great that the concept of accountability can degenerate to the level of shibboleth. Critics with axes to grind will find it a convenient rallying cry for witch-hunting forays and for economy drives destructive to the school.

Components. The elements of the accountability concept that cause the least dissension are those dealing with finances and with things. The financial bookkeeping and the auditing of accounts in accordance with strict business and legal procedures are laudatory American virtues. It is expected that in any kind of institution those officials charged with handling funds and discharging moneys will be honest. When inaccuracies are revealed, traceable either to chicanery or poor business practices, dismissal or prosecution should follow.

In the same light appear the inventorying of things and the discharging of responsibility for their care and preservation. Unless such an accounting process begins to consume an inordinate amount of instruction time and begins to assume more importance than it should rightfully command, it is generally accepted by everyone involved as a matter of course.

The elements which create divergence of opinions are those dealing with accountability for deeds, such as teaching style, or classroom routines, and account-

[5] DeNovellis and Lewis, op. cit., p. 6.

ability for results in terms of test scores of students randomly grouped for class work. In these immaterial areas, the chances for making unwarranted conclusions are vast; the propensity to make indefensible decisions on the basis of inconclusive, even unavailable, evidence is extremely tempting.

Programs designed so far to secure accountable behavior on the part of school personnel appear to differ considerably, but most seem to share the following features in common:

1. Instructional objectives of the school program are stated in performance terms, that is, in terms of specific student learning outcomes.
2. The instructional program is designed by the instructional staff to attain the stated objectives.
3. An evaluation program is designed to measure the extent to which students achieve the stipulated outcomes.
4. A communication system is devised to provide for informing all who are concerned—pupils, parents, school authorities, and state department personnel—of the results achieved.
5. Provisions are made for correcting phases of the program which do not produce satisfactory results.[6]

The master-servant, employer-employee relationship appears as an essential part of each program. Those employed to operate the schools are obligated to report to, or to justify, or to explain to those persons who are superior within the system how well the school is doing, what it is doing, whether it is doing those things that it should be doing, and the alternative possibilities that can be resorted to if success is delayed in coming. In turn, these superiors will justify the performance to those legally vested with higher authority, such as boards of education, state department officials, and legislators, and, when it pertains, to federal authorities.

Legislation Regarding Accountability. The momentum of the accountability movement can be seen in the fact that by 1973 all but a few states had educational accountability programs under consideration. Table 5-1 presents information on the status of legislative action as of autumn of that year.

In this table, states were listed as having some aspect of accountability if they had acted in one or more of the following areas:[7]

1. Established state-wide goals or objectives. In some instances, the legislation has been prescriptive in specifying explicit goals (e.g., Mississippi). In others (e.g., Massachusetts), the legislation has been general enough to permit a wide degree of latitude.
2. Instituted state-wide programs to assess student achievement. In several states the results are used in attempts to isolate factors that influence learning. In several, the results are used for state-wide decision making.
3. Provisions for allocation of state resources. In Colorado, for example, the law provides for a loss of 10 per cent of the amount it would otherwise receive if a district fails to establish and maintain a program accounting

---

[6] Norman E. Gronlund, *Determining Accountability for Classroom Instruction* (New York: Macmillan Publishing Co., Inc., 1974), p. 1.
[7] DeNovellis and Lewis, op. cit., p. 8.

Table 5-1   Status of Accountability Legislation, 1973

State	Legislation Enacted	No Legislation
Alabama		X
Alaska	X	
Arizona	X	
Arkansas	X	
California	X	
Colorado	X	
Connecticut	X	
Delaware		X
District of Columbia		X
Florida	X	
Georgia		X
Hawaii	X	
Idaho		X
Illinois	X	
Indiana	X	
Iowa		X
Kansas	X	
Kentucky		X
Louisiana		X
Maine		X
Maryland	X	
Massachusetts	X	
Michigan	X	
Minnesota		X
Mississippi		X
Missouri		X
Montana		X
Nebraska	X	
Nevada	Joint Resolution	No Statute
New Hampshire		X
New Jersey	X	
New Mexico	X	
New York	X	
North Carolina		X
North Dakota		X
Ohio	X	
Oklahoma	Joint Resolution	No Statute
Oregon	X	
Pennsylvania	X	
Rhode Island	X	
South Carolina		X
South Dakota	X	
Tennessee		X
Texas	X	
Utah		X
Vermont		X
Virginia	X	
Washington	X	
West Virginia		X
Wisconsin	X	
Wyoming		X
Total	27	24

system. In other states, encouragement to become fiscally effective or efficient is offered through the promise of extra resources.

4. Establishment of some kind of accounting system that relates program, management, and budget. The prescriptive states have legislated specific procedures; the permissive states have directed state departments of education to work with school districts in developing appropriate systems for management of information. As a consequence, some districts have begun to utilize PPBS (Planned Program Budget System), or MIS (Management Information System), or some other uniform accounting system.

5. Evaluation of professional personnel. Some states directly relate teacher evaluation and accountability. For example, the California legislation specifies that all local teacher evaluation systems must include standards of expected student progress in each area of study. Certificated personnel are to be assessed in relation to the established standards. The Kansas legislation, on the other hand, provides simply that each school district shall develop procedures for personnel evaluation within general guidelines.

Problems Encountered. So far, programs of accountability appear to have generated opposition and uneasiness among educators. Some programs have been installed in organizational settings that lack the necessary background and organizational traditions to assimilate them. These programs were initiated before psychometric theory was well developed and were imposed from above on unwilling or uncomprehending supervisors. In most cases, they became embedded in unrealistic management and legislative mandates and came to be viewed as ends rather than means. Few early groups had taken the time and effort to evolve a philosophy of accountability before attempting the implementation process.[8] There have also been efforts which suffered from trying to make programs accomplish a great deal with oversimplified procedures. Some of the systems introduced do not appear to have been designed to gain the acceptance of those who are affected by them or by those that have had to implement them. Many programs appear to lack the capacity for determining the extent of influence of any teacher upon any student in a quantifiable form. Although tests currently used are assumed to reveal achievement resulting from a teacher's efforts, no shred of proof is available to warrant the assumption that progress or lack of progress is attributable to a single teacher. Such an assumption ignores the potential influences of the school setting, the peer group, the school administration, the curriculum, various materials in the classroom, the attitude of parents, the intelligence of the student, the motivation of the student, class, and teacher, the amount of government support, the temperature of the room, the presence of uncorrected physical problems of sight or hearing, the amount of pressure the local press might have placed upon the schools, or one or more of a hundred other possibilities.

The Accountable Classroom Teacher. In these state systems, the scope of accountability ranges all the way from those that hold the school accountable only for behavioral objectives, which the school system designs and communicates for itself and which can be measured in quantifiable terms, to those that include a myriad of functions and purposes which properly are assigned in assessment of

[8] Felix M. Lopez, "Accountability in Education," *Phi Delta Kappan,* **52:**231 (Dec. 1970).

schools. Those opting for the narrow kind of accountability do not repudiate the broader functions or goals of the school, but wish to establish only this degree of accountability because they can justify only this amount of responsibility. Believing that every child can acquire the basic skills of reading, writing, and arithmetic and recognizing that these skills are demonstrable, those who limit accountability narrowly support holding the school responsible for showing proof of accomplishment. In the broader areas concerning attitudes, appreciation, values, and knowledge, the search is still on for evaluation procedures which yield dependable data concerning demonstrated mastery. Three of the ways in which teachers may be held accountable are described by Gronlund as programs which any state or any school district might utilize:[9]

1. Product accountability programs which stress the amount learned by the student. Representing by far the most common view about schooling, such observers conclude that if the specified learning outcomes have been achieved, the teaching has been effective, and if they have not, it has been ineffective. The error in this kind of simplistic thinking, of course, is that
   a. Student mental ability, student past achievement, physical condition, and self-concept generally are not satisfactorily considered as contributors to the results.
   b. Student acceptance or rejection of the role of the school in the learning process has often not been weighed.
   c. The impact of the rest of the school and of a single teacher in a solitary classroom in relation to the total faculty, the specialists, and the general staff have not been analyzed.
   d. The influence of out-of-school conditions and environments of home and community has not been considered significant.
   e. School conditions, pupil-teacher ratio, and pupil interaction have not been considered.
2. Process accountability programs in which teachers are held accountable for the professional knowledge and skill they demonstrate.
   In general, teachers support process accountability programs because such programs acknowledge that failures in learning cannot be imputed solely to the teacher. Process accountability recognizes that, similar to the doctor who performs brilliant surgery only to lose the patient, so some students may not succeed in spite of dedicated efforts by the teacher. The stress in process accountability on teachers "knowing their subject, knowing their students, knowing the factors that influence learning, and using professionally sound instructional procedures" is acceptable in general so long as the in-school and out-of-school factors and other individual differences are also considered.
3. Experimental accountability program in which teachers are expected to try out different approaches to improve learning and instruction.
   In this kind of system, teachers would be judged on the basis of their participation with others in planning, carrying out, and evaluating experimental programs on a school-wide basis and in their own classrooms.

[9] Gronlund, op. cit., p. 5.

Assigning Responsibility. The pattern of responsibility that is operational in most school districts in the United States is illustrated in Figure 5-1. Each group shown in Figure 5-1 has major responsibility for some phase of the school program. Teachers are held responsible for instruction, administrators for facilitating and evaluating the program and personnel, school boards for policy making, and the public for financing the schools. In Henry Dyer's hour-glass model, presented in Figure 5-2, the accountability indicated by the arrows shows everyone responsible to someone immediately superior to him for carrying out orders to make the system work. At any point in this hierarchical scheme, any individual who is displeased with the orders he is given can circumvent his immediate superior and take his case through provided channels to the next higher level of authority. In point of fact, however, as Dyer notes, the lines of authority are frequently so tangled that almost no one in the system could respond with simplicity to the query, "Who is really the boss?"

The problem concerning accountability for deeds appears to be the establishment of balance between conflicting points of view. On the one hand, teachers are expected upon being hired to bring with them their personal philosophies of education to serve as guides in their work in the classroom, in teaching their subject, in interacting with students, peers, and parents. On the other hand, it is an accepted fact that the professional staff is hired to implement the wishes and designs of the electorate. The balance that must be struck concerns the day-to-day, class-to-class freedom that each teacher must feel in order to discharge professional obligations while operating within guidelines, perhaps contradictory to personal philosophy, laid down by the majority of voters. The school must move forward; the major goals must be realized while less crucial differences about process prevail. Not all subsidiary goals are achieved, but discussions are continued and student progress is not impeded. Dyer calls this system "the chain of accountability." Each person in a superior position obligates himself to help each subordinate to discover the appropriate action to take in order to benefit each learner. He then helps in procurement of materials and equipment needed for performances. Teachers in the classroom will be accountable for the students, the school principal for each teacher, and so on up the line.

Lopez describes how a similar system, called a "charter of accountability" (described in the Rationale section of this module), which worked for the

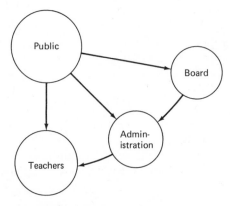

Figure 5-1 *Chain of Responsibility in U.S. School Systems.*

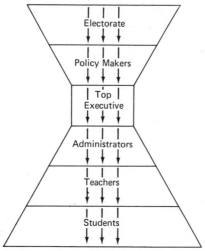

Figure 5-2 *Hierarchy of Accountability. Source:* Henry Dyer, *How to Achieve Accountability in the Public Schools* (Bloomington, Indiana: Phi Delta Kappa Educational Foundation, 1973), p. 15.

Ground Systems Group of the Hughes Aircraft Company, could be adapted for any school system. In this approach the individual charter is agreed upon by two individuals or groups after consultation, discussion, and negotiation. Ultimately, the entire organization is covered by a series of charters, beginning at the top with a major organization unit, such as the English department in a local high school. "Each teacher's goals are shaped by his unit's charter of accountability. Each unit head is held accountable for the results specified in his charter, which he draws up and which he and his superiors sign. Ultimately, all charters are combined into a system-wide charter that provides the basis of accountability for the board of education and the superintendent of schools."[10]

In most good school systems, accountability of this kind has prevailed for some time. There are trust, freedom of movement, assumption of responsibility, conscientious exercise of judgment, and provision of resources, within limits. The desire for improvement keeps such school systems striving to better past accomplishment, extend services, and upgrade equipment and material. It is recognized that even good systems may never be able to indicate with certitude which process is the cause of which desirable aspect of the product, but they continue to utilize all processes that appear to have had positive effects previously and to search for something better. It must always be recognized that each educator has little control over many of the external factors which significantly affect the learning of individuals. Schools may not be judged in isolation because learning is enhanced or inhibited by many factors impinging upon students both from outside as well as inside the classroom.

Educated Opinions Concerning Accountability. The consensus among professional educators, who will be affected by the action ultimately taken, appears to support teacher accountability under the following conditions:

[10] Lopez, op. cit., p. 232.

1. If the public supports education generously. Failures to achieve because of lack of equipment, material, qualified personnel, or adequate space are thus eliminated from consideration.
2. If the school board and administrators announce clearly defined areas of teachers' responsibility. Vague references to what constitutes adequate progress for a year's work are eliminated. Until it becomes possible to describe the stage of achievement arrived at by a student before he is assigned to a teacher, it will not be possible to measure the advances he makes.
3. If the goals of the school system are realistic, clearly defined, and stated in measurable terms. The impediment to progress toward the goal of accountability has been a lack of agreement in particulars about the purpose of the schools. As a result, the curriculum that has emerged has not been appropriate for some of the student body. In addition, when vague and general descriptions of goals have been used, the selection of appropriate testing material has been made difficult, and conclusions about success or failure in goal achievement have been debatable.
4. If the teachers who will be affected by the policy are encouraged and permitted to participate in the policy making. Errors made by misguided policy makers, by members of the electorate who are lacking in knowledge about growth and development of children, or by ambitious, politically motivated participants, must be avoided.
5. If the teachers involved are provided with inservice instruction designed for retooling, periodically, and are given adequate time to plan, prepare, and execute their tasks.
6. If teachers are required to teach only in their particular areas of specialization.
7. If the professional staff, teachers and administrators can merge into a mutually supportive educational team.
8. If the means are provided that will enable those involved to diagnose needs of students and evaluate strengths.
9. If all factors that influence learning are taken into account when assigning responsibility for students' educational growth. In this regard each participant in the educational process should be held responsible for only those educational outcomes that he can effect by his actions and only to the extent that he can effect them.
10. If the evaluation conferences held between supervisor and teacher are handled fairly and professionally, motivated by the objective of improving the teaching process toward the enhancement of learning.
11. If the evaluation system adopted is broad-based and comprehensive. Paper and pencil tests may constitute the bulk of the system, but other types of evaluation should also be used and considered as important.

Conclusions. At this time, the concept of accountability appears to be winning many supporters and to be stimulating conversations among diverse groups concerned with American education. Since most people hold manufacturers, tradesmen, and people in other professions accountable for the performances of their cars, homes, and home services, they naturally conclude that educators should be so held, because public moneys support the schools. In education it could become a catchall for the frustrations of some people, because many supporters of accountability assume it will cure everything that has ever been and is now wrong with education.

The problem as to the extent of the responsibility of each participant in the educational process—teacher, principal, chief administrator—will remain perplexing. Much research and investigation yet needs to be done to supply answers to the many subtle questions surrounding each facet of the concept. Assuming that accountability is not a fad and will not soon disappear, it may be that in a few years a great many educational systems will have more precisely defined objectives, indices and measures compatible with those objectives, systems for collecting and analyzing data longitudinally, and better identification of who is accountable for what is happening.

Already, some interesting effects on education have resulted from efforts that have been made, even if all of the ills that exist in our schools have not been solved. For example, educators are now greatly concerned with having objectives for activities in classrooms stated in behavioral terms. Classroom teachers are becoming more concerned with performance. Another outcome is that administrators are more concerned with personnel assignments and selection. They are realizing that not everyone can teach elementary school, or reading, or social studies, or any other subject area without proper training. More money is also being put into improved resources for the classroom in contrast to the many curriculum projects which were the favorite attraction for the money dispensers during the 1960s.

Performance Contracts

Performance contracting establishes a contract between a school district and an outside firm for a level of payment based on the level of student performance delivered. The contractor is usually a commercial firm that frequently has educational curriculum products to offer. So far, this arrangement has been tried only in a few school districts throughout the country. Therefore, it is still an unproven innovation in which private corporations and teachers will be paid according to their ability, as assessed by pretesting and posttesting with standardized achievement tests, to improve specified skills of a given group of students.

History. Performance contracting is associated more with training in the industrial world than in education, but its backers feel that the concept can be successfully transferred to the educational world.

The rationale behind performance contracting is very simple: You pay for what you get and only for what you get. You are not concerned with the cost to the supplier to produce what you are buying, and you do not care how he produces it so long as the product meets your quality specifications. This idea works fine in the business world, dealing with material things, but when it is applied to education, simplicity vanishes.

Background. National attention was first focused on performance contracting after preliminary reports from a project in Texarkana, Arkansas, indicated that a private firm had improved the reading and mathematics skills of underachieving students. In addition, the daily attendance rate of children participating had improved and fewer of them were dropping out of school.

It must be pointed out that the Texarkana project was a dropout prevention program to help children to succeed in school by improving their mathematics and reading skills and thus stay in school. The target group was achieving at least two years or more below grade level as measured by the Iowa Test of Basic Skills, and had been diagnosed as potential dropouts. It must also be stated that the Texarkana project was not set up as an experiment, for it did not include the evaluation design or administrative controls necessary to assess the capabilities of performance contracting in any reliable fashion.

The project, however, looked promising, so the Office of Economic Opportunity (OEO) decided to expand the program to eighteen school districts. In the expanded program, six firms worked with over 15,000 children in a $5 million one-year, experimental contract with OEO. The contractors' pay was to be determined solely by their success in improving the skills of specified underachieving students in reading and mathematics. The contractors were not to be reimbursed even for expenses until the students' skill levels improved by an average of one grade level in both subjects.

In setting up the conditions for these grants, OEO included criterion-referenced tests as well as normative tests as evaluation instruments. Criterion-referenced tests enable an individual to discover where he stands in terms of content mastered rather than simply in relation to other students in the class. Normative tests inform him of his performance in relation to others. Students had to perform well on both kinds of tests. Payment for improvement was based on how well individual students did in their skill improvement. All students did not have to improve at the same rate or be at the same level by the end of the year. Students who were achieving at a normal rate or above were not included in the program. Since many of the students lived in neighborhoods with high family mobility, a formula was worked out to adjust payment according to the length of time a student was in a class. As a precaution for the contracting firm, it was further stipulated that students must attend class for at least 150 days and all students must have a minimum I.Q. of seventy-five.

Results. One thing that must be done in evaluating this kind of project is to separate the factors accounting for the achievement from those resulting from the Hawthorne effect. This refers to gains made because of psychological factors unrelated to improved teaching or improved learning. Just being part of the experimental group or just receiving some attention from supervisors effects the change. The latter often produces immediate gains but, for various reasons, these gains are not sustained over a period of time. In the Texarkana project, incentives, such as Green Stamps, transistor radios, free time to listen to records and to read paperbacks and magazines were used to help students do better on periodic tests. The contractor, the Dorsett Company, postulated that after students began to see that they could achieve success, they would not need the tangible incentives.

Two recent studies, however, have confirmed that standardized tests do not measure real gains in student learning. They found that a student's test-taking behavior can be influenced by simply offering him rewards for improved test performance. At Indiana University, Donald Farr and associates found that students achieved higher grades on standardized tests in mathematics and reading when offered financial rewards for greatest score improvement between pretests and posttests. Sheldon Sofer, director of Detroit's "Section Three" program, concluded that monetary incentives can improve the performance of some students on standardized tests.

In the original letter of intent, the Dorsett Company and the Texarkana School District agreed to retest the students after six months to determine the degree of retention. Subsequently, this condition was dropped because of problems that arose regarding the administration of the retest.

On the average, students in the Texarkana program progressed more than one grade level in mathematics and reading skills and the dropout rate declined from 12 per cent to 1 per cent. But, when it was time to terminate the contract, allegations were made by the school district that the teachers involved in the project had "taught for the test." School officials felt that this practice inflated the students' scores and they therefore withheld some of the payment money. The Dorsett Company has since filed a $30,000 lawsuit against school officials, seeking payment of the withheld funds.

After the 1971–72 school year, OEO was very critical of the results shown in many of the eighteen school districts utilizing performance contracting and did not fund the projects again.

Research about the effectiveness of performance contracts is conflicting. If any conclusions are to be made about failure of the OEO's projects to produce significant student achievement gains, they must be qualified in terms of the unique characteristics and conditions that existed at each site. In some programs, students with low I.Q.'s did significantly better than those with higher I.Q.'s. Different results were obtained when different standardized tests were used. Some students apparently gained one grade level during the summer following completion of the project. In some projects, even though the OEO stated that they went badly, the teachers and students not only liked the programs, but have defended them to skeptical administrators and other groups.

Performance contractors usually provide a great deal of inservice training for participating teachers. Whether or not this training has something to do with the performance of the teachers and the achievement of their students is not known. Most of the contracting firms have worked to avoid the traditional classroom structure of the self-contained variety in which the teacher is the most important source of knowledge. The teacher becomes the manager of learning and resource systems, facilitating the students' search for knowledge through diagnosis and prescription. Consequently, contractors feel it necessary to provide preservice training which stresses attitudinal and classroom management dimensions.

Those firms that rely heavily upon automated instruction prefer to hire paraprofessionals instead of fully qualified teachers for their programs. Eliminating the certification requirement provides them with a larger reservoir of potential personnel and reduces the cost considerably. Much of the money saved on personnel is invested in modifying the appearance of the traditional classroom. Electrical wiring for the automated devices and furniture for individual or small group instruction must be installed. Since each room serves as a learning center to which no student brings instructional materials, each must be furnished with prescribed library materials, programmed texts, cassette-type recorders, teaching machines, carpeting, and study carrels.

Students are encouraged to look upon the teacher as a "partner to help them learn." The typical concept of teacher who "stands apart," "talks to," or "teaches at" is discouraged. Incentives offered to these teachers in several projects range from $45 to $90 for raising a student one grade level. In four sites sponsored by OEO, "teachers could earn up to $1,200 per class and parents $100 per child, based upon performance above the class expected gain."[11]

Since 1970, some companies that were involved in the OEO project have accused OEO of deliberately "failing" performance contracting. They claim that OEO was responsible for problems that arose pertaining to the limited time for proposal submission, contract negotiations, school-contractor familiarization, program startup, overreaction to concerns about "teaching to the test," test-content mismatches, inadequacy of standardized tests, and unrealistic minimum grade-level gain requirements. These criticisms point out the fact that all parties involved in future performance contracts must be satisfied about the conditions and about which party is responsible for them, before a project is started.

Conclusions. So far, organized teacher groups have lobbied hard to discredit performance contracting. One reason is that these groups feel that it is another step toward "merit pay." Another reason is their concern that performance contracting will take the determination of educational policy out of the hands of the public and possibly establish a new monopoly of education.

Opponents also feel that performance contracting is predicated on the false assumption that educational achievement can be improved in the laboratory of a machine-oriented classroom alone without changing the wider environment of the poverty-stricken child. One of the greatest dangers is that important educational objectives will be lost if "teaching for the test" becomes too important.

There is also a possibility that school districts might run into legal problems if and when they enter into a performance contract. School boards will have to check such things as whether (1) they have the right to delegate authority to an outside firm; (2) collective bargaining agreements are being violated; (3) the party responsible for classroom accidents is the private corporation or the school district; (4) the teachers will be employed by the school district or by the contracting firm, and whether the pay scale and the teacher fringe benefits will be determined by the former or the latter; (5) it is legal to provide public facilities to private corporations for the making of money; and (6) what obligations each party will have in the turnkey phase of the contract.

The *turnkey phase* refers to the transferring of the program back to the school system when the contract has expired. It may be that, in some cases, the private firms will be brought in only to conduct special training sessions for teachers. In other instances, the firms may be asked only to prepare new curriculum packages for the schools, or to implement in the schools programs which the schools have prepared themselves. Each situation, it appears, will be unique and therefore the extent of the firm's involvement will vary among programs.

One of the good results of performance contracting is that it has forced teachers, administrators, and school board members to talk to each other and establish goals and objectives for the students in their districts.

More research on performance contracting has to take place. Perhaps the

---

[11] Charles Blaschke, *Performance Contracting: Who Profits Most?* (Bloomington, Ind.: Phi Delta Kappa Educational Foundation, 1972), p. 26.

major problem to be investigated is the relationship between pupil potential and actual performance on standardized tests.

Obviously, performance contracting is not an easy way for a commercial firm to make money, and it isn't a cure-all for the learning problems of disadvantaged youngsters, regardless of the early results of some projects.

Alternative Schools

An *alternative school* is one started primarily for the purpose of providing students with an alternative to what would have been their regular public school. Most existing alternative schools have been created for the secondary-level student.

Rationale. Alternative schools are a result of the dissatisfaction of some people with the traditional public schools. Some of the reasons for this discontent are that schools are too regimented, administrators are too unsympathetic, teachers are too hamstrung by administrators or by the prescribed curriculum, and the learning climates are too sterile. Some of the creators of alternative schools have been inspired by the writings of such anti-public school authors as Glasser, Herdon, Holt, Leonard, Kohl, and Kozol. Most of them believe that public education is not humane. They feel compelled to "humanize" the schools.

There are differences among individual alternative schools, but the common bond among almost all of them is a feeling that the public schools have not proved themselves worthy of the trust of parents who turn their children over to be educated. They believe something has to be created to replace the public schools, which, for their children, have failed in their educational duties. If other people still retain trust, they should be allowed to continue to patronize the established school. Those who have lost faith, however, resent being coerced by the existence of only one type of school and urge the alternative establishment as a solution.

What Is Happening. In 1970, there were more than 700 alternative schools. In 1973, more than 3,000 were reported. One projection claims that by 1976, close to 20,000 such schools will be in operation in this country. Some of them have not lasted more than a year or two because they were not well planned. Many were considered super-Summerhills; others were directed towards specific cultural development or trade development. Most of these schools were private, and were supported either by tuition or donations or a combination of both. They were located in all areas from the inner-city to upper-class neighborhoods.

However, not all of the schools were private, for some public school districts have begun to investigate the idea of alternative schools for some of their children. One of the most noteworthy examples is Philadelphia's Parkway Program (Schools Without Walls), where certain students attend classes which are not held in a typical school. They are located where students and instructors can find the best setting for the class. The City Hall, a neighborhood repair garage, a newspaper office, the central art museum, and other similar locations have been used to date, because they met the specifications of the class and subject.

Common Types of Alternative Schools. Some of the more common types of alternative schools reported extant in 1973 include the following:[12]

OPEN SCHOOLS. Learning activities in these schools are more individualized and are organized around learning centers within a classroom or within the school building. The St. Paul Open School in St. Paul, Minnesota, and the Brown Open School in Louisville, Kentucky, are two instances. Each enrolls about 400 elementary and secondary school students.

MAGNET SCHOOLS AND LEARNING CENTERS. Some alternative schools are oriented toward a specific interest area, such as the visual and performing arts, the musical arts, the sciences, or environmental studies. Sometimes these schools are designed for particularly gifted young people. The Berkeley High School of the Arts in Berkeley, California, is a foremost example of this type of school.

DROP-OUT, DROP-IN SCHOOLS. Drop-out, drop-in schools are for youngsters who have dropped out of regular high schools and for potential dropouts. Sometimes the educational program is combined with a community-living center. Number Nine in New Haven, Connecticut, was one of the first efforts to provide this kind of educational opportunity.

ALTERNATIVES FOR DISRUPTIVE STUDENTS. Some school systems are trying to stabilize their conventional schools by creating alternative schools with programs designed to give school-rejects—disruptive students—enhanced self-images and other kinds of help. Philadelphia has opened some thirty alternative schools that are designed explicitly to salvage the disruptive student.

FREE SCHOOLS. Free schools tend to be more radical in ideology and looser in structure than other alternative forms. They strive to help young people and adults learn to live together in an atmosphere of freedom. Pacific High School in Palo Alto, California, is a current example. Most free schools are nonpublic.

FREEDOM SCHOOLS. Chiefly community-based and developed, freedom schools are operated by and for Blacks and other ethnic minorities. They stress ethnic studies and basic learning skills. Harlem Prep in New York City was one of the first and is probably the best known of this type of alternative school. Most freedom schools are nonpublic.

CAREER SCHOOLS. These newly developed alternatives are trying to find new ways for young people to gain greater knowledge of careers and to acquire more useful job skills. The Career Academy, operated by Research for Better Schools, is one of several such schools that have been funded by the U.S. Office of Education.

SURVIVAL SCHOOLS. Survival schools are not really schools in any usual sense of the word. Rather, they are groups of adults who take young people into challenging natural environments to teach them how to get along together, how to brave the elements, and how to discover who they really are. Outward Bound was one of the first such efforts, and it has spawned a host of followers.

Attractions of Alternative Schools. There is little research on the success or failure of alternative schools. But many public school people are attracted by what is happening in some alternative schools, because some students who would not be regular in attendance if enrolled in a public school are eagerly attending

[12] Curriculum Report, from the Curriculum Service Center, *National Association of Secondary School Principals Bulletin,* Vol. 2, No. 3 (March 1973), p. 2.

classes; some students are taking more class hours a week than they would have otherwise; and many students, parents, and other supporters of alternative schools are those who come from the social and economic stratum that has traditionally supported public education, both financially and philosophically.

Assumptions. An almost universal feature of the alternative school is the emphasis on the students' assumption of an active role in their own educational programs. Students are treated as adults.

Directors of alternative schools believe that education is better when some of the institutional barriers between students, teachers, and administrators are removed. They also believe that students should be given freedom to pursue their own areas of interest because they are more aware of what is meaningful to them than are most public school administrators or teachers. As a result, most of the hierarchical staffing arrangements that create separations in public education between the top administration, the classroom teacher, and the students are eliminated in alternative schools. Schools are put in control of those who are most affected by them—students and parents. Students have roles to play in setting their own learning tasks. Efforts are made by all to create classrooms that have a loving, accepting environment. In the appropriate climate, emotional needs can be met, students feel free to grow, to follow their natural curiosity, and to do whatever is necessary to satisfy their intellectual drives.

Suggestions. Following are listed some guidelines used by various successful alternative schools for change in the public school curriculum and in the operations of administrators, teachers, and others affected.

1. Place the focus on the individual student. Place less emphasis on national curriculum developmental projects. Most curriculum work should be done at the local level.
2. Readjust some of the rigid structure of the typical school administration so that students, teachers, and administrators will interact. Involve students in decision making, so that they can learn to become independent.
3. Operate schools as a part of student life, not as adult living. Students should feel they belong and should become active participants.
4. Base the curriculum on the realities of the students' situations. An interdisciplinary curriculum is necessary.
5. Work out programs in which objectives for individual achievement are designed by the student in consultation with the teacher.
6. Develop techniques that help teachers become facilitators of learning instead of dictators, and that enable them to direct and assist students instead of being the providers of information.
7. Arrange for some of the school activities to take place outside of the school, where the action is. If education is to become an integral part of a student's life process, he must be given an opportunity to experience cultural institutions, public buildings, and neighborhoods other than where he lives.
8. Accept the employment of personnel lacking in academic credentials. It is not vital for all instructors to be certified. Lawyers, doctors, plumbers, truck drivers, and electricians should be called upon as needed.

9. Capitalize upon the backgrounds of the students as a resource for other students' education. Students have knowledge of language, culture, hobbies, crafts, and other skills that can help educate others.

Conclusions. Whether or not the charges brought against public education are warranted, the growth of alternative schools is causing a reexamination of the relationship between the institution of the school and the student population that is served by that institution.

Riordan[13] offers the following as major tasks for all individuals and groups interested in establishing viable, "flexible, responsive institutions committed to change."

1. Secure the field. The alternative school must stake out its claim, secure its ground. It must gain the time, the space, and the autonomy—the security from external threat—to devote the major portion of its energies to the clarification and active pursuit of its goals.
2. Clarify goals, priorities, constraints, and limits for everyone. This process will require that the implications of the goals are understood and that the limitations on what can be done are understood and accepted.
3. Develop alternative structures and practices, consistent with goals and constraints. "Alternative schools must realize that structure and discipline, far from being antithetical to their principles, are the prerequisites to building a viable alternative setting. In the absence of bureaucratic structures, clear delineation of responsibilities is still a necessity, including students' rights, exclusion procedures, required courses (if any) and provision of decision-making procedures."
4. Develop procedures for systematic, supportive evaluation feedback. Standard evaluation procedures may not measure what the alternative school is trying to accomplish; therefore, ways must be found or invented to evaluate alternative goals.
5. Establish communication networks with other alternative institutions. Clearing houses have already been established but have not yet achieved the systematic dissemination necessary if the movement is to prove effective.

It must be pointed out that the alternative school idea is not looked upon as a cure-all for all students. Many students require a situation in which there is structure and they profit from pedagogical techniques similar to those now in use. The main concern of the supporters of alternative schools is that the students be given a chance to select how they want to be educated and be able to make meaningful choices about the process.

Educational Vouchers

Definition. Probably the most radical proposal for achieving better education through improved accountability is the educational *voucher* plan. In such a plan, parents receive vouchers—checks, script, declarations—of a specific value, based

[13] Robert C. Riordan, *Alternative Schools in Action* (Bloomington, Ind.: Phi Delta Kappa Educational Foundation, 1972), pp. 42–43.

upon an amount equivalent to the local school system's per pupil cost of education. They then use the voucher to pay for the education of their children in the school of their choice. The school may be public or private, traditional or alternative, local or distant. This system would allow the education of children to be purchased by parents in a free market system through payment provided by school districts or government agencies.

Rationale. The rationale for this consumer choice solution is that there would be direct and immediate accountability by the school to the parent. Improved public relations would keep parents constantly informed, or reports by students about the absence of learning or of dereliction on the part of the staff would result in negative consequences. Dissatisfied parents would be able to move a child and funds to another school where better conditions for learning are promised. In this system, it would be up to the parent to become informed and to be able to evaluate the schools. The necessity of choosing a school is not considered a drawback because parents have generally been concerned about finding good schools whenever they have changed their residence.

The voucher plan is associated primarily with Professor James Coleman, economist Milton Friedman, and the Harvard Center for the Study of Public Policy. It implies, in various of its proposed forms, regulations relating to a selection of students, access to the schools for financial and program audit, standards of educational quality, and availability of evaluative data to potential purchaser-parents. Essentially a response to the need for equality of education for minority groups and ghetto dwellers, the plan has appealed to many interested in religious education and also to some supporting the accountability movement.

Implications. At present, there has been very little experience with educational voucher systems. This means there is little basis for judging how well a voucher system might operate or what effect it might have on the quality of education.

Problems. Despite the attractiveness and apparent logic of the rationale supporting the concept, there appear to be several weak spots which have generated opposition. One foreseeable problem is that it could become impossible for school districts to plan their programs and work on curriculum improvement because of potential parental reaction. If parents can pull children out of a school whenever they are disturbed with what is going on in a particular school, some schools will never institute new programs. Sometimes parents get angry about things that have no relation to how well children are doing in school, and if it becomes easy to put children in a school and just as easy to withdraw them, the entire process could turn into one giant push me-pull you contest. Social considerations such as the school with the best team or with the most popular celebrity could induce fickleness of judgment by some parents.

Perhaps the most serious weakness is that popular schools would have to find ways to limit enrollment by discrimination of some sort. Other schools might gain in popularity by featuring discrimination of another sort. Still other schools would have to close down with great loss of investment in buildings, personnel, and equipment.

The consensus at present appears to be that the voucher system represents a mixed blessing which, while solving some of the knotty problems confronting schools today, creates some new knotty problems for tomorrow. If solutions can be devised to make it possible for parents and children to become more free in selecting a school while refraining from impinging upon the freedom of the school and the right of educators to survive and function, vouchers may satisfy a need for the future.

A Final Comment. The innovations treated in this module are products of their time. They appear to be

1. Aimed at accelerating and cementing recent social and civic gains. If they are successfully implemented, they may help to resolve the problems attendant upon de facto segregation, upon the inferiority of equipment, facilities, and materials that accompany inner-city blight, and upon the cultural impediments to education found among some minority groups in some closed neighborhoods.
2. Designed to exploit the Yankee concept of competition. If one teacher is not doing a satisfactory job, clients will move to another. If one school falls out of touch with the needs and wants of its pupils, parents will transfer them to another. Only the "fittest" will survive.
3. Creations of new participatory roles for parents and students in the administration and curriculum development. Decentralization beyond the scope envisioned by most activists to date would take place automatically.
4. Attractive lures to segments of society which have in the past paid only scant attention to the educational enterprise. As potential profit-making ventures, schools could become the recipients of the imaginative thinking and almost unlimited financial resources which have characterized the business and industrial sectors of American society. The promise is great. The drawbacks and difficulties discussed in the text will have to be overcome, it is true, but in the light of such potentially huge gains, the effort required to accelerate the evolution assumes considerably less importance.

SUGGESTED READING

"Accountability, Vouchers, and Performance Contracting." *Today's Education* (Research Division), **60**:13 (Dec. 1971).

"Almost Everything You Need to Know About Performance Contracting." *American School Board Journal,* **159** (Oct. 1971), 28–35.

Barrilleaux, Louis E. "Accountability Through Performance Objectives." *NASSP Bulletin,* **56** (May 1972), 103–110.

Barrow, Stephen M. "An Approach to Developing Accountability Measures for the Public Schools." *Phi Delta Kappan,* **52** (Dec. 1970), 196–205.

Blackman, Nathaniel. "The Community as Classroom: Three Experiments." *NASSP Bulletin,* **55** (May 1971), 147–150.

Browder, Lesley H., Jr., William A. Atkins, Jr., and Esin Kaya. *Developing An Educationally Accountable Program.* Berkeley, Calif.: McCutchan, 1973.

Center for the Study of Public Policy. *Educational Vouchers: A Preliminary Report on Financing Education by Payment to Parents.* Cambridge, Mass.: The Center, March, 1970.

Domyahn, Roger A. "Annotated Bibliography on Accountability." *Audio-Visual In-struction,* **16** (May 1971), 93–101.

Illich, Ivan, et al., *After Deschooling, What?* New York: Harper & Row Publishers, 1973.

Inlow, Gail M. *The Emergent Curriculum.* New York: John Wiley & Sons, Inc., 1972.

Lucas, Christopher J. *Challenge and Choice in Contemporary Education: Six Major Ideological Perspectives.* New York: Macmillan Publishing Co., Inc., 1976.

MacDonald, James B., Bernice J. Wolfson, and Esther Zaret. *Reschooling Society: A Conceptional Model.* Washington, D.C.: Association for Supervision and Curriculum Development, 1974.

Millman, Jason, "Reporting Student Progress: A Case for a Criterion Referenced Marking System." *Phi Delta Kappan,* **52** (Dec. 1970), 226–230.

Reynolds, Jerry D. "Performance Contracting . . . Proceed with Caution." **60** *English Journal,* (Jan. 1971), 102–110.

Robinson, Donald W. "Alternative Schools: Challenge to Traditional Education?" *Phi Delta Kappan,* **51** (March 1970), 374–375.

Schiller, Jeffrey. "Performance Contracting: Some Questions and Answers." *American Education* **7** (May 1971), 3–5.

POST TEST

Select the best answer to complete each statement and put the correct letter in the space provided.

_____ **1.** The main difference between accountability in business and in education is that
   a. education cannot be evaluated.
   b. in industry, it is always possible by testing to identify where a mistake has been made in a product, and this is not true in education.
   c. in education, it is possible by testing to identify where a mistake has been made, and this is not true in industry.
   d. both 1 and 2 are true.
   e. both 2 and 3 are true.

_____ **2.** Professional accountability differs from educational accountability in that
   a. doctors and lawyers have more clearly defined performance objectives.
   b. the American Bar Association and the American Medical Association are more careful in their screening of practitioners than is true in the field of education.
   c. doctors and lawyers are held accountable for their efforts, but not for their results.
   d. all of these reasons are true.
   e. none of these reasons is true.

_____ **3.** Educational accountability is defined as an agreement between a school district and a public or private agent which includes the following criteria:

a. input **b.** measurement **c.** objectives **d.** payment **e.** time limits.
Which of the following responses lists these criteria in the order in
which they occur?
(1.) c, a, b, e, d, b.
(2.) a, b, c, d, e, c.
(3.) c, e, b, a, b, d.
(4.) b, c, e, a, b, d.
(5.) d, a, b, c, e, c.

——— **4.** The main belief held by people who favor educational accountability
is that
   a. schools should teach everything students will need in our society.
   b. accountability is the answer to most of the things that are wrong
   in education.
   c. parents should have more of a say in what is taught.
   d. students should take more tests and have more homework so parents could check on their progress.
   e. educators should be held responsible for what happens to the students in school.

——— **5.** The two areas of the curriculum that have been selected as the most
important by supporters of accountability are
   a. reading and social studies.
   b. mathematics and science.
   c. science and reading.
   d. language arts and social studies.
   e. mathematics and reading.

——— **6.** In school districts in which accountability has been tried, educators
have found some reasons why accountability has not worked as well
as expected. Which three statements have been offered as reasons for
this problem?
   a. not enough money has been put into accountability programs.
   b. the schools have tried to do too much before the district was ready
   for the program.
   c. the organization and objectives were not suited for what was to take
   place.
   d. the teaching organizations have always been against any form of
   accountability.
   e. programs have been pushed on teachers without their consultation.

——— **7.** Which two major facts do supporters of educational accountability
tend to overlook?
   a. children do not learn everything from a teacher.
   b. administrators have as much impact on children as do teachers.
   c. there are more subjects in the curriculum than reading and mathematics.
   d. teachers should have more to say about the curriculum than anyone
   else.
   e. peer groups have as much influence on children as does school.

———— **8.** In most of the accountability projects that have been tried so far, which group has been held most accountable?
   a. school boards.
   b. superintendents.
   c. parents.
   d. principals.
   e. teachers.

———— **9.** If too much pressure is put on teachers to help students do well on their final evaluation, the nonsupporters of accountability believe that the main result will be that
   a. the teaching organizations will demand that it be stopped.
   b. teachers will teach for the test.
   c. teachers will refuse to be held solely accountable.
   d. the extra financial burden will destroy public education.
   e. merit pay will destroy the harmony in school faculties.

————**10.** So far the programs that have tried accountability have stressed the learning of what level or levels?
   a. cognitive.
   b. affective.
   c. psychomotor.
   d. cognitive and psychomotor.
   e. cognitive and affective.

————**11.** When a formal contract is drawn between a school district and another agency which guarantees that the agency increase the learning of students or they will receive no pay, it is called
   a. educational accountability.
   b. educational vouchers.
   c. alternative schools.
   d. performance contracting.
   e. all of these.

————**12.** So far, performance contracting projects have been
   a. mostly successful.
   b. mostly unsuccessful.
   c. slightly successful.
   d. slightly unsuccessful.
   e. labeled both successful and unsuccessful, depending on who is evaluating the project.

————**13.** The reason usually given for success in performance contract projects is
   a. the ratio between teachers and students.
   b. the standardized tests used in the evaluation of the projects.
   c. the amount of inservice training given to teachers in the projects.
   d. the ability level of students picked for these projects.
   e. none of these.

————**14.** When parents take children out of the school they normally would attend to place them in a school with a different philosophy, they deal with
   a. parental preference.
   b. educational vouchers.
   c. alternative schools.
   d. performance contracting.
   e. educational accountability.

_____15. Backers of alternative schools are members of which group?
   a. students.
   b. teachers.
   c. school administrators.
   d. parents.
   e. all of these.

_____16. When parents are allowed to put their children in a public or private school of their choice with the government providing the funds, this is called
   a. communism.
   b. educational accountability.
   c. performance contracting.
   d. educational voucher.
   e. alternative schools.

Crucial Social Issues

Manouchehr Pedram

Graceland College

module 6

Racism in American Education / Desegregating the Schools / Urban School System

RATIONALE

American urban centers are in the midst of a series of profound, complex changes. The most notable of all are the changes affecting the racial make-up of the city, the economic welfare and social integration of its citizens, the housing conditions of the laboring class, and the financial plight of municipalities. Although these problems are interrelated, the most nagging of them all is the change in racial make-up of the city, and the changing life style accompanying it. The racial composition of most large metropolitan areas has shifted to the point that many cities are referred to as black cities. Edmonia Davidson reports that, by the start of 1970, three out of every five blacks or fifty-eight per cent of the total black population lived in a major metropolitan area. Washington, D.C., Detroit, Newark, Atlanta, and Richmond are a few examples of black cities.[1] The trend that began just before the 1950s, with the immigration of blacks from the South and their redistribution in Northern cities, led to eventual flight of middle-class, white Americans to the suburbs.

In this process of change, schools in the urban metropolitan centers found themselves facing problems that were similar to those of the city within which they were located. In the minds of many, big city schools became equated with dilapidated physical facilities, lack of up-to-date library resources, visual aids and modern technological alternatives. The basic issue appeared to be whether the city's existing schools with all their limitations could meet the needs of the urban community, with its multiethnic, multiracial population. It is apparent that even though urban centers have changed in their racial compositions, they still provide a center of heterogeneous cultural variations. The survival and stability of the cities, because of their pluralistic nature, depend upon an educational system that can promote a vehicle for exposure to, and an understanding and appreciation of cultural variations and ethnic diversity. To achieve the desired goals, there must be a change in the segregation and racial imbalance of the urban school system in respect to both students and staffs attending those schools. There also must be greater participation on the part of the various ethnic groups so that decisions can be made in educational matters relevant to their life styles. Finally, a high quality, multiracial, multiethnic education must include a core of well-prepared and sensitive teachers who are able to cope with the serious educational problems facing the urban community.

This module, therefore, will focus basically on these three issues and related topics.

GENERAL PURPOSE

This module is designed to enable participants to gain insight into kaleidoscopic aspects of urban educational problems and to demonstrate knowledge of underlying concepts:

[1] Edmonia W. Davidson, "Education and Black Cities: Demographic Background," *The Journal of Negro Education*, **42**:233–260 (Summer 1973).

1. Racism and segregation.
2. Problems emerging from attempts at resolving conflict:
    a. Busing controversy.
    b. Remedial alternatives.
    c. Struggle for a voice in educational decision making.
    d. New teachers in desegregated schools.

These concepts have caused persistent problems which have almost defied solution.

Specific Behavioral Objectives

Upon completion of study of this module, you will be able to

1. Note the distinction between *racism* and *segregation*.
2. Rationalize the relationship between multiethnicity and cultural pluralism in American society.
3. List the causes of segregation, as enumerated in this unit, and describe its interrelation with the total problem.
4. Using a map of the local area, be able to locate major housing patterns in accordance with racial and ethnic groups (blacks, whites, Chicanos, Indians, Puerto Ricans, and other groups with various national origins).
5. Compare and contrast according to the given instructions the three court decisions in regard to desegregation:
    a. *Brown* v. *Topeka Board of Education.*
    b. *Bradley* v. *School Board of City of Richmond, Virginia.*
    c. *Keyes* v. *School District No. 1, Denver, Colorado.*
6. Cite the difference between the Supreme Court decision in *Plessy* v. *Ferguson* and *Brown* v. *Topeka Board of Education.*
7. Enumerate at least four reasons given by proponents of support and four by opponents of support for busing.
8. Cite the rationale behind community desire for a role in formulating major educational policies and practices.
9. Select one of the alternatives listed for desegregating a big city school system and write a one-half page view supporting or rejecting it as a real alternative (self-analysis and view).
10. Write a paragraph or two in defense or rejection of accusations made against teachers in the central city school system.
11. Complete the Post Test without missing more than two answers.

ACTIVITIES

After completion of study of this unit, complete the activity in section I and two of the activities listed in section II, in order to satisfy the experiential base for relating the concept to practice.

Section I

Using a map of the local area and with the help of census materials, shade the major housing patterns in your metropolitan area in accordance with racial and ethnic concentration (blacks, whites, Chicanos, Puerto Ricans, Indians, Italians, and other foreign-born groups).

Section II

1. Visit at least one agency or organization in your local urban area, such as Model Cities, Urban Renewal, Human Relations, Civil Rights organization, Legal Aid, or welfare agency, and note the function or the services available in such an agency or organization in accordance with the provided guideline of activities.

2. Visit a community center, storefront church, or similar center in the central city area, and learn about the role it plays or services it provides in that community, using the provided activities guideline.

3. Make a visit to a neighborhood that has a concentration of low socioeconomic groups, and write your impressions.

4. Arrange, if possible, to visit a classroom in a central city school (minimum one-half day) with a concentration of racial or ethnic minority students, and observe teacher behavior toward various ethnic children. Write your impressions.

After completion of your observation, if possible, talk to a couple of persons in the neighborhood, or pupils in the classroom, and ask their reactions to the agency, organization or school.

Observation Guidelines

1. Agencies, organizations and centers:
   a. Major function and services the organization provides.
   b. Boundary limits of the services including geographical, legal, budget, and staff.
   c. The groups or clientele benefiting from the services.
   d. Reaction of various individuals you have talked to, as they perceive their roles and functions.
2. Central city neighborhood:
   a. Neighborhood's general racial make-up.
   b. Physical condition of neighborhood (dilapidated, deteriorated, well-kept, clean, noisy, calm, trash piled up or lack of it).
   c. Noticeable recreational facilities, if any.
   d. Available transportation facilities.
   e. Any other relevant information.
3. Classroom observation:
   a. Teacher's racial or ethnic background.
   b. Teacher's exhibited general attitude toward various ethnic or racial groups or subgroups during your visit.
   c. The percentage (approximate) of positive or negative reinforcement provided by the teacher.

d. The teacher's general positive or negative relationship or rapport with pupils.
e. Flexibility, rigidity, consistency, affecting the classroom climate.
f. Relevance of activities, methods, and resources as you observed.
g. Classroom appearance (neatly organized, messy and overcrowded, lack or abundance of resources).
h. Reactions of pupils to teacher as well as to your visit, if any.

MODULE TEXT

Racism in American Education

The American Heritage Dictionary defines *racism* as "the notion that one's own ethnic stock is superior," and *segregation* as "the policy and practice of imposing the social separation of races." Based on these definitions, racism and segregation are contradictory to the principle of pluralism and multiethnic society. In practice, however, one can see the existence of the two contradictory elements in all aspects of American social, economic, political, and educational processes. It is not surprising that to many minorities, particularly blacks and Chicanos, the urban school system is a racist institution, reflecting the attitudes, values, and bigotry of the larger, white, American society. The general policies of school systems, the teachers' attitudes, the insensitivity in general of school personnel toward minority children, and the lack of systematic effort for genuine integration of the total educational system are given as reasons for these allegations. Accusers point to the containment of various ethnic minority children in a substandard system as an expression of the majority's will to provide separate and unequal education for ethnic minorities. Whether these allegations are true or false, it is apparent that the flight of the white, middle-class majority to the suburbs and an increase in minority population in the big metropolitan centers have caused the isolation of races and seclusion of ethnic minorities in de facto segregated systems. In addition, the following practices and policies on the local level have encouraged segregation and have effectively separated races: (1) gerrymandering of school attendance zones to keep separate races in selected schools; (2) building new schools or expanding the old ones in areas that either promoted or preserved segregation; and (3) organizing and manipulating grade levels in order to keep the balance of races in accordance with a desired level.

The exclusion and containment of minorities have led to a surge of protest, in both violent and nonviolent forms, to demonstrate discontent with the imposed limitations and to support the struggle for equal opportunity and treatment. Some people, either for psychological or other reasons (such as their sense of white supremacy or their fear for job security), are unprepared to face the challenges of minority demands and therefore offer active or passive resistance. The struggle for equal rights has brought the attention of many to the fact that a multicultural, multiracial society cannot survive without mutual respect, understanding, and a mutually receptive atmosphere in which there is appreciation of the positives in a diversified culture.

Some Causes of Racial Isolation. The racial isolation and containment of various ethnic minorities, particularly blacks, in the central city, is not an accidental happening, but has been a long process. Although the very basis of the racial isolation has been racism on the part of the majority, there are practices on the part of government or private institutions that have had an influence on racial isolation. One of the most influential factors in this process and a very major cause of separation of races can be traced to the discriminatory policies of the housing industries and real estate agencies. Governmental policies, in general, with their power of eminent domain, ordinances, and zoning powers have been an encouraging factor in this process. Federal Housing Authority regulations for years were based upon the principle of homogeneous neighborhoods which resulted in racial imbalance. Housing projects, even until the mid-1960s, were assigned on a blacks or whites basis by governmentally supported policy. Suburban fights to keep out low-income housing have made it difficult even today to break the racial separation which has divided American society.

Segregation and Its Consequences. In practice, no pluralistic society can afford division and the isolation of its races. They leave it without sufficient interaction among all racial elements, which is detrimental to a free society. Segregation is un-American in the full definition of the term. The United States was built upon cultural variations and ethnic diversity. In this kind of multiethnic, pluralistic society, each group brings a culture and set of values of its own for interplay. Cross-cultural contacts and constructive participation in a culture different from one's own is essential to strengthen the multicultural, multiracial society. Study after study has pointed to the harmful effects of segregation, not only to ethnic minority children but to all races, including whites. They show that segregation and isolation of races foster a "false sense of superiority" in white children and a sense of "alienation" and "inferiority" in isolated minorities. The Coleman report was very specific in pointing out that pupils' achievement increases in a system in which there is integration both of races and social classes.

Negro children as a group evince and sustain substantially greater academic achievement if they are members of a predominantly white classroom. This effect is especially strong if the child begins his interracial education in the first three grades. And the achievement of white children in such classrooms is not lowered when contrasted with that of comparable white children in all-white classrooms. . . . Desegregation is the prerequisite of the ideal condition—the true cross-racial acceptance of integration. In other words, a desegregated school is merely an institution with an interracial student body, usually mostly white; it implies nothing about the quality of the interracial interaction. By contrast, an integrated school is a desegregated one with numerous cross-racial friendships and little or no racial tension. The Commission on Civil Rights, in closer examination of the Coleman data, discovered that the chief academic benefits of interracial education occurred primarily in the genuinely integrated schools.[2]

Ewald Nyquist, Commissioner of Education in New York State, testified before a subcommittee of the United States House of Representatives about evidence that

[2] Robert Schwartz, Thomas Pettigrew, and Marshall Smith, "Desegregating: Assessing the Alternatives," in Emanuel Hurwitz, Jr., and Robert Maidment, eds., *Criticism, Conflict, and Change* (New York: Dodd, Mead & Co., 1972), p. 110.

indicates that isolation in schools is harmful to academic achievement of students. Pointing to the merits of desegregation and eventual integration, Nyquist stated that in integrated schools children learn "to live in a multiracial society in a multiracial world" in which a majority of the world population is "non-white." He emphasized that children learn to judge people for what they are rather than for their color or group association. It is true that integration is more than a superficial interaction of races. It should be a process of permanently cementing the racial bonds. Interaction, though, even in its superficial form, does provide a climate that otherwise is not available. Levine, et al., in a study of interracial attitudes in Kansas City, discovered that children of the same age but of varied racial background did develop "positive racial attitudes" after they were placed together.[3] It is, therefore, imperative that efforts to desegregate both schools and the total community should not be abandoned, but rather should be broadened. If the structure of multiracial, multicultural society is to be stabilized and protected, cultural diversity needs to be examined and appreciated. Where there is racial isolation, it is doubtful that a true appreciation of others' cultures can be experienced. Morally, legally, and educationally, America as a nation is obligated to provide a climate for integration. This requires that ethnic groups work together in good faith. Desegregation and integration are pillars of quality education and are parallel processes; one without the other is incomplete. It is time, therefore, to take a realistic look at the educational system in the metropolitan centers and reorient our educational priorities as a means toward achieving a truly integrated society. To endorse the recent declaration by the American Association of Colleges for Teacher Education (AACTE) that there is no "one model American," is in fact recognition of the principle that there are "many models" in American society. No one race, color or culture has superiority over other races, colors or cultures. Because of this diversity and multiplicity, value differences and cultural varieties are to be appreciated and accentuated. This, no doubt, requires an examination of attitudes and behaviors by all who are involved in the educational process. Until the changes occur, voices of discontent, accusations, and struggle will continue.

Desegregating the Schools

Desegregation and the Courts. The basic issue facing the courts has been whether a school system is racially balanced in accordance with the racial composition of a specific area. Although there have been cases in the lower federal and state courts as well as in the Supreme Court, one case can be considered the turning point. That key decision is the Supreme Court decision in the case of *Brown* v. *The Board of Education of Topeka, Kansas,* on May 17, 1954. Chief Justice Earl Warren, in delivering the opinion of the court, struck down the doctrine of "separate but equal" in education. The court indicated that separate educational facilities violate the Fourteenth Amendment of the United States Constitution because they are inherently unequal. That decision in essence reversed the doctrine laid down by *Plessy* v. *Ferguson* fifty-eight years earlier, in 1896. The

[3] Daniel U. Levine, et al., "Interracial Attitudes and Contact Among a Sample of White Students in Suburban Secondary Schools," Center for the Study of Metropolitan Problems in Education (Kansas City, Mo.: University of Missouri–Kansas City, 1969).

basic mandate of the high court in the Brown case was that, legally as well as morally, an equal education requires a racially balanced system. It is, however, apparent that the 1954 decision, although it had an impact upon Southern and border states because of their racially explicit state laws, did not eliminate de facto segregation across the nation. With the exodus of white population to the suburbs, the urban centers, particularly the major central cities, became predominately black. As a result, a variety of cases since 1954 have challenged de facto segregation policies. Courts across the nation have spelled out a variety of opinions in reference to de facto segregation in such cases as *Keyes* v. *School District No. 1, Denver, Colorado* (1972), and *Bradley* v. *School Board of the City of Richmond, Virginia* (1973). The Denver case was significant in that it involved a city in the North rather than in the South. In this case, the Supreme Court held that the Denver school district provided educationally inferior, intentionally segregated schools with such devices as manipulation of student attendance zones and school site selections. In the Richmond case, the emphasis was upon the permissibility of a "metropolitan" approach or crossing boundary lines for the purpose of desegregation. The decision of the high court, with Justice Powell not participating, was divided.

The National Association for the Advancement of Colored People (NAACP), the Southern Christian Leadership Conference (SCLC), and parents and school administrators are tangled in a civil rights battle to achieve racially balanced and integrated school systems in major metropolitan areas. The 1970s appear to be a decade in which the battle for civil liberties will continue and probably will become stronger than ever before. Courts are asked to pave the way for major desegregation of schools by mandating more flexible boundary lines which will provide for the integration of big city and suburban areas. It is no secret, however, that court decisions have left the states basically responsible for providing each youngster with an equal educational opportunity, in which each child, regardless of his race, social class, color, or national background, is given the same opportunity as all other children in the states. Such a state responsibility in essence should assure that state resources are available to all children on an equal basis without discrimination.

As the year 1975 passed its midpoint, school desegregation was making slow progress, with busing as a top alternative in the desegregation process. In the absence of any consistent federal enforcement policies, and foot-dragging by the Department of Health, Education, and Welfare, 1975 witnessed only a few desegregation efforts of any magnitude. Court suits appeared to be a major instrument in school desegregation of Northern cities, as they had been in Detroit, Boston, Louisville, Washington, Denver, Indianapolis, Wilmington, and Springfield, Massachusetts, to name but a few. Boston, among the listed cities, was a symbol of white resistance, racial turmoil, and violent opposition. Parents demonstrated in the streets, buses had been stoned, and blacks had been beaten when they ventured into South Boston. Because all evidence pointed to a similar happening in the fall of 1975 school opening, Boston city officials mobilized riot-trained federal marshals, state and local police, and the National Guard to enforce phase two of the school desegregation plan. Under phase two, it was expected to bus one third of the city's 84,000 pupils.

In Louisville, when the United States Supreme Court Justices Blackman and Powell rejected requests for a delay in scheduled busing for desegregation, school officials began busing 130,000 students in the city and Jefferson County school systems, which were merged in July 1975.

In contrast to Boston, Denver has demonstrated that community cooperation and leadership can provide a successful nonviolent approach to integration.

Busing Controversy. Busing is a side effect of desegregation and a band-aid approach to a very stubborn, bleeding problem, desegregation. Busing has become an emotional and political issue, especially when politicians have tried to make it so for their own specific purposes. The existing residential pattern emphasizes neighborhood schools or locates schools geographically close to home. Busing has become an emotional issue then when the white parents are faced with having their children transported to schools with a black majority.

The real issue is, however, whether busing can be an effective alternative in the desegregation process. It is ironic that busing has been officially part of American education since the early part of 1900. It has been used without much objection from parents since the 1860s for a variety of reasons. In fact, if it had not been for busing, the dual system of education would not have occurred. Statistically, 40 per cent of the school-aged population or over twenty million youngsters are bused daily; only about three per cent of this number are bused for desegregation purposes. The United States House of Representatives has voted to limit the application of busing for overcoming segregation. Interestingly enough, opposition to busing comes not only from whites but also from Blacks who have found a new sense of identity, and find it insulting to have it implied that their children learn only by sitting next to white children.

OPPONENTS' VIEW. The opponents of busing have been very vocal and generally well organized in making their views known. Their major emphasis for opposing busing can be summarized as follows:

1. Too many children ride too long a time in buses instead of being in the classroom.
2. Children and their parents are subjected to massive busing in order to achieve racial balance.
3. Racial differences result in racial disagreements and clashes in desegregated schools.
4. Neighborhood schools, besides their convenience because of their close proximity to a child's home, provide a sense of community pride and cohesiveness.

In general, opponents challenge the idea that racially balanced schools provide higher academic achievement, positive self-concept, or better race relations. They point to the incidents that have resulted in confusion, polarization of races, and disruption of schools' operation. Citing the financial plight and budget limitations of urban school systems, opponents of busing argue that the money used for busing can upgrade the school resources and, as a result, the quality of education.

PROPONENTS' VIEW. Proponents of busing, on the other hand, maintain that

1. Busing has been part of American education since 1860, and it is only the element of racial fear that has triggered the controversy.
2. The National Safety Council's report reveals that children are safer riding buses than walking to school.

3. The neighborhood concept is relatively new and has little foundation in American education. In a highly mobile society such as ours, the advocating of a neighborhood school constitutes a double standard.
4. Busing has been used to achieve racial balance only when there has been deliberate racial segregation and then only on a minimum degree basis. (Only about three per cent of the total population of children are bused for this reason.)
5. Busing will result in integration of races and upgrade the quality of education. Integration leads to a preference among both white and Negro children for integration, while segregation promotes further segregation.
6. Busing has resulted in a reduction of tardiness and absenteeism.
7. There is no evidence that busing is either psychologically, physically, emotionally, or educationally harmful to children.

The United States Supreme Court has upheld the constitutionality of busing as a means of eliminating the dual school system in *Swann* v. *Charlotte-Mecklenburg Board of Education* as late as April 1971. However, the high court has clearly ruled that this decision does not apply in de facto segregation situations.

Remedial Alternatives. Busing was described as a band-aid approach to the solution of the desegregation problem. Several other alternatives have been suggested. Although none of the alternatives has proved to be 100 per cent successful in relieving racial imbalance, each of the following approaches has contributed something toward the reduction of existing problems, and therefore merits consideration.

OPEN ENROLLMENT. The open enrollment plan permits parents to enroll their children in any school they desire as long as space is available. From the beginning, this approach has been controversial because it tends to increase segregation, rather than desegregation. Designed to provide minority youngsters with the option of attending a white school, it also equally provides an opportunity for whites who live in mixed districts to move out of their neighborhood schools. In addition, even though this plan may improve the racial balance of a receiving school, it does not affect the racial composition of the sending school and so does not provide for a real desegregation of races.

Almost every city involved in desegregation has utilized the open enrollment approach as a first step toward desegregation. But the effect in most cases has been minimal, yielding only limited success.

EDUCATION PARKS. This approach features a single, large, centrally located campus that receives students from a wide variety of neighborhoods throughout the city. Because of its inclusion of children from a large geographical area without limitation of race or color, the education park seemed to be a unique approach to desegregation. By pooling building facilities, faculties, and resources, it was expected that equal education of superior quality would become a reality for all youth from kindergarten through the first two years of college. However, for a variety of reasons, particularly financial, the plan has not gained popularity.

There are no systematic reports as to the success or the failure of education parks. Major cities, such as Pittsburgh, Syracuse, or Berkeley, which have experimented with the plan, have had degrees of success, particularly in being able to attract students from both central cities and adjacent suburban communities. The latest reports, however, point out that because of financial limitations both Pittsburgh and Syracuse have abandoned their projects.

SUPPLEMENTARY AND MAGNET SCHOOLS. This plan proposed attendance by children at their neighborhood schools for part of the day, followed by attendance at a supplementary school in which various races meet for the other part of the day. A number of cities with large black populations have been offering special programs in certain schools referred to as *magnet schools*. The purpose has been to attract both white and black students from a wide geographical area and to achieve partial desegregation.

Boston, Cleveland, Philadelphia, and Los Angeles are among cities experimenting with the magnet school idea. This plan has had minimal effect, since it attracts only a limited number of students of various racial backgrounds.

PRINCETON PLAN. Sometimes referred to as Pairing Schools Plan, the *Princeton Plan* offers a building in a community where all students of a certain grade level are combined in one school to provide for racial balance. For example, in a community where there is an all-white and an all-black school, one of the two schools would enroll all the students who are in grades one, two, and three, while the other school would house all students in grades four, five, and six. Children from both black and white neighborhoods would attend the designated school according to grade level. In some districts that have a single junior high school, neighborhood units have continued to enroll students as usual up to grade five. One building has been designated to receive all grade six students from the entire community, thereby insuring a racial mix one year earlier than the first year of junior high school.

The success of the Princeton plan in the desegregation process has been limited to smaller communities such as Princeton, New Jersey; Coatesville, Pennsylvania, and Greensburgh, New York.

METROPOLITAN APPROACH. Originally suggested by Robert Havighurst for reorganization of Chicago schools, the *Metropolitan Approach* was designed to integrate big city and suburban schools into one metropolitan system. The merged district resulting would function as a unit for taxation as well as for desegregation efforts. So far, community pressure and court cases have prevented any widespread implementation of this idea. However, this alternative has been considered by many to be the real answer to the racial balance problem.

Cases involving the merger of suburban and urban school districts are before the courts across the country. This alternative is suggested because it is impractical to expect a city to desegregate when its racial composition is one-sided, unless it can draw on the suburbs in its proximity.

The metropolitan approach appears to be the most promising of all alternatives so far practiced or suggested for desegregation of an education system. Metropolitanism in practice may also prevent further flight of whites to suburbia to escape racial integration. The real challenge to metropolitanism came in the Detroit case in which the United States Supreme Court in a 5 to 4 ruling threw out a cross district integration for the city and 52 suburban districts. However, the high court left the door partially open by ruling that multidistrict integration plans may be imposed when there is evidence that districts involved have deliberately failed to operate an integrated school system. As a result, federal courts in some cases have declared a merger of the city schools and outlying districts. A federal court judge ordered that the Indianapolis public school corporation transfer

6,500 black pupils to eight outlying schools in the fall of the 1975 school year, and prepare a plan for elimination of all schools with 80 per cent or more black enrollment. In Louisville, after four years of suits and countersuits over school desegregation, the United States District Court judge, under order from an appeal court, ordered the merger of Louisville and Jefferson County and busing of 22,600 students in a joint city and county school involvement.

Without cross-district busing and with present housing patterns, many large urban areas will remain black.

STATUS OF ALTERNATIVES. Although each alternative has its own merits and liabilities, one point should be emphasized: all of the five alternatives cited provide for a change in the organizational structure of a school in order to bring various ethnic and racial groups together. However, none provides for a change in policies, practices, and intellectual structure which relate to total education, such as pupil placement, school attendance, disciplinary practices, and, especially, curriculum and extracurricular matters. A true desegregation alternative would need to consider both the organizational change as well as policy and practice changes facilitating the shift in population. The real solution to eventual racial balance cannot be achieved without determination, commitment, sacrifice, and a willingness to change on the part of the total population, particularly the dominant majority. The change should embrace change in behavior, attitude, and opinion in relation to one another, a generating of psychological togetherness, and recognition of minority rights in the decision making process.

Urban School System

Struggle for Decision-making Role. Aware of the existing inequalities in education, parents, lay residents, and students in the big city schools are exerting pressure for community participation and a voice in decision making in crucial matters related to school policies and practices. The desire of the minority population to share in leadership on issues related to education, such as curriculum, budget, personnel selection, and related matters, has become a political issue of our time. Community control has been an effective means by which the alienated parents of minority children can make their voices heard. Blacks, Chicanos, and Puerto Ricans have been very vocal in demanding power in control of their schools. The significant Ocean Hill-Brownsville controversy in New York City is a case in point. This cause célèbre has been analyzed, discussed, and written about extensively. The basic issues appear to have been the control of the school and the exertion of power in crucial decisions affecting the children of the community. Educators have believed for some time that there is a significant relationship between community participation in decisions regarding school policies and practices and genuine quality education in a multiethnic, multiracial society. In the large urban areas, school affairs, budgets, policies, officials, and administrators over the years had become far removed from the public, in general. Unlike the situation in neighboring smaller communities where the school board is an elected body and where the policies, budgets, and administrators are components of everyday affairs, large city school-related happenings suffer the curse of bureaucratic giantism and, almost per force, become remote to all except the active few. The citizens of Ocean Hill-Brownsville, a section of Brooklyn, in their dispute were only demanding the right exercised by citizens of other American communities to control their own destiny.

In response to this demand, Mayor John Lindsay appointed a commission on decentralization, headed by McGeorge Bundy, president of the Ford Foundation. The Commission report, generally known as the Bundy Report, among a number of suggestions, recommended the reorganization of New York City schools into thirty-six autonomous community schools with a governing board of education elected in each district. Based on the Bundy report and with funding from the Ford Foundation, the Board of Education created demonstration sites, the Two Bridges district and the Ocean Hill-Brownsville district. The governing board of Ocean Hill-Brownsville sought a greater degree of control and power and, with the support of the militants in the community, they dismissed thirteen teachers and six administrators. The governing board refused to submit the issue for arbitration and accused those dismissed of sabotaging the demonstration site. The dispute continued with charges and countercharges. The Teachers Union (U.F.T.), considering the dismissal of teachers as a threat, voted to strike and demanded the dismissal of the Ocean Hill-Brownsville Board and Rhody McCoy, its administrator. After compromises and promises, the local board agreed to accept the rights of teachers who were dismissed and who wished to return to their job. The strike ended with the union in return dropping its demands for the dismissal of the Ocean Hill-Brownsville board and Rhody McCoy. But the situation remained tense and was followed by another teacher strike and violence. The controversy seriously affected the strength of U.F.T. and its community relations even though the union repeatedly supported decentralization.

New Teachers in the Desegregated School System. With the emphasis upon desegregation in urban systems across the nation, it appears that there is need for a new kind of teacher: those who have special sensitivity and understanding of various ethnic and racial groups. The new teacher must have the competency and commitment to face the new challenge of teaching in schools with a concentration of nonwhite children. There are ample evidences that the congruity or incongruity of a teacher's attitude and behavior with that of his pupils makes a difference between the success or failure of youngsters involved. Experiences discussed in *Death at an Early Age* by Jonathan Kozol or Nat Hentoff's *Our Children Are Dying* point to the results of teacher insensitivity and prejudices displayed toward minority children of various racial backgrounds. In general, since many teachers come from the middle class, their value system and frame of reference reflect their social class, and therefore, fail to encompass knowledge and understanding of other racial, ethnic, and socioeconomic groups. For this reason, the teachers in the urban school systems, particularly those teaching in the core central city, have been under attack, not only for their middle-class backgrounds, but for their lack of insight into the norms and educational needs of minority youngsters, whose behavior and practices have been shaped by other cultures and other social classes. These accusations have led to the cry of "unqualified," "inexperienced," and "unresponsive" concerning teachers assigned to the core city schools. Although it is dangerous to generalize and to assume that all or even a majority of teachers in the big city schools are unqualified or unresponsive, there is evidence pointing to the fact that a substantial number of teachers consciously or unconsciously demonstrate negative attitudes in their relationships with children of minorities, because of a lack of understanding of the life styles of the children. Parents of minority youngsters have rightly pointed to the large faculty turnover and to the expressed desire on the part of many teachers in city schools to transfer to a "better neighborhood." They have been distressed by the inability of some teachers to function in the classroom containing their children and the apparent inability to understand or accept the minority culture.

Prospective teachers must recognize clearly that although a teacher's understanding, empathy, and sensitivity are necessary in any teaching situation, they are essential qualities in central city schools where there is a concentration of various racial and ethnic minorities. The sensitivity process, if it is to be effective, should bring teachers into contact at a personal level with the varying cultures, value systems, and life styles. It should spotlight the fact that the local school system's philosophy, methodology, approach, values, and meaning may be farfetched and remote for the target population. The sensitivity process may also reveal that more effort in updating, more self control in implementing, and more divergent adaptation of the usual curriculum is required if schooling is to yield its promise.

Classroom Climate. The most noticeable teacher failure in the core city schools has been the inability to control pupils' behavior in the classroom. Those who accuse teachers of being "ineffective" and "unqualified" have successfully cited the teacher's inability in matters of establishing discipline and control to substantiate their accusation. Many urban teachers have been deficient in establishing a relaxed classroom climate and standards for behavior which would facilitate the teaching-learning process.

Factors influencing the climate of any classroom are many and varied. The most influential factor is a teacher's understanding of the youngsters' cognitive life style, degree of interest, motivation, and behavior. Behaviors exhibited by children of various racial and ethnic backgrounds can be interpreted differently. Certain behavior may be normal in a particular cultural setting and abnormal in others. A teacher's individual personality, his capacity for interpersonal relationships, his enthusiasm, and effort to establish with his students a feeling of mutual respect are also essential contributing factors in the production of cohesiveness between teacher and pupils. In his relationship with youngsters, a teacher should be firm, fair, friendly, consistent, and well prepared. Firmness does not mean authoritarian and rigid. It means that the teacher takes time and expends the effort to establish appropriate levels of expectation. Fairness implies that a teacher plays no favoritism and is prudent in his or her judgmental decisions. Friendliness is not to be interpreted as descending to the level of children. It is made up of tolerance and sincerity and should produce a relaxed climate for interaction and communication with students. Consistency is important in setting the stage so the youngsters know the level of a teacher's expectations.

A teacher's understanding of students' backgrounds and cognitive norms implies the planning of relevant activities to meet the needs of a specific group. Providing relevant and concrete materials related to ethnic minority culture and experience is an important element in any classroom. Teachers who are aware of their children's norms utilize various techniques such as brainstorming, feeling level discussion, and expression of ideas and opinions to motivate classroom learning. Providing room for expression of views, opinions, and concerns, and giving students responsibility in the classroom are examples of ways to elicit communication and enhance the climate for the teaching-learning process. Much classroom chaos and many problems result from lack of planning or of faulty planning and lack of organization and imagination on the part of the teacher. Teachers who do care make it known to their students by their behavior, by establishing an atmosphere of success, and by exhibiting a conviction about the ability of each student to learn. When the teacher has a belief in his own ability to teach, in the importance of the subject he is teaching, and when he brings about a climate that encourages effort, his progress toward his instructional goals will suffer fewer setbacks and disruptions than when he lacks convictions and neglects to build a supportive classroom climate.

A Final Comment. Efforts to eliminate segregation will continue. In this struggle, the moral consciousness of majority Americans is at stake. As the efforts for desegregation slowly progress, black frustration on one side and white resentment on the other side are also growing. Racial tensions and events such as those at Little Rock, Pontiac, and Boston are each a challenge to the fabric of American society. More than two decades have passed since *Brown* v. *Topeka Board of Education,* but the struggle to eliminate dual school systems is still in its infancy. The issue is no longer a Southern issue, but national in scope. Northern cities are plagued by court cases challenging the de facto dual system of education. Racism as well as violent opposition to busing for desegregation has resulted in resentments, hatred, and violence. Busing is an emotional national issue and whether it is the only way to achieve desegregation remains an open question. But the general consensus is that schools must provide equal education for all children regardless of their race or ethnic background. Accepting racial and ethnic diversity must remain a high goal in a multicultural, multiracial society. Tolerance for ethnic and racial differences is an educational function with interaction and interrelation of members of various groups essential. Prerequisite to true integration is desegregation of schools as well as of the total community. American society with its pluralistic population has no alternative. The road is rocky, and alternatives limited, but there is only one way to move ahead.

SUGGESTED READING

Cronin, Joseph M. *The Control of Urban Schools.* New York: The Free Press, 1973.

Cuban, Larry. *To Make a Difference: Teaching In the Inner-City.* New York: The Free Press, 1970.

Fantini, Mario D., and Gerald Weinstein. *The Disadvantaged: Challenge to Education.* New York: Harper & Row, Publishers, 1968.

Glasser, William. *Schools Without Failure.* New York: Harper & Row, Publishers, 1969.

Glazer, N., and Daniel P. Moynihan. *Beyond the Melting Pot.* Cambridge, Mass.: Harvard University Press, 1963.

Green, Robert L. "Community Control and Desegregation." *School Review,* **81** (May 1973), 347–356.

Hogan, John C. "School Desegregation—North, South, East, West: Trends in Court Decisions, 1849–1973." *Phi Delta Kappan,* **55** (Sept. 1973), 58–63.

Hogg, Thomas C., and Marlin McComb. "Cultural Pluralism: Its Implications for Education." *Educational Leadership,* **27** (Dec. 1969), 235–238.

Liebow, Elliot. *Tally's Corner*. Boston: Little, Brown and Company, 1967.

Marcus, Sheldon, and Phillip D. Vairo. *Urban Education: Crisis or Opportunity?* Metuchen, N.J.: The Scarecrow Press, 1972.

Nyquist, Ewald B. "Busing? The Real Issue Is Racial Integration . . ." *Educational Leadership*, **30** (Jan. 1973), 302–304.

Taylor, William L. "The Legal Battle for Metropolitanism." *School Review,* **81** (May 1973), 331–345.

White, Louise R. "Effective Teachers for Inner-City Schools. *The Journal of Negro Education*, **42** (Summer, 1973), 308–314.

White, William F. *Tactics for Teaching the Disadvantaged*. New York: McGraw-Hill Book Company, 1971.

POST TEST

Circle the correct answer for each question.

1. The most profound and noticeable change in American urban centers is
   a. Increase in freeways in the last decade.
   b. Decrease in parks and recreational facilities.
   c. A shift in the racial make-up of the population.
   d. A shift of government and financial institutions to the suburbs.

2. An example of a black city or city with 50 per cent or more black population is
   a. Denver, Colorado.
   b. Atlanta, Georgia.
   c. San Francisco, California.
   d. Miami, Florida.

3. The most persistent problem facing a big city school system is
   a. Election of minorities to the school board.
   b. Frequent striking teachers.
   c. Insufficient energy to operate the schools.
   d. Desegregation of staff and students.

4. The big city school systems have been under attack by minorities for
   a. Lack of systematic effort toward genuine integration.
   b. Not establishing educational parks.
   c. Busing substantial numbers of children.
   d. Using behavioral modification in disciplinary cases.

5. The most influential factor in separation of races has been
   a. Discriminatory practices of the housing industry.
   b. Financial inability of minorities to purchase suburban houses.
   c. Desire of minorities to live together.
   d. Insufficient government housing projects for minorities.

6. The nonrelevant factor in de facto segregated urban school is
   a. Gerrymandering of school attendance zones.
   b. Building new schools in segregated areas.
   c. Manipulating grade levels.
   d. Emphasizing the open enrollment plan.

7. Government housing policies and practices traditionally tended toward
   a. Establishment of homogeneous communities.
   b. Establishment of heterogeneous communities.
   c. Establishment of cosmopolitan communities.
   d. None of these.

8. In the *Brown* case, the United States Supreme Court mandate was that the Topeka Board of Education violated
   a. The equal protection clause.
   b. Affirmative action clause.
   c. Racial imbalance clause.
   d. None of these.

9. Busing children for racial balance, opponents say, has an adverse effect because
   a. It is safer to walk than to ride.
   b. Busing increases tardiness and absenteeism.
   c. Busing eliminates community pride and cohesiveness.
   d. Busing is wrong regardless of the reason.

10. A true pluralistic society should promote
   a. A melting pot concept of culture.
   b. A many model concept of culture.
   c. A monolithic concept of culture.
   d. A majority race concept of culture.

11. Segregation of races has an adverse effect because it
   a. Builds a false sense of superiority among minority population.
   b. Fosters alienation of segregated population.
   c. Fosters alienation of majority population.
   d. Encourages assimilation of various racial populations.

12. The alternative desegregation technique that provides pupils with special academic programs in neighborhood schools is known as
   a. Open enrollment plan.
   b. Metropolitan plan.
   c. Magnet school plan.
   d. Princeton plan.

13. The metropolitan approach to desegregation provides for
   a. Redrawing neighborhood lines to draw attendance to a certain school.
   b. Drawing attendance from the entire city.
   c. Merging suburban and urban school districts.
   d. Assigning pupils to a neighborhood magnet and supplementary school.

14. The Bundy Report recommended reorganization of
   a. Pittsburgh high schools into a cluster of new schools large enough to serve the entire city.
   b. Boston schools to attract students from a wide geographical area into their magnet schools.
   c. Atlanta schools with extensive compensatory education for both white and black children.
   d. New York schools into a number of autonomous community schools.

15. Central city teachers are accused of
   a. Deviating from conventional classroom approaches.
   b. Unresponsiveness to the needs of minority children.
   c. Compromising their middle-class values too often.
   d. None of these.

16. The most frequent contributing factor to a teacher's classroom problems is
   a. Lack of understanding of children's cognitive life style.
   b. Lack of knowledge of their subject area.
   c. Age differences of students and teacher.
   d. Student desire to keep their distance.

17. An effective approach in sensitizing teachers to a minority's life style is
   a. Requiring additional sociology courses on the campus.
   b. Requiring additional psychology courses on the campus.
   c. Increasing the student teaching duration.
   d. Involving teachers in personal contact with various ethnic groups and their cultures.

18. Effective classroom control is generally attributed to a teacher's ability to
   a. Demand obedience and quiet in the classroom.
   b. Ignore the problems and let the youngsters do what they desire.
   c. Show mutual respect and develop positive interpersonal relationships.
   d. Keep youngsters constantly involved with busy work.

19. The first test of the metropolitan approach came in the United States Supreme Court ruling involving the city of
   a. Louisville, Kentucky.
   b. Richmond, Virginia.
   c. Detroit, Michigan.
   d. Indianapolis, Indiana.

20. By the fall of 1972, the two cities utilizing a cross-boundary approach were
   a. Boston and Pontiac.
   b. San Francisco and Pasedena.
   c. Union Township and Atlanta.
   d. Indianapolis and Louisville.

Crucial Educational Issues

Leo Auerbach

Jersey City State College

module 7

Traditionalism vs Modernism / Censorship / Race and Ethnic Relations / Financing the Schools / Compulsory Attendance / Community School / Impact of Leisure / Role of Athletics

RATIONALE

The major purpose of Modules 7 and 8 is to help you acquire skill in grappling with controversial issues, so that you can identify the problems and the facts surrounding them, recognize their importance for pupils, teachers, and the community, and work out your own relationship to the issues. No one can hope to become an expert on all of them, but we can all develop a frame of reference for analyzing the issues and a set of criteria for judging various efforts to resolve the problems. You will find some issues more familiar than others, but all are examples of present-day challenges to education with a special bearing on us as teachers.

John and Mary Q. Public look at education in the news. They find boycotts, strikes, and demonstrations; court cases, budget problems, and reading scores; vandalism, personal violence, and school attendance figures; busing, censorship, and taxes; drugs, alcohol, and sex. Whenever events are dramatic, we expect the media to focus on them. If much of the news is gloomy and unsettling, the media claim that they do not create it, but merely report it. Fortunately, school sports events, scholastic awards, and dramatic or musical performances usually offer a brighter side of the picture. Clearly, though, one reason for the visibility of education is that the schools are a significant social institution. As such they are affected by the general conditions of society—the state of the economy, political events, the cultural scene, science and technology, population changes, ethnic awareness and group movements—in short, every facet of our civilization. Especially are the schools confronted with the unsolved problems each new generation inherits, and these form part of the issues pressing for attention. The way education reacts to its problems, whether as rapid adaptation to change or as institutional inertia, is a vital factor in their solution.

Education is expected to help in the socialization of the young, mainly through developing skills and attitudes and guiding ideas and behavior. At other times and places, the task of reflecting and transmitting the values and patterns of society to children and adolescents may have been simple, direct, and unchallenged. In these days of rapid and profound change, however, values are not self-evident, socially pervasive, or static. Various groups in the community, organized or merely united in sentiment and orientation, see their needs and interests differently. Confrontation and conflict in opinions, attitudes, and beliefs lead to struggle for power, for input and influence in decision making, in the schools as in all social institutions.

Teaching today is not the placid backwater of Ichabod Crane's milieu. Internally there are pressures and movements for change, not merely because innovation is fashionable, but because it may be urgent. As previous modules have indicated, such changes as team teaching, differentiated staffing, flexible scheduling, and curriculum revisions are proposed and introduced to improve education. Methods and techniques as well as materials and resources are being constantly evaluated and revised in response to new demands. All teachers recognize the need to participate in these professional activities.

However, in turning to the more external issues, a beginning teacher might feel totally unwilling to become involved. She might prefer to stay out of the politics of the community. Concentrating on her work, her students, lesson preparation, marking papers and tests, and taking graduate courses seem more than enough to keep her busy without bothering about problems such as student power, busing, censorship, or unions. She may feel uninformed about many situations, disturbed by the strong emotions of individuals and groups in confrontation, and ready to leave the decisions to the school board, the state legislature, and the courts. She has heard the familiar advice: "Don't stick your neck out. Don't be militant. You're not going to change anything." Yet, keeping a job and earning the respect of students, parents, or colleagues may involve expressing sympathy or support for specific actions.

We can appreciate the young teacher's dilemma and understand her reactions. Recent history, however, has demonstrated that events and issues may be thrust upon us, regardless of the nature of the community. We can try to ignore to avoid the problems, but they remain. For us as teachers and citizens, the alternatives seem to be not between having an opinion or dodging a conclusion, but between being well-informed and being poorly informed.

This responsibility entails (1) knowing the specific issue; (2) understanding some of its background and circumstances which gave rise to the problem; (3) identifying the groups interested in the issue; (4) identifying the arguments they advance in support of their position; (5) identifying their relative power and effectiveness; (6) identifying the methods they rely on to advance their cause, and (7) identifying their successes and setbacks.

We can then try to predict the possible consequences of actions already under way or of proposals being urged for adoption. This is a tall order. Yet we have a guide. We can agree that all conflict should be resolved in the best interests of the students, the community, and the total society. Only well-informed participants can make democratic and constructive decisions prevail in education. Teachers who can analyze and clarify problems and issues and act together on the best available judgment can make a calm, reasonable, effective, and worthwhile contribution. Recognizing the profound implications and urgency of various situations, they can offer well-formulated opinions and desirable alternatives. Rather than following the easy way, choosing the position which is most popular at the moment, it is possible to rely on different criteria, such as these: What choice of action would be most conducive to pupil growth, intellectual, physical, social, emotional, and moral? What will enrich the pupils' educational experience, involving them in greater personal and social responsibilities, widening their interests and perspective, and encouraging desirable attitudes?

Which proposal is the most democratic and which the least democratic? Which might better expand the possibilities of national growth and progress? If education intends to cultivate the potential of all our people, regardless of sex, race, color, religion, national origin, or socioeconomic status, how would different proposals contribute to this goal, militate against it, or completely ignore it? Specifically, how do various proposals relate to the principle of equal educational opportunity?

Using such a framework of questions, we can evaluate the community's readiness to act to improve education. Since society expects a return from the schools in the form of student behavior and attitudes, of citizenship, of preparation for economic productivity and social living, we teachers work to effect these by supporting the best solutions to the internal and external problems of the schools. These two modules touch on some highlights of representative controversial issues in contemporary education.

In order to keep the discussion manageable, facts about groups and events are generally omitted. Attention is centered on the importance of each issue, the proposals for change, and the arguments advanced by the main contenders. It is hoped that you will acquire an approach that includes an impartial analysis of the problems, a seeking out and weighing of evidence and opinions, and finally arrive at independent decisions and judgments. Above all, you can keep in sight what is sometimes lost in the arguments—namely, the power to evaluate issues and proposals by how they contribute to helping all children to function in a democratic society.

SPECIFIC OBJECTIVES

After working through this module, you should be able to perform in the following five ways regarding each of the issues included in this module:

1. State the main problems regarding each issue.
2. State, in an objective and neutral manner, at least two different positions on each issue.
3. Present at least three arguments in support of each viewpoint.
4. Indicate the proposals you find most worthy of support and your reasons for approving them.
5. Offer a prediction as to the possible consequences of
   a. selecting one or another proposal, and
   b. doing nothing about the issue.

MODULE TEXT

Traditionalism versus Modernism

Critics of the schools have been so active in the past decade that you can almost hear the complaints: "The schools are not turning out students who are prepared to take their place in the life of our country. They don't read well, write well, or speak well. They don't have a serious attitude toward work; they expect everything to be provided for them. They are too dependent; they're too soft. And they don't respect the rights of others. They are rude and abrasive. Their appearance! They try to look as sloppy as they can. They jump from one crazy fashion to another. Look at their tastes in clothes, hair styles, music, room decorations. And when they're criticized, their reply is: 'We're young. We have new ideas. We have a right to be different.' To them being different can mean drugs, premarital sex, obscene language, fighting, stealing—anything goes."

"Why have the schools failed us? They must have been encouraging all this, or at least they have done very little about standards. When are the schools going to do their proper job of training the young in basic skills, decent behavior, good manners, and respect for others, in accepting responsibilities like work and not just talking about their rights? What young people need is more discipline, living by rules, measuring up to tests, caring about marks and grades. Schools must return to their old ways. That's what we're paying for, and the schools must be held accountable for all this."

On the other hand, a completely different indictment of education runs as follows: "Most schools are grim, joyless places, like prisons. Students are not respected as human beings. Their potentials are not being developed because they are not encouraged to express themselves. Young people are not stimulated or encouraged to be original, creative, imaginative, curious, and independent. As a result, they are bored and uninvolved, restless, 'turned off.' Students are confronted with content that is unrelated to life, either to their present experiences or to the ever-changing demands of a rapidly moving world. They turn away from school just because it has so little to offer them. When are the schools going to challenge students to think for themselves, to become excited and enthusiastic about learning new material, discovering new facts, trying out their skills, testing their mastery of processes? Why aren't pupils given responsibility in sharing the planning of their own activity? How can school experiences be enriched and made more realistic? What use can be made of the pupils' ideas, imagination, artistic talents? Only when deep changes in this direction occur will our school children be constructively occupied, happy, and self-disciplined. This is also the way to developing their good judgment and tastes. This is the solution to the crisis in the classroom."

Suppose we did not accept either view. We could point out that many students are serious and hard-working, enjoy learning, cooperate readily, behave well, express themselves creatively, prepare for higher education or become more immediately productive, and are law-abiding and considerate of others. We could claim that the schools by and large are doing the job society requires of them. Yet we must admit that many important problems arise in the relationships between the schools and society. The perspective from which we examine various problems and proposals is affected by our attitude toward contending viewpoints. Unfortunately, there is no single satisfactory way of labeling the major positions. The contrast may be made between traditional and modern, formal and informal, content-centered and student-centered, repetitive and creative, basic and experimental, or conventional and developmental, but no dichotomy fully and fairly captures the difference. Therefore, when the terms *traditionalist* and *modernist* are used, the reader should recognize the limitations of the labels and keep in mind the more complete picture.

The traditionalist maintains that one way to improve education is to concentrate on basic skills. Literacy and command of computation (mastery of the three R's) are essential for both academic achievement and later life, since these skills are used to acquire the body of knowledge and set of values which constitute our cultural heritage, painstakingly accumulated over the centuries. He maintains that time-honored and time-tested subject matter and procedures, when properly transmitted to the young, produce desirable and successful pupil performance, readily observable and measurable. Whatever the subject matter, the material should be logically organized in orderly, meaningful sequence and presented in familiar, easily reproducible ways so that the pupils can be constructively occupied. Nor is everything old-fashioned, since innovations such as programmed learning or audio-visual presentations can be readily accommodated to methods using workbooks, drill materials, and textbook assignments.

In this approach, all pupils are regarded as needing the same foundation, being helped to acquire a similar background to the level of their capacity. They should be grouped by ability and encouraged to choose careers for which the adult school personnel believes them to be best fitted. Proper guidance involves helping students adjust to their own capacities rather than courting unrealizable expectations. With this kind of education, students are able to read, write, and perform other necessary activities, are well socialized and productive citizens, and are adequately prepared for the adult world. They score well on tests, are interested in grades, and have a strong sense of accomplishment. In sum, the traditional approach claims to be fundamental, practical, realistic, visible, and proven, disciplining yet democratic.

Some critics of this viewpoint have maintained that reading and writing are more adequately acquired when students work on materials meaningful to them. Boredom or hostility defeat the acquisition of skills. They say that rather than using the adult culture, the young should be working with personal experiences and content related more immediately to their own lives. Since learning depends on interest and since education nowadays has strong competition from television for student time and attention, more student-oriented materials are essential. Of course, their own culture is to be treated as the starting point, rather than the end result of education. Besides, learning proceeds psychologically rather than logically, so that all content must be organized differently. In addition, critics say that mass education built on the traditional model emphasizes memorization at the expense of thinking, requires conformity without questioning, adjustment and adaptation rather than criticism and flexibility. They charge that traditional education ignores individual learning styles by insisting on uniform patterns. It narrowly measures student growth and development by test scores and grades, rather than by qualitative changes which, they say, are just as real and usually more significant. Such training as it provides is totally inadequate for a modern, fast-moving world in which initiative and originality are vital: the facts that are so laboriously learned are either forgotten or no longer valid in a short time. Finally by its use of ability grouping, tracking, or streaming, traditional education predetermines, in an undemocratic or unscientific way, the future of all pupils. The criticism can be briefly summarized as stating that traditional education does not fully develop student abilities, it ignores their interests, and it fails to meet their needs.

The modernist maintains that pupils learn best when they are interested. They will acquire all necessary skills in the process of meeting situations that stimulate curiosity and problem solving, encourage exploration and discovery, and tap creativity and self-expression. He sees the school purposes of student growth and development as based on independence and self-discipline. He urges that enthusiasm for and pleasure in learning should replace anxiety and fear. To him, the most immediate and basic material is student experience, with the teacher guiding toward and facilitating ever-widening types of experience, a constant enlargement of interests, and cultivation of student potential. In this approach, conventional subject matter designations are not as important as the feeling on the learner's part that content is worth knowing. This is the way to making it his possession. If such exploration leads naturally to aspects of the cultural heritage, this is fine. If it does not lead that way, but instead encompasses other meaningful areas of learning, it is still the most positive approach. What students are developmentally capable of is more important than adult-selected and adult-organized content. Thus, presentation and acquisition of content becomes more informal and individualized.

Working to achieve willing cooperation and mutual respect, the modernist sets democratic participation as the goal and uses pupil-teacher and pupil planning, the sharing of decision making, as the means for achieving it. Rather than competing for higher test scores and grades than one's peers, the pupil directs his competitiveness toward excelling his own previous performance. In addition, modernist education does not settle for training, which may be mechanical and repetitive, but prepares pupils for novelty and change, since it rewards creativity and emphasizes self-confidence. In brief, this approach claims to make learning a happy experience by building on pupil interest, satisfying important pupil needs, and cultivating pupil abilities.

Critics of this position have maintained that the benefits asserted in support of modernist education cannot be measured objectively. For instance, self-reliance or cooperativeness may or may not be evident to all observers. Meanwhile, the students do not really acquire basic skills in the rather indirect, unstructured way on which this kind of education relies. Without sequence and logical organization, learning becomes too vague and accidental. Also, by neglecting or minimizing test scores and grades, this approach does not adequately prepare students for competition, either for jobs or for admission to higher education. When frustration and feelings of insecurity set in, the students suffer. With pupils too young, immature, and inexperienced to make important decisions about what to learn, teacher control must take over. Critics also charge that under mass education, the experimental approach is impractical, unrealistic, or unfair. They say that many individuals can be lost, not helped, allowed to "mark time," while teacher attention is monopolized by more assertive or more aggressive students. When brighter students are attended to, slower ones suffer from inability to keep up, and when slower ones are attended to, brighter ones are bored or left to their own devices. Furthermore, the critics say that the excessive permissiveness of this approach is a fundamental cause of the lack of discipline prevalent among today's young people. All in all, the charge is that modernist education fails the pupils by drastically reducing adult planning and responsibility.

Both traditionalists and modernists believe they have answers to the criticisms leveled against them. Before deciding on the values and drawbacks of the two viewpoints so briefly sketched, consider your own educational experiences. Try to remember activities that gave you a sense of accomplishment, a feeling that you were learning how to do something, or learning about something meaningful or interesting. Recall the circumstances, the teacher's behavior, attitudes, and personality, the subject matter and activities, the people you worked with, and the atmosphere all these factors generated. Which aspects do you consider most important? Which experiences were most positive and which would you have preferred changed? While you might prefer to select the advantages of the various approaches while eliminating its disadvantages, you should realize that different groups in a community, as well as many educators, regard the approaches as mutually exclusive. They believe a clear and decisive choice must be made.

Essentially, agreement on what the schools should be doing and how they should be doing it is difficult to reach because of varying responses to problems. Suppose it is agreed that schools should help students think and live democratically. The question becomes how they should go about achieving it, by providing direct experience or by making it a subject to study. Should schools concentrate on training for measurable skills, processes, and content, and treat values and attitude formation as incidental? Is it possible to achieve a balance between discipline and self-discipline? Should all students be expected to develop the same skills, with some allowance for individual differences in talents or interests? What does equal educational opportunity really mean, and is it realizable in a practical way with a heterogeneous population? Can the materials of learning be the same for all learning styles, backgrounds, preferences, and needs? Finally, what are the responsibilities of the schools, of the adults who run them, of the adults who support them, and of the students who attend them? Different philosophies, such as the traditionalist vs. the modernist, lead to different perspectives and priorities.

Censorship

A different dichotomy between traditionalists and modernists appears on the issue of censorship versus professional freedom in the selection and assignment of books and materials. These differences center on the role of the school as perpetuators of tradition versus their role as critics of social ills. The conflict emerges between a section of the community and members of the teaching staff, with community forces sticking to the "tried and true," while educators introduce the experimental or new. Such disagreement may surface when controversial social, moral, or political questions are being debated, such as political issues during the 1950s or problems of race relations and civil rights, or sexual behavior and taboo language in the 1960s and 1970s. Frequently, the disputes involve the availability of library materials and the teaching of English and social studies. The conflict may become wide enough to involve entire communities and larger organizations, especially when firings and resignations occur. Occasionally, there are burnings as well as bannings of books and, more rarely, the kind of violence that occurred in Kanawha County, West Virginia. Most often, teachers and entire school systems accommodate themselves to the most conservative sectors of the community. Yet, situations when opposition appears always raise the question of professional competence and judgment versus lay supervision and community concern.

Proponents of community power point out that their children are the ones receiving the education and parents retain the right to supervise and approve the content of their learning. They regard teachers as public servants whose authority is limited to performing carefully circumscribed tasks. Some communities extend their intervention by applying strict standards of personal conduct to teacher behavior outside of school. They expect teachers to serve as models worthy of imitation by the young. At least equally important in this view is that the schools must fulfill the job of maintaining and preserving society. Presenting critical questions to immature pupils is dangerous and to be avoided in school. Essentially, public scrutiny of teacher performance and public exercise of pressure and power are claimed as inherent rights of parents, school boards, religious leaders, and political officeholders.

In opposition to these claims, educators have asserted that their selection of books, materials, curriculum, and subjects for student discussion is a matter of professional expertise. They say that they are hired because of their special training, knowledge, and experience to provide the best education for the children. Teachers are qualified to estimate pupil needs, for example, whether it is useful to discuss a contemporary adolescent novel that includes pregnancy or to deal with racial or ethnic prejudice affecting the locality or any other area. Furthermore, maintaining pupil interest by using current, topical materials is standard educational practice. In fact, teachers may point out that preparation for life requires consideration of real problems. Also, in order for the schools to transmit the cultural heritage, it is only by exercising freedom of thought and expression that this heritage can be demonstrated and kept alive. For the schools to be guardians of democracy, they must practice it and provide pupils with concrete, living experience. The danger is not in opening the doors for the children's minds but in closing them.

At stake here is a fundamental issue of control and supervision of educational materials. The contenders are those outside and those inside the teaching, learning process. Involved in the dispute is the extent of public confidence in the schools. When there is general satisfaction with the job that schools are doing, very few incidents tend to occur. However, in each specific instance, it is essential to identify the forces involved, the philosophy they espouse, and their relative power. These are more cogent than any scientific measuring of the effects of using the materials in question. What one group in one community may object to, another in a different community will completely ignore. This is one controversial area in which there are no absolute, clear-cut standards.

Race and Ethnic Relations

Walt Whitman, the great poet of American democracy, once hailed the United States as a "teeming nation of nations." Yet, more recently, the National Advisory Commission on Civil Disorders noted that "Our nation is moving toward two societies, one black, one white—separate and unequal." The Commission warned that this polarization would lead to "the destruction of basic democratic values." The schools, as we know, are expected to help make this "one nation indivisible." If this goal is accepted by all, questions arise as to what kind of unity can be achieved and how much diversity can be tolerated. Only a few aspects of this great range of problems can be dealt with at this point.

At least two major conflicting viewpoints have been advanced. One insists that all people dwelling within our borders become assimilated or acculturated to the dominant culture. Sometimes called the melting pot theory, this is said to have worked well in the past with most immigrant groups. The other theory regards the United States as a multicultural country, in which cultural pluralism is essential to genuine unity and is based on respect for diversity among our people. This is said to be vital for survival, progress, and mutual enrichment.

Consider the more numerous groups which constitute ethnic or racial minorities—Blacks, Spanish-speaking Americans (such as Mexican Americans or Chicanos, Puerto Ricans, or Cuban Americans), Native Americans (or American Indians), and Asian Americans. Under the melting pot theory, all students are expected to conform to prevailing social and educational requirements, such as adapting to white, middle-class life styles and values, using only Standard American English, and competing equally for higher education and careers. Under the cultural pluralist approach, the schools would accept and utilize cultural and linguistic variability among the learners. All sectors, majority and minority, would benefit culturally from the differences, and the schools would guarantee equal educational opportunity, compensating for past or existing discrimination and deprivation. Clearly, the choice between the two theories, whether made explicitly or implicitly, has profound consequences.

Ethnic and racial differences underlie basic issues, such as what the schools should teach, who is to teach, how teaching and learning can be made most effective, how learning is measured, how pupils are categorized and classified, and what educational and vocational aspirations are developed. Curriculum changes, for example, have been proposed to include Black studies, Hispanic studies, and the like, with some educators recommending that these are valuable for all students, not only for those of minority background. In literature and in history classes, it has been urged that contributions of all groups be studied. History texts would have to be written to deal more fully and more objectively with the relations between Native Americans and later Americans. The new awareness also has raised the question of the recruitment of teachers and administrators of minority background. A mere reference to these issues reveals how complex and far-reaching the problem is.

One deep question revolves around the dialect barriers to reading comprehension. Handling these barriers from the very beginning of reading instruction is crucial. Besides appropriate methods and attitudes, the question of reading materials has been raised, with some urging the use of stories and situations that reflect the life experiences of culturally diverse children. Because of language differences between the schools and the communities, some children from minority backgrounds have been variously labeled as uneducable, slow learners, learning-disabled, suffering from cognitive defects, incapable of logical thinking, or genetically inferior. Yet, all the while, the operative factors may have been the materials, especially so-called standardized tests, which were developed for white, middle-class children and which penalize those who are different by describing them as deficient. Some educators have recommended that the schools use a cultural filter through which teachers learn a more accurate way to observe the children.

Since language is fundamental to academic achievement, a central problem is that all children are expected to become proficient users of Standard American English. How this can best be achieved and what knowledge of language, including other varieties of English, is needed by teachers in order to assist in such mastery are at present unresolved questions. As an example of the way the issue may be met, one very large school system with a large Spanish-speaking student population has received pressure from the community to maintain students' native language and culture. The school board has proposed to have fourth-grade pupils spend 50 per cent of the school day in classes conducted in Spanish. To this proposal, the teachers' organization, recognized as collective bargaining representative, has raised strenuous objection, stating that this will unjustly prevent the integration of students into the mainstream of American life. The conflict between theories goes on in many real ways.

No one disagrees with the need to hire or train teachers who have positive attitudes toward their students, teachers who recognize student potential and build on it. But it is claimed that stereotyping of minority children has prevailed in many schools, with harmful consequences. How to eliminate such stereotyping has been posed as a major task for the educators. One suggestion has been to increase everyone's familiarity with the range of differences found within each racially or ethnically identified community. Another fact meant to influence teacher attitudes is the observation that many isolated or segregated communities have developed as a result of some form of discrimination, especially in housing or employment opportunities. Such treatment, as well as language, cultural, or social bonds, has kept communities together and conscious of their common needs. While segregated education has been a product of these social forces, many look to desegregated education to help solve the broader problems. Minorities who reject the melting pot theory, insisting on the validity of their culture and language varieties, may succeed in projecting a demand for multicultural education and in the process influence the criteria for teacher education, such as knowledge of and attitudes toward minority children. It may be significant to note that even at a time of economic stress the federal government is willing to provide funds for bilingual education.

All minorities seem agreed on the program for more education in order to achieve both survival and progress. Faith in education is strong among them. This accounts for their vigorous political activity to overcome the deficiencies of the past—inadequate schools, financial restrictions on personnel, equipment, and supplies. The cry for quality education, for equal educational opportunity, has not diminished and would seem to be shared by all democratically minded Americans. Yet there are serious disputes over what school integration is or should be, whether it is practical and feasible, and whether it can achieve the goal of equal educational opportunity.

In the famous 1954 United States Supreme Court decision, the court decided that separate education could not be equal in quality and that separation of races during formative educational years was psychologically harmful to all children. Such education violated constitutional rights. Recognizing the problems of overcoming decades of segregated schooling, the court urged "all deliberate speed" in changing the total set-up. However, evidence in later court cases revealed that little or no change was instituted voluntarily. To save new generations from inferior education, federal judges throughout the country have ordered school districts to plan for and accomplish integrated education. In the absence of geographically located schools which could easily achieve integration, the courts have mandated the busing of school children for the purpose of "racial balance." This action has sparked demonstrations, such as those in Pontiac, Denver, Canarsie, and Boston, affected the Florida primaries prior to the 1972 elections, and led to demands for federal legislation. As a limited case study of the controversial problems arising from racial and ethnic relations, this issue of court-directed busing is indicative of forces, positions, and attitudes running through the entire question.

About 95 per cent of current school busing has nothing to do with integration, but is used for geographically scattered children. In some instances, available schools are centrally located; in others, consolidated schools may provide special types of education or special services. Pupil transportation had nineteenth century origins, and by 1964 busing had become its chief means. At present nearly twenty million pupils are transported at public expense for all purposes other than integration, without any public opposition. This should help keep the busing issue in perspective.

Advocates of busing for integration, who recognize its temporary, stop-gap nature, maintain that immediate steps are necessary to achieve equal educational opportunity. Continuing segregation, while waiting for new schools to be built to end segregation, condemns generations of school children to inferior, low-quality education, as the courts have recognized. Substandard schooling perpetuates the cycle of limited job possibilities, narrow cultural horizons, and inadequate preparation for higher education. Both immediately and in the long run, society as a whole suffers from the failure to develop and utilize student potential in all sectors of the population. The school systems' defense that they cannot solve social problems and that housing patterns are the basis of segregation has been rejected by the courts. In decisions involving Richmond and Pontiac, for example, the court indicated that this was no excuse for the zoning which prevents integration. Whatever help busing can make to equalizing and improving education, proponents of busing urge its implementation. In answer to the complaint that busing is expensive and that the money would be better spent on improving schools, these advocates reply that no one objected to the cost of busing for other educational purposes. Besides, segregated education has always suffered severe inequality in past allocation of school funds. In fact, busing is cheaper than investing in equalizing educational services, requiring buildings, equipment, faculty, and other expenses. Above all, supporters of busing believe their campaign focuses attention on the problem of separate education, which is a violation of constitutional guarantees.

Critics of busing, rather than dealing with this aspect of legal or constitutional rights, have sometimes maintained that busing is an infringement on the rights of white parents and students. Unwilling to accept the transported children, some critics have directed attention to the problem of adjusting the newcomers and the receivers, both pupils and teachers. Friction, suspicion, and hostility, opponents of busing point out, do not provide a good educational atmosphere. Frequently thought of but left unsaid is the fear of crime and violence supposedly connected with the bused children, although in publicized confrontations, some critics of busing have apparently been the ones resorting to violence. Another fear has been that standards of educational achievement may decline. Sometimes this is restated in terms that competition among students is unfair to the more poorly prepared incoming students. Critics have pointed to the disruption and inconvenience busing introduces into the lives of the bused children and their parents. Insisting that the expense of busing would be better diverted to more substantive educational needs, the opponents of busing have insisted that there is no substitute for the long-range solution of new housing patterns.

Confronted with such strongly opposed viewpoints, one must reexamine his position on the entire question of integration—social, economic, and educational. Is busing too simple a solution, a patchwork bandage that leaves basic inequality untouched? How committed are we to a policy of equal educational opportunity as an essential part of democratic principles? What is the school's responsibility as a social institution for achieving better human relations, social cohesiveness, "with liberty and justice for all"?

Financing the Schools

Two prominent issues regarding money for education are voting on school budgets and improving urban education. Even prior to severe inflation and economic recession, many communities were voting down proposed school budgets. Sometimes the resulting pinch was serious enough to force the closing of schools for extended periods. Quite often, the action grew out of opposition to school board contracts which had granted increased teacher salaries. In some areas, money was not approved for school site purchasing or school construction, or for special programs or innovations in curriculum and materials. Objection to so-called frills in education occasionally meant refusing to support what some regarded as making the school into agencies of social change. Perhaps more than any other democratic activity, voting on school budgets has been a major form of community involvement in decision making.

By far the most serious crisis in school financing, however, has arisen in connection with urban education. Population shifts, bringing large groups of former rural dwellers to the cities, have placed a tremendous burden on the schools. Formerly leaders in education, urban school systems have lost out because they have been called upon to provide more services to more pupils than before, have been competing for money with other urgent problems such as housing, health care, transportation, and air pollution, and have been confronted with rising costs and changes in the tax base. Around the question of priorities, ongoing political struggles have been and are being fought in defense of education's role in society.

In the most recent period, major attention has been directed to the taxes used to pay for the schools. Although the federal government has increased its financial support for education, well over 80 per cent of the money for elementary and secondary schools still comes from state and local taxes. The most common source of revenue is the local property tax, which is then supplemented by more or less extensive state aid. Poor school districts have been taxing themselves at a higher rate than the wealthy school districts, but their efforts do not compensate for deficiencies in the tax base. In addition, state aid to schools, which might be expected to redress the imbalance, has for many years discriminated against the cities. It is small wonder that the Education Commission of the States has described the current system of financing the public schools as "chaotic and unjust." In states relying on local property taxes, the ratio of assessed valuation per pupil between the wealthiest and poorest districts ranges from 1.7 to 1 to 182.8 to 1. Other reasons for inequity include methods of property assessment and tax exemptions. As a result of these wide differences, which render any equal educational opportunities impossible, legal action in many states has been used to bring relief.

In 1971, a landmark decision of the California Supreme Court ruled that since education is a "fundamental interest," its quality should not depend on the relative wealth of school districts. Measured against the equal protection clause of the Fourteenth Amendment to the United States Constitution, existing forms of educational financing were declared unsatisfactory. Immediately thereafter, courts in Minnesota, Texas, and New Jersey decided cases along similar lines. However, in 1975, the United States Supreme Court, by a 5 to 4 vote, ruled that "where wealth is involved, the Equal Protection Clause does not require absolute equality or precisely equal advantages." The issue of school financing then remains unresolved.

State governments, wrestling with proposals for changing the tax structure affecting funds for education, have been stymied by interests that benefit from existing laws. This type of funding runs counter to majority opinion which has stressed the need for tax reform and for not relying on the local property tax. In some areas, voters have been faced with detailed, elaborate referenda on such problems: Should the property tax be replaced by more income and sales taxes? Should property taxes be distributed on a state-wide basis?

Underlying the debate is the question of commitment to equal educational opportunity versus defense of the status quo. Those favoring the existing system point out that parents work hard to provide their children a better education. Frequently, this goal has involved moving their families to communities, usually suburban, which strive for excellence in education. Through taxpayer associations, these parents defend the principle of local control of the schools, an ideal which they claim would suffer as a result of any change in methods of school financing. They believe that their willingness to tax themselves on a local basis should be emulated by others. Often, they express strong opposition to supporting the needs of the large cities. In their presentation, they may omit the issue of equal educational opportunity or may insist that equal expenditures would not ensure equal educational quality. Sometimes, the taxpayer groups express the desire that more funds should be available to all schools, regardless of district, but they usually oppose tax increases or changes in existing tax structure.

Those who believe in changing the tax structure to allocate funds for the purpose of equal educational opportunity advance a number of arguments besides the constitutional one argued in the courts. Developing the potential of all children is in everyone's interest, since the entire society suffers when inadequate or inferior education is the lot of the poor or of the racial and ethnic minorities. The process of urban decay, including deterioration of the schools, has victimized those people most powerless to overcome the problems. Perpetuating the set-up means condemning generations to low-paying, dead-end jobs, substandard, over-crowded housing, and increased possibilities of socially disruptive violence. Historically, amounts spent on better education have more than compensated for savings on social welfare or prison funds. Although all observers agree that by itself more money does not guarantee better education, advocates of equal educational opportunity argue that without more funds there can be no improvements in urban education. Recognizing the essential need for economy and efficiency in the schools, these reformers insist that the real and growing problems are just too great to be met by belt-tightening and reallocation of existing resources. More federal funds are part of the answer, they admit, but the main assistance must come from increased state aid. However this is to be accomplished, through new or different taxes or changed formulas for distribution, they say this aid is necessary to make our educational system a truly democratic one.

Compulsory Attendance

Nations pride themselves on the amount of free public education they provide to all their children. Besides the number and types of schools offered, they also point to the steady rise in the compulsory attendance age. Some have challenged the need to enforce free public education by complusion, but a look at history, involving political, economic, and moral aspects, illuminates the reasons for making parents legally responsible for their children's education. Moreover, when society provides schools, it recognizes the fact that ensuring attendance is part of making education effective.

Massachusetts by 1647 required towns to provide schools and schoolmasters, but most colonies had no compulsory education laws. Even after the American Revolution, only New England states had a public primary school system. In most places, fees were charged or free schools were maintained by charity. Education remained largely the privilege of the rich, since many parents were too poor to pay fees or too proud or indifferent to accept charity. When free public high schools were set up, accompanied by strong truancy laws, opposition arose. One historian comments, "The argument against compulsory school attendance, which time and experience gradually overcame, now sounds odd: it was then compared with compulsory church attendance, infringing on the rights of parents to the use of all their children's time."[1]

Free public schools were established only after bitter political fights, since the people of property often opposed them because of taxation and the loss of child labor. In other places, groups feared the loss of their transplanted language and culture. By 1850, to a limited extent, the principle was established "that all children be required to attend school up to a certain age, but not necessarily the free public school, since religious schools existed. These privileges as yet were only imperfectly extended to women, and even less to Negroes."[2] Although a major motive force driving for secondary and higher education in the United States prior to the Civil War was religious, another impulse was the drive for economic and cultural improvement. Part of the educational awakening noted by all visitors was the movement for adult education.

The conception of an equal, free education for all had been implicit in the political theory of the Founding Fathers, some of whom saw schooling as a selector of talent. Later democratic theory viewed the schools as great equalizers and guarantors of good government, since only an educated citizenry could participate well in the political process. Thus, for example, the Reconstruction governments in the South immediately after the Civil War for the first time established free public education for all children by 1870.[3]

Nationwide, the greatest advance in compulsory attendance laws was related to the influx of immigrants, especially into the cities. Discussing this phenomenon, one historian writes, "Partly from fear and partly from compassion, thirty-one states enacted some form of compulsory education by 1900.[4] The schools were expected to serve an Americanizing, socializing, and moral function, first of all for the young. They also served as community centers. With regard to their basic student body, the schools contributed to occupational mobility, as well as the more traditional academic or intellectual development. No matter how well or indifferently all these functions have been performed, the need for public schools and for compulsory attendance has been largely unchallenged for at least half a century.

[1] Samuel Eliot Morison, *The Oxford History of the American People* (New York: Oxford University Press, Inc., 1965), pp. 330–331.
[2] Ibid., p. 532.
[3] Ibid., p. 719.
[4] Henry J. Perkinson, *The Imperfect Panacea: American Faith in Education, 1865–1965* (New York: Random House, Inc., 1968), p. 70.

However, in recent years, critics of the public schools have attacked them from at least four different angles. Some claim that the schools have failed to provide education appropriate to the economic needs of modern society and that on-the-job training is much more valuable and interesting. These critics refer to the evidence that many graduates end up in jobs which make little use of their school training. They also point to a high drop-out rate, especially when students are expected to contribute to family support or earn a living as quickly as possible. Such students may be slow learners, academically unsuccessful, bored, or potentially disruptive—in any event, they are reluctant learners who might be more usefully and happily occupied outside of school. A few critics have claimed that only a certain amount of training in basic skills, the three R's, is sufficient for many pupils and that the schools should never have undertaken a vocational-preparation function. Some even add the opinion that the home and family should fulfill the socializing function.

Other critics have focused on what they regard as the repressive aspects of current education. They insist that the schools stifle the freedom and creativity of students who should explore the community and the world with more reliance on their own curiosity and interests. Still other critics deplore the high cost and difficulty of enforcing compulsory attendance laws. Besides stressing the savings that would ensue if the laws were changed, these critics would also make the teacher responsible for motivating student attendance. Although the groups and individuals opposed to compulsory attendance differ on almost every other facet of education, they agree on calling for an end to this historic component of American education. They admit that they favor the decline or drastic reduction of the public schools.

In response, defenders of free public education maintain that much of the criticism really deals with the content and quality of education rather than the feature of compulsory attendance. No one can disagree, they say, with the need to improve education, regardless of the time pupils are required to spend in school. But, they maintain, there is no substitute for the free public schools. The defenders believe that content, for example, is determined by function and purpose. Since schools are meant to educate and not merely train children, the necessary three R's are not enough to produce democratically reared, intellectually stimulated, fully developed young people. Limiting further education to those children whose parents may recognize its advantages is to foster an elite and is a retreat from the function of preparing good citizens. Letting children and parents choose how much education they prefer is to make child and adolescent development haphazard and accidental. Rather than psychological, sociological, cultural, and ethical improvement of the young, society would be faced with the danger of deterioration.

Even with regard to vocational education, the defenders say that the schools can do better than industry, perhaps not in terms of specific jobs or a narrow range of skills, but in helping young people prepare for a world of industrial change, in encouraging and helping students to develop more rounded skills, abilities, and interests. With today's technology, the schools can assume the task of making job preparation truly realistic and beneficial, all the while attending to the needs and many-sided growth of the students. Finally, with regard to saving money, defenders of compulsory attendance challenge the assumption that young people not compelled to attend school will be engaged in socially constructive activity. Experience seems to indicate that far from economizing, an end to compulsory attendance may increase the cost to society in over-all law enforcement, not to mention the economic waste in human potential.

The issue of compulsory attendance relates to the fundamental questions of how one judges the best interests of the young and the role and functions delegated to the educational system. Serving a public purpose of promoting the general welfare in a democratic society, the schools insure that knowledge and understanding are both made freely available and are actively inculcated.

Community School

In the movement for educational reform, a unique position is held by the community education plan. Approved by many political, professional, and civic leaders, this approach to learning has been implemented in 700 school districts. The community education system extends the use of the school plant, of all learning facilities, and services to all members of the community, not just the traditional school population. It proposes to help all people meet their learning needs. Some educators look to it for help in solving current social problems and not merely educational ones. Breaking large cities into smaller, more manageable units makes it possible to involve people in problem solving, as well as to promote personal identity and a community spirit. In addition to their primary educational mission, community schools have an expanded role which is said to make economic, educational, and social sense, using public buildings, facilities, and professional expertise in new ways.

Its proponents insist, however, that the community education concept is not synonymous with adult education, public relations, extended activities for students, continuing higher education, neighborhood schools, community control, vocational training, social work programs, recreation programs, or compensatory education. These different streams and movements may have fed the mainstream, but are not to be confused with the guiding philosophy which makes the school responsible for all aspects of education as it relates to the community.

In order to guarantee total community involvement, recommended size is the community surrounding an elementary school building. Organized to work on community problems, representative groups develop community power, identify community resources, and then mobilize and coordinate them. Besides the traditional school program, community education expands activities for school-age children to additional hours of the day, week, and year. It brings the community into the classroom and the classroom into the community. It includes equal educational opportunities for adults in all areas of education: academic, recreational, vocational, and social. Also new is the fact that the learners are involved in deciding what is to be learned, when it is to be learned, and how it is to be learned. All in the community are learners, just as all are potential teachers.

Proponents of the community education approach defend it as a truly democratic approach to the solution of many problems. Community education enables people to participate in meaningful decision making in areas of direct concern to them. It fosters positive self-image and makes education a lifetime endeavor, since it focuses on problem solving. Its defenders claim that its widespread support makes it the most feasible reform, despite its confrontation with the restrictive practices of the educational bureaucracy. Citizen involvement can make the schools more responsive to the needs, desires, and aspirations of the people. Not being bound by traditional organization and procedure, community education looks beyond the schools to guarantee use of many varied facilities in a total education program. Such attention to all community resources for learning purposes highlights their potential benefit to all levels. Whether designed for rejuvenating American cities or providing rural enrichment, its supporters call community education a social imperative.

Unlike other issues about which proponents and opponents contend vigorously, community education encounters a criticism that deals less with its purported advantages or benefits. Instead, its critics usually point to what they regard as extravagant or exaggerated claims. They say that the evangelistic promise with regard to social problems is greater than the movement can deliver. Stressing the need for realism, these critics maintain that, perhaps because of its diverse origins, community education has no consistent, clearly defined system of ideas, and that it sometimes seems to include the entire universe in its concept. Besides, the schools have enough to do to reform themselves without undertaking to work on all community problems. Furthermore, the critics charge that by emphasizing learning as a process instead of the educational product learned, community education leaves its outcomes vague or it tries to conceal the fact that much of its work is really an expansion of traditional adult or recreation education. If it were really social problem-oriented or attempted to establish itself outside the existing educational administrative framework, the critics predict that it would lose its major support. So long as its services and expenditures are modest, community education will retain a place as an adjunct, a supplement to traditional education, having little or no reforming influence on education as a whole.

Impact of Leisure

It seems paradoxical that when our society suffers from such social, political, and economic problems as poverty, unemployment, inflation, urban decay, and official corruption, it also has a problem at the opposite end of the spectrum, namely, the problem of effective use of leisure. Leisure on a mass scale, rather than leisure for the few, seems to be a new phenomenon. And an increasingly leisure-oriented society cannot rely on chance, but needs education for leisure—planning, development, and maximum utilization. Society needs a different perspective on the quality of life when it moves from a work ethic to a leisure ethic. A shorter work week and longer vacations made possible by the scientific and technological revolution affect our psychological needs. Freedom from household chores and an increase in longevity add to the challenge to develop new possibilities, to guide our changing values.

It would appear obvious that young people should be educated in the worthwhile use of leisure time, helping them acquire skills, attitudes, knowledge, and appreciations so that they may continue to enjoy a wide variety of beneficial activities throughout life. Some activities depend on an early start, and creative use of leisure is part of realizing everyone's potential. Providing opportunities for those with abundant leisure time, especially teenagers and older people, is part of any national goal for leisure. Unlike old programs for "keeping the kids off the street," preventing juvenile delinquency, or providing therapy, new programs would emphasize life enrichment. In the enthusiastic words of some leaders in recreation education, "If work is necessary but not all that important, then the ultimate maturation of the leisure ethic is likely to be expressed in the human values of a harmonious combination life style in which work, recreation, education, and creature comforts blend into a conscious existence more compatible with human nature than any plan so far designed by the mind of man."[5] Leadership by the schools implies enormously expanding education for leisure in order to help develop fully integrated people.

Proponents of this view emphasize the need for reorienting and reeducating educators to the importance of the total recreation program. Under the motto "Education is recreation," required classroom lessons in art and music, and even in science and literature, become voluntary activities involving recreation leaders and participants in the congenial environment of the playground or center. Interest in and enthusiasm for learning and self-improvement become fundamental. In this way, proponents of recreation education claim to contribute to intellectual as well as to physical and emotional growth. Of course, they also add the fact that vandalism, arson, and theft cost public schools more than $80 million a year, and claim that at least some destructive activities may be defused by absorbing youngsters' energies in recreation. Hence, significant social benefits, as well as the obvious personal benefits, are ascribed to an expanded, publicly provided education for leisure.

Opponents of expanding the work of the schools center their fire on the so-called frills of education. They believe the schools should adhere to their limited historic function. In one of its brochures, for instance, the Council for Basic Education states that schools exist to provide the essential skills of language, numbers, and orderly thought and to transmit in a reasoned pattern the intellectual, moral, and aesthetic heritage of civilized man. However, in practice, the opponents of increased leisure education narrow the transmission of the aesthetic heritage. Economic boom times usually see little overt opposition to school minors such as art and music, but during periods of financial strain, these areas are usually the earliest victims of cuts in education budgets. For instance, school bands are among the first casualties. Physical education in general is also pinched. A major argument of the critics of all forms of recreation education is that opportunities should be provided by each family for its members, rather than be the burden of the total taxpaying public. Critics claim that although leisure education benefits individuals directly, it brings society extremely limited returns. As we all know, the traditionalists often succeed in convincing large segments of the American public that the chief purpose of the schools is to make young people literate in word and number and in historical knowledge. This really means that formal, publicly provided education should stop at that point.

Role of Athletics

From the Bowl games of New Year's Day through major and minor events of each successive season, from prime time on television through magazine and

---

[5] Ted Gordon, et al., "The Community Education View of Health, Physical Education and Recreation," *Phi Delta Kappan,* **54:**180 (Nov. 1972).

newspaper publicity for various national "heroes and heroines" of popular sport, athletics are such an integral part of American life that it may come as a surprise to find anyone challenging its role in the schools. It all seems so positive, beneficial, healthful, invigorating, or exciting, a source of inspiration to the young and of pride to people of all ages. Yet the issue has been seriously raised: Are athletics and education compatible?

Those who raise this question do not mean to limit physical education programs. Nor do they challenge the role of sports in our national life. Among other things, they are referring to the enormous pressure for schools to develop prize-winning teams at the expense of involving all students in athletic participation at the level of their skill. Some question the concentration on victory at all costs and competition for the prestige of the school and community. They sometimes refer to the readiness to sacrifice academic standards to guarantee having the best players available for the teams. They also mention decisions whereby limited funds are apportioned according to anticipated returns in revenue or reputation rather than in educational benefits. Some point to catering to the demands of the college rather than to the needs of secondary school students in the operation of the teams and their schedules.

In essence, the critics offer evidence suggesting that athletics programs in the schools do not have the interests of the students at heart, certainly not the interests of all the students. For purpose of majority involvement, intramural sports would seem preferable to interscholastic competition. The latter allows only a handful to participate, while the rest are assigned spectator roles. Also, if athletics are intended to provide healthful exercise and fun, the drive to win usually overwhelms this purpose; the physical and psychological pressures, say the critics, are too obvious to require elaboration. No one denies the strenuous efforts, the tension, the occasional recklessness generated in school sports. Intense, artificially cultivated rivalries have even led, at times, to ugly outbreaks of violence among spectators. To all this is added the distortion of value, in which some fundamental aims of education may be lost—equal participation, growth and development of all, a balance of physical, intellectual, emotional, social, and cultural improvement. As part of the unpleasant story, cases of changing students' grades over a teacher's objection and of falsification of records to gain athletic scholarships are reported in the press.

Not too long ago, in various parts of the country, racial discrimination occurred in school sports, and only now is the drive to end sex discrimination gaining momentum. Some schools have failed to provide equal athletic opportunities to those interested in and capable of benefiting from sports. Rather than serving as a democratic model, in the hands of some who were not so motivated, school sports have perpetuated undemocratic attitudes and practices. Competition has not been fair competition. The over-all claim of the devotees, then, of character-building of youth through cooperation in action, honesty, and fair play, has not been substantiated in real life. The critics conclude that only by placing athletics in a new perspective, reevaluating the programs and the way they are carried out, can they be made to serve their proper educational functions. Only by curtailing interscholastic athletics and by encouraging participation by all students can school sports be educationally justified.

The defenders of athletics admit some of the shortcomings, but insist that these are minor blemishes and not an inevitable part of any school's program.

They claim that the benefits, in terms of student interest, school spirit, and morale, are far too important to be undermined by such substantial change. They believe school sports are essential for the well-being of all, students in the first place, but adults as well. To reduce interscholastic competition, to curtail prize-winning football, baseball, or basketball teams, would be to remove a powerful asset, without providing a meaningful replacement.

So far as competition is concerned, these advocates maintain that this is the best preparation for life, that exertion to win is the source of progress in all fields, that this stimulates the keenest thinking and the marshaling of everyone's best efforts. True, only a handful make the top position, but these serve as a model and a goal for others. Winning, it is claimed, is mainly the result of clean living, co-operation, concentration, perseverance, alertness, quick decision making, and drive, all commendable qualities.

Furthermore, a school's interscholastic schedule does not preclude an active intramural program. In an atmosphere in which athletics are supported and encouraged, more students, rather than fewer, tend to be involved as participants. Such an interest is wholesome, despite the stigma sometimes attached to the sordid aspects of professional sports. School athletics must be judged on their own terms, the boosters say, and these are overwhelmingly positive. Social conditions generated in the larger society are not the fault of the schools, which may be in a position to provide a counter example. In the view of their defenders, school sports have too many essential values to be sacrificed to the changes proposed by the critics.

Evidence in this debate is sparse and inconclusive. With the current inadequate level of research into important aspects of this problem, each community and each school can only arrive at decisions based on its own experiences and observations, its own needs and interests. The only guide we can hope for is to make policy based on educational values for all students.

A Final Comment

Many people might prefer to select the best features of different proposals and thus to compromise on controversial issues. However, in actual practice, communities, through their school boards, commit themselves to specific choices. These decisions often bring the school boards into conflict with groups, sometimes with educators, who see things differently. Competing philosophies—traditionalism versus modernism, academic freedom versus censorship, "melting pot" versus cultural pluralism—may touch all phases of school life: selection of teachers and administrators, courses of study, materials and methods, classification and grouping of students, testing and grading, individualization, and the like. How vigorous the disagreements are depends on time, place, the groups in control, the forces in opposition, and the meaning of the issue.

Constant interaction between the schools as an institution and society as a whole is clearly evident from the effect of economic fluctuation on how much education is provided, as well as what kind, to whom, and how its effectiveness is measured. Population changes, political demands and action, cultural patterns, and shifts in values all generate new problems for education and force us to take a fresh look at old ones. Seeing opponents lined up on strongly competing sides of a controversial issue—be it busing or school financing—makes us realize that it is imperative to be well informed about the issues, their origins, background, and present status. Knowledgeable and concerned teachers can and must contribute to an understanding and solution of the many touchy and critical questions in education.

SUGGESTED READING

Adams, Don, and Gerald Reagan. *Schooling and Social Change in Modern America.* New York: David McKay Co., Inc., 1972.

Cox, Donald. *The City As Schoolhouse: The Story of the Parkway Program.* Valley Forge, Pa.: Judson Press, 1972.

Fantini, Mario S. *Public Schools of Choice.* New York: Simon & Schuster, Inc., 1974.

Full, Harold. *Controversy in American Education: An Anthology of Crucial Issues.* New York: Macmillan Publishing Co., Inc., 1972.

Lucas, Christopher J. *Challenge and Choice in Contemporary Education: Six Major Ideological Perspectives.* New York: Macmillan Publishing Co., Inc., 1976.

Macdonald, James B., Bernice J. Wolfson, and Esther Zaret. *Reschooling Society: A Conceptional Model.* Washington, D.C.: Association for Supervision and Curriculum Development, 1974.

Pearl, Arthur. *The Atrocity of Education.* St. Louis: New Critics Press, 1972.

Tanner, Daniel. *Secondary Education: Perspectives and Prospects.* New York: **Macmil**lan Publishing Co., 1972.

Journals

Because of the nature of the issues involved, the most valuable sources of information are the periodicals. Among the most useful for this purpose are the following journals.

American School Board Journal
Bulletin of the National Association of Secondary School Principals
Changing Education
Chronicle of Higher Education
Council-Grams of the National Council of Teachers of English
Education U.S.A.
The Educational Forum
Phi Delta Kappan
The School Review
Today's Education

POST TEST

Circle the most satisfactory answer.

1. Traditionalist education does not emphasize
   a. acquisition of basic skills.
   b. independent self-expression by the pupils.

    c. logical rather than psychological organization of content.
    d. testing and ability grouping.
    e. preparation for productive performance in the adult world.

2. Modernist education does not emphasize
    a. original and creative self-expression.
    b. student interests as a central component of curriculum.
    c. joint planning by teachers and pupils.
    d. logical rather than psychological organization of content.
    e. emotional and social growth of pupils.

3. Traditionalist and modernist views of education cannot be compared because
    a. they disagree on too many features.
    b. there is no suitable measure for judging them.
    c. no critics are unbiased.
    d. they set different goals and objectives.
    e. they are both useful in different ways.

4. Censorship becomes a problem since
    a. educators wish to introduce contemporary or realistic materials.
    b. school boards have to demonstrate their power.
    c. educators do not trust nonprofessionals.
    d. children show the immediate effects of uncensored materials.
    e. publishers push to sell their products.

5. Proponents of the melting pot theory consider their most important claim the fact that
    a. it has worked perfectly throughout our history.
    b. it is the only realistic way to unify people in troubled times.
    c. it is the most efficient and most economical approach.
    d. the schools should help minorities assimilate to the majority culture.
    e. assimilation is the only hope for the future.

6. Defenders of cultural pluralism stress the point that
    a. only respect for different cultures can unite all people.
    b. white, middle-class life styles will be most readily adopted in this way.
    c. we can ignore past discrimination and look hopefully to the future.
    d. each group should concentrate on its own culture.
    e. language differences make it impossible to appreciate other cultures.

7. Teacher stereotyping of minority children
    a. has never really affected anyone seriously.
    b. may have been true in the past but has been eliminated.
    c. has been helpful in understanding and grouping the children.
    d. has been necessary as part of the melting pot theory.
    e. has become a significant issue in minority communities.

8. Busing to achieve integration in the schools
    a. will be permanent because it is the most satisfactory remedy.
    b. has been received like all other school busing.
    c. has only been supported by the courts.

    d. has largely overbalanced other school busing.
    e. is only a partial, temporary remedy.

9. Critics of busing to achieve integration
    a. usually propose simpler ways to desegregate education.
    b. always favor integrated housing as a prior condition.
    c. ignore the social advantages of segregated schools.
    d. support quality education through large appropriations for new schools.
    e. have aroused strong community feeling.

10. School budgets and problems of school financing
    a. interest very few people with specialized knowledge.
    b. find most people in substantial agreement.
    c. have little effect on the quality of education.
    d. produce considerable community involvement.
    e. are understandable only by tax experts.

11. Financing urban education
    a. has suffered greatly in recent years.
    b. has received sympathetic treatment on all levels of government.
    c. has depended on income taxes more than on property taxes.
    d. has been well planned, well organized, and equitable.
    e. has reduced the differences between wealthy and poor school districts.

12. Critics of compulsory attendance laws believe that
    a. without legal pressure schools would compete better with industry.
    b. such laws were necessary only in dealing with immigrant children.
    c. reluctant students will be more productive outside of school.
    d. schools should replace the community in stimulating curiosity and creativity.
    e. savings resulting from repeal of the laws would be unimportant.

13. The community education movement
    a. has already been implemented in many school districts.
    b. has set itself very modest goals and therefore limits its claims.
    c. does not basically alter or expand the role and function of schools.
    d. offers a problem-free, preplanned, noncontroversial set-up.
    e. leaves untouched any existing community resources.

14. Proponents of education for leisure believe that
    a. all education should be recreation.
    b. recreation education cannot be expected to reduce juvenile delinquency.
    c. helping youngsters is more important than helping older people.
    d. intellectual growth has been overemphasized.
    e. the full costs of recreation education should be met privately.

15. Opponents of present-day athletics programs
    a. really hope to eliminate school sports altogether.
    b. believe that sports are overstressed in our national life.
    c. want more attention paid to intramural sports programs.
    d. freely admit that competitive pressure is a major benefit of these programs.
    e. are concerned because not enough revenue is raised through existing sports activities.

Crucial Emerging Issues

Leo Auerbach

Jersey City State College

module 8

Student Power / Teacher Power / Role of the Courts / Sex Education / Religion and the Schools / Alternative Education

RATIONALE

A major theme running through the previous module was the conflict concerning aims, purposes, and philosophies of education. Some newer sources of controversy are such recent developments as the movement for student rights, the growth of teacher militancy and power, the increasing intervention of the courts, and the wave of reform using the catch-all term, alternative models of education.

All social institutions are subject to fluctuations in the exercise of power, and the schools are an arena for competing forces. Perhaps today's pressures for change are greater, more dynamic, more urgent than in the past, but transitions are not easy. Demands by the critics are widespread and insistent, and frequently the conflicts are between rival proposals for reform. Amidst the clamor of voices, including those of defenders of the status quo, we may try to determine the following: In these recommendations, whose interests are being advanced? How will these proposals affect the pupils, parents, teachers, community, and larger society?

How much attention do the changes give to growth and progress? To the solution of other problems? Does each specific proposal represent a broad view or a narrow view of the problem? If this is adopted, who has to give up something, and if so, what? Would this lead to a genuine improvement or a formal but nonsubstantive change, or even a step backward?

Specific Behavioral Objectives

After working through this module, you should be able to do the following regarding each of the issues included in this module:

1. State the main problems regarding each issue.
2. State, in an objective and neutral manner, at least two different positions on each issue.
3. Present at least three arguments in support of each viewpoint.
4. Indicate the proposals you find most worthy of support and your reasons for approving them.
5. Offer a prediction as to the possible consequences of
   a) selecting one or another proposal; and
   b) doing nothing about the issue.

MODULE TEXT

Student Power

Try dropping the expression "student rights" in the midst of a social gathering. One reaction may be, "Never mind 'student rights.' What about student responsibilities? What has happened to that time-honored expression, 'Children should be seen and not heard?' All this trouble from student radicals, this defiance of their elders, this rebellion against the things we cherish, the things we have built so carefully over the years. All of it comes from too much concern about student rights. They have to grow up first. They have to do more listening. They need more discipline, more obedience. Permissiveness is not good for them or for anyone else. They are immature and irresponsible. They must accept adult guidance, and if we don't insist on it, we're almost as much to blame as they are."

Another may respond, "How are children supposed to learn the right way if they are not allowed to try things on their own? Blind obedience never helped anyone grow up to be independent. Besides, if we don't listen to them, to what's bothering them, we can't expect them to listen to us. Sure, we can use our authority to make them conform. We don't have to reason with them. But we can only expect resentment and resistance from the best and brightest among them. How can we get them to accept our standards if they see hypocrisy and corruption among adults? Do we preach one set of values and practice another as adults? We can't hope that somehow they'll learn the right way by listening to us tell them things."

If we examine the issue more closely than this, however, we find that these general statements and viewpoints are important but not very helpful. Under the heading of student rights, the following matters have become significant: (1) access to school records; (2) rules governing discipline; (3) suspension, expulsion, and involuntary transfer; (4) equal educational opportunity; (5) classification and grouping; (6) freedom of religion; (7) freedom of expression and assembly; (8) rules governing search; and (9) possession and distribution of literature.

Besides revealing the range of subquestions, this partial list helps us recognize the fact that the problems are not equally significant, nor do they arise simultaneously in all schools and for all age levels. Federal legislation was adopted in August 1974 concerning access to student records. Applying to schools receiving federal funds, the law gave parents the right to inspect, challenge, and protect their children's school records. Immediately, groups lined up on opposite sides. Those favoring access believe that the law will safeguard against inaccurate, irrelevant, or obsolete material entering and remaining on record. They also believe it necessary to control the dissemination of school records, that is, by requiring student or parent consent, limiting divulgence of data to private and government agencies, colleges and universities, branches of the military, credit bureaus, and businesses. The groups who object to the law focus on the fact that many records, such as letters of recommendation, were obtained under a pledge of confidentiality. They also fear the divulgence of psychological records. Whatever future amendments are adopted in response to the critics, the outcome seems likely to remain an extension of student rights.

Those viewpoints tend to deal with the second subquestion, the rules governing discipline. Disputes over clothing and hair styles have been widely publicized to the exclusion of more significant matters such as disruptive, violent, or dangerous behavior. Drug abuse, vandalism, and racial fighting characterize some schools, and it seems to be in everyone's interest to spell out the rules for discipline since a code of behavior includes both rights and responsibilities. Yet, disagreements have arisen over the type of rules that should be enumerated and whether such enumeration would restrict the power that administrators need to enforce any rules. Those who call for detailed specification argue that rules have to be explicit in order to guarantee that they are public information, are enforced consistently and fairly, and that everyone understands their value, as a protection against abuse. Supporters of this viewpoint tend to emphasize individual worth and dignity. They also believe repressive approaches do not succeed because they are negative.

Those who oppose enumeration of student rights claim that schools are not miniature political institutions with equality between teachers and students. For these people, formal education retains the traditional master-pupil relationship, legally identified with the master-servant relationship. In this viewpoint, student responsibility cannot become self-directed since students are socially and intellectually immature. Decision making and governance remain the sole property of administrators who are charged with maintaining order and control. To some of these people, the very suggestion of a code of behavior is a source of conflict since such guidelines may encourage the young to express various demands. They regard socialization as adaptation to circumstances, acceptance, and adjustment, leaving the details of standards of behavior in the hands of responsible adults. It is not clear whether the public, which regards discipline as the number one problem of the schools, fully shares every aspect of this traditional viewpoint.

Between the two opposite poles there seems little hope for compromise and reconciliation, so we can foresee a prolonged period of disagreement. This extends to the question of punishment. Only a minority supports the use of corporal punishment. But there is also disagreement over such other forms of punishment as suspension, expulsion, and involuntary transfer. At one time, no one challenged these administrative actions. Now the courts have supported the idea of due process and, in various places, principals have been restricted, and now must provide notice, hearing, and reasons for such penalties. Of course, the different states have different regulations granting authority to school officials to suspend and expel pupils, but the problem has become the length of temporary suspension as well as the number of suspensions within a given time. Some critics of existing procedures urge that as disciplinary measures become more severe, their harmful effects on students make it important to strengthen safeguards. A clear description of prohibited activity and of appropriate penalties would be the first step. Providing other opportunities for learning—use of textbooks, access to assignments and tests, use of alternative instruction such as night school, tutoring, televised instruction, or correspondence courses—would minimize the most serious consequences of exclusion.

Summing up the central issue, one attorney writes, "It has been argued for some time that suspensions and expulsions merely exacerbate a student's disciplinary problems by alienating him from his peers, retarding his academic progress, and breeding distrust of the school system. But it is argued just as vehemently that education can be improved and safety maintained only if the disruptive pupil is barred from the classroom."[1]

While the argument over disciplinary measures may be more dramatic, the issue of equal educational opportunity may be important for many more people. True, no one would openly urge discrimination in public education. However,

---

[1] Thomas J. Flygare, "Two Suspension Cases the Supreme Court Must Decide," *Phi Delta Kappan,* **56:**258 (Dec. 1974).

disputes continue over the concrete ways in which participation in classroom instruction or extracurricular activities may be limited because of age, sex, race, religion, national origin, pregnancy, parenthood, marriage, or other reasons. Some claim that lip service is given to equal educational opportunity whereas actual school practice fosters inequality by perpetuating majority standards, unfair tests, or obsolete customs that exclude individuals regardless of their abilities or potential. These people maintain that years of discrimination or neglect require special efforts to achieve genuine equality. Recognizing the importance of teacher expectations and judgment as influencing student performance, they stress the fact that bias of any kind affects success or failure. On the other hand, defenders of existing arrangements concentrate on what they regard as fundamental in education: maintaining quality, preventing the lowering of standards of achievement, and rewarding merit in open competition. They rely on test scores and claim that objective data must determine how much and what kind of education can benefit a given student. Disagreement on this issue may remain a deeply divisive feature of American education for many years.

The procedure for classifying and grouping students may soon surface as a challenge to educators. Both I.Q. tests and standardized reading and arithmetic tests for determining a student's placement—a decision that affects his entire educational and vocational future—may be questioned in the near future by more and more people. By and large, parents have left the decisions unquestioned, treating them as professional matters. Communities express concern about improving their children's scores. Even when classification implies emotional or behavioral handicaps, it is accepted. However, if open enrollment continues to bring educationally limited students into higher education and if the campaign that depicts higher education as the key to higher social and economic status persists, a new look may be taken at present practices of classification and ability grouping. The construction, use, and interpretation of the tests will then become a potential center for controversy. This dimension of student rights will then involve all the thorny questions of intelligence vis-à-vis race and social background, and the school's undertaking to provide the maximum development of each individual's capabilities.

The final group of student rights resemble the adult area of civil rights. Freedom of religion in a public school setting includes the right to refrain from participating in any form of religious activity: prayers, songs, readings, meditations, or seasonal programs. Efforts to reestablish religious observances in the schools persist. Besides opposing these, some educators insist that school officials have a responsibility to protect students who exercise their right to refuse participation in religious activities.

According to a number of court rulings, students are protected in their right to express themselves by speaking, writing, wearing, or displaying symbols of ethnic, cultural, or political values. They also have the right to assemble in a nondisruptive time, place, and manner. Nevertheless, a principal may regulate both expression and assembly if he has a factual basis for believing the exercise of these rights by students may cause substantial disruption of school activities.

Protection against indiscriminate or general search without prior notification may require obtaining a valid search warrant. The principal has to have a reasonable basis for believing a student is concealing material which is prohibited either by federal, state, or local law or by a code of school bylaws and regulations. Obviously, drugs or weapons come under legal prohibition. But the right of privacy is also defended.

In recent years, student "underground" publications, usually critical of some official policies and practices, have led to incidents involving the possession and distribution of literature. Some educators maintain that student rights include the right to possess and distribute controversial material, even material containing language offensive to part of the community. In their view, only extraordinary circumstances which might materially endanger the normal functions of the school would justify a principal's suppressing a specific issue of a specific publication. Students might be required to submit a copy of a piece of literature to the principal, but mere possession could not be questioned. Under this suggested procedure, regulations for distribution would apply uniformly to all literature, and times and places for prohibiting distribution would be specified. Thus any person would have the right to accept or reject any literature distributed according to the rules. On the other hand, other adults, school officials, faculty, and parents have objected that permitting distribution is sometimes mistaken for approval and can therefore be dangerously misleading. They insist on maintaining complete control (prior restraint or censorship) over any literature distributed in or near school buildings. By and large, these forces appear to have succeeded in limiting the appearance of controversial student publications.

Student rights in many areas have either been extended or more clearly spelled out. Controversy over their content and exercise very likely will continue to flare up as one or another of these rights occupies the center of attention.

Teacher Power

No one can say how much the old stereotype of the timid, dedicated, self-effacing teacher-public servant still remains in the minds of the public or of the teachers themselves. Recent years have witnessed teacher strikes and lockouts, jailing of teachers and their leaders, organizational drives, and vigorous political activity. The new image is different. The two leading organizations, the National Education Association (NEA), with 1,700,000 members, and the American Federation of Teachers (AFT), with 414,000 members, generally compete as to which can organize more teachers and conduct militant actions to win substantial gains. Every year in different areas, negotiations break down over salaries or working conditions such as class size and tenure. Then, teachers may form picket lines, close down school operations, and publicize their demands to win general support from the community. At school opening in September 1974, for instance, strikes were reported in fourteen states, despite the fact that the number of teacher strikes was more than 40 per cent fewer than for the same period in 1973.

Teachers join unions for various reasons, but apparently the leading cause is economic. Although inflation affects everyone, teachers appear to be among the prime victims, almost as powerless to control their economic conditions as retirees on fixed incomes. During a few years of intensive teacher organization and militant activity, salary increases were won. Then the highest increases continued in those states such as Michigan and Minnesota where teachers were well organized and collective negotiations were well developed. Most recently, teachers have been affected by increases in class size, reduction in personnel, elimination of programs and services, and cutbacks in materials and equipment. These problems are essentially economic in origin and are usually grouped together as working conditions. Since no individual teacher can negotiate on such matters, only collective bargaining is appropriate. Regardless of the name—union, teachers' association, educational organization—when teachers unite for group action and empower their representatives to negotiate a contract or collective agreement, that is teacher unionism or teacher power. When and if an agreement is signed with a school agency, usually a local board of education, the contract may cover many possible sources of friction, such as tenure, promotion, ratings, and academic freedom, as well as the usual items of absences, leaves, holidays, vacations, pensions, and welfare coverage.

Defenders of teacher organization insist that bargaining and ongoing management-labor liaison provide a stable framework for professional performance. The teacher feels free of the fear of economic pressures or arbitrary treatment. In providing some measure of job security as well as input on aspects of policy making, teacher unionism claims to make improved teaching possible, thereby benefiting everyone. Despite the unfavorable publicity about teacher strikes, unionists indicate that these are weapons of last resort, used unwillingly, and only after all other forms of discussion and persuasion have failed. They believe the shorter the strike, the better, and that in the long run, the benefits outweigh the immediate inconveniences. They maintain that their major activities are virtually ignored. For example, with more organization, teachers have pressed more successfully for larger education budgets, and have pleaded that education deserves a high rank among social priorities. Campaigning for political candidates sympathetic to education has increased teacher influence to the advantage of the schools, not the selfish interests of the organized, according to unionists. Far from reducing the professional aspects of teacher behavior, they say, organization has put it on a sound basis. Nothing that has been won has weakened the schools, but has instead made their operation more democratic and more responsive to social needs. A representative voice from the immediate producers, the teachers, is a guarantee of meeting all interests fairly, and all talk about the menace of "teacher power" is a distortion of the truth.

Critics of teacher organization and activism complain that the dignity of the profession is impaired, both in the public image (a lowering of prestige or status) and in practical support. Gains in salary and improvements in working conditions are undeniable facts, but the critics maintain that the price has been too high. Furthermore, they attack strikes as contrary to public interest, since they place the heaviest burden on the students, the immediate consumers, rather than on the opponents, the school boards with whom teachers negotiate. A school situation is not comparable to industry or trade in which an employer is deprived of production and sales. In addition, some critics claim that teacher input regarding tenure, ratings, or academic freedom encroaches on the prerogatives of management. Contracts may protect teachers who fail to maintain professional standards of performance and may make it difficult for school boards to act. Such an acquisition of power, the critics believe, is dangerous. Should the two competing national organizations merge, their unified strength would dwarf the influence of any other groups concerned with education.

Each person must decide for himself whether teacher unionism has advanced education or has the potentiality for doing so. Facing outward, teacher organizations contend with all the economic and political forces that affect the schools. Facing inward, the question of keeping teacher organizations democratic and responsive to public needs as their numbers grow will be decided by the members. Acceptance or opposition of the role of teacher organizations by such bodies as state legislatures, school boards, and parents' organizations will help determine the role they can fulfill in the school system, positive or negative, leading or retarding. Wisconsin in 1959 pioneered the first legislation authorizing collective bargaining by teachers and school boards. By mid 1974, 38 of the 50 states had sanctioned by law teacher-school board bargaining. It took only fifteen years, then, to reverse a public policy that originally denied teachers the right to bargain collectively with school boards about wages, hours, working conditions, or anything else. From now on, adjusting to change, resisting it, or helping to shape it will be the choice of all individuals and organizations involved in education, including teacher unions.

Role of the Courts

Local school boards adopt fundamental policies regarding education. Their decisions deal with building schools (what kind, where and when to build, how much to spend), hiring personnel (administrators, teachers, and staff), curriculum guidelines, purchasing policies, school zoning, and a thousand and one other details of running a major operation. Yet, in recent years, the idea that school boards really control policy has been branded a myth. Essentially this charge stems from the fact that court decisions affecting the schools have become very prominent in the past two decades.

From the United States Supreme Court decision in the 1954 *Brown* case to the present, public attention has been drawn to the civil rights cases, the judicial attack on racial segregation in the public schools. The issue of property taxes and inequitable apportionment of funds for education has also come under review. Similarly, protection of constitutional rights, as stated in the First, Fifth, and Fourteenth Amendments, has been the basis for suits dealing, among other things, with flag salute, religious instruction, and state aid to nonpublic schools; free speech and assembly; due process for students and teachers in suspensions, expulsions, and transfers; and sex discrimination. Although collective bargaining rights have been handled largely by legislative action, specific issues, such as forced leaves of absence for pregnant teachers, have been brought to court.

As long as laws and finances have related to the schools, government intervention on policy has existed. State budgets have always circumscribed expenditures on education. Accepting federal funds for higher education, vocational and agricultural education, veterans' education, scientific and technical education, and compensatory education has involved accepting federal guidelines. But extensive intervention by the courts is a comparatively recent phenomenon. Previously, most policy making was left to local school boards, since the courts were reluctant to enter areas in which they believed professional expertise was essential. Also, it was believed that remedies for overcoming inequities or alleged injustices were readily available in the intimate, democratic atmosphere of community participation in education. When the civil rights cases took the national spotlight, other constitutional issues came under scrutiny. Although the Supreme Court does not regard education as a constitutional right, it has declared it a "fundamental interest." This serves as the legal basis for court review of education decisions.

Defenders of judicial intervention point out that the courts have entered quite unwillingly into the area of school policy making. Only after hearing convincing evidence that individual rights or the rights of groups, such as the poor and minorities, have been violated have the courts agreed to act. With school boards maintaining or very slightly modifying the status quo, some people contended that discrimination and inequality remained intolerable and dangerous. Virtually all court decisions affecting education have the common theme that existing practices in the schools, adopted and enforced by school boards, have been undemocratic. As a result, either no remedies or very inadequate remedies were available to the relatively powerless individuals and groups seeking to overcome restrictive or inferior schooling. It was argued that without court action other generations of students would also be condemned to suffer the same handicaps.

Those who apply to the courts for help state that the American tradition includes reliance on the courts as impartial agencies. Unlike other public bodies, they are not regarded as politically motivated or influenced. More circumspect judgments can be made, considerate of the public good rather than limited to narrow, local, or partial interests. Their decisions are said to include both immediate and long-range effects of policies. Sensitive to precedent and custom, judges are expected to be rational, not rash; balanced, not biased, and free to protect those whose backgrounds may be completely different from their own. They have undertaken to intervene in the interests of justice.

Critics of court intervention claim that judges have pre-empted the powers of local school boards or other properly delegated authorities. Reviewing board decisions in order to pinpoint abuses may be all right, but actually shaping policies is very different. The critics maintain that courts have gone far beyond finding legality or illegality in school practices by issuing mandates outside their jurisdiction. Attendance zones, ability grouping schemes, personnel policies, pupil activity in religious observances, wearing buttons and armbands, and hair styles, for example, have all received court attention. Although courts have refrained from establishing content and curriculum, the judges' willingness to examine disputed policies has influenced school board decisions. The critics call this coercion and claim it is harmful to education, since it leads to manipulation of school populations. Besides, it is easier to mandate a change than to implement it. Furthermore, the critics assert that the courts should not require schools to serve as major agents of social change. By making education contribute to solving social and economic problems, the courts (and the legislatures, in this instance) impose burdens on the local schools that they cannot carry. Some critics have even charged that disruptive or poorly achieving students have been encouraged to flout school standards because of sympathetic or tolerant judges. The conclusion urged by the critics is that the courts must adopt more of a hands-off policy.

The line-up on this issue illustrates the problem of responsibility, the relative domains of different social and political institutions, and their vision of the way the others operate. The courts have indicated they would not review school policies and practices if there were no evidence of violation of individual and group rights. They would gladly entrust full authority to the schools to manage their own affairs if their decisions were just, equitable, and democratic. On the other hand, school boards believe they represent their communities and should be left free to carry out the needs and demands of their constituents. They insist that court intervention strips them of their rightful powers and interferes with their proper services.

Sex Education

Historians of American education have traced a pendulum action regarding sex education in the schools. Periods of freer discussion and more open treatment have alternated with times of extremely limited references in the curriculum. There have also been wide differences between communities. One reason is that school systems respond differently to the needs of the students. Recognizing that the family and church may find it difficult to provide accurate, up-to-date information on human sexuality, some communities may rely on the schools for help with problems such as pregnancies, venereal diseases, or psychological difficulties. Early physical maturing of girls in our society, revealed in the earlier onset of menarche, has made some observers recommend earlier education. An increase in youthful marriages and in divorces may demonstrate the need to develop greater understanding of infatuation, parenthood responsibilities, and formation of attitudes and values. In the area of defining sex roles and sex expectations, new currents of thought surround the young. Confronted with the image-making by the mass media, they derive standards of physical attractiveness and patterns of sexual behavior that make sexual consciousness pervasive enough to appear as a national obsession. How to cope with these phenomena and how to integrate personal fantasies with the world of reality, become problems for our school population. Yet a considerable amount of information and misinformation, and of trust or secrecy, has been acquired by the young at an early age. Drawing on parents and peers, on observation and curiosity, our young people build a framework of beliefs, attitudes, and responses on the subject of sex. What responsibility do the schools have?

It may be helpful to agree on what is meant by a program of sex education in the schools. Most programs familiarize students with a scientific vocabulary for anatomy and sexual activity. American schools commonly teach the reproductive system of vertebrates, although frequently using species other than the human. Many programs stress the seriousness and responsibilities of marriage. Through concern for student health, many schools introduce information about venereal diseases. Social aspects of relationships, such as dating courtesy, are included in many programs. Some include a discussion of love. Often, programs deal with the development of masculine and feminine roles. A common denominator of many programs is the acknowledgement of the individuality of the human being: what is right for one person may not be right for another. Besides considering those who oppose sex education in the schools, we must recognize those who want it expanded as well as those who wish to maintain these present programs.

Some proponents of sex education regard existing programs as inadequate, and therefore urge various changes. One would be the inclusion of emotionally-laden street terms, presented in a straightforward manner, in order to dull the impact of nonscientific language and to clarify many misunderstandings. Such education would also investigate data about various life-styles including nonmarriage or about the gap between engagement and child-bearing. Further, the timing of programs would be changed, since the young people who need information about venereal diseases include school dropouts and most programs do not present the facts until after dropouts have left school. Teaching about sexual health within the context of human sexuality, these people believe, could be appropriate, serious, and realistic for younger pupils. Enlarged programs could undo misleading ideas and information about differences between animal and human mating. With regards to social relationships, these programs would gear their material to the developmental level of the students. Some educators believe that many myths and fallacies are left uncorrected in existing sex education programs because social forces outside the school tend to reinforce errors. They point out that value systems are rarely discussed, although they are an integral part of the transition between the childhood approach and the adult approach to sex, with adolescence representing a crucial period in this process. Investigating anthropological and sociological data would be extremely helpful. Such a modified program would clearly necessitate a substantial change in teacher education, not to speak of changes in community acceptance of extensive sex education.

For present sex education programs, defenders claim numerous advantages. They refer to the important ways these supplement the work of the family and church. While the latter deal with personal values, moral standards, judgments, and emotional components, the schools can be more objective. Schools have no problems of personal involvement and embarrassment; they have no pressure to impose or mandate specific patterns of behavior. Instead, schools can be more factual and scientific, more concerned with the accuracy of information. Presenting the material within a framework of total education of the child, schools effectively introduce appropriate biological, anthropological, sociological, and psychological perspectives. Not only can a school program be more inclusive this way, but it can also reach all students, rather than leaving education to chance. By attending to quality and quantity, sex education in school can treat both the knowledge and the clarification of values sequentially, gearing the content to the developmental needs of the pupils. As a contribution to the physical, emotional, and social well-being of all, proponents of sex education urge the continuation of these programs.

Opponents of sex education regard it as a challenge to morality, a political issue used to manipulate the young, and a threat to religious upbringing. Believing it to be the responsibility of parents and religious teachers, these critics want to remove from the public schools all control over sex information and sex discussion. Some fear that the schools will move into phases of emotional and moral development that they consider their exclusive province. As a result, school boards have sometimes yielded to the opposition of parents. Superintendents and principals have been hired or fired because of their opinions regarding sex education.

At the present time, in various places, there is no agreement as to how sex education should be taught, where it should be taught, and by whom. With so much confusion surrounding the programs, it would appear most worthwhile if the subject could be discussed in a calm, careful, and knowledgeable way. If a common need to inform the young about human sexuality is recognized, cooperative efforts may lead to the best decisions for sharing adult responsibility.

Religion and the Schools

When the United States of America proclaimed the separation of church and state as the first item in the Bill of Rights, it set a powerful democratic example for the rest of the world. Following this principle has kept public education completely secular, so that no religious group has had advantages over any other and no student has been required to participate in any form of religious education. However, there has been strong historic connection between religion and education, especially in higher education and, to some extent, in secondary education. The first American colleges were founded, in most instances, primarily to prepare clergymen; and, as new denominations grew, they formed their own colleges. Quite naturally theology was an important subject from the earliest days. In addition, reading, which is the first of the three R's, was emphasized as necessary preparation for reading the Bible. When compulsory attendance laws were adopted, attendance at private schools, usually religious ones, was accepted as a legal substitute. Furthermore, all schools have been expected to transmit traditional values, including a respect for religion as a matter of individual conscience. Occasionally, religious groups have influenced state legislatures to specify religious inclusions and exclusions, perhaps the most famous example being the state of Tennessee's prohibition of the teaching of evolution. But this has been rare.

Most recently, some issues involving the relationship between religion and the schools have included the following: (1) financial aid to parochial (religious) schools; (2) released time from public school to receive religious instructions; (3) flag salute and the pledge of allegiance; (4) inclusion of prayers and other religious content in school programs; and (5) the use of the Bible in literature study.

Most of these cases have gone as far as the United States Supreme Court, since the constitutional question of the First Amendment has been raised. Major pressure has usually come from those who want more religious content and instruction, either mandated, approved, or tolerated. Opposition has come from those who believe the original separation of church and state must be maintained, especially in the area of education. In general, the courts have ruled that religious content should be excluded, although the Bible has received approval if handled strictly as a literary document. Individual conscience and the right to privacy have been strongly and consistently upheld.

Defenders of the exclusion of religion from the public schools begin by stressing the need to guarantee all constitutional rights as a bulwark of democratic practice. In the area of civil rights, they urge vigilance and strengthening of protection as a safeguard against abuse. They warn that introducing religious content or observance would raise the danger of discrimination, ostracism, and social disapproval. Teachers, zealous on behalf of their own beliefs, would be encouraged to foster viewpoints and doctrines in conflict with those of the family and church of the pupils. Proponents of strict separation cite evidence of social ostracism and the propagation of sectarian outlooks. Some claim that religion has been an enemy of free inquiry, an obstacle to human enlightenment and intellectual advance. They mention opposition to progress in science. Another historic lesson they point to is the social divisiveness of religion, ranging from religious wars to more everyday forms of intolerance, bigotry, and prejudice.

With regard to aid to parochial schools, the separationists who oppose it maintain that parents voluntarily select such education, despite the availability of free public education. In doing so, parents agree to bear the expense of such education, perhaps sharing the burden with their own religious group. To expect more aid from public taxes, the separationists say, is to expect all citizens to contribute to the propagation of various groups' religious views, which would be retrogressive.

As matters stand now, religious property is tax-exempt, already a special privilege. Recognizing the concern over the quality of public education, the separationists point out that the return of the best students to the public schools, rather than their flight to private schools, would make for a significant improvement. With a larger constituency working for increased school budgets, education for all would improve, since facilities would not be duplicated and religious instruction would not compete with general education. The separationists also point out that on a practical level, religious groups seeking financial assistance from government agencies would have to accept policy input, that is, government control over the use of the funds which religious groups are unwilling to agree to as conditions for the aid.

Advocates of change in the direction of more religious content in education claim that it is an essential part of character education and moral development of the young. They believe that neglect of this aspect of education has led to a decline in moral values and ethical conduct, that a secular basis is inadequate for cultivating worthy social ideals, and that the schools should provide both models and reinforcement for the best behavior. They regard religion as a major component of education, that has inspired some of humanity's greatest cultural achievements in art, architecture, literature, music, and philosophy. If the schools are to serve as transmitters of this rich heritage, they must not neglect religion.

Concerning increased financial aid to parochial schools, the proponents of change point out that the bulk of education deals with nonreligious instruction, from the three R's up to the most advanced mathematics. Providing such an educational service is socially useful, yet expensive, so these groups believe all citizens should share the financial burden. Purchase of textbooks and supplies used for general education, in subjects such as language arts, science, vocational education, and health education, relieves the public schools of the need to supply the same quantity to these pupils if they had been attending the public schools. Only the place where they are being used is different. A similar argument is offered with regard to virtually all facilities. Recognizing the special nature of religious instruction, some advocates of "parochiad" confine their requests for public funds to those educational services and structures that duplicate those of the public schools.

It may be noted that in certain respects the two sides in these debates—religious content in the public schools and public funds for parochial schools—often do not address themselves to the same points so that one side does not attempt to answer the claims of the other. In such circumstances, decisions are usually made on the basis of what one believes is most compelling, on what one is willing to consider as valid and relevant by way of ideas, experiences, or evidence in formulating a judgment.

Alternative Education

For most people, the question, What is education? conjures up a familiar, simple image. It is the activity that goes on inside classrooms in a readily recognizable school building. The process involves a teacher, textbooks or other equipment, and children being instructed or supervised in certain tasks. As a result of the process, the children increase their information, develop physical and intellectual abilities, and practice those skills which are needed to survive in and contribute to the society they were born into. Yet, throughout the history of education, perhaps its most important figures have been the reformers, critical of existing arrangements and procedures. Innovations in any period may involve the school setting, the content and curriculum, the selection of students and their treatment, attitudes and methods, and any combination of factors.

Although education may take place in a classroom, every individual's learning is a product of his total experience, in school, at home, in the community, anywhere and everywhere. Even the school building is a learning area greater than the sum of its separate classrooms, as is obvious from any look at the same pupils in different rooms, the gymnasium, the school cafeteria, the auditorium, and the school yard. However, conventional school administration has been mainly concerned with moving masses of children quietly and efficiently from one area to another and keeping them there for fixed periods of time. This is one source of the steady movement for changes in education.

Some advocates of change have been critical of the stress on order and organization which they believe has been unproductive of learning and oppressive. Some critics have urged different settings and procedures, providing warm, friendly, and pleasant learning environments, allowing freer individual movement to interest centers. Some have taken students out of school buildings, into unconventional "street academies" or "schools without walls," conducting extensive learning activities in the community. Others have worked for educational parks or learning centers with a concentration of resources available to all students in the community. Still others have worked to organize "open education" within existing school buildings. So-called "free schools," emphasizing the greatest physical freedom, have been almost exclusively outside the public school system.

Alternative education has usually stressed voluntary participation by students, parents, and teachers. It has claimed to be more responsive to the needs of communities and individuals and has been more flexible, more open to modification and change. In this way more multicultural, bilingual, or ethnic schools have been set up. Advocates of alternative education also claim to fulfill more comprehensive goals and objectives than conventional education does. Their common purpose has been to focus on student choice, interest, and feelings. However, some maintain that they combine a concern for basic skills development and college and vocational preparation with "the improvement of self-concept, the development of individual talent and uniqueness, the understanding and encouragement of cultural plurality and diversity, and the preparation of students for various roles in our society."[2] A major stress has been the claim that the alternatives can be more humane to students and teachers, since they are smaller and have fewer rules and bureaucratic constraints.

In support of alternative education, its advocates insist that it makes freedom and diversity a democratic reality in education. As an option within the community, it does not require consensus, but rather provides choice plus an opportunity for parental involvement. Some suggest that a positive by-product of the alternative education movement has been an increase in subject matter elections, in diversified curricula, materials, and methods within traditional schools. With regard to the problem of equal, quality education, some point to successful racial

[2] Vernon H. Smith, "Options in Public Education: The Quiet Revolution," *Phi Delta Kappan,* **55:**435 (March 1973).

integration models on a voluntary basis. On psychological grounds, proponents of alternatives refer to the fact that different children have different learning styles, and only a plurality of modes of education can meet varied needs. They believe different teaching styles must be developed and encouraged. By responding to community needs quickly, drawing on community resources, and involving community people in education, the alternatives strengthen school-community ties and enrich the students. Hence, the claims are made that the environment appears more humane and that problems such as juvenile crime, truancy, and vandalism are reduced.

Critics of alternative education have charged that frequently change has been introduced for its own sake, at the expense of simpler, more feasible improvements. One charge has been that reformers have been unrealistic and utopian, proposing innovations for which conditions are not right or appropriate. They have imposed their views and policies on those who are powerless or unprepared to challenge them. Students, parents, and communities must pay for the follies of the visionaries. Change is not always for the better, and while experimenting is going on, the students involved lose the benefit of a traditional education. Some critics claim that since society provides public education, it has to use the criterion of the public good. (This usually means majority decision.) Guaranteeing free choice may satisfy individuals, but the value of education is tested by its benefit to all. Critics of alternatives usually urge that decision making remain in the hands of school leaders who are most responsible and best informed. Especially do some express fear of a loss of commitment to formal schooling in the face of easier, less rigid, less demanding options. Some critics are concerned that trivial novelties will appear most attractive. Recalling the fact that educational fads have come and gone, without the benefits of creativity and originality claimed as their objectives, critics warn against the destructive consequences of most alternatives.

One group of opponents claims that the alternative education movement rejects an essential purpose of the schools, transmitting the cultural heritage, and that many segments within the alternatives do not adequately handle the three R's. These critics charge that in promoting cultural pluralism the reformers are losing sight of cultural unity and undervaluing the shared interests and ideals of society. Some opponents also insist that many reformers are more interested in manipulating the schools and the children for the purpose of changing society. These critics condemn the anti-intellectualism which they claim results from the alternatives' stress on informality, on students' feelings, on the importance of joy, and on the absence of structure, standards, or discipline in education. They believe it desirable and practical to keep education compulsory and formalized, with sequential courses and schedules. In their view, the teacher is an authority and not an equal partner of the student, ability grouping is fair and beneficial to all students, and tests and measurements are always necessary to judge teaching and learning. In summary, the critics believe that alternative education looks at the wrong aspects of education in need of change and is proposing the wrong ways to reform the schools.

A Final Comment

Having glanced at some current controversial issues in education, we can safely predict that more problems will arise in the future, even as some issues lose their urgency. The typical questions presented in these modules demonstrate the fact that the schools as social institutions are subject to constant reexamination and reappraisal. We may all share the hope that controversy is a sign of health rather than evidence of crisis. Inevitably in our society, different individuals and groups will identify different needs and different features of education they wish to change. The alternative education movement may focus on areas such as curriculum, the student population, school procedures, methods and techniques, or learning environments. Achieving equal educational opportunity may demand more immediate or more drastic treatment than other problems. But all aspects need constant review and criticism as part of the process of vitality and renewal. Central to any improvement in education is the preparation of teachers. Becoming informed about issues and problems, investigating sources and proposals, arriving at well-reasoned and balanced judgments, and participating actively in advancing the profession, the teacher makes a contribution both to his personal growth and to the democratic progress of society.

SUGGESTED READING

Bremer, John, and Michael Von Moschzisker. *The School Without Walls.* New York: Holt, Rinehart & Winston, Inc., 1971.

Dropkin, Stan, Ernest Schwarcz, and Harold Full. *Contemporary American Education: An Anthology of Issues, Problems, and Challenges.* New York: Macmillan Publishing Co., Inc., 1975.

Frymier, Jack R. *A School for Tomorrow.* Berkeley, Calif.: McCutchan Publishing Corporation, 1973.

Full, Harold. *Controversy in American Education: An Anthology of Crucial Issues.* New York: Macmillan Publishing Co., Inc., 1972.

James, Charity. *Young Lives at Stake: The Education of Adolescents.* New York: Agathon Press, 1972.

Rist, Ray. *Reconstructing American Education: Innovation and Alternatives.* New Brunswick, N.J.: Transaction Books, 1972.

Saxe, Richard W., Ed. *Opening the Schools: Alternative Ways of Learning.* Berkeley, Calif.: McCutchan Publishing Corporation, 1972.

Student Involvement in Decision Making in An Alternative High School. Chicago: Center for New Schools, 1971.

POST TEST

Circle the most satisfactory answer. Determine what makes the other responses inadequate or inappropriate. Some choices or explanations will depend on your ability to interpret the text of the module.

1. The right of student and parent access to school records
   a. has been universally welcome.
   b. is really nothing new.

   c. is meant to safeguard against inaccurate or misleading material.
   d. will open up all special data, like psychological records.
   e. is expected to reduce the number of confidential recommendations.

2. Enumerating and specifying rules of student behavior is defended on the grounds that this will
   a. guarantee that the rules are enforced consistently and fairly.
   b. restrict the power of administrators.
   c. maintain the traditional master-pupil relationship.
   d. make corporal punishment unnecessary.
   e. reduce the need for suspension or expulsion.

3. The use of standardized tests as a basis for classification and grouping
   a. has been challenged as a means for restricting equal educational opportunity.
   b. is usually ignored by the community at large.
   c. has no effect on preparation for higher education or careers.
   d. is the only fair way to compare different ethnic or racial groups.
   e. genuinely reveals both pupil intelligence and achievement in reading and mathematics.

4. Teacher unionism and teacher power
   a. have increased enormously only in recent years.
   b. have been welcomed by school officials as a breath of fresh air.
   c. have made militant action less necessary.
   d. are presently professional rather than economic or political in nature.
   e. are not affected by social changes outside of the schools.

5. Local school boards
   a. have gladly shared power with groups such as teachers or judges.
   b. have preferred to concentrate on the minor, everyday operations of the schools.
   c. have been responsible for virtually all policy decisions affecting education.
   d. have maintained undisputed control over all features of school life.
   e. have had their legal position strengthened by the state legislatures.

6. The courts have intervened in school issues because they
   a. enjoy the opportunity to use this power.
   b. believe the rights of powerless individuals and groups have been violated.
   c. have always regarded education as a special interest of theirs.
   d. use the occasion to display their impartiality.
   e. believe their decisions are most important for the immediate future.

7. Critics of the courts have
   a. admitted that judges are usually very conservative in their decisions.
   b. said that courts should limit their review to the most important issues.
   c. claimed that the schools will work for social change even without court approval.
   d. charged that judges are mandating content and curriculum.
   e. believed that judges have imposed unfair and unwise burdens on the schools.

8. Sex education in the public schools has
   a. had a constant, steady growth in this country.
   b. been welcomed by most families, churches, and other institutions.
   c. varied according to different community attitudes and beliefs.
   d. not been related to specific problems such as venereal diseases.
   e. always had the greatest benefit for those who need it most.

9. Programs of sex education all include
   a. information about the reproductive system of vertebrates.
   b. the latest relevant information in physiology, anthropology, and sociology.
   c. adequate discussion of various life styles.
   d. extensive material on personal values and moral standards.
   e. opportunities for emotional growth and development.

10. Opponents of sex education in the schools have
    a. challenged the scientific accuracy of the information in these programs.
    b. charged that it is a political issue used to manipulate the young.
    c. usually trusted school boards to decide the matter free of outside pressure.
    d. agreed to share responsibility for instructing the young.
    e. claimed that parents and religious leaders do a better job.

11. Decisions regarding religion in the public schools have included
    a. use of the Bible as a literary document.
    b. approval of religious programs and prayers as not violating any student's rights.
    c. denial that flag salute and pledge of allegiance infringe on anyone's beliefs.
    d. siding with the teaching of science in a nonreligious way.
    e. recommended that religion be stressed in teaching traditional values.

12. The use of public funds for parochial schools
    a. has aroused very little controversy because it is necessary and helpful.
    b. has aroused considerable controversy because it draws funds away from public education.
    c. is defended on the grounds that they handle the most difficult pupils.
    d. is criticized as being inadequate to support their special services.
    e. is slated for immediate, substantial increase.

13. Alternative education
    a. is a completely new development in the history of education.
    b. has assumed forms very similar to conventional education.
    c. has been urged by critics with widely varying philosophies.
    d. is taking place almost exclusively outside of the public school system.
    e. has concentrated on content rather than goals and methods in education.

14. Advocates of alternative education have usually
    a. believed that only limited goals and objectives can be accomplished realistically.
    b. believed that student interests and choices have guided too much of their education.
    c. claimed that too much diversity impedes school achievement.
    d. stressed that smaller units and fewer restraints make it more humane.
    e. believed that community involvement is not very important.

15. Opponents of alternative education have frequently criticized it for
  a. concentrating on formalities such as the cultural heritage.
  b. ignoring the need to change society rather than the schools.
  c. imposing too many compulsory features in a rigid schedule.
  d. spending too much time testing students or preparing them for tests.
  e. introducing innovations more for the sake of change than for improving education.

Organizational Innovations

Joseph F. Callahan

Jersey City State College

module 9

Mini-courses / School Within a School / Block-of-Time Scheduling / Career Education Concept

RATIONALE

Several years ago, an amusing and topical television series entitled, "This Is the Week That Was," captured the attention of viewers and the ratings of critics. For a meteoric moment, it became a conversation piece and when it finally was replaced, it left only its name as a marker of its existence.

In the Modules 9, 10, and 11, an attempt will be made to capture some of the highlights of the "weeks that were" in the recent past, primarily of secondary education. It is intended that the presentation of what occurred in those weeks will bring you up to the present in your thinking about the schools of today and further expand your understanding of the process of schooling.

Sprinkled among the units about what was are also some units about what may be. For some time, in various "lighthouse" districts which have become accustomed to beaming the way for the rest of the educational world, enterprising educators have been busily cultivating their various curriculum projects. Some of these projects have been described in the periodical literature and have demonstrated enough vitality and merit as to have already collected scattered bunches of followers. While it is possible for the climate supporting their further implementation and development to change, it appears at this time that interest and support is still on the rise and should merit our attention.

Caution

Sometimes, future-gazing is disconcerting to teachers in training. It is unsettling, discouraging, and perhaps self-defeating because preservice teachers are not always equipped to respond sensitively and professionally. To begin with, future-gazing for them involves "deferred satisfaction" and "deferred action." Many preservice teachers find themselves unable to entertain the concept of modifying that which they have yet to plunge into. In addition, many of the future actions can be presented in such a way as to appear almost self-evident. "Why, indeed, not make the classrooms of the late 1970s more humanistic in goal and practice?" Without an understanding of the structure of schooling in the past and present, the impact of a proposed innovation for the future in any school district may be poorly discerned.

It is a fact that educational trends have a propensity for emerging, waxing or waning, and then either becoming universal or disappearing completely. Promising and well-supported trends that appear on the threshold of current acceptance can, because of some change in the political climate, the economy, world relations, or scientific breakthrough, either burst upon the educational scene as full blown action now phenomena or disappear totally from focus. At this writing, the trend toward career education occupies such a position. Currently, there is political support, scholarly interest, worker activity at the grass roots level, and a readiness on the part of some segments of society to support curriculum changes suggested. Decline of interest or support on the part of any of these groups, however, could quickly lead to the eclipse of the concept and its disappearance from the scene for another period of gestation.

Younger teachers, unfamiliar with the causes of past failures, may find themselves at a loss when experienced teachers cite historical data to support their predictions of failure.

The theory upon which each of the innovations in this module is based is presented so that the reasons for the waning can be isolated and safeguards constructed in the future to ward off recurrence of decline of promising efforts.

Specific Behavioral Objectives

Upon completion of your study of this module, you should be able to perform all of the following objectives:

1. Cite at least two reasons for keeping current in reading about educational trends and innovations.
2. Describe the significance of the waxing and waning cycle of innovations.
3. State the purpose of interest-centered mini-courses and describe how they have benefited the curriculum in some schools.
4. Cite four of the five major premises upon which the case for successful mini-course programs has been based.
5. Substantiate with illustrations the reasons given for departments to develop a rationale as a guide in the adding of mini-courses.
6. Explain how the introduction of mini-courses will bring about an increase in interaction between teacher and student and will effectuate improved advisement sessions.
7. Describe two ways in which the offering of mini-courses will improve the teaching profession.
8. Explain why many schools offering mini-courses use natural-order grouping in creating classes.
9. Cite three advantages and three disadvantages associated with bigness in a school.
10. Describe how the house plan can help to secure the benefits of bigness and keep the benefits of smallness.
11. Explain the difference between horizontal and vertical organization of houses.
12. Explain why the guidance function can be discharged more effectively in the house plan.
13. Explain why student behavior should improve in the house plan.
14. Describe what advantages there are for faculty in the house plan.
15. Distinguish between a conventional school schedule and a variable schedule.
16. Specify five reasons for using a block-of-time schedule.
17. Describe how two-phase scheduling works.
18. Explain the need for career education as specified by the United States Commissioner of Education.

19. Describe the consequences associated with discrete separation of vocational and academic curriculums in the school.
20. Describe how the Hackensack model functions at the fourth to sixth grade level, seventh to ninth grade level, and tenth to twelfth grade level.

MODULE TEXT

Mini-courses

Most of the innovations in the tryout period today, such as modular scheduling, team teaching, or independent study, offer little more than organizational change as the means of achieving a more productive, more satisfying, and more relevant school experience. In each, students are regrouped, or a varying amount of class time is allotted to groups, or the teacher's role is modified somewhat from what it conventionally has been. In general, the curriculum and the curriculum process have not been directly touched, so only the form but not the function of the school has been affected.

An Exception. At least one of the new wrinkles attempting to reverse this pattern is the interest-centered curriculum with its electives of varying length. In place of constant courses, which formerly were required for all students of a particular grade, some schools are now offering groups of elective courses from which students select according to their interest, need or career intention.

In this plan, teachers with particular strengths in a subject area design and offer short courses that have high interest for them and, it is hoped, great motivational appeal to the students. Personal commitment of the teacher insures enthusiasm for the class presentations, and the elective option, the short-term life span of the course, and student interest help to guarantee active student participation. The success of these mini-courses or multielective programs has been such in recent years as to augur that the trend will continue, will spread, and will accelerate as time goes by.

Premises and Argument. The major premises and the arguments in support of them, upon which the case for these multiple offerings is based, are as follows:

1. Interest, morale, effort, and achievement will be improved if students are permitted to pick electives from a broad range of selections that are high in interest values.

In schools where this innovation has been tried, the report is that notable changes of attitude have occurred, among both students and teachers. There has been a shift of emphasis from concern about grades to a striving for continuous progress and an almost casual reaction to testing situations; a shift from awe or fear of or revolt against school regulations to a greater reliance upon individual judgment and responsibility; and a shift from lassitude and apathy toward learning to a desire for active involvement in school processes.[1]

[1] Herman Ohme, "Steps Toward Relevance," in Glen Haas, Joseph Bondi, and Jon Wiles, eds., *Curriculum Planning: A New Approach*. (Boston: Allyn & Bacon, Inc., 1974), p. 415.

As a consequence of these shifts, not only are teachers demonstrating more enthusiasm for their work, but also student failures have diminished and student behavior problems have declined.

2. Teachers can make more valuable contributions to student schooling if they are permitted to develop the courses they want to teach, drawing upon their own areas of interest in their specialization.

The tendency on the part of teachers to fall into a formalistic rut in the classroom will decline as each teacher begins to accept personal responsibility for attracting students. The temptation to teach as one has been taught will cease to exist since many of the new courses will be without precedent. Following the table of contents in a standard text, of course, will be completely out of the question because text-books will not be available for many of the new courses.

Successful teachers will attract enthusiastic students and their classes will be well attended. Less effective teachers will stand out conspicuously in an unfavorable light. Those who are capable but who have not produced in the past will be pressured by circumstances to work harder to achieve the success that survival will demand. Those who are ineffective because they are incapable will probably be encouraged to leave the profession.

The absence of textbooks will cause great difficulty for the traditional teacher who may have leaned too heavily on the sequence of an author's presentation. The teacher of the new mini-course will not be able, nor will he desire to assign the "next ten pages for homework." The course will be so unique an entity, the chance is great that written material will be scarce. Even when accompanying text matter can be found, the individualized approach of each teacher to the general topic will force discriminating use of the text. Unless ample guidance is provided by the teacher in cases of this sort, the student in the short-term course will not be able to profit from the daily instruction.

3. Courses will be offered in varying lengths—from three weeks to twelve weeks—based upon the nature of the course and the particular goals sought.

The semester-length and the year-length courses will be reexamined for possible modification. Most of the longer courses as presently offered are so heavily weighted with fact or convention that, it is postulated, it is difficult to generate spontaneity and enthusiasm in presenting them and almost impossible to sustain group motivation for the length scheduled.

The short-term elective will require acceptance of the philosophic concept that all successful students should be able to carry on by themselves after they have developed adequate skills and have accumulated the requisite knowledge of the course content. Since, with the explosion of knowledge, it is impossible to cover any field in its entirety in a year of study, skillful selecting of attractive facets will become necessary with the expectation that the student, actively engaged in learning, will fill in the gaps through personal application.

Not as much will be lost when courses are compressed as might appear on first consideration. The shortness of total time will force each curriculum worker to select his content with greater care, enhancing those parts that are of high interest, and eliminating those parts that are busy work or of low interest. Instead of one long, rather spotty survey course with frequent testing sessions, it will be possible, for example, to offer four or more interest courses comprised of only the most essential concepts.

4. Students can profit from interacting with each other. Grouping for the multielective courses can be of the natural order, based upon interest, not grade level or student age.

Neither homogeneous nor heterogeneous grouping will need to be considered with offerings of this sort, nor college preparatory nor general studies nor remedial instruction. Since the course selection will be based upon the interest of the student, the grouping will resemble more closely that found in adult society. Even among the faculty, natural selectivity will become the mode for scheduling teachers. Each teacher, having proposed his course for consideration, will prepare his own course outline and materials, and recruit students who have an active interest in the topic. The staff seniority system, which traditionally gave privileged status to senior staff members, whereas less experienced teachers earned their spurs with remedial or reluctant scholar groups, will no longer prevail. Teachers will be engaged with topics that attract them, will be following the course guide that they have prepared, and will be interacting with students who have volunteered their presence because of their interest.

5. Teachers serving as course leaders can be held responsible not only for advisement of students but also for attracting potential students.

The success of this kind of program will be contingent upon the growth of active interest of students in learning and active participation in the course selection process. Since the survival of any offering will depend upon the number of students who want to take the course, teachers will have to stay in tune with student needs and desires through interactive dialogue to insure subscribers.

The plethora of offerings resulting will tend to confuse students. Teachers will be forced to become well informed about the offerings both in their own department and in other departments of the school. Those teachers who have gained insights into student needs, desires, likes, and dislikes in order to keep their own offerings current will be in a good position to render an excellent service during advisement periods. Student course elections will thus become acts of intelligence, made with foreknowledge about course content and course appropriateness in the light of personal interest and need. The routine following of predetermined sequences will become a happening of the past.

Curriculum Development Changes. If it takes hold, the multielective minicourse curriculum movement will force many teachers to participate much more actively than ever before in the curriculum process in each school. They will face provoking questions which in the past were answered by people and groups much farther removed from the individual classroom. When they are vitally involved as promoters and designers of courses that they trust will attract, teachers will be forced to address themselves to concepts that previously were considered only by department chairmen or curriculum directors:

1. What will be the content of the short course?
2. How will it be integrated into what has been presented previously in this subject or contribute to what has been planned to follow? How will it contribute to progress in other areas in the curriculum?
3. What skills and knowledge are prerequisite for success in the course? What skills will be developed in the course?
4. What may be legitimate expectations—cognitive and affective—of students who take the course?
5. Is it possible for a student to sequence short courses in each subject so that he is exposed to the important concepts in that subject?
6. Where may appropriate materials for studying the course be found? Can a text be provided? Need a text be written? Can support materials be duplicated?
7. What procedures will be followed to evaluate the course? What provisions have been made for introducing modifications when evaluations reveal the need?
8. What are the general objectives of the department as a whole? Of each specific course, in particular?

Program Rationale a Requisite. The benefits claimed for mini-courses may not be automatic. If the movement is to be successful in a school, each department participating in the offering of multielectives must not only respond to these curriculum questions posed, but also must develop a consistent set of beliefs concerning what the subject is all about, a rationale. Without such a set of beliefs for guidance, peculiar assortments of course offerings may result because in curriculum based mainly on teacher interest courses may range widely without focus. A 1973 NASSP *Curriculum Report* that examined some 2,000 courses reveals evidence of what can occur:[2]

Programs were discovered that contained two or three courses on the novel, but none in drama; programs existed that offered two or more courses in Shakespeare, but no courses focusing on any other writer; not a single one of the courses examined "focused on such an important American writer as Mark Twain"; and no program gave any rationale for a course on a single author at the high school level.

Courses on political economists were listed and offered by English departments, as were courses on sports in which coaches and players explained their sport, but in which students were not asked to do any reading or writing.

Departmental rationales that reflect systematic analysis of the various levels of difficulty, that specify the objectives of the department in general and of specific courses in particular, and that enumerate the fundamental concepts to be mastered will establish department boundaries and provide guidelines for additions and deletions. Haphazard growth and course accretion will thus be severely curtailed.

School Response. The National Association of Secondary School Principals' survey found elective programs to be popular. "Teachers and administrators in charge of elective programs are very pleased with results. They feel that students are happier with the English courses they are taking and that teachers are happier

---

[2] *Curriculum Report* (Washington, D.C.: National Association of Secondary School Principals, May 1973), p. 1.

in teaching courses which represent their personal interests."[3] "The long corridor of failure" associated with annual or semi-annual organization has become a thing of the past in many of these schools. Students who do poorly discover in a much shorter time that credit will not be granted, and they are forced to lose only a few weeks of time instead of an entire year if they must repeat a course. In some schools, forced repetition of the same course has been eliminated. Because the electives are many and because the reason for failure may be built into the course failed, students are permitted to substitute other short-term courses in the same subject as replacements.

Sequential skill subjects such as mathematics and foreign languages are using the mini-course movement to justify and introduce "attenuated" courses which now become possible. One school that operates on a five-cycle year with each cycle consisting of seven weeks of classes, offers subjects in a normal five-phase span (one year), a seven-phase span (one and one-half years) and a ten-phase span (two years).[4] In a design of this sort, repeating can occur when lack of success begins to set in so that longer periods of repetition can be avoided.

Other courses exercise different options, in an effort to capitalize on the factor of student interest. One social studies department, for example, offers a series of six-week segments from which students select their individual sequence. A six-week series in World Studies consists of (1) religious movements; (2) revolution: military and social; and (3) major political movements. In its American Studies series, the offerings are (1) the Al Capone era; (2) yesterday, today, and tomorrow; (3) war and peace.[5]

Another school offers forty-seven mini-courses in five general social studies areas: history, economics, cultural, social, and political science. Courses last for nine weeks or less and receive one quarter of a Carnegie unit for each course successfully completed. Four Carnegie units must be completed in four years for graduation and thus all students select a minimum of sixteen of the total courses presented.

The Lexington, Massachusetts High School offers thirteen elective courses in writing, but students must take a writing workshop, preferably before taking any other composition course. All students who plan to go to college are expected to take a course in writing research papers.[6]

In general, the interest-centered curriculum in any subject area cannot help but excite and motivate students and teachers. The openness of the enrollment will usually provide the bigness required to support acceptable class size. When registration for courses is confined to one grade level, or to students in a particular stream, smaller schools have difficulty recruiting enough students for a special class to make the effort defensible economically. When the restrictions are removed and the whole school is eligible for registration in every course, enough student support can probably be generated to warrant some of the new offerings. The teacher's familiarity with the subject and the students' interest will be depended upon for

[3] Ibid, Part Two, p. 7.
[4] Sol Levine, "The John Dewey High School Adventure," *Phi Delta Kappan,* **52:**109 (Oct. 1971).
[5] James A. Burns, "McGavock: A Model School," *Educational Leadership,* **29:**530 (March 1972).
[6] Bernarr Folta, "English Teaching—Yesterday, Today, and Tomorrow," *Today's Education* (March–April 1975), p. 87.

determining the depth of the coverage. To be successful, teachers will have to find ways to cope with the variations in ability level and maturity among the mixed group of students who elect a course. Theoretically at least, the interest-centered curriculum approach will force teachers to listen to and interact with students and administrators to engage both teachers and students in grass roots curriculum growth and development.

The necessity for teacher participation in public relations is also looked upon as a benefit. Unless the teacher advertises the content that is to be covered, registration for any course may be slight. Giving thought to what will attract students and cultivating teacher sensitivities to student needs and aspirations appear to be effective ways to encourage students to study and learn.

School Within a School

The school-within-a-school organization is also known as the house plan, the campus school, and the decentralized school. As an organizational device, it is implemented in large high schools when it is deemed that the institution has become too big to allow for personal considerations. When students and faculty appear to be getting lost in the magnitude of an institution, and when educational leaders are so beset with administrative problems that they can find little time to lead, it is probable that the institution is too large. In theory, the intent of the school within a school is to capitalize upon the advantages that accompany bigness while at the same time to risk the loss of none of the virtues of smallness.

Horizontal Structure. Very often, the school within a school is set up on a total grade basis. Each grade is organized and administered as a completely self-contained, self-sufficient school. In some cases, this school has its own building (in a campus set-up), its own wing, or its own floor, and students frequent other parts of the larger institution only for special events, such as athletic contests, auditorium sessions, or all-school convocations.

Vertical Structure. The other arrangement is the grouping of students into houses or schools, representing one fourth, for example, of the total school population. Students for each small school are drawn from each of the grades housed in the total institution, so they represent a cross section of the large school. These subschools may be housed in separate quarters and be almost totally self-contained and self-sufficient. They choose names such as Washington House, Jefferson House, Lincoln House, or Roosevelt House, by which they are identified; they sponsor their own clubs, dances, and activities, and elect their own student house government representatives.

Advantages. Advocates of school-within-a-school type of organization postulate that in the subschools more attention can be paid to the needs of the individual student. The portion of faculty attached to the house can get to know all of its students by interacting more frequently with them and so build an identity and esprit which is not possible in the large institution. Subschools attempt to maintain the advantages of the large school by sharing and pooling students, staff, and facilities. No one house, for example, might have a large enough student demand to justify the hiring of a specialized teacher but, by pooling students from all the houses, a sufficiently large class roster can be collected to substantiate the employment of a specialist to meet the need. As a rule, gymnasiums, laboratories, shops, media services, and other expensive facilities and equipment are shared by all subschools.

Attention is generally focused upon building an identity within the subschool. To facilitate this goal, administrators, teaching faculty, and guidance counselors remain constant throughout the years in the school. In horizontally structured schools, for example, the staff may begin at grade nine with its students and remain with them until graduation, moving as a unit into the tenth grade, then the eleventh grade, and the twelfth grade. This subschool remains essentially a closed unit, once established, until the students graduate. Then, the process is begun anew with the incoming new ninth grade.

Although it is conceded that this design limits the exposure of students to relatively few teachers, and forces teachers to prepare new course outlines annually since they will be advancing with their students, its advocates consider that the resulting benefits are worth the sacrifice. Students profit from the feelings of warmth and security associated with dealing with friends and acquaintances. They also are spared the annual bewilderment and strangeness associated with adjustment to a new staff each September. Teachers get to know the strengths and weaknesses of students and can carry over their prescriptions from year to year. Students with problems can continue remedial or developmental treatment without waiting to be rediscovered when the new year begins. The retiring student and the loner are preserved from getting lost among the crowd. The vertical organization can resolve the problem associated with teaching specialities by establishing a very flexible attitude toward change of teacher each year. When it serves a purpose, teachers can advance with their students.

The house plan attempts to short-cut the bureaucratic organization of the large school by locating the administrative leadership for each subunit in the office of the housemaster. The housemaster's scope of operation is broadened to encompass all that happens within the house, and he becomes the administrative leader for all the students and all the faculty assigned to that house. He is proximate and real. He is expected to know, and be known by, the students in his house.

To further the identification process, homeroom teachers, homeroom groups, and guidance counselors are often kept constant. Except when personality conflicts arise, no need is seen for changing these relationships. In addition to enhancing students' feelings of security, long-range associations of this sort also yield knowledge about students for the professional staff with whom they interact.

The remoteness of the school principal, as a consequence, is no longer a formidable problem. Daily affairs can be conducted at the local level. The chief administrator of the total school can function as the educational leader of the institution, coordinating the leadership of the housemasters and charting the prospective educational route for the total institution.

It should then follow, it is hoped, that

1. Counseling and guidance can be provided more effectively. Inducting and orienting new students to the school and the house, and arousing the interest of all students in house activities should be facilitated. Remaining with the same students for a period of years and limiting the number for

whom he is responsible should enable each counselor to know well the talents and aspirations of each student. Advisement can be available to all students in a house on a regular basis and not reserved just for upper-classmen about to select a college.

2. Pupil-personnel records can be stored much closer to the area of use. Because of proximity and ease of access, teachers will make more frequent use of these records.

3. The possibility for anonymous misbehavior is severely curtailed. As with society in a previous century, the student should find himself in a milieu in which he is known by everyone and many discharge their responsibility for his demeanor.

4. House activities can be kept so small and so intimate as to need the services of all who become interested. At the same time, all-school activities can be refined to the point of excellence in which even the most sophisticated can find challenge enough to maintain their interest.

5. The potential for anonymity is considerably reduced. When the hectic pace induced by size is avoided, when there are people directly responsible for the welfare and success of small groups, and when there is continuity of staff in the same position from year to year, it becomes harder for quiet and self-effacing students to get lost.

6. Teachers are encouraged to discharge their instructional duties more systematically to their students because of their familiarity with student strengths and weaknesses. They also are able to remain more active professionally because of their affiliations with the all-school staff, the house staff, and the all-school departmental staff.

A Trend. Administrators of big schools will probably continue to implement or examine the school-within-a-school concept whenever they become concerned about the depersonalization and institutionalization of their unit. Districts that have used the plan for years find it has improved the spirit in the school and gained for them some of the benefits of smallness.

Block-of-Time Scheduling

Secondary school daily schedules are of two general types, the conventional and the variable. The predominant type, the conventional, provides for class periods of fixed length for class groups that meet at the same fixed hour each day, for teacher-supervised study halls for students not attending a class, and for a set of uniform provisions that apply to the entire student body.

Most conventional schedules have either six, seven, or eight periods per day, each lasting forty to sixty minutes. The long-term trend has been toward longer periods because they (1) provide time for both recitation and directed study under the same teacher; (2) make unnecessary the scheduling of double periods for laboratory and shop sessions; (3) allow time for projects, audio-visual procedures, demonstrations, and panels; (4) provide more instructional time during the year; and (5) appear to be preferred by teachers.

Critics of the conventional schedule maintain that it does not facilitate adaptation of time to needs of different subjects and types of instruction. They contend that longer periods impede individualization of instruction through rigid time provisions, interfere with new cooperative teaching arrangements for large and small groups, and result in too much regimentation of students. They also discourage independent study and the development of self-responsibility.

Variable Scheduling. The variable schedule, introduced to permit flexibility, features functional variations in period length, in time of meeting, and in number of meetings per week. Block-of-time classes, floating or revolving classes, and time modules are introduced to achieve flexibility.

The floating class is designed to achieve equal status for every class instead of dooming some of them to the less acceptable slots in the daily schedule for the entire year. Thus, classes that meet first period on Monday, move to second period on Tuesday, third period on Wednesday and consequently share equally the benefits that placement in the school day has to offer.

Use of modules of varying lengths of time to accommodate learning activities is currently the vogue in some districts. When team teaching is utilized and when large and small groups of students are called for, very short periods and very long periods of time are made possible by using modules to help fit the length of period to the method used and the goal sought. Modular scheduling is described in detail in Module 1.

The block-of-time method used to achieve variability is probably the longest-lived alternative of the three. An offshoot of the core curriculum movement of the 1930s, it allows for two or three consecutive periods with one teacher or one team. When correlation of subject matter is the objective, two or more subjects such as English and social studies may be taught during the extended period. When student personal growth is the goal, the block can be used to accommodate group guidance activities, and student-teacher and parent-teacher conferences. When used at the junior high school or middle-school level, it is frequently proposed as the easiest and most sensible time distribution to facilitate transition from the self-contained elementary to the departmentalized secondary school.

In the middle-school organization, the objective of the block of time is to win for the students and their teachers some immediate control over their schedule destiny. To accomplish this end, some middle-school organizations practice two-phase scheduling. The administrative scheduling team (principal, assistant principal, and others) begins the process by scheduling all classes that meet in specialized or limited facilities. They then assign groups of classes to teams of teachers for large blocks of time. Each student then, as a member of a group, has a teacher or a room that he reports to at the beginning of the school term. The second phase of the scheduling process is the responsibility of the teaching team. On a daily, weekly, or some other basis, the teachers of the team shift individual students around within the time block in ways judged best to achieve their goals. The variations and combinations possible are limited only by the desires or imagination of the team members. The length of the block of time depends generally upon the number of teachers in the team. Therefore, for example, the block of time for a four-teacher team ordinarily would be four periods long. If single periods are each forty-five minutes, the block of time becomes approximately 180 minutes long.

Through team planning, it is possible to regroup students. Committees can be formed to meet for a specified period of time each day. Students with similar problems can be grouped to receive attention from particular teachers for remedial work. Students ready for advanced study can be clustered for extended sessions in the library or laboratory while the remaining students continue in regular class sessions.

Rationale for Block-of-Time Scheduling. Block-of-time schedules have been used by proponents to solve a number of problems and to dissipate a number of concerns. The block facilitates the integration and correlation of courses. Teachers or teaching teams who teach combinations of courses (for example, English language arts and social studies, or science and mathematics) to a group of students can eliminate overlapping and unnecessary repetition and insure the application of skills learned in one subject to the performance of assignments in the other (by requiring, for example, the utilization of acceptable writing skills in submitting reports in history).

The block of time is also helpful in the teaching of problem-centered courses in which the content is drawn from a number of fields rather than from single subjects for the reasons already given: integration and application of content.

The block-of-time method also makes it possible for teachers to get to know their students better than does the traditional departmentalized scheduling. To know intimately 125 to 150 students a day is unrealistic. The block of time reduces the volume to a more manageable number of students. This reduction in student load permits each teacher to devote more time to individual assistance and individual guidance without affecting the allotted class time.

Such scheduling permits more effective teaching. Not only does the augmented time permit clean-up and storage time for classes which use materials in a laboratory fashion, but also it adapts itself well to short field trips, lengthy film viewing sessions, visits of guest speakers, and use of panel discussions.

More than anything else, though, the selling factor appears to be the block's potential for meeting individual needs and attending to individual differences among the students. When the scheduling process is shared by teachers and students, and when the teaching team can shuffle membership in student groups based upon intimate knowledge of student needs and interests, the tyranny of the clock and the bell is diminished.

Career Education Concept

In the wake of the pursuit of excellence theme, the effort in the post-Sputnik era directed toward the top 20 per cent of the student body, state and federal officials have become concerned about the remaining 80 per cent whose needs are not being met. Sobering statistics from the Department of Labor and elsewhere appear to support and encourage this change in emphasis. The general condition, reported by Hoyt, which finds 80 per cent of secondary school students taking courses that are prerequisite for college attendance when less than 20 per cent of the jobs in this decade will require a college degree, is symptomatic of the problem.[7] Twenty years ago, 25 per cent of the jobs required only muscle and a willingness to work; today, only five per cent of the jobs available require no

---

[7] Kenneth B. Hoyt, "Career Education: Myth or Magic," *National Association of Secondary School Principals Bulletin*, **57**:22–30 (March 1973).

education and no specific job skills.[8] By the end of this decade, according to the Labor Department, although four out of every five jobs will not require a four-year degree, most of them will require training beyond high school. Blue-collar jobs, it appears, as we have known them in the past, will rapidly vanish.

In Ohio, in 1969, a State Department of Education study revealed that of every 100 students entering first grade, 95 enter ninth grade; 76 graduate from high school; 32 enter college; 14 graduate from college; 31 enter the labor force, trained through vocational programs or college; and 69 enter the work force without adequate training.

The 1970 United States Office of Education study placed the number of youths who annually enter society without adequate preparation in terms of vocation, occupàtion, or profession at nearly two and a half million.[9] In their average employed life of forty-six years, these individuals will each hold twelve different jobs. Only one worker in five of this group will remain in the same general occupation category during the working years.[10]

The new technologies and service industries are now in the process of creating a new middle ground of job opportunities that will require specialized, but not college, training. Millions of current job holders without the proper specialized training will find themselves heading in a dead-end direction. A new relationship will spring up between man, his education, and his work. Whereas, historically, this relationship has always existed for the scholar and the professional man, the need for specialized education as a preparation for all vocations will be imperative for all workers.

Rehabilitation and retraining are becoming an important priority, not just during the change-over period in education, but for all workers from this time forward. By 1985, one college president states, "one-half of the labor force will be working on jobs which have not yet been invented. The average person will have more than one occupation in his lifetime. He will need to be provided with linkages to other jobs."[11]

The concern of many civic, social, and educational leaders was severely intensified after the upheavals, which occurred in the 1960s, associated with the civil rights movement. They began to echo the cry for "relevancy in education" and to demand the establishment of some direct relationship between the study required by the curriculum and the knowledge and skills demanded in the working world of adults. The heaviest insistence for change was directed at schools in the urban areas where "the swelling numbers of young American boys and girls [are] listlessly, apparently hopelessly entering their names on the rolls of the unemployed, not because they lack talent, but because the schools have not given them a decent or fair preparation for the hard competitive business of life— including, of course, job skills, but certainly not limited to that area."[12] These leaders viewed with alarm the school systems which appeared to them to be producing "an entire generation of boys and girls (who are) rapidly becoming

[8] Grant Venn, "Career Education in Perspective," *National Association of Secondary School Principals Bulletin,* **57:**11–21 (March 1973).

[9] John B. Stevenson, *An Introduction to Career Education* (Belmont, Calif.: Wadsworth Publishing Co., Inc., 1973), p. 5.

[10] Ibid, p. 9.

[11] Ibid, p. 8.

[12] Sidney Marland, Jr., "Career Education: A Report," *National Association of Secondary School Principals Bulletin,* **57:**3–10 (March 1973).

men and women and who fail to understand what they are to do when the transition to adulthood is complete."[13]

The Change. Traditionally, there has been minimal acceptance by our school systems of the responsibility for placing every student in a "next step" after leaving school, whether for a job or for the next educational round. Knowledge has been offered in the curriculum for its value as an end worthwhile in itself. In 1963, after Congress passed a broad Vocational Education Act, interest was stimulated in career development theory, and new attention was focused on preparing the individual student for job performance and mobility. By July 1970, when the National Advisory Council on Vocational Education issued a report calling for a complete reform of the American education system to include Career Education, the trend had begun toward pursuit of knowledge for its applicative and instrumental value so that it could be used in solving problems and meeting students' needs.

The Career Concept. The first public giant step in the direction of Career Education concepts was taken by the United States Office of Education in 1971. Since then, that office has continued to urge, "not a rejection of the liberal, humanistic tradition in favor of a strictly pragmatic utilitarian approach," but rather that "all educational experiences—curriculum, instruction, counseling— should be geared to preparation for economic independence, personal fulfillment, and an appreciation for the dignity of work."[14]

The U.S. Office of Education urged an active partnership for the school and the community. Each should help the other to make "preparation for making a living" as worthy a goal of education as some of the other lofty or more dignified aims of the school. The ultimate objective of this partnership would be the integration of the values of a work-oriented society into the personal value structure of each student in such a way that work would become possible, meaningful, and satisfying to each child. Teachers would focus on and emphasize the career implications of their subject content so that students could begin to see some relationship between what they were assigned to study and the careers they might follow in the future. The school would modify its traditional offerings in vocational education and would begin to create a different image for vocational education. Skills programs of all sorts would replace some of the trades courses previously offered, and all classes would stress the occupational skills required for getting and keeping employment. Courses would aim at maximum adaptability in order to satisfy the new aspirations, new jobs, new careers, and new national objectives. The business-labor-industrial community would provide observational opportunities, work experience, and work-study opportunities in addition to advising school administrators and teachers about emerging needs.

The intention of these changes would be to modify or eliminate the "absurd partitioning of the house of education" in which students are separated from each other in accordance with the curriculum they elect. Students would not be labeled superior because they followed the liberal arts tradition, nor inferior either intellectually or socially because they sought vocational training. By rendering it

[13] Ibid.
[14] Ibid.

honorable for all students to engage in preparation for a career and by making it possible for all students to cross disciplinary lines to take courses of interest to them, the high school, it was hoped, would become a more viable, vibrant institution.

In addition to a reemphasis on the National Education Association's Cardinal Principles of Education (health, command of fundamental processes, worthy home membership, vocation, citizenship, worthy use of leisure, and ethical character), the career education movement stressed (1) a need for practice in career decision making, (2) increased motivation for learning in the school curriculum, (3) the importance of work to society, and (4) the need for preparation for work.

Some saw the functioning of the traditional school as actually having served to discourage decision making by students. Tradition decreed that course sequences should be predetermined in large measure by the faculty. Little room remained for the exercise of judgment or for decision making by the students. Students who did make early decisions about careers that attracted them might even be warned about "premature commitments" and about their lack of the experiential background upon which to base such conclusions. Some high school graduates found themselves forced to become college students or post-graduate students because they lacked the skills requisite for a career, or because they had given inadequate thought to the selection of their life's work. Deprived of the opportunity to practice decision making throughout their school career, many students responded at graduation time by deferring the decision to enter the world of work. They therefore repeated the process which their schooling had taught them to do.

As to motivation for learning, too many students, it appeared, were failing to see the connection between life in school and life after schooling. Career educationists urged that schools start demonstrating the social relevance of school learnings for this, the "most socially concerned of all generations of American students." By illustrating and relating topics of study to socially relevant careers and to the continued existence of society, students would better achieve a mastery of the subject being taught. They would develop some of the concepts about careers and career change that would be required of them in the future. Capitalizing upon early vocational choices as evidence of interest would provide an additional positive factor in gaining student support for school subjects. The subject matter would make sense and, consequently, would be more easily remembered.

In yet another area, educators faced a unique phenomenon. They had grown up in a milieu which believed that no society could exist without work. Literary works describing societies in which machines produced the food, shelter, and other necessities of life were listed as science fiction and the societies were described as utopias. In the era of the 1960s, a youth subculture that rejected work came into existence. Largely, perhaps, because its members did not understand the contributions of work to society and to individual well-being in more than a monetary sense, many of these rebels "dropped out." It became obvious that if this attitude was to be checked, the cultivation of positive attitudes regarding work would have to be introduced during the early school years and concentrated upon throughout school life, along with cultivation of the other positive attitudes sought.

Schools traditionally furnished extensive preparation for work in only a certain few occupations; they provided little or none in most occupations. The academic and professional occupations for which college preparation and even graduate school are prerequisite have generally been adequately served. Far fewer opportunities are available for preparing to work in occupations requiring less than a four-year college degree for admission. In fact, except for business and secretarial courses, most secondary schools offer nothing for those students who discontinue their schooling at age sixteen or before.

The gaining of personal satisfaction through growth toward self-fulfillment in a democratic society was proposed as one of the great goals of career education. By making education more relevant and meaningful to students as they are in the process of becoming educated, and by preparing individuals to meet ongoing needs in the world of work, future citizens could be helped to control the effect of technological change, rather than succumb to control by it. The skills of self-analysis, self-evaluation, and self-determination that would be cultivated throughout the school years would help human beings in the educational process to keep abreast of changes occurring in their society. They could thus avoid the fears associated with human obsolescence at subsequent points in career maturation.

Office of Education Proposals. Early in 1971, the U.S.O.E. created a research and engineering action to verify the promise which Marland envisioned for career education. Four experimental models were established, to be independently developed. Each with its own peculiar thrust would search out the possibilities for successful development in one of four different directions. One model was to be school-based and operate through the machinery already in existence. A second model would be home- or family-based; a third, employer-based; and the fourth, residential- or community-based.

Ohio State University was awarded the contract as project manager for the school-based model. In June 1971, its Center for Vocational and Technical Education received $2 million (supplemented by an additional $1.7 million four months later) for the developmental phase lasting through March 1972.

Six local education agencies were selected from those that entered the competition to function as experimental sites: Atlanta, Georgia; Hackensack, New Jersey; Jefferson County, Colorado; Los Angeles, California; Mesa, Arizona; and Pontiac, Michigan. Resident C.V.T.E. (Center for Vocational and Technical Education) project teams were established in each local district, and arrangements were made for on-site consultations with researchers and experts from the University in Columbus, Ohio. The following description of the Hackensack project will illustrate the work of the project teams.

Hackensack Model. The Hackensack project team established for itself a "reorientation of the goals and a changing of the value system of American education" to the extent of establishing career education as an essential ingredient in every curriculum design. As one objective, this project sought to make career inquiry an integral part of classroom studies in every discipline at every grade level. The intent of this effort was to be that all students, regardless of their status or post-graduation plans, would receive entry-level job skills training in a field of their choice before leaving high school.

The Hackensack design called for beginning with an exposure to the world of work. In the primary grades, students would be introduced to workers from various local occupations and professions, would relate their classroom learning to the jobs performed by these people, and would begin thinking about and discussing potential roles they might play as future workers. The division of all work into goods production or service vocations furnished the framework for the learning at this stage.

In fourth through sixth grades, the theme of awareness to work was broadened to include a study of five basic occupational clusters—industry, commerce, social science, services, and arts.

During the junior high years, seventh through ninth grades, the career study theme was changed to exploration. The list of clusters was broadened to twelve, and from this list, each student was to select the eight that held most interest for him. Those eight he would explore in a systematic fashion for the three years he remained at the junior high level, interspersing them through his academic curriculum, and combining field experiences with classroom demonstrations and individual guidance sessions.

The tenth through twelfth grades would constitute a "career prep" phase of the program. By this level, the student would be able to narrow his interest to just one of the eight clusters for an in-depth study over the three-year period. Training would be scheduled into open periods in the student's program or programmed for out-of-school time. Sometimes, such arrangements might involve sharing time with local vocational or proprietary schools, or using the training resources of business and industrial firms, or special sessions with private individuals in the community who have particular expertise in some occupational skill.

In summary, the aim is to have each student leave high school better prepared to face the world, whatever his plans. He should have greater insight into his

Table 9-1 Occupational Clusters for Delivering the Comprehensive Career Education Model*

(CCEM) Objectives by Grade Level

GRADES K–3	GRADES 4–6	GRADES 7–9	GRADES 10–12
Goods ——————— Industry		Natural resources / Construction and / Manufacturing	This level permits a continuation of the 7–9 twelve clusters
	Commerce	Transportation and communication / Trade and finance	
Services	Social science	Government / Education / Health and welfare	
	Services	Personal services / Product services	
	Arts	Arts and humanities / Recreation and entertainment	

* A. J. Miller, *The Emerging School-Based Comprehensive Education Model* (Columbus, Ohio: The Center for Vocational and Technical Education, Ohio State University, 1972), p. 25.

career goals and have developed a salable skill without having sacrificed any academic preparation. He will have examined the possibilities and have learned a process of career inquiry that he can continue to apply throughout his life. If the program is successful, the skills, the process, and the knowledge learned in it will facilitate his finding a satisfying adult life role.

Special Features. Among the major criticisms of the career education movement have been the vagueness of its definition and the paucity of clear-cut instructions on how to achieve it. As a consequence, the movement could fail or could fall short of its potential and be abandoned as another abortive attempt to change the schools.

The leaders of the movement, however, are in favor of the amorphous definitions. They fear that clear definition and narrowing of focus will diminish the impact of the movement and will render it eligible for quick dismissal.

In keeping with the philosophy of the comprehensive high school

1. The career education movement could be used to unify the institution. It could influence students in the general, vocational, and academic curricula and lead them back and forth across lines which formerly separated and divided them into groups with more or less status than other groups.
2. Infusion of knowledge would be the tactic for implementation. Tacking on another program would overload an already full day. Adding classes would tend to alienate some of the regular staff, who would resent the diminishing of time for their particular courses. But using concepts germane to the world of work in the teaching of academic subjects, on the other hand, would introduce relevancy to courses which may have depreciated in meaning and significance. It might help motivation for study.
3. The community and the school, the parents and the students, the teachers and employers would all be brought closer together in a cooperative venture.
4. No student would leave school to an occupation or to further education, lacking a salable skill.
5. Special provisions for cooperative work-study programs would become possible. In addition, adjusted programs that lead to certification in technological areas could be accommodated as new tracks, specially prepared for college-bound students with industrial interests.
6. Responsibility for student progress would not be forgotten upon graduation. Placement offices would not only be involved in identifying and recording the next step each student intended to take but also would follow up regularly and seek feedback about the school program.
7. The resulting education would be a blending of general, vocational, and college preparatory education. It would not serve as a substitute for any or all of these.
   a. It would be "designed for students of all ability levels, not just for low ability students."
   b. It would be an "integrated part of the entire spectrum of education from K throughout life, not a course offered at a set specific time in education of youth."

c. It would reveal to students "the great range of career options open to them with the correlative development of positive attitudes toward work rather than demanding a permanent bondage to a single career goal and its correlative dead-end effect."

d. It would focus "attention on needs as perceived by the individual, society, economy, and employer, not just the meeting of an educational goal which was perceived by educators."

e. It would focus upon the development of "the decision-making process in the individual, not a one-course, one-semester, stop-gap measure."

f. It would emphasize "relevancy, the law of readiness, and instructional motivation, not the redundant exposition of an island of information."[15]

Trends in Career Education. The trend in this movement could profoundly affect the organization of the school, as we know it. The philosophy of the institution may be modified in subtle more than in overt ways. But if the support, intellectual and financial, for the concept remain constant, the result could well be the emergence of a new institution, referred to by some as the "Community High School," which promises features not currently associated with existing institutions. Hoyt includes the following among such changes:

1. The creation of a true open-entry, open-exit system of education in which the term *school dropout* becomes obsolete.

2. The installation of performance evaluation as a primary basis for evaluating educational accomplishment.

3. The creation of a twelve-month school year, a six-day school week, and an eighteen-hour school day in which both youth and adults can learn together in courses that run for varying lengths of time under some form of flexible scheduling.

4. An increased emphasis on a project- or activity-oriented approach to instruction that will allow greater individualization of instruction and demand relatively small class sizes.

5. The offering of twelve-month contracts to all professional educators. Part of the year would be spent in the world of work outside of education or in other kinds of learning activities.

6. The creation of comprehensive career guidance, counseling, placement, and follow-up programs that serve both in-school and out-of-school youth and adults.

7. The creation of methods for granting educational credit to students for tasks performed outside the walls of the school and under supervision of persons who do not possess standard teaching certificates.[16]

SUGGESTED READING

Alpern, Morton, Ed. *The Subject Curriculum: Grades K–12.* Columbus, Ohio: Charles E. Merrill Publishers, 1967.

[15] From John B. Stevenson, *An Introduction to Career Education* (Belmont, Calif.: Wadsworth Publishing Co., Inc., 1973), p. 3. Reprinted with permission of the publisher and the Conference of Area Education, Wisconsin, 1972.

[16] Hoyt, op. cit., p. 29.

Dunn, Rita, and Kenneth Dunn. *Practical Approaches to Individualizing Instruction.* West Nyack, N.Y.: Parker Publishing Company, Inc., 1972.

Flanagan, John C., William M. Shanner, and Robert F. Mager. *Behavioral Objectives: A Guide for Individualizing Learning.* New York: Westinghouse Learning Corporation, 1970.

Hass, Glenn, Joseph Bondi, and Jon Wiles, Eds. *Curriculum Planning: A New Approach* Boston: Allyn & Bacon, Inc., 1974.

Heath, Robert W., Ed. *New Curricula.* New York: Harper & Row, Publishers, 1964.

Heidenreich, Richard R., Ed. *Urban Education.* Arlington, Va.: College Readings, Inc., 1971.

Hoyt, Kenneth B., et al. *Career Education: What It Is and How To Do It.* Salt Lake City: Olympus Publishing Company, 1972.

Hurwitz, Emanual, Jr., and Robert Maidment, Eds. *Criticism, Conflict and Change.* New York: Dodd, Mead & Co., 1972.

Kembrough, Ralph B., and Michael Y. Nunnery. *Education Administration: An Introduction.* New York: Macmillan Publishing Co., Inc., 1976.

Renner, John W., Robert F. Bibens, and Gene D. Shepherd. *Guiding Learning in the Secondary School.* New York: Harper & Row Publishers, 1972.

Sund, Robert B., and Leslie W. Trowbridge. *Student-Centered Teaching in the Secondary School.* Columbus, Ohio: Charles E. Merrill Publishers, 1974.

Trump, J. Lloyd, and Delmas F. Miller. *Secondary School Curriculum Improvement.* Boston: Allyn & Bacon, Inc., 1968.

Unruh, Glenys G., and William M. Alexander. *Innovations in Secondary Education.* New York: Holt, Rinehart & Winston, Inc., 1970.

Weisgerber, Robert A., Ed. *Developmental Efforts in Individualizing Learning.* Itasca, Ill.: F. E. Peacock Publishers, Inc., 1971.

POST TEST

1. Cite at least two reasons teachers should keep current in their reading about innovative practices.

   _____

   _____

2. Cite at least two things to be learned from "waxing and waning" cycles of innovative effort in schools.

   _____

   _____

3. List four consequences of the introduction of mini-courses.

   _____

   _____

   _____

   _____

4. State five reasons for insisting upon a departmental rationale pertaining to control of mini-courses.

_____

_____

_____

_____

_____

5. Cite three ways mini-courses improve interaction.

_____

_____

_____

6. What effect related to the laws of supply and demand will mini-courses have on teachers?

_____

_____

_____

_____

_____

_____

7. Write a short paragraph describing natural-order grouping.

_____

_____

_____

_____

_____

_____

_____

_____

8. Cite four advantages proposed by supporters of the five-cycle year.

_____

_____

9. List four of the advantages connected with bigness.

10. List four disadvantages of bigness.

11. List four advantages of the house plan.

12. Distinguish between the vertical house plan and the horizontal house plan in the school-within-a-school organization.

13. Describe what is expected to happen to the guidance function when the house-plan is adopted.

_____

_____

_____

_____

_____

_____

14. List some additional advantages of the house plan organization.

_____

_____

_____

_____

_____

_____

_____

_____

_____

_____

15. Cite some of the advantages of the variable schedule.

_____

_____

_____

16. Specify why the block-of-time schedule is desired for the middle school.

_____

_____

_____

_____

_____

_____

_____

_____

_____

17. Point out at least five things which the Commissioner of the United States Office of Education indicated career education should strive to accomplish.

_____

_____

_____

_____

_____

_____

18. Outline, in brief, the Hackensack model for a career education program.

_____

_____

_____

_____

_____

_____

_____

_____

_____

_____

Trends in Organizing for Instruction

Joseph F. Callahan

Jersey City State College

module 10

Comprehensive High School / Regional Vocational Technical Variation / Middle School / Tracking and Phasing

RATIONALE

Since 1821 when the English Classical School was established, the American high school has withstood many periods of stress and strain. Since then, its leaders have confronted a multitude of dilemmas involving adolescents of postelementary school age. Should the high school concentrate on service to the great masses of students, or should they concentrate on the students with outstanding potential? Should the curriculum include only those courses looked upon as respectable by the colleges, or should it include a multitude of courses that promise to meet more of the needs that students seem to have? Should students be mingled in classes in a heterogeneous fashion the way adults are distributed in a community? Or is there value in separating students so that the intellectuals go one way and the laborers go another? Can, should, must an institution integrate preparation for the professions with preparations for the worlds of business and trades in order to satisfy its mission? Can all students of the same age be taught effectively in the same class? Or can more progress be expected if students are admitted only into those specific programs for which their intellectual gifts equip them?

Some of the efforts made to answer these questions are examined in the units of this module. Your study should cause you to examine your convictions on the questions raised and enable you to reach decisions on how you feel about each topic.

Specific Behavioral Objectives

Upon completion of your study of this module, you should be able to perform all of the following objectives:

1. State the grades commonly included in a middle school.
2. List at least four traits or characteristics which mark middle-school students as different from students older or younger.
3. Describe briefly how the teacher in the middle school should differ from teachers for the other grades.
4. State at least three characteristics of the emergent middle schools which appear to meet the needs of the pre- and early adolescent student.
5. Show how the innovations—team teaching, nongrading, flexible scheduling, and newer media—contribute to the success and growth of the middle school.
6. Give a simple definition of block-of-time scheduling, and state three advantages of this type of time organization in the middle school.
7. Give at least ten guidelines for planning a middle school.
8. Cite the substance of the research upon which the location of grade nine is based.
9. Describe the role of the comprehensive high school.
10. Differentiate between a multiple curriculum organization and a single curriculum organization.

11. Show how the conventional school schedule supports or impedes team teaching.
12. Explain how the comprehensive high school has been affected in the urban areas.
13. Explain how a vocational-academic dichotomy opposes the original premise upon which the comprehensive high school was established.
14. Explain Conant's reference to "social dynamite" smouldering in the schools in 1961 as supportive of the comprehensive school concept.
15. List at least four programs that the innovative schools have included in their curriculums in order to eliminate the vocational-academic dichotomy.
16. List and give a brief explanation for each of the five types of curriculum organization used in secondary schools.
17. Define *tracking* and state at least three assumptions made to justify its use by its proponents.
18. List at least three weaknesses of the track system offered by its opponents.
19. Respond positively or negatively to *phasing* in the open curriculum.

MODULE TEXT

Comprehensive High School

The universalization of secondary education is a phenomenon of the twentieth century in the United States. Although Massachusetts had enacted a law in 1827 making compulsory the financial support of secondary education in communities containing more than 500 families, and another law in 1852 making attendance for youth compulsory, it was not until the turn of the century that progressive educators began to succeed in harmonizing within the schools their humanitarian ideals and the social precepts of democracy. In 1918, one group, the Commission on the Reorganization of Secondary Education, succeeded in redefining the goals of secondary education. They advocated the establishment of the comprehensive high school, which would combine all curriculums in one unified organization as the standard type of secondary school in the United States.

By 1925, the high school, which previously had been highly selective in character, had begun to serve a larger segment of adolescents from a greater variety of backgrounds. No longer was it patronized primarily by the upper socio-economic classes nor aimed predominantly toward preparation for college and the professions. It had expanded its curriculum to include a wider range of subjects and was attempting to attract and retain also those students who intended to terminate their schooling upon graduation.

It had assumed a comprehensive role and had become an institution "which has no counterpart in any other country."[1] Because of our economic history and our devotion to the ideals of equality of opportunity and equality of status, the all-inclusive school with a common program of general education, as well as specialized programs for those with particular interests and particular goals, became the model characteristic of our society. A number of specialized high

[1] James B. Conant, *The American High School Today* (New York: McGraw-Hill Book Company, 1959), p. 7.

schools continued to exist and still do exist in some communities. These special schools offer particular programs adapted to specific groups of students and require evidence of certain aptitudes on the part of candidates for admission. In New York City, there is the Bronx High School of Science, for example; in Philadelphia, Central High School; and in Boston, the Boston Latin School—all of which offer programs that are strictly academic in nature. In many cities, there are also specialized vocational high schools, which direct their efforts toward a different group of students with a different set of special interests and abilities, or attempt to meet the needs of a dominant local trade or industry, as, for example, the School for the Performing Arts in New York City.

In general, though, the high schools in the United States have developed with varying degrees of comprehensiveness depending upon the extent of interests in some communities in certain types of programs, and the zeal of student demand in others in support of other types of programs. Large and well-equipped schools that could perform all of the functions of a comprehensive high school flourished and multiplied in the more heavily populated areas. However, even small school districts supported the multipurpose kind of institution for adolescents. Regardless of difficulties, endorsements were given for program designs, which were flexible enough to meet interests and needs of all students and which purported to train all youth to function effectively in the society in which they lived.

General Description. The American high school is called comprehensive "because it offers, under one administration and under one roof (or series of roofs) secondary education for almost all the high school age children of one's town or neighborhood. It is responsible for educating the boy who will be the atomic scientist and the girl who will marry at eighteen; the prospective captain of a ship and the future captain of industry. It is responsible for educating the bright and the not so bright children with different vocational and professional ambitions and with various motivations. It is responsible, in sum, for providing good and appropriate education, both academic and vocational, for all young people within a democratic environment which the American people believe serves the principles they cherish."[2] It provides learning opportunities for all adolescents within a range from barely educable to the gifted and talented. Its purpose is to enable each pupil to develop his greatest potential for success and happiness and to make a maximum contribution to the American society of which he is a part.

To provide educational opportunities for all types of youth, the comprehensive high school offers basic general courses for all students, a wide range of elective courses in special fields—academic, vocational and avocational—and a broad program of extraclass activities, guidance, and community-related experiences. It differs from the specialized high school that provides a program designed for a selected and relatively homogeneous body of students with a dominant educational objective, such as college preparation, vocational specialization, or scientific or fine arts concentrations.

General Education Component. The general education component of the comprehensive secondary school's curriculum embraces all of those courses which

[2] Ibid, James B. Conant, *The American High School Today* (New York: The New American Library, 1964), p. ix.

must be completed satisfactorily by all students, no matter what their career plans. Its aim is to develop the traits and understandings that men must have in common to sustain a democracy, despite the differences among them as individuals. Although specifying requirements in terms of courses, the intent is to cut across subject matter lines, to draw upon material from all sources that will assist youth in becoming responsible citizens, and to develop the competency and knowledge they will require to meet their subsequent needs. The Harvard Committee Report compared general education "to the palm of a hand, the five fingers of which are as many kinds of special interest—mathematics and science, literature and language, society and social studies, the arts, the vocations"[3] that stretch beyond the common core. Not all students need to pursue exactly the same special courses, but their general education should embrace common aims and ideals. Those students planning to attend college should pursue further studies in one or more of the special areas. Students with other life goals would take work in other courses of the specialized areas. General education is intended to be general in at least three respects:

1. It should be intended for everyone. Unlike other components of the school curriculum, it should not be pointed especially towards the future scholar, the potential members of the learned professions, or the prospective woodworker. Instead, it should be planned to meet the varied needs of all young people of the community that is served by the comprehensive school.
2. It is concerned with the total personality of the students. The emotions, the habits, the attitudes, as well as the intellect are the targets of instruction. All students are viewed as single unified beings rather than as compartmented creatures whose separate facets are educable in an exclusive fashion, each in isolation from the other.
3. It is concerned with the nonspecialized activities of students, that is, with preparation for living regardless of vocational choice. It is not antivocational nor does it encourage a sharp division between special courses and general courses in actual conduct of any educational program. Since each person is expected to contribute to society and also to earn his own living, general education points toward the choosing of a vocation in relation to one's aptitudes and interests and the needs of society, but not toward training in a specific vocation.

Conant Recommendation. In 1959, James B. Conant, former United States Ambassador to Germany, released his report of a study of the American High School in which he endorsed the comprehensive high school concept. His recommendation concerning the general education program called for "four years of English, three or four years of social studies—including two years of history (one of which should be American history), and a senior course in American problems or American government—one year of mathematics in the ninth grade (algebra or general mathematics); and at least one year of science in the ninth or tenth grade which might well be biology or general physical science."[4] This academic

[3] Report of the Harvard Committee, "General Education in a Free Society," (Cambridge, Mass.: Harvard University Press, 1945).
[4] James B. Conant, *The American High School Today* (New York: The New American Library, 1964), p. 47.

program of general education would account for more than half of every student's total course work.

The end sought in this kind of program Conant described in referring to social studies classes. Each course, he declared, "should be a cross section of the school: the class should be heterogeneously grouped. Teachers should encourage all students to participate in discussions. This course should develop not only an understanding of the American form of government and of the economic basis of our free society, but also mutual respect and understanding between different types of students. Current topics should be included; free discussion of controversial issues should be encouraged. This approach is one significant way in which our schools distinguish themselves from those in totalitarian nations. This course, as well as well-organized homerooms and certain activities, can contribute a great deal to the development of future citizens of our democracy who will be intelligent voters, stand firm under trying national conditions, and not be beguiled by the oratory of those who appeal to special interests."[5]

For other required courses that are outside of the general program and also for those elective courses chosen by students with a wide range of ability, he recommended that ability grouping should be used, on a subject-by-subject basis. For these courses, at least three kinds of groupings should be provided: "one for the more able in the subject, another for the large group whose ability is about average, and another for the very slow readers who should be handled by special teachers."[6]

Conant's recommendations strongly favored including vocational work in the comprehensive high school instead of providing for it in a separate secondary school. His reasons were largely social rather than educational. He believed that it was important for the future of American democracy to create as close a relationship as possible in high school between the future professional man, the future craftsman, the future manager of industry, the future labor leader, the future salesman, and the future engineer, so that the fundamental doctrines of American society concerning equality of status in all forms of honest labor as well as equality of opportunity could be learned by all at the same time.

Necessary Characteristics. To be effective, the comprehensive high school should not only serve a cross section of the youth of the community, but also present a rich and varied curriculum. It must develop strong relationships with community life, include programs that lead to employment in skilled occupations as well as to college admission, have a competent faculty and staff, and provide extensive resources.

Balance in the curriculum is the first essential among the other characteristics of the comprehensive school. In addition to courses of all levels of difficulty in the basic academic fields, there must also be programs in the fine and practical arts, in health and physical fitness to develop the abilities and meet the needs in other areas. Heterogeneous grouping in the general courses and in activities such as student government, service clubs, social functions, and athletic contests can be used to develop the qualities of mutual understanding. Homogeneous grouping,

---

[5] James B. Conant, *The Comprehensive High School,* (New York: McGraw-Hill Book Company, 1967), p. 33.
[6] Ibid, p. 30.

based upon levels of achievement and expressed student interest, in the specialized classes of electives will provide the competitive academic motivation.

Depth in the curriculum is stressed next as a requisite. Watered-down courses that cover the text in a shallow way cannot be accommodated by this concept. In each study, the ability to think through problems must be cultivated and the capacity for sensing relationships and clarifying values must be developed. Academically talented students should have available sequences that challenge their abilities and opportunities to qualify for advanced placement. Enrichment study should be available through summer study opportunities and utilization of a seven- or eight-period day in the regular schedule.

Individualized education assumes a very important position in comprehensive schools. Despite the stress upon preparation for adult citizenship and the objective of intelligent group interaction in a free society, the needs and interests of the individual must not be overlooked. Each pupil's program should be planned specifically for him and should include, in addition to general education courses, those elective courses which meet his interests and abilities. Testing programs should be used to assess strengths and disclose weaknesses and to provide parents as well as students with the data needed for course selection purposes. In support of the individualization concept, Conant stressed the need for each student to retain the same guidance counsellor and to be a member of at least one continuing group throughout his high school career.

Functional learning has a position of respectability in the ideal comprehensive school. Classroom learning is related to life outside of the classroom. The school functions as an integral part of the community, and the faculty cooperates with parents to create a school environment that encourages the practical application of whatever is learned in any subject. Diversified programs for the development of marketable skills are offered consonant with the employment opportunities in the community.

Social Dynamite Warning. The comprehensive high school idea, as defined and favored by Conant, has found only limited applicability in the big cities, despite the conclusion in a NASSP study of large city high schools that schools of this type were the healthiest and most satisfactory of the four kinds extant.[7] Big city schools appear to be succumbing to the threat of neighborhood change and to be suffering from the spread of the inner city slums and of racial and economic segregation.

According to the national study by NASSP, the types of schools that seem to be increasing in size as big cities lose middle-class students to the suburbs are "Lower Middle-Class Working Class Schools" and "Working Class Schools." Students in these schools lack the advantage of competition with those who have greater academic motivation, and evidently the teachers frequently transfer to neighborhoods they consider more favorable, once they have accumulated sufficient seniority.

The type of school most typical of the country at large and which Conant names "the Suburban school," no matter where it happens to be located, is main-

[7] Robert J. Havighurst, "Big-City Schools, Present and Future," in William M. Alexander, ed., *The Changing High School Curriculum* (New York: Holt, Rinehart, & Winston, Inc., 1972), p. 100.

tained as a high-status school in the city. It lacks a major ingredient of the democratic school structure since students from low-income and minority group families are usually missing. The neighborhoods from which this type of school draws its students lure parents who can afford to move to insure excellent schooling for their children, while the rest of the city suffers a decline in quality. In the communities outside the large cities, because of the socioeconomic status of the population served, the suburban schools send a large majority of their graduates on to college. They appear to meet the needs of their academic students and to satisfy the desires of parents who are ambitious for their children, but in the process may put a stigma upon the practical courses that help students get jobs immediately upon graduation.

In 1961, James Conant warned in *Slums and Suburbs* of the "social dynamite" smoldering among the out-of-work, disadvantaged, and noncollege-bound high school students in large cities. It was evident to him that employment prospects were quite dismal not only for those who would drop out, but also for those who would earn a high school diploma through a general curriculum. Those lacking in technical skills necessary for gainful employment, it appeared, were heading for a life of social disaffection and servile dependence.[8]

School administrators and boards of education during that decade made great efforts to bring their high schools into agreement with Conant's recommendations. They added courses and equipment to satisfy the criterion of breadth, and permitted and encouraged cross discipline course selection to satisfy the flexibility criterion. In many school districts, much progress towards comprehensiveness was made. In large city districts where other factors were causing problems, progress was slower in coming.

Trends Toward Comprehensiveness. The equilibrium of the comprehensive school can be maintained only if the dichotomy between the academic and the vocational programs is minimized. Only if both are planned as educationally sound sequences, are equally well staffed, and are equally accessible to all members of the student body can the respectability of each be insured. All students must be advised and guided in their selection of courses so that their needs are met and their future selections facilitated no matter which direction they intend to travel.

In 1971, the United States Commissioner of Education pleaded for the development of programs for the disadvantaged that would avoid separating them from the mainstream of education. He urged the American high school to become truly comprehensive in goals and functions, purged of the fragmentation which divided its several parts from one another. In attempting to reach this goal, New York City, which has operated specialized vocational and academic high schools for many years, is in the process of eliminating most of its vocational schools in favor of comprehensive schools, in recognition of the racial and socioeconomic stratification perpetuated by a dual system of secondary schooling.[9]

Innovative schools today are adding work-study programs, cooperative education programs, tutorial or independent study programs, advanced placement pro-

[8] James B. Conant, *Slums and Suburbs* (New York: McGraw-Hill Book Company, 1961).

[9] Morton Alpern, ed., *The Subject Curriculum: Grades K-12.* (Columbus, Ohio: Charles E. Merrill Publishers, 1967), p. 357.

grams, all within the same framework, facilitating a free intermingling and over-lapping of students. Some students who leave the building to spend the afternoon hours in a place of employment, and others who are involved in preparing for the professions by way of "cadet" participation of an apprentice nature elect common courses during the hours they spend on campus. The emotional climate in schools of this sort supports and encourages the election of courses which satisfy some need. It discourages the election of courses simply because of the status position they occupy.

Regional-Vocational-Technical Variation

One innovation that appears to exploit imaginatively the comprehensive concept is the regional-vocational-technical school which draws students from a geographical area larger than that of the typical school district. Pupils from co-operating school districts spend about half their time in this regional school and the other half in their home high school. When half time daily in each school becomes unmanageable because of distance and travel factors, a "weeks-about" arrangement has been recommended. Such plans maximize the opportunities offered by curriculum, facilities, and specialized staff while simultaneously maintaining the local community identity.[10]

The successful vocational-technical schools currently flourishing in many states appear to have respected the following guidelines:

1. A variety of representative occupational areas is available for students to select from. Today a program of fewer than ten activities is considered inadequate in contrast to past programs that tolerated fewer than six. A more generally desirable number would range between twenty or forty or more.
2. Courses are provided for both girls and boys and all courses are made available to either.
3. Courses include a range from the least to the most demanding so that there may be occupational preparation for persons of diverse abilities.
4. Courses are offered at more than one level of difficulty. In this fashion, vocational courses can be offered on an enriched, regular, or slow basis.
5. Some courses offered require from one to three years of study for completion. Other courses are of shorter duration, intended for those interested in immediate employability.
6. Some sequences permit the combination of two or more vocational areas into a single program. When there are common skills and knowledge in the areas, student progress can be facilitated by recognizing the common content in a synthesis of the areas.
7. The practical arts are used as an important part of prevocational experience for all students.
8. Special emphasis is given to those areas that relate most directly to national needs of the moment, such as the distributive trades, and the technical, health, and office occupation programs.

[10] Daniel Tanner, *Secondary Education: Perspectives and Prospects* (New York: Macmillan Publishing Co., Inc., 1972), pp. 426–428.

Programs meeting these guidelines should help students remain in school longer, help them to become more employable when they seek work, and permit them to contribute more effectively to their personal development and to society.

Middle School

As a discrete entity, the school for students in the ten to fourteen year age bracket dates from the early 1900s. At that time, it was named the junior high school, and it was created to facilitate transition into secondary education. Too many students had begun accepting the terminal point of the elementary school, grade eight, as the terminal point of education for them and were complicating the employment picture in urban areas by swelling the ranks of job-seekers. One of the goals of this new institution was to create grade twelve as a new terminal point by bridging the gap between the elementary school and the high school, thereby postponing the point of decision until after the possibilities of early specialization had been introduced. When the junior high schools were erected, grades seven, eight, and nine were combined into new administrative units, self-contained classrooms were changed into departmentalized classrooms, and new laboratory subjects such as industrial arts and home economics were added to meet the needs of the manually-oriented student.

As the movement gathered momentum, and as the years passed, the junior high school, new to many communities, began to lose some of the characteristics and innovative spirit that had distinguished it earlier. The exploration and integration functions, upon which the theory supporting the junior high school concept was based, began to succumb to rigidifying standards set by the upper-level schools. Gradually, in many communities, schools that had been flexible and free were functioning very much as little high schools and binding themselves with an even more prescriptive curriculum.

The relatively new replacement institution introduced to meet the needs of the intermediate-aged child but avoiding the rigidifying structure of the junior high school has become known as the *Middle School*. In this institution, grade nine is released to join the senior high school while grade six and sometimes grade five from the lower grades are annexed to form the middle unit. School systems which include grade five in the middle unit are identified as *K–4–4–4* systems. Other systems are *K–5–3–4* in which the middle school includes grades six, seven, and eight; and the *K–6–2–4* in which the middle school includes only grades seven and eight. Whatever the system adopted, it is the general trend to separate the grade nine students from the prepubescent youngsters below that grade.

To many observers who remember the promise of the junior high school when it was new, the trend toward middle schools appears to be a return to a previous era. The new middle school concept seems to be emphasizing the same kind of special purposes and to be pointing toward eliminating the same kinds of paralyzing curriculum structures which typified the earlier junior high school movement. The new movement is attracting much attention and winning many converts. It will probably gather increasing support as the decade continues.

In many districts, the in-between school has been ignored as a separate entity. Until a population spurt or a new housing development in the community has created a need for additional classroom space, the middle grades have been housed wherever there has been room. No one in these districts has been able to convince the community that the group of students eligible for the in-between grades is uniquely different from any other group of students.

In terms of numbers of schools involved, the most frequent pattern of grade organization found as recently as 1967 was the *6–6* arrangement,[11] in which the secondary school was an undivided six-year unit. Perhaps the popularity of this pattern stems from the fact that there are many very small schools in the country. Housing less than six grades in any secondary school of small size tends to diminish flexibility and to reduce the program to the level of austerity. In terms of numbers of students enrolled, the leading patterns in 1967 were the *K–6–3–3*, followed by the *K–6–2–4*. Each of these forms provided a separate unit, either a junior high or a middle school, between the lower- and upper-level grades.

Today the trend is in the direction of the *4–4–4* and *5–3–4* patterns. When changes are being contemplated, educational leaders appear to be offering rationales in defense of administrative units that are flexible and exciting, that encourage learning in many modes and that include teachers and students in the planning in a great many ways.

Students. Students for the new middle school differ greatly from youth in other brackets. Almost all are undergoing a period of accelerated physical growth which results in tremendous variations between individuals in the group. Puberty is reached at different times by the girls and the boys, and the awkwardness that they reveal is probably due as much to self-consciousness as to sudden growth. Physical and mental endurance are limited. Possibly because of the draining of energy by the process of growth and the disproportionately small size of the heart, junior high students are prone to exhibit signs of listlessness and lassitude and, at times, an inability to prolong concentration for extended periods.

In social activities, the peer group becomes the source of general rules of behavior. When conflict arises between the adult code and the peer code, the former is likely to be violated since deviation from the latter may result in banishment from the group. This groping toward independence and freedom from the adult domination of earlier years often results in conformity to the crowd and the establishment of cliques. The good opinion of friends and acquaintances is intensely sought and best friends are often used to replace parents as confidants. Girls, who generally mature earlier and who are generally more advanced socially than boys, tend to gravitate toward boys in the upper grades. Frequently, the boys, in an attempt to camouflage their lack of maturity and confidence, resort to teasing and aggressive behavior toward girls. The disparity among the individual members of any group at this age in terms of interests, social maturity, and mental maturity is probably as great, though not as visible, as the differences among them in height, weight, and social maturity.

Both sexes are likely to be moody and unpredictable, partly as a result of the biological changes taking place within them and partly because of their own confusion concerning their child-adult status. Their lack of self-confidence can trigger

---

[11] Weldon Beckner, *National Association of Secondary School Principals Bulletin,* **51:**68–70 (Feb. 1967).

outbursts of anger and boisterous and opinionated expressions of points of view in attempts to intimidate those not in agreement.

They are more volatile as a group than youth in other age brackets. They strive for, demand, and need opportunities to act independently similar to the older students in the senior high school. However, at times, their need for solicitude, for decision making by the adults in their lives, and for tender loving care is as great as or greater than that required by the children in the primary grades. Naive idealism motivates much of their positive behavior; despair, panic, and fear of failure haunt their interaction with their peers, lest they be found different and wanting and suffer rejection.

Flights of fantasy and daydreams of glory are common. Their desires for acceptance and for success often lead them into vague periods of wool-gathering because they are unable to achieve in actuality the status to which they aspire or because the dawn of the real day of accomplishment is still so many years away in the distant future. Although some students are still functioning in the area of concrete operations in grade seven, it is generally concluded that most will be capable of functioning at the abstract level before they finish the middle school.

Parents and teachers of middle school students have frequently expressed their concern about the plight of this group of students in an age of rapid change. They view with alarm the fact that today adolescence seems to begin earlier than ever before and yet, because of social conditions, youth's period of dependence is prolonged. Although parents and teachers recognize that factors in the economic picture nationally and internationally, as well as shifts in mores at the community level, have helped to effect these changes, they express concern that the cultivation of heterosexual interests appears to be starting very early while critical decisions about careers and marriage are being postponed until very late.

The consequence, they feel, is that there is no escape from the need for a rich educational experience for middle school pupils. Additionally, since these youths need to be prepared to make decisions about course selection prerequisite for career preparation, the opportunity to gain appropriate experiences must be provided. The middle school purports to provide this richness through the use of specialized teachers and facilities, and through special attention to the articulation of course sequences between the elementary and the senior high school.

Teachers for the Middle School. Some educational leaders of the middle school movement have indicated a preference for a unique kind of teacher for this type of school. The typical secondary teacher, they postulate, is too subject-oriented to function well among these mercurial students who, at times, adopt a disparaging attitude toward accumulated knowledge. At the same time, the typical elementary teacher, despite her "whole child" orientation, appears to them to be lacking in the depth of subject matter preparation required to meet the sometimes profound and sometimes precocious inquiry of the almost adult adolescent. The need, as they see it, has been demonstrated for a hybrid professional, trained to function as scholar as well as teacher, who possesses the personal qualities that can tolerate the shifting from one role to the other. The ability to stimulate curiosity and to guide inquiry in great depth is important, but no more so than the ability and willingness to supervise study with a gentle hand and to respond positively to needs for guidance, created by personal, emotional, and physical moments of trauma.

Emergent Middle School. When the junior high school movement was young, the ninth grade was considered to be a vital part of the unit because fifteen-year-olds were considered to have more in common with younger students than they had with older adolescents. In addition, the break that occurred between the self-contained eighth grade in the grammar school and the ninth grade in the high school seemed to be accepted as the logical place for dropping out of school. By linking grade nine with grades seven and eight, and by introducing departmentalization and career preparation programs in the in-between unit, proponents of the junior high school movement hoped that the best of two worlds could be gained: like students could be grouped together, potential dropouts might be retained, and the growth of heterosexual interests and activities might be delayed.

Since the early days of the junior high school movement, researchers have contributed additional data which modifies somewhat the rationale of the intermediate unit. Social psychologists and anthropologists have reported that children in growing up faster today have become sophisticated and more aware of the reality of human nature and society. They reach adulthood earlier, are permitted by parents to do adult things earlier, and mature socially earlier. They are also, they say, more difficult to teach, more unwilling to remain in the position of learner, less patient with teachers, and not so apt to regard school personnel as acceptable authorities.[12]

One study of students in grades five through ten, using as criteria measures of social, emotional, and physical maturity and opposite sex choices, contributes insights which tend to contradict earlier convictions about age grouping. The least amount of differences, according to William Dacus, exists between students in grades six and seven and between students in grades nine and ten. "The most noticeable feature of the male sample was the marked differences in social and emotional maturity between grades eight and nine, while there were no observed differences between grades nine and ten; this is precisely where the 6–3–3 plan divides them."[13]

The debate about the optimum points for separation may never be resolved, and decisions in each community may continue to be made more in accordance with local peculiar housing circumstances than upon research data. Whether the emerging middle school becomes "a junior high school without a football team," or a leaven causing the reorganization of the total educational ladder will depend upon the educational convictions and dynamic leadership, or lack of it, in active communities.

Educational Change. In the school year of 1965–66, 500 middle schools were in existence; in 1969–70, more than 1300.[14] The announced intention of some large city school systems, such as New York City, to abandon the junior high school format may have contributed to the increase in the tempo of change. In addition, though, for new communities deciding for the first time about grade groupings beyond the early elementary, research on individual differences relating to nongraded structures has appeared to endorse the concept of flexibility.

---

[12] Alvin W. Howard, *Teaching in Middle Schools* (Scranton, Pa.: Intext, Inc., 1968), pp. 5–6.

[13] Ibid, p. 4.

[14] Ronald Tyrell, "The Open Middle School," *National Association of Secondary School Principals Bulletin,* **58:**6 (April 1974).

One shared characteristic of these many new institutions has been the attempt to combine the best features of specialization of the secondary school. The result, in many instances, particularly in the East, has been schools with self-contained classes for grades five and six and essentially departmentalized classed for grades seven and eight.

Another characteristic appears to be the emphasis placed on self-understanding. The modified curriculum of these new schools contains instructional units about special concerns of adolescents. In these units, topics and issues identified by students are discussed under the leadership of community and school adults specially trained in the particular area. Medical doctors have taught about sex education; former drug addicts have focused on the drug problem; juvenile conference authorities have attacked problems of delinquency and vandalism.

A third characteristic has been the emphasis on greater student self-direction and self-responsibility for learning. As contrasted to earlier schools, middle schools intend to involve the students very heavily in decision making. Required courses are kept to a minimum. Students are permitted to exercise options based upon interests, needs, and career intentions. Study is motivated by the intrinsic value of the subject matter and not coerced by grades and threats of failure. Independent study, contract learning, or independent research become important processes for all to use who are mature enough to handle them. Most middle schools have built into their plans space and personnel for resource centers. In some schools, one large center, perhaps the library, has been modified into a resource center, equipped with audio and video devices which students are encouraged to operate themselves. In other schools, separate rooms have been equipped to serve as resource centers for each subject. Paraprofessional help has been employed to staff these centers and to help students doing independent study. In addition, each teacher in the department devotes a specified number of hours weekly to advisement duty in the center.

A fourth characteristic has been the expanded number of electives to support the exploratory function. Mini-courses of various descriptions have been added to induce inquiry in breadth. One of the objectives in repackaging the regular courses has been to capitalize upon student interest. In the traditional curriculum in which courses were identically prescribed for all, individual student interest was allowed to play a very modest role. Every student, like it or not, took the courses listed. With the rise of interest in student self-understanding and the search for opportunities to develop skill in decision making, student interest becomes very important. Now the student must be informed about course content and course instructor as part of the process. To capture his attention, attractive titles are adopted and planning is devoted to selecting units for study. Although essentially course content remains what it previously had been, the introduction of some flexibility into the selection process is expected to predispose pupils toward studying.

Rationale for Middle Schools. Some of the reasons given for the acceleration of educational change in the direction of the emerging middle schools are

1. The structures imposed by the upper-level units prohibits the realization of the praiseworthy goals toward which the junior high school once directed its efforts. The imposition prematurely of senior high school type academic

activities and the resulting unwholesome pressures of the interscholastic academic and social rat race, tends to dissipate the freedom involved in the exploratory function of the junior school. The middle school, by excluding grade nine, moves decidedly in the direction of the flexibility required and insures the school's freedom to act.

2. Some of the educational innovations that are being proposed, examined, and introduced—team teaching, nongrading, flexible scheduling, newer media—are peculiarly adaptable to the middle school goals of flexibility and personal responsibility.

3. The findings of researchers pertaining to individual differences have prompted many middle units to espouse the continuous progress route. Whereas formerly high school standards deterred school faculties from fully implementing the educational philosophy they professed, the middle school concept seems to encourage its implementation. Annual promotions had forced secondary schools to accept the position that teachers should pick up students at the point at which they found them and carry them as far as time and student ability permitted. In no other way could some students of limited ability in a graded school be retained with other students of similar age. However, when students who never quite mastered some subjects were promoted to grade nine, the prescriptions of the Carnegie unit system of granting credit created problems. Not only could these socially promoted students not keep pace, but in addition some of the courses introduced to permit nonachieving students to avoid dropping out had lost some of their respectability and left the student with no place to go. The legitimatizing of differentiated rates of progress enables students who are tardy in their academic maturation to remain with their social peers while they work toward mastery of subject matter at a lower level.

4. The trend toward humanized classrooms, the open school concept, and the concomitant change in school architecture began making possible the implementation of many methods not previously feasible. New structures rising to accommodate the middle grades were built with flexibility in mind. Programs and curriculums were designed first and then schools were planned to accommodate the activities. Large rooms were provided to facilitate the operations of the teaching team. Many smaller than usual classroom spaces were provided to permit small groups to accomplish their purposes. The addition of resource centers, budgeting for departmental materials, providing of packets facilitating individualization of effort, and the building into daily schedules of time for planning instruction all set the stage for the rapid progress of the movement.

New Directions. The most promising change has been the substitution of teaching teams which work as units in place of departments.[15] Each teacher in these teams has his own home base group of approximately twenty-five children for whom he acts as teacher-counselor. In addition, he serves as a specialist in one of the four major areas of language arts, social studies, mathematics, or science. Four such teachers with respective specialties in the four areas assume joint re-

[15] William Alexander, "Background of the Middle School Movement," in Glen Hass, Kimball Wiles, Arthur Roberts, eds. *Readings in Secondary Teaching* (Boston: Allyn & Bacon, Inc., 1970), p. 537.

sponsibility for perhaps 100 students. Together they plan the kind of schedule arrangements that they deem most effective for their students. This arrangement gives each teacher the best chance to use the individual competencies he possesses and, at the same time, allows him to call upon other special teachers as needed.

Seventeen characteristics are listed and described as guidelines for planning middle schools in the NASSP *Bulletin* for April 1974.[16] In addition to the characteristics already described in this module, such as continuous progress, flexible schedules, exploratory and enrichment studies, guidance services, independent study, security factor, basic skill repair and extension, creative experiences, and auxiliary staffing, the authors indicate the need for special social experiences and special physical and intramural activities. They also believe that community relations, student services, and positive and nonthreatening evaluation can flourish best in the climate of the middle school.

The final guideline which they feature, multimaterial approach, stresses the need for a "wide range of easily accessible instructional materials, a number of explanations, and a choice of approaches to a topic." Classroom activities should be planned around a multimaterial approach in the middle school rather than around the conventional, basic textbook technique.

Maturity levels, interest areas, and student backgrounds vary greatly at this age (ten to fourteen), and these variables need to be considered when materials for instruction are selected. The middle-school-age youngster, viewed from either biological or psychological point of view, has a range that extends from seven to nineteen years of age. His cognitive development, according to Piaget, progresses through different levels, too. Consequently, "variation in approach and variable materials should be available in the school program to meet the various needs and abilities and to help the teachers retain the students' interest."[17]

While there is a great deal more that needs to be explored and verified about the emerging adolescent child and the school program appropriate for him, the interest shown to date in his peculiar transitional problems almost insures that future educational changes will include increased focus on the middle school as an appropriate institution for his growth and development.

Tracking and Phasing

Before the turn of the century, when the high school was still the people's college, planning a curriculum for a school for adolescents was a relatively uncomplicated matter. Not until the new century was well started, when a more highly differentiated body of adolescents presented themselves for education, and when enrollments in schools began to double each decade did it become necessary to set up programs of many kinds to meet the varying needs of the increased numbers.

Approximately five types of curriculum organization have been used during the 300-year history of secondary education in America:

[16] Nicholas P. Georgiady, Jack D. Riegle, and Louis G. Romano, "What Are the Characteristics of the Middle School?" *National Association of Secondary School Principals Bulletin*, **58**:72–77 (April 1974).

[17] Ibid, p. 73.

1. Single curriculum: The single curriculum is the traditional European pattern employed in the German Gymnasium and the French lycee. The same courses are provided and prescribed for all students. Students with different interests select different special schools to attend.
2. Multiple curriculum: The multiple curriculum is a more flexible pattern, designed to serve a more diverse student population. Two or more parallel sequences of courses are established to coexist. Each of these sequences offers subjects designed to help the student toward common as well as particularized objectives such as the college preparatory sequence and the trades sequence. In some cases, all of the courses within a sequence are prescribed. Students are prohibited from taking courses in both sequences at the same time.
3. Constant with variable: The constant with variable curriculum has been the most common type of curriculum organization since early in this century. Certain courses are required for all students (constants): English, social studies, science, and mathematics. Other courses (variables) may be freely elected, based upon interest or career plans: foreign languages or advanced mathematics. In the past, student grade level has often been the discriminating factor regarding sequence of variable election.
4. Advisory or combination pattern: The advisory or combination curriculum pattern is a combination of the multiple and the constant with variable types. It permits crossing lines and making elections at various grade levels, prohibited by both of the other types; for example, a college prep student may take courses in the business sequence.
5. Open curriculum: Essentially, the open curriculum consists of the constants with variable structure that has been liberalized to permit much personal choice. For example, it permits the substitution of several mini-courses or semester-length courses for a required constant of a year's length, or permits free election with disregard of grade level.

The Problem. The big difficulty for secondary schools has been to provide for individual differences among students who elect any of the sequences permitted and, at the same time, to meet the needs which students share in common as they prepare to function as fellow citizens in a free society. Although elective options are available, at best they leave much to be desired because instruction is often the same for all students although wide differences are known to exist among pupils within elective classes.

As a consequence, schools have devised various administrative plans to help eliminate the problems resulting from individual inadequacies that deter progress when students are massed or grouped for instruction. Some have tried ability grouping, and others have introduced advanced placement courses, nongraded programs, special education classes, flexible, personalized programs, and multiple track plans.

Multiple Tracks. In comprehensive high schools, an early effort to differentiate instruction was the assignment of each student to one of several curriculum sequences, such as college preparatory, business, agriculture, or general. Access to any sequence was determined by a student's ability to meet the qualifications established by the designers of the program. Each school established its own set of admissions criteria—some very simple and others quite comprehensive—against which every applicant was measured for potential before permission to enter was granted or denied. Certain courses within each of these sequences were elective, but the requirements and electives in any one curriculum usually differed markedly from those in the others.

Multiple tracks as a pattern of curriculum organization consisted of procedures for organizing the curriculum into levels and placing students in the specified levels according to their ability, past achievement, and interest.

Judgments about the need for establishing different instructional levels and for separating students into groups appear to be based upon a series of assumptions such as the following:

1. All students need instruction in the basic skills.
2. Instruction in basic areas can be more effective when the range of differences in ability and achievement among students is narrow.
3. Schools can remedy deficiencies of the slow or dull students by treating them apart from the others. The achievement of the average and above average can be increased by not holding them back.
4. For success in future life, college-bound students need subject matter that is different from that needed by noncollege-bound students.
5. Unless preventive action is taken, many able students will elect easy courses in order to make high grades with little effort.
6. It is necessary to prohibit students from wasting time by electing courses that do not fit stated career plans.
7. It is possible to measure accurately educational potential and to determine a track which will meet the needs of particular students.

Multiple-track programs differ from school to school. The following example, offering four curriculum sequences, is somewhat typical: (1) honors—for the more able student; (2) college preparatory—for the college-bound student not qualified or not desiring the honors program; (3) general—for the student not qualified or not desiring the college preparatory curriculum; and (4) basic—for the academically retarded student. In mathematics the sequence of courses might be arranged into the tracks as illustrated in Table 10-1.

Another example of the multiple-track program as used by a school system in Ohio is illustrated in Table 10-2.[18] This system uses "Accelerated" for honors students and "Slow Program" or "Track III" for Basic. A student in this school, admitted to the depth enrichment program in the primary school, continued his education at the upper levels in sequences for which Track I students were eligible. "Slow Program" students were limited to Track III courses or could transfer to an occupational school at the upper levels. "Regular Program" students to whom something happened—i.e. who began to over achieve or fall behind—in the elementary years could move up to Track I or down to Track III as they progressed through the system. The accelerated courses above Track I were reserved for the capable students who had demonstrated the ability to handle the rigor of advanced

---

[18] Morton Alpren, ed. *The Subject Curriculum* Grades K-12 (Columbus, Ohio: Charles E. Merrill Publishers, 1967), p. 363.

Table 10-1 A Typical Multiple-Track Arrangement in Mathematics

GRADE	HONORS	STANDARD	BASAL	REMEDIAL
9	Intermediate Algebra	Algebra I	Basic Math	Computational Skills
10	Integrated Geometry	Plane Geometry	Algebra I	Consumer Math
11	Advanced Placement Algebra	Intermediate Algebra	Refresher Math	——
12	Advanced Placement Trigonometry and Analytic Math Analysis	——	——	——

work. By using the constants-with-variable curriculum pattern, one basic set of prescribed courses in English and social studies might be established for all students. Subsequently, with the guidance of teachers, parents, and counselors, each student would be required to elect the remainder of his subjects, keeping in mind the track limitations, the entrance requirements of the college he hoped to enter, or the other needs he anticipated meeting upon leaving school.

Rationale for Multiple Tracks. The objectives of the four-track curriculum as presented by Carl F. Hansen, the superintendent who introduced the system in the Washington, D.C. schools, are

1. To provide a planned curriculum for individual differences. Haphazard, incidental, or improvised planning to solve difficulties created by obvious differences would become a thing of the past.
2. To provide a total rather than a partial curriculum for students of different

Table 10-2 The Multiple-Track System of an Ohio School District

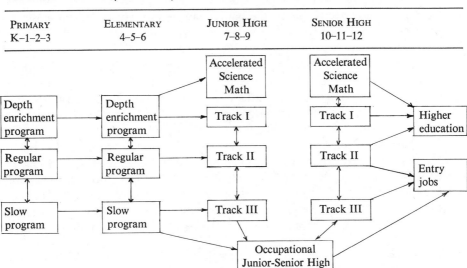

PRIMARY K–1–2–3	ELEMENTARY 4–5–6	JUNIOR HIGH 7–8–9	SENIOR HIGH 10–11–12

ability levels. For example, instead of only a remedial English class for retarded readers, there would also be classes in history and arithmetic. There would also be an across-the-board program of studies for the academically gifted.

3. To reduce the range of differences in academic abilities in each class so that group teaching could be made more effective.

4. To stress the fundamental subjects. Instruction in the basic academic content for bright, average, and slow students would discharge the common learnings requirement at varying levels of difficulty. The bright are not to be encouraged to loaf through school by electing easy courses, nor the slow to waste their time in improvised nonacademic subjects.

5. To encourage bright students to excel in classes with students of similar capacity.

6. To encourage slow learners to remain in school until completion of high school by presenting programs that are realistically within their grasp. Achievement can be upgraded and motivation stimulated when students are challenged to accomplish but are not obligated to satisfy requirements beyond their capacity.

7. To preserve the democracy of the comprehensive high school and to preserve it as a viable organization by challenging educational achievement at the various levels within it.[19]

Since a major problem in secondary schools appeared to stem from diversity of student ability, the solution proposed by tracking enthusiasts concerned ways to delimit the spread of differences so that group sessions could be made more effective. Accordingly, students were to be selected for placement in the various tracks with considerable care. Results from standardized aptitude and achievement tests would have to be evaluated, and data concerning judgments of previous teachers, previous educational experience, social maturity, and pupil preference of interest would have to be examined before the decision was made about a particular track.

Opposition to Tracking. It appears that although tracking may have administrative and management benefits, the gains may be outweighed by the costs to students. Not all the students in the school profit from the typing and programming that takes place.

1. Students from the lower-income or minority-group families appear to suffer from discrimination in this system. The track tests seem to be weighted in favor of white, middle-class youths so that the others sift naturally to the least demanding, least respectable, least desirable of the streams. The bottom track, then, fails to prepare students for effective living in an open multiethnic society.

2. There is a tendency to lock students prematurely into particular educational and occupational career lines. Advanced courses, for example, require prerequisites which must be taken early in the high school program. Delayed decisions made by students who are late in blooming must be accompanied by a willingness to take freshman or sophomore courses to qualify for upper-level instruction. Many students, rather than suffer the humiliation of moving down or brook the intimidation

[19] Carl F. Hansen, *The Four-Track Curriculum in Today's High School* (Englewood Cliffs, N.J.: Prentice-Hall, Inc., 1964), p. vi.

inherent in moving up resolve to keep the status they have. The risks involved appear too great to be worth the effort.

In some cases, the difficulty stems from the rigidity of the tracks in which students are placed. Students, for example, in a vocational track may not have access to or may be discouraged from taking a course in the college preparatory track. Similarly, a student in the college preparatory track may find it difficult to arrange to take a course in the vocational track.

3. Lower-track courses may be inferior in quality. In some large urban high schools, the general curriculum is reserved for those students who fail to make it into one of the other tracks. It becomes the "dumping ground" that prepares students neither for further education nor for the world of work. The low expectations of teachers in this track, the damaged self-esteem of the students, the poor peer models, the nature of the subject matter, and the ineffective teaching all contribute to make this track the school trouble spot. The fact that, with malice on the part of no one and with the purest of intentions on the part of all involved in the process, such a situation develops prompts opponents of tracking to campaign against it. Their contention is that the comprehensive high school can offer diversified programs without tracking students within the various programs. They endorse the trend "in recent years (of) the high schools (which) have come to recognize that tracking serves no useful purpose and only tends to accentuate differences along social class lines. The curriculum of the comprehensive high school must be diversified to meet the needs of all youth, but it need not lock students into curriculum tracks."[20]

The United States Federal Court in *Hobson* v. *Hansen,* 1967, ruled against tracking as practiced by the school district of Washington, D.C. Although the basic question concerned the constitutionality of the district's actions regarding the "District's Negro and poor public school children," some of the court's findings which related to tracking were that

1. The track system as used is a form of ability grouping.
2. The aptitude tests used to assign children to the various tracks are standardized primarily on white, middle-class children. Since these tests do not relate to the Negro and disadvantaged child, track assignment based on such tests relegates Negro and disadvantaged children to the lower tracks from which the chance of escape is remote because of the reduced curricula, the absence of adequate remedial and compensatory education, and continued inappropriate testing.
3. Education in the lower tracks is geared to what Dr. Hansen, designer of the track system, calls the blue-collar student. Such children, so stigmatized by inappropriate aptitude testing procedures, are denied equal opportunity to obtain the white-collar education available to the white and more affluent children.
4. As they proceed through the District of Columbia school system, the reading scores of the Negro and poor children, but not of the white and middle-class pupils, fall increasingly behind the national norm. By senior high school, the width of the discrepancy amounts to several grade levels.

[20] Daniel Tanner, *Secondary Education: Perspectives and Prospects* (New York: Macmillan Publishing Co., Inc., 1972), p. 321.

5. Racially and socially homogeneous schools damage the minds and spirits of all children who attend them—the Negro, the white, the poor, and the affluent—and block the attainment of the broader goals of democratic education, whether the segregation occurs by law or by fact.[21]

The defendants in the Hansen case argued that the track system "always has been a legitimate pedagogical method of providing maximum educational opportunity for children of widely ranging ability levels, and that any racial effect is but an innocent and unavoidable coincidence of ability grouping."[22] It provided, they protested, the means for systematically organizing and structuring the comprehensive high school so as to provide the differing levels of education needed. In their estimation, the usual two-level method (bright-dull) of ability grouping did a disservice to those at either end of the ability spectrum. They favored "searching for the gifted student, to place him with others of his own kind, thereby stimulating him through this select association as well as by the rigorous, demanding curriculum designed to develop his intellectual talent. Indeed, the academically capable student was required as a public necessity to take the academically challenging honors curriculum."[23] For the retarded student, the potential dropout who becomes increasingly frustrated with every failure, they advocated a "special curriculum geared to his limited abilities and designed to give him a useful basic education— one which makes no pretense of equaling traditionally taught curricula."[24]

In its decision, the court struck down the District of Columbia track system because they judged that it stigmatized the disadvantaged child and relegated him to its lower levels without providing adequately for egress up and out. In concept it was found "undemocratic and discriminatory" and failing in its obligation to bring the great majority of children into the mainstream of public education.

Phasing. The open curriculum, which currently is receiving attention and which promises to resolve some of the problems pertaining to individual differences in the future, appears to avoid many of the negative social aspects of tracking. By using the concepts of continuous progress and independent study, it attempts to achieve the flexibility and individuality found missing in earlier attempts to organize effectively for instruction.

In some nongraded efforts, students study the same subject content as they would in the graded school except that it is possible for each to proceed at his own rate within divisions or phases developed for each course. In other schools, such as the Melbourne, Florida High School, as many as five levels or phases of curriculum programs are offered—remedial, basic, standard, honors, and quest— with no compulsion to pass from one phase to the next. At the same time, there are no impediments to transferring from one to the other if and when a student is ready. Students are permitted to enter a particular phase of a course or pursue a particular track according to their needs and stage of growth, rather than because they have reached a specific age. They then progress from one assignment level to

---

[21] Emanuel Hurwitz and Robert Maidment, *Criticism, Conflict and Change,* (United States Federal Court 269, Federal Supplement 401, 1967), p. 271.

[22] Ibid, p. 274.

[23] Ibid, p. 277.

[24] Ibid.

the next as they demonstrate achievement, following individual rates of progression. Failures do not exist since students continue to study until mastery. Brown cites the dispersal of achievement among students in a regular tenth grade class "in English which will range from grade three through grade thirteen"[25] in support of his concept of phasing. The range in other subjects, especially in mathematics, he affirms, is equally great or greater. Assigning students, then, to "fluid learning situations in each subject on the basis of their individual potential and competencies"[26] permits some to begin college-level work when they become tenth graders while others may continue to receive substantial amounts of remedial work through grade twelve. The temporary "fluid learning situations" called *phases* in the Melbourne, Florida nongraded school are stages of development with varying time elements. Students may remain in lower phases indefinitely, or progress to higher phases in some subjects but not in others, but "must always find open the paths to deeper learning."

Upon entry in the school, each student is scheduled on an individual basis into one of five groups or phases, designed to group students in relation to their knowledge of skills as low, minimal, medium, high, or superior. Basic subjects such as English and mathematics are given first consideration. New students who are weak in these areas are required to devote double time, two periods a day, to each of these subjects until such time as they are up to standard. Subsequently, all students are scheduled by subjects and by depth of subject according to their achievement as measured by standardized tests. It is possible for students to distribute themselves across five regular phases:[27] In Phase I, courses are designed for students who need special assistance in small classes; Phase II courses are designed for students who need more emphasis on the basic skills; Phase III courses are designed for students with average ability in the subject matter; Phase IV courses are designed for capable students desiring education in depth; and in Phase V, challenging courses are offered for exceptional students.

In Melbourne, it is possible for a student to be scheduled into Phase I in one subject but scheduled into Phase V in another. In Phase I mathematics, for example, he would address himself to fundamentals that should have been learned in the elementary school, and at the same time school companions of the same age and school experience in Phase V will address themselves to calculus during the third year in high school. His presence in Phase I mathematics will not interfere at all with his enrollment in Phase V in another subject such as English or social studies. Lower-phase students are guided into cluster groups for basic or remedial instruction, and upper-phased students possessing academic maturity are programmed into depth education situations in which they assume more personal responsibility for their progress.

Similar to the other plans of grouping that have been tried, the open curriculum has its problems and has generated its corps of critics. Limitations of staff, time, and facilities, and lack of familiarity with some of the concepts because of the newness of the effort appear responsible for some of the problems dealing with

---

[25] H. Frank Brown, *The Nongraded High School* (Englewood Cliffs, N.J.: Prentice-Hall, Inc., 1963), p. 49.

[26] Ibid.

[27] Ibid, p. 50.

delay of student movement from one phase to the next. In addition, it appears that downgrading from one phase to a lower phase occurs less regularly than might be expected. Probably, the most common criticism is that "too much stress is placed on tests over mastery of content as the basis for progress, and other important educational outcomes—attitudes, creativeness, social interaction, and demonstrated responsibility—are given too little weight."[28]

If the present trend of consideration of individual differences continues, the next decade should witness increased experimentation in the direction of the open curriculum and the solution to many of the administrative and technical problems currently discouraging continuous progress efforts. As the technical problems diminish, the expectation of some observers is that the philosophical climate among citizens will become more supportive. When that happens, the graded school we have known with its tracks and streams will yield to the newer open organization. In the continuous progress plan, no student will be taxed beyond his capacity to perform, and no gifted student will be deprived of the opportunity for study in depth in the area of his strength.

SUGGESTED READING

Alexander, William M., Emmett L. Williams, Mary Compton, Vynce A. Hines, and Dan Prescott. *The Emergent Middle School*. New York: Holt, Rinehart & Winston, Inc., 1968.

Allen, Dwight W., and Eli Seifman, Eds. *The Teacher's Handbook*. Glenview, Ill.: Scott, Foresman and Company, 1971.

Anderson, Lest W., and Lauren A. Van Dyke, *Secondary School Administration*. Boston: Houghton Mifflin Company, 1972.

Brown, B. Frank. *New Directions for the Comprehensive High School*. West Nyack, N.Y.: Parker Publishing Company, 1972.

Bush, Robert N., and Dwight W. Allen. *A New Design for High School Education*. New York: McGraw-Hill Book Company, 1964.

Conant, James B. *The American High School Today: A First Report to Interested Citizens*. New York: McGraw-Hill Book Company, 1959.

Conant, James Bryant. *The Comprehensive High School*. New York: McGraw-Hill Book Company, 1967.

Goodlad, John I., Renata Von Stoephasius, and M. Frances Klein. *The Changing School Curriculum*. New York: The Fund for the Advancement of Education, 1966.

Inlow, Gail M. *The Emergent Curriculum*. New York: John Wiley & Sons, Inc., 1972.

McNally, Harold J., and A. Harry Passow. *Improving the Quality of Public School Programs*. New York: Teachers College Press, Columbia University, 1960.

Palardy, J. Michael, *Teaching Today: Tasks and Challenges*. New York: Macmillan Publishing Co., Inc., 1975.

Stoumbis, George C., and Alvin W. Howard, Eds. *Schools for the Middle Years*. Scranton, Pa.: International Textbook Company, 1969.

Weisgerber, Robert A., Ed. *Developmental Efforts in Individualized Learning*. Itasca, Ill.: F. E. Peacock Publishers, Inc., 1971.

[28] Anderson and Van Dyke, op. cit., p. 137.

POST TEST

1. (*Circle one.*) The unique child in the middle, the emerging adolescent differs from students in the high school in
   a. sexual maturity.
   b. mental maturity.
   c. social maturity.
   d. ambivalence about dependence and independence.
   e. exaggerated fears regarding lack of peer acceptance.
   f. all of these; or
   g. the first three of these.

2. List some (five) characteristics of the emergent middle school that help the in-between child.

   _____

   _____

   _____

   _____

   _____

3. The teacher in the middle school must be a hybrid professional. List some of the characteristics he must possess.

   _____

   _____

   _____

   _____

   _____

   _____

   _____

   _____

   _____

4. What are the grades commonly included in the middle school?

   _____

   _____

   _____

5. In planning a middle school, what are five important guidelines?

_____

_____

_____

_____

_____

6. Cite some (five) of the purposes of independent study, increased course electives, and student participation in course-planning in the middle school.

_____

_____

_____

7. State at least three ways in which the substitution of teaching teams for subject-matter departments contributes to the success of the middle school.

_____

_____

_____

8. Cite at least three advantages claimed for block-of-time scheduling in the middle school.

_____

_____

_____

9. Write a short definition or description of a comprehensive high school.

_____

_____

_____

_____

_____

10. Cite three things that have affected the comprehensive high school in the urban area.

_____

_____

_____

11. Explain in a short paragraph Conant's reference to the "social dynamite" smoldering in the schools in 1961.

_____

_____

_____

_____

_____

_____

_____

_____

_____

12. Match the two columns by placing a letter next to a number to link each curriculum title to an appropriate description.

Title	*Description*
1. advisory or combination	**a.** two or more sequences of courses
2. single	**b.** mini-courses as substitution for year-length courses
3. constant with variables	**c.** certain required courses in which students can cross grade lines and sequences
4. open	**d.** same courses for all
5. multiple	**e.** certain required courses for all, electives at specific grade level
	f. based on ability grouping

13. Describe the viewpoint of this module regarding the vocational-academic dichotomy in the comprehensive high school.

_____

_____

_____

_____

_____

_____

_____

_____

_____

_____

14. Cite three advantages of the track plan according to the educators who supported it.

_____

_____

_____

15. In a short paragraph, describe the position taken by the opponents of the track system.

_____

_____

_____

_____

_____

_____

_____

_____

_____

16. Does phasing appear to you to offer a solution to the grouping problem? Answer Yes or No. In one or two sentences substantiate your answer.

_____

_____

_____

Curriculum-Based Trends

Joseph F. Callahan

Jersey City State College

module 11

Structure of Discipline Movement / Discovery and Inquiry Method / Humanism
and the Humanities

RATIONALE

With relation to the curriculum of the schools, the majority of citizens of a community can be described as leaning in the direction of conservatism. Not only are they the products of their society and culture but also, in this regard, they are the products of their schooling. For twelve years of their youth they have been processed through the classrooms of the schools in their communities. They have been exposed to the ideas, the ideals, the mores, the values, the skills, and the accumulation of learning of each of their teachers and have become accustomed to the expectations of their communities concerning the meaning of success. Upon assuming their positions in the adult community, they have found that they have been more quickly assimilated if they reflected the attitudes and views that they had learned in school and that represented the majority views in most communities.

Bringing about change in the curriculum frequently necessitates some "violence" to cherished beliefs. Habits of thinking developed over many years are not changed, no matter how slightly, by concerned citizens without due cause and much consideration. Consequently, when innovative procedures are proposed, sincere and involved thinkers are prone to demand evidence that the new will be better than the old, that the shift from one to the other can be made in a painless and non-traumatic fashion, and that present benefits will not be lost in the change. The school as a last bastion of defense against disconcerting change in the larger social environment sometimes has been forced to function anachronistically until community forces and emotional and intellectual climates temper opposition to proposals and become supportive of change.

Prospective teachers are not immune to the drift toward perpetuation of the status quo. Although the liberalizing exposures which they experience on the college campus tend to move them in many respects away from the very conservative end of the change continuum, they frequently do not move them as far regarding the education process. Newly certificated teachers, in general, appear to have the same tendencies "to teach as they have been taught" as had their predecessors. Now that they have plunged into their area of specialization and have become enamored of accumulating learning in their major field, they reveal the same urges to transmit their enthusiasms and affections for their subject to others. Their youthful idealism, it is true, prompts them to believe that they will be more successful than their predecessors, and their proximity in age to their potential pupils tempts them to conclude that they will discover quickly the way to build the bridges necessary for communication. But, in general, the humanistic impulses which they experience appear to support efforts to improve the doing of what has been previously done rather than to focus their efforts on a change in the accepted system.

This module considers three innovations which have attracted and are currently attracting considerable attention: the structure of the discipline movement, the discovery and inquiry method movement, and the humanist and humanities movement. Citizens and teachers who have favored the subject-matter curriculum, in particular, have examined the thesis of the supporters of the discipline movement, because it appeared to offer the support to put the quietus on the alleged mushy thinkers favoring "Progressive Education," "The Imperative Needs of Youth," and student interest-oriented programs. The theory of the inquiry and discovery method of teaching needed little documentation for most good subject-matter teachers, because it already existed as an acceptable method.

What will happen to the humanities and the humane school movement still awaits resolution. The changes which have occurred in society, especially the re-treat from some of the values and mores previously venerated in the culture, have begun to precondition society toward changes in a direction supportive of the humanities. Much study, experimentation, and time will be required to keep this movement on the right track. Sentimental attitudes and wishful thinking about the humanities and humaneness may lead to many kinds of excesses. Especially vulnerable to misdirection in this regard are teachers in training. With only their own experiences as students to rely upon and with their natural youthful propensity for idealistic thinking, the temptation may well be great to promote or engage in soft, goalless programs which are destined to fail to yield the results expected.

Examine critically the component parts of these movements, as presented here, and read generously from the Suggested Reading list at the end of the module. Evaluate your mastery of the objectives by taking the test at the end of the module. It should serve as motivation to remember that the social climate which inhibited change in the past is still in the process of change itself. By the time you are in a position to engage yourself actively in the process, the climate may be ready—if you are.

Specific Behavioral Objectives

Upon completion of your study of this module, you should be able to perform all of the following objectives:

1. Give a brief description of the *structure of a discipline* theory.
2. Differentiate between the organization of a subject-centered curriculum and that of a discipline-centered curriculum.
3. Explain the value of the discipline approach for the learner.
4. Cite three of the five fundamental premises upon which the new programs, designed to replace out-of-date content, were based.
5. List four of the five areas of dissatisfaction which were offered by op-ponents of the discipline movement.
6. Explain the effect that "teacher-proofing" materials had on the ecological nature of the school and on the life of the discipline movement.
7. List at least ten of the changes of emphasis effected by the discipline move-ment during the last decade that probably will be retained wholly or with some modification in the future.
8. Describe learning by the discovery or inquiry method.
9. List five of the nine advantages for users of the inquiry or discovery method as claimed by its proponents.
10. Give three disadvantages of the use of the discovery and inquiry methods that have been pointed out by the critics.
11. Describe the probable role of the inquiry or discovery method in the class-rooms of the next decade.

12. State at least three specific reasons why the critics opposed the discipline movement as it affected the learner.
13. State the basic purpose of the humanities movement and explain how *interdisciplinarity* is fundamental to the movement.
14. Explain why it is claimed that the humanities cannot be taught in a linear fashion.
15. Explain how the humanities program is a catalyst to "unfreezing the schools."
16. List five of the ten common characteristics of today's school which the humane school will change when it becomes a reality.

MODULE TEXT

Structure of Discipline Movement

Beginning of the Movement. "The structure of the Discipline Movement in American education arose after World War II as part of an emphasis on competence, proficiency, power, and excellence stressed by political, military, and business leaders, and by scholars—particularly in the natural and technical sciences. A central notion in this theory was that teaching should stress the underlying concepts and processes characteristic of each field of scholarly inquiry, such as mathematics, language, physics, chemistry, biology, history."[1]

In the late 1950s it became common to evaluate schooling more in accordance with its contribution to national needs and national policies and less on its focus upon the individual and the total nurture of the person. For the teacher, the movement in this direction meant the de-emphasizing of his role as counselor, guide, and parent-surrogate and the focusing upon the specifically intellectual functions he performed in the pursuit of excellence.

It is now generally recognized that a conference of scientists and psychologists held at Woods Hole, Massachusetts, in 1959 gave impetus to the movement. It brought together scholars in primary fields of human knowledge and active teacher educators; it attempted to establish a common meeting ground between the two which would aid students in their quest for knowledge and understanding.

The decade that followed that conference was alive with curriculum alteration, modification of the teaching act, band wagon activity, and frantic publication of textbooks and materials. Teachers returned to college campuses for retooling, and workshops of all sorts, sponsored with financial support from federal sources and private philanthropic foundations, were conducted almost everywhere.

Not until the start of the 1970s did support for the movement begin to show any appreciable signs of abating. But by then it was becoming evident that the pendulum had reached its ultimate sweep and was about to start its journey in the other direction.

Description of the Movement. "Grasping the structure of a subject is understanding it in a way that permits many other things to be related to it meaningfully.

---

[1] Robert E. Mason, *Contemporary Educational Theory* (New York: David McKay, Co., Inc., 1972), p. 136.

To learn structure, in short, is to learn how things are related."[2] Jerome Bruner, a leader at the Woods Hole Conference, maintained that each discipline has a structure, an internal connectedness, a meaningfulness, which, if understood, would allow the student to draw implications and relationships from his study instead of just memorizing a body of factual subject knowledge that he might neither understand nor be able to use intelligently.

Traditionally, the subject-centered organization of the curriculum has been the basic plan in our nation's schools. Although many schools have introduced new and challenging organizations—the experience curriculum and the core curriculum —the majority of schools has continued to organize its curriculum on some variation of the subject-centered approach.

Advocates of the discipline-centered approach claimed that knowledge should play a different role in the curriculum from that which it formerly had played in the subject-centered curriculum. Subject matter should be presented in such a way, they believed, as to introduce students to the ways of life required by the fields of scholarship and to engage them in activities patterned after those of practicing scholars. Instead of stressing factual and descriptive content, emphasis should be placed upon basic concepts and conceptual relationships that scholars in the various fields use as intellectual tools. The result of this change would be an economy of effort in learning, a minimizing of the impact of the knowledge explosion, and an establishing of the generalizations, principles, and techniques which might be applied in learning throughout a lifetime. The learner would be led to discover the structure of the subject being studied, would be encouraged to use the method and style of inquiry peculiar to that discipline, and would be expected to simulate the role of the scholar in that discipline. The goal of the learner would be the integration of knowledge and a search for a wholeness in all that is studied to facilitate future learning.

The value of the discipline approach, its advocates maintain, would be that each new idea could be related to the family of ideas to which it belonged. Since ideas presented in isolation tend to vanish while ideas comprehended within the unity of the discipline tend to remain vivid and powerful within the understanding, the progress of the learner would be more substantial and more lasting.

Components of the Movement. A discipline is defined as an "organized branch of knowledge resulting from study, research, imagination, and contemplation." Each discipline has its own content, its own structure, and its own method of inquiry. The content refers to the data and factual information which are combined in a logical and natural way. The structure is the combination of concepts, principles, and generalizations, based upon the content and the interrelationship of these concepts and generalizations which facilitates the discovery and incorporation of additional facts. To have a grasp of the structure of an area of knowledge is to be able to relate other things to it. This method of the discipline refers to the disciplinary tools and procedures for discovering and ordering information—the style of inquiry.

Beliefs Supporting the Movement. An examination of the publications and activities of the various learned groups that prepared programs of study in their

[2] Jerome S. Bruner, *The Process of Education* (Cambridge, Mass.: Harvard University Press, 1960), p. 7.

disciplines to replace allegedly out-of-date programs in the curriculum of the public schools reveals a set of premises that each appears to have accepted as fundamental.

1. The cognitive style of the immature learner differs from the style of the mature scholar only in degree; fundamentally, the styles are identical; they are the same "in kind."
2. The intellectual pursuits of the scholar in any field can be made appropriate for learners at every level in that field because intellectual activity is everywhere the same.
3. The scholar on the forefront of knowledge discovery is concerned with the principal structural elements of his discipline. Consequently, the subject matter content for school boys and girls should also be determined through the structure of the discipline.
4. Since the scholar is the one who is most competent to determine the structure of his discipline, he should play a central role in devising the subject matter in his discipline at all levels of schooling—not the educationist, not the textbook publishers, not the layman or the teacher, but the master-scholar engaged in researching his discipline!
5. Since the scholar is engaged in the process of inquiry-discovery in order to develop new knowledge, the appropriate mode of learning for the school boys and girls should be that of inquiry-discovery.

Teams of scholars, teachers, psychologists, and curriculum specialists in collaboration created a number of curriculum projects based on these premises. In these projects, outmoded units were eliminated, inaccurate and misleading information was brought up to date, and new material, substituting search and discovery for memorization, was added. The preference of the learned scholar replaced student interest as a criterion for selecting curriculum material.

Reform of the Subject Curriculum. The artificial and largely arbitrary nature of much academic subject matter was the target of reform efforts. Teachers, reformers believed, tended to place excessive emphasis on manipulation and memory and to give inadequate attention to meaning and understanding. Only a few schools attempted to coordinate or articulate one course with another even in the same subject area. In addition, the revolutionary developments in science and technology during the first half of the century had outstripped the capacity of most teachers to keep pace with the adaptations needed. Relatively unimportant topics received considerable attention in classrooms daily, while newer, more useful, and more accurate topics were ignored. Some subject matter that could serve a beneficial function if taught earlier in the school life of a student was reserved for upper-level school years. The language and symbols used in classrooms were lacking in precision, which contributed to the difficulty in defining concepts, and the expository method of teaching cultivated a passive attitude toward knowledge. Little time in the regular day could be found for exploration and discovery or for the more time-consuming deductive processes associated with aggressive and active learning. In sum, it was the conviction of reformers that the schools "taught prosody in the name of poetry thus killing an interest in poetry . . . had taught grammar in the name of composition, destroying the possibility of a widespread ability to write good essays or even good expository prose . . . have taught computation in the name of mathematics . . . phonics in the name of reading, and have produced in the early grades word-callers, not readers . . . have taught place geography in the name of geography, almost killing this subject in the schools . . . have taught dates and battles in the name of history . . . have taught facts and principles in the name of science; but science is a mode of inquiry, and the scientists now say what (they) are doing is not only out of date, but it is not science."[3]

New findings, new departures, new theories, new programs, and new methods, which promised the changes that many had looked and hoped for, were accepted and introduced. Learned journals began featuring descriptions of new programs, and school systems began developing their own materials and techniques for implementing the innovations.

Specific Programs. Perhaps a look at a few examples of the new programs will provide an understanding of what the reformers were trying to do. Among the first of the new courses devised was a revision of the high school physics course under the auspices of the Physical Science Study Committee (PSSC). Under the leadership of Jarrold Zacharias, a prominent Massachusetts Institute of Technology physicist, the committee offered revised texts, adapted visual aids, problem books, and question and answer cards, designed to present the structure and quality of the most advanced thinking in physics. The approach, they urged, differed from the conventional in that there were no directions to follow and no predetermined "correct" results to get from laboratory tests. Instead of memorizing Newton's three laws of motion, for instance, they insisted that students should work as physicists and conduct laboratory experiments to discover for themselves the laws that Newton talked about. With the minimal directions they were supplied in their PSSC courses, students had to decide upon the efficacy of experimentation versus arriving at conclusions based upon concepts already at hand. Since the course deemphasized technological applications in favor of fundamental concepts of classical and modern physics, more atomic and nuclear physics could be presented in the high school course.

The concepts selected as foundational by the Biological Sciences Curriculum Study (BSCS) led that group to the development of three courses in high school biology. All had the same goals, conceptual themes, and objectives, and overlapped about 70 per cent in topics but differed somewhat in the treatment of the topics. The Blue version showed a prime concern for physiological-biological aspects and, consequently, had its emphasis at the molecular level. The Green version stressed ecology and focused on the community, and the Yellow version took the genetic approach emphasizing cellular aspects.

In revising the chemistry program, the Chemical Education Material Study (CHEM Study) group followed the idea that important concepts and generalizations of chemistry should be developed inductively. By use of the "open-ended" laboratory in which he was allowed to evaluate and interpret the results of his work, the student was expected to seek regularities in what he observed and then raise questions about his observations. The goals of the course specify that students

[3] Arthur W. Foshay, "Education and the Nature of a Discipline," in Walter B. Waetjen, ed., *New Dimensions of Learning,* (Washington, D.C.: Association for Supervision and Curriculum Development, National Education Association, 1962), pp. 5–6.

should be expected to (1) accumulate information through experimental observations; (2) organize information, observe regularities, evaluate, and interpret data; (3) appreciate the meaning of uncertainty in science and recognize why certainty is not possible; (4) demonstrate ability to use the simplest cycle of scientific activity—observe, find regularity, and find explanations; and (5) recognize that science could not advance if the overwhelming mass of available knowledge were not ordered with the aid of theories and laws.

In all the new mathematics programs, greater attention was given to basic structure and less attention to mere operational facility. Common among these programs were (1) replacement of those topics that were relatively unimportant with more useful content, such as probability theory and statistics; (2) some shifting of content to lower grades and earlier introduction of abstract concepts; (3) use of more precise language and symbols to refine definitions and facilitate concept formation; and (4) more emphasis upon the deductive process in teaching method, whereby students were expected to develop ingenuity by discovering mathematical relations on their own, working their way through carefully designed sequences of questions.

The University of Illinois Committee on School Mathematics (UICSM), for example, instead of supplying rules, organized materials in such a way that learners could work on solving simple problems, for which their prior experience would provide solutions. In approaching their work, students were expected not to apply a given or specific computing rule but to find the underlying properties that applied to all the computing rules. Familiarity with the properties and the student's experience in combining the properties, it was expected, would enable each student to design his own rules when necessary.

The Greater Cleveland Mathematics Project stressed the logic of mathematical thinking; the learning of mathematical concepts rather than mere skill in performance became most important. Reasoning, thinking, and understanding were made paramount, and routine performance, though important, assumed a subordinate role.

Reaction to New Programs. The years of activity involving reform produced some unexpected outcomes as the decade of the 1960s came to a close. The discipline doctrine, which had triggered the activity during the era of the cold war and space race, suddenly appeared to many students to have little relevance to a society torn by domestic and international conflict. In addition, even though the curriculum reforms in the sciences were supported by the federal government as a means of inducing more talented boys and girls to embark on careers in science and engineering, the proportion of high school students taking physics courses declined during the 1960s. Some of the new high school courses in the sciences, it turned out, were more abstract and difficult than the corresponding introductory college courses, and therefore scared off applicants. As experience was gained with the newly introduced courses, many educators, parents, and students began to raise questions concerning the wisdom of the new high compression curriculum packages. The consideration of the high school student as a miniature adult capable of the same kind of pursuit of knowledge as the scholar-specialist once again provoked question and debate.

Added to these bits of dissatisfaction, the disjointed fashion in which many programs were introduced into the curriculum generated resentment and opposi-

Table 11-1   Future Curriculum Trends*

FROM	TO
1. Local responsibility for curriculum development guided by high school teachers.	1. National responsibility for curriculum development guided by specialists working with high school teachers.
2. Major emphasis upon informational aspects of the discipline and minimal attention to the processes.	2. An emphasis upon the discipline "as a way of knowing," emphasizing the processes of the discipline as they relate to what is known.
3. A survey of many topics to acquaint students with the range of knowledge in a subject.	3. A few topics explored in depth and taught to the point of understanding.
4. Descriptive and applied subject matter.	4. Interpretive and theoretical subject matter.
5. Established knowledge with emphasis upon basic facts.	5. Knowledge in the mainstreams of modern thinking, with emphasis upon models and theories.
6. Rote learning and memorization.	6. Concept formation and systematic thinking.
7. Group learning, teacher directed, telling, and drill.	7. Individual learning, student-centered, guided discovery, and contemplation.
8. The opinion that learning has occurred if information can be repeated.	8. The opinion that learning has occurred if the pupil can use his knowledge in an explanatory or interpretive manner.
9. Subject matter chosen by teachers or textbook authors.	9. Subject matter chosen by research or professional specialists.
10. Personal-social needs of pupils as the criterion base for choosing course content.	10. Use of the conceptual schemes of the discipline for choosing course content.
11. Testing mostly on factual information with a "right" answer.	11. Testing mostly on the use of concepts to interpret observations or provide explanations.
12. Laboratory exercises to demonstrate, visualize, or verify known information.	12. Laboratory experiments to raise problems, test inquiry skills, and provide discovery opportunities.
13. Laboratory sessions to follow class discussion of topics and be largely divorced from classroom learning.	13. Laboratory work as an integral part of class work with pre- and post-laboratory discussion.
14. Learning capability depending almost entirely on student effort and teacher telling; a passive process.	14. Learning capability to depend upon organization of curriculum and ability of teacher to match a teaching style with stated goals; an active process.
15. Education focused upon the world as it is today.	15. Education for change and for the future.
16. Sequence of learning opportunities dependent upon teacher's arbitrary choice.	16. Sequence of learning opportunities dependent upon logical structure of the discipline.
17. Curriculum improvement through revision and refinement.	17. Curriculum improvement through reform and innovation.
18. Courses built of instructional units representing a logical organization of information.	18. Courses built around conceptual schemes in a coherent sequence, stressing logical unity of the discipline.
19. Instruction as information giving.	19. Instruction as information processing.
20. Courses written at a uniform level of conceptualization.	20. Courses written at increasingly higher levels of meaning, building upon previously learned concepts.

* Based on Paul DeHart Hurd, *New Directions in Teaching Secondary School Science* (Chicago: Rand McNally & Co., 1969), pp. 52–54. Cited in Weldon Beckner and Joe D. Cornett, eds., *The Secondary School Curriculum: Content and Structure* (Scranton, Pa.: Intext, Inc., 1972), pp. 239–240.

tion. For years, educators had been working toward the consideration of wholeness concerning the curriculum offerings in the school. Their thrust had been in the direction of scope and sequence, continuity and articulation, and grass roots participation in curriculum modification. In contrast to change in the curriculum by autocratic administrative fiat, the trend had been toward change only with the help, effort, and guidance of the teacher who would be called upon to implement the change. Earlier experiences had revealed that teachers who were knowledgeable about proposed modifications because they had participated in the process of deciding would be willing and able to work for interrelatedness of knowledge and would almost instinctively avoid segmentation, fragmentation, and compartmentalization.

Most of the new programs were offered in contradiction to these principles. They appeared to be presented as modules that could "merely be plugged in" to any curriculum because they had been "teacher-proofed." The packaged programs were supposedly so well engineered and so self-contained with specifications concerning content and methodology as to promise effective instruction despite the presence of mediocre teachers. Little effort was expended on the details of integrating the new programs into the school curriculum, and few innovators appeared concerned enough to plan for reconstruction of the total curriculum necessitated by the addition of new parts. Consequently, the focus on separate domains of knowledge aggravated the previous problem of fragmentation and gradually disrupted "the ecological nature of the school."

Trend of Curriculum Activity. It is likely that adjustments will be made periodically in the years to come through the revision of the major curriculum projects. Gradually, the favored position granted mathematics and the sciences will diminish, and the other disciplines will be provided a more prominent place in the curriculum. New alternative projects will be forthcoming and future modifications will be made to those already extant by evolutionary rather than revolutionary adjustment. The effort will be directed at retaining the gains that have been made but helping to fit them into a curriculum that will be more responsive to the needs and interests of students and that will use the special talents and insights of the teachers.

It is probable that future efforts in all disciplines will be made, on a gradual basis, to continue most of the changes of emphasis so dramatically introduced during the last decade. Table 11-1 shows how one authority expects the trends to go.

Discovery and Inquiry Method

Most of the new programs developed by scholar-educator teams for use in the elementary and secondary schools have placed stress upon helping the student to think systematically, critically, and creatively. Some, such as the mathematics programs, have stressed the student's discovery of generalizations so that the solution of future problems can be based upon sound reasoning by the student instead of upon the application of a memorized formula. Others, such as the BSCS program, involve students in activities that require using controls, determining cause and effect relationships, and using and interpreting quantitative data to help them develop competency in strategies used in solving scientific problems.

In these programs, the inquiry and discovery method is important. In addition to the accumulation of knowledge, other goals are sought, such as the cultivation of skill in the use of the scientific and scholarly processes and the development of particular attitudes. Through learning by discovery, it is postulated, the pupil will behave as a scholar and will learn, as a scholar, to suspend judgment until all data is in, to cope with new situations caused by the addition of new data, and to synthesize new discoveries into the body of knowledge learned previously.

Revival of Interest in Method. Teaching by discovery and inquiry was not a new process invented to accompany the proposals for new curriculum additions. It had been an essential part of Dewey's theories on learning, adopted by many good teachers during the progressive era. What was new was the resurgence of interest in it, approximating a band wagon phenomenon, following the publication of Jerome Bruner's *The Process of Education* in 1960.

Of significance in this resurgence movement was the emphasis placed upon helping the student develop his ability to function as a scholar. Although reformers recognized the need for an essential academic background, they focused on the rational powers of the student, the heuristic methods of teaching, the opportunity to practice critical thinking, and the transfer of knowledge, attitudes, and procedures from one content to another.

Particularly offensive to new program planners were educational practices that treated the student's mind as a storehouse to be filled with information, or that featured "thoughtless ingestion and repetition of facts." They rejected the old assumption that if students could learn and recall in verbal form all of the knowledge prescribed, then all good things in life would follow. In their opinion, the assign, discuss, and test method did not suffice at all.

Instead, they placed their emphasis on learning how to learn, on developing the arts and skills by means of which the student could teach himself, and on when and how to question, and where to find the answers. In lieu of passive, docile learning and dependence upon teacher and textbook, they supported an active, doing process, which sought interpretation rather than replication, and which used the textbook and the teacher as guides, subject always to challenge.[4] The right answer to questions was not to be the objective in classrooms but, rather, the probable answer or the most defensible answer among the many examined critically on the way toward the solution of a problem.

Some classrooms were turned into learning laboratories where teachers served as discussion leaders, inquiry advisors, or devil's advocates. Questions for which no one had an answer became a matter for inquiry rather than the next unit in the text. Bruner referred to this kind of teaching as the "hypothetical mode" (in contrast to the "expository mode") in which the student was not the "bench-bound listener" but an active participant, providing feedback with his verbal and nonverbal behavior upon which the teacher based his own performance.

Advantages of Discovery and Inquiry Method. Proponents of these investigative methods list many philosophical and psychological advantages resulting from their use.[5] They claim that these methods (1) increase intellectual potency; (2)

---

[4] Weldon Beckner and Joe D. Cornett, *The Secondary School Curriculum: Content and Structure* (Scranton, Pa.: Intext, Inc., 1972), p. 29.

[5] Robert B. Sund and Leslie W. Trowbridge, *Student-centered Teaching in the Secondary School* (Columbus, Ohio: Charles E. Merrill Publishers, 1974), p. 54.

cause a shift from extrinsic to intrinsic motivation; (3) help students to learn how to learn in investigative ways; (4) increase memory retention; (5) make instruction student-centered thereby contributing better to a person's self-concept; (6) increase expectancy levels; (7) develop multiple, not just academic talents; (8) avoid learning only on the verbal level; and (9) allow more needed time for students to assimilate and accommodate information.

The process involved in this kind of learning is the real content of the teaching. Through the use of guided opportunities to think and act as a scholar, the student is expected to learn as a scholar and use his rational capacities. He is expected to learn the techniques of investigating by discovering how to organize and carry out investigations, and then by actually investigating. By experiencing the thrill of discovering a solution, he is expected to enjoy the intrinsic satisfaction of learning. He remembers better what he learns because having reasoned to his conclusions and having put the parts together himself, he develops a much greater understanding of what has been learned.

The slower pace required for discovery teaching forces teachers to abandon the compulsion to "cover" the text in order to provide time for focus upon insights into concepts and principles. It also imposes a need for more teacher silence, for less lecture, and for the providing of guidance only when needed.

Criticism of Discovery Teaching. Critics of the discovery and inquiry methods of teaching point out a number of disadvantages to the use of these approaches:

1. They are time-consuming and inefficient. Students who are exposed only to this way of learning may not be able to learn enough in their years of schooling to qualify them for their next career step, such as college admission. Although what is learned may be more lasting, the process promotes and tolerates such fitful efforts that the accumulation of knowledge may be meager. Too much time may be spent in rediscovering the wheel, while the heritage of the culture is bypassed in favor of the creative process.
2. The teacher is placed in an ambiguous position. He must pretend ignorance of the solution sought, claim knowledge but refuse to divulge his answer, or select as topics to teach only those topics about which he has little knowledge. In class discussions he must guard more zealously against monopolization by the more insightful students to the detriment of the slower students and he must devote considerable planning time in contriving compatible buzz groups in which each student will find the time and climate for verbal inquiry.
3. The methods place great responsibility upon the teacher for discharging his duties conscientiously and great weight upon his judgment in guiding the learner. If a student follows the wrong route, then the teacher is faced with the problem of insuring unlearning. The latitude possible when using these methods is broad enough to permit the poor teacher to absolve himself of a sense of failure since instruction in the traditional sense is unnecessary.

Future Use. Learning by discovery has been an admirable tool in the repertoire of techniques used by effective teachers throughout history. For certain purposes and under certain conditions, it has always been recognized as having a defensible rationale and undoubted advantages. Learning by discovery has constituted the main method used with the curriculum projects that have stressed active experimentation and that have made deliberate attempts to develop in students the same sort of "investigatory set" found in the scholar who works on the frontier of knowledge. The designers of these new programs have recommended confronting the student with a problematical situation and allowing him to draw upon his own research skill and his own intuitive judgment in seeking a solution.

Since the emerging emphasis in secondary education appears to still favor active learning, the trend will probably continue to support the inquiry and discovery method. Instead of constituting the sole method utilized in the development of inquiring minds and in mastery of the scholarly disciplines, inquiry and discovery will assume an important position in the hierarchy of methods so that the teacher may be able to select that which he feels most appropriate for his purpose, whether it is the cultivation of intellectual skills or of the intuitive sense.

Humanism and the Humanities

Resistance to Disciplines. The peaking of the structure of the discipline movement appears to have occurred in the early 1970s. With the start of that new decade, as program after program evaluated the results of several years of trial, opposition spokesmen began to express their misgivings concerning schools and the curriculum. Some of these spokesmen based their disenchantment upon the frantic and almost exclusive support given to the cultivation of future scientists and mathematicians, which appeared to have absorbed the attention of the schools. The fact that the social sciences, literature, and the arts were not likewise receiving attention and support planted the fear that important facets of student development would consequently be neglected. Since the thrust of the disciplinarians had been toward knowledge and the disciplines, this rising opposition group appeared to stress the learner in the learning process.

Some educators voiced disappointment with the divisions of knowledge and the compartmentalization of the disciplines approach. They now proclaimed the need to seek the adoption of a unified theory of learning which would facilitate the transfer of learning from one narrow field to the other. The transfer that was brightly envisioned by Bruner for the disciplines and that educators had been led to expect had apparently failed to survive the transplantation from university campus to the public school system. Instead of excited, self-motivated learning by all students, teachers were confronted, especially in the case of the so-called average student, with learners who found that the new disciplinary programs were either too abstract to master or simply too remote and unrelated to capture their interest.

Broadening the Focus. The big educational movement that these spokesmen appear to be heralding has been termed the *humanistic movement* because of its concern for the student as an individual person capable of creative thought and action. Today more educators in more journals are urging schools to a concern for "man as man" and to action upon the student's "total educational diet" than at any time since before World War II. In this vein too, convention speakers and popular journalists are addressing themselves to the concerns of the total individual rather than so exclusively to the concerns of the future scholar, lawyer, physician, or merchant.

The structure of the entire instructional program and the interrelationships of its parts have been suggested as the hub for this new movement, in contrast to the structure of each specific discipline. The effort will be to relate what is learned in school to the world of human affairs: to strive for understanding of the relevance of each of the disciplines to the student fulfilling his role as worker, as citizen, and as individual searching for fulfillment.

Interdisciplinary movements are being encouraged as replacements for single-focus study on separate subjects. As one author puts it, "In the social sciences, the economist is preoccupied with the concept of scarcity, the political scientist with the concept of power and authority, the anthropologist with the motion of culture, and the sociologist with social functions and social systems. Man's social life, however, as it is actually lived is far more complex than the limited image of it reflected in the concepts and generalizations of any one of the social disciplines. Only by combining the various points of view of the various disciplines can anything approaching a complete anticipation of future occurrences be achieved."[6] In his estimation, the time has arrived when natural science scholars, social science scholars, mathematics, and humanities scholars should begin to search as a group for new structures for teaching. The new structures resulting from their team work must respect the integrity of the individual fields but, at the same time, help these fields find their place in a pattern of studies that provides a substantial measure of coherence and relatedness to the program as a whole. As a group, these subjects will promote the study of man as being other than a biological product and different from a social or sociological entity. They will examine the activities of man to provoke the discovery of relatedness among his activities. They will involve considerable attention to values, ethics, and morals not only as they have been and are but also as they should be.

Relevance and Values. The increased concern for human values, for human interests, and for the individual student represents a change of emphasis in thinking for the various groups that influence the direction of curriculum development. The effect of the flash fire, social revolution, which took place in the summer of 1969 and was brought on by the national draft, the conditions in the ghetto, the threat of the dope epidemic, and the impact of rapid technological development, among other things, has forced these groups to reexamine the programs of the schools which produced the citizens involved either as victims, perpetrators, or participants in the social unrest.

Scope of New Programs. Some high schools have already introduced humanities programs on a limited scale. Primarily designed for seniors or upper-level students, these standard programs consist mostly of single course offerings that focus upon teaching more about literature and the arts. The trend, however, appears to be in the direction of a further broadening of the scope of such standard humanities courses. To be effective, it is believed, these courses will have to become integrated streams that run through all the years of the secondary school and encompass more than the infusion of art, music, and philosophy into the literature

[6] Arno A. Bellack, "What Knowledge Is of Most Worth?" in William M. Alexander, ed. *The Changing Secondary School Curriculum* (New York: Holt, Rinehart & Winston, Inc., 1967), p. 221.

program. It is envisioned that aspects of the behavioral sciences, such as psychology, social anthropology, economics, and archaeology will also gradually be included; that multigrading will be welcomed; and that emphasis will be on problem solving rather than on fact accumulating.

Considerable attention also must be given in each course to the nature of human involvement with the human world, in contrast to the detached and objective treatment of evidence which was stressed by the disciplines. The emphasis will be upon the interrelatedness of knowledge and the continuity and repetitive quality of the thoughts, creations, and actions of predecessors which affect and are related in the work of contemporaries.

The fact that the humanities cannot be taught in a linear fashion, as can mathematics, will force program planners into a broad focus. The goal will be not to merely know about but to incorporate into daily life the concepts focused upon. Care will have to be exercised to keep the focus on mankind and on the individual's purpose in becoming educated, for, as in the past, this innovation could follow the pattern set by all of its predecessors if the purpose is ignored. Once structure is introduced and sequencing of streams occurs, there is always a tendency to permit the deadly hand of bureaucracy to crush lively programs. In the past, to sequence courses efficiently, course guides have been prepared and then used for freezing the content instead of as resources to open and broaden inquiry. Also, tests have been devised to measure progress and readiness for the next step. Naturally, in short order, studying to pass the test and attempting to amass cognitive knowledge have become paramount concerns for students. The goals of enriching their personal lives, of transmitting the most noble aspects of the race, and of alleviating some of their adolescent fears concerning the emergence of the "brave new world" have become almost incidental.

Program Design. The promise of the trend toward the humanities lies in its potential for making education a relevant happening in the lives of youth. Wilhelms feels that "it may well be the most significant development of our times in secondary education,"[7] which educators should be backing with all their strength. He feels that just as there is a valid reason "to have a special program, the social studies, to cultivate the civic person; so it is also valid to create a special program to cultivate the inner private person." Students need "free time and sympathetic guidance to look at life, to look at themselves, to grasp the human condition, and slowly to decide how they mean to spend themselves and by what values they choose to govern their years upon this earth."[8]

The function of this course should not be for students to become acquainted with certain bodies of content but that "they should use these great treasure houses of our culture to find what speaks to them and helps them to grow in their innermost selves."[9] With a balanced team of resource people, cooperating in a carefully cultivated environment, it will be possible, using new teaching techniques that stress team learning, block scheduling, student-teacher planning and post-holing, to achieve the cynergistic goals envisioned.

[7] Fred T. Wilhelms, "Multiple Ways to a More Humane School," *The Bulletin of the National Association of Secondary School Principals* **56**:1–8 (Feb. 1972).

[8] Ibid, p. 7.

[9] Ibid.

In this type of humanities program, the components that will require the most attention to effect the appropriate blend are[10]

1. The creation of a climate of questioning, creativity, emotional involvement, and individuality which must characterize the teaching-learning act.
2. The skillful avoidance of accenting too heavily any purely literary works lest fact accumulation and verbalization assume larger roles than planned.
3. The maintenance of flexibility in use of methods and materials of instruction.
4. The recognition and insistence that affective learning is just as important as cognitive learning.
5. The utilization of team teaching to secure the talents and rich backgrounds and services of a variety of members of the staff so that burdens may be avoided for any particular individuals.
6. The investigation of the fundamentals of logic and philosophy and aesthetics and, in some cases, religion as a link with our cultural heritage.
7. The emphasis upon cultivating habits of reading serious selections as well as recreational genres as a lifelong practice.
8. The refinement of tastes for the fine arts—music, the theatre, literature, architecture, the dance as an art form. Familiarity with some of the great names, structures, paintings, and other art works will follow naturally.
9. The exposure to the cultural development of the Eastern world as well as of the Western world, including their philosophies and religions.

Course Organization. The most common way in which new humanities programs are being organized appears to be by topic or theme such as "The Individual and Society," "Freedom and Authority," or "God and Man." Some teachers attempt to correlate their teaching efforts with teachers in other subjects to achieve the integration of knowledge. Others interchange classes for certain units, or invite art, music, or religion specialists to lecture on particular phases of their study. In some schools in which programs have been established to explore knowledge from a chronological base, guests of all sorts are utilized for particular periods of history or for examination of some cultural epochs. But whatever pattern of organization evolves in a school, the major goal of the developing humanities programs appears to be the growth of the individual student and his self-actualization, rather than the mastery of knowledge. Openness to experiences, imagination, and fantasy are encouraged. Mass testing is decreased; so are other teaching situations which encourage competitive endeavors in a climate of anxiety. The primary emphasis appears to be on the person as learner and not on the learning program. Teachers strive to build positive relationships between themselves and their students, to minimize the use of ability groups, and to encourage pupil participation.

So far, there appears to be no over-all pattern to the emerging humanities programs and courses. They seem to grow out of interests and talents of teachers and students and the resources of the community. Many of them appear to accommodate as much activity outside of the traditional classroom—inside the school, out in the community, on field trips—as they do in it. Many also appear to be rendering catalytic services in the process of unfreezing schools and promoting a

[10] Beckner and Cornett, op. cit., p. 308.

more human atmosphere, in which the substitution of discussion of issues vital to man has replaced the lecture, and in which the examination and probing of values and the resulting growth in self-discovery appear to be flourishing. The settling in of a human relationship between students and teacher has been the desired consequence.

Humanity. Even in schools in which the "humanities as a discrete body of knowledge" are not receiving any emphasis, a concern for, a respect of, and a search for the human being in each child is being exhibited. Classrooms have changed in appearance, dramatically in some schools and only subtly in others. In many schools, there appears to be a change of climate which, it is hoped, will affect the teaching and the learning acts significantly.

The ecology of the schools of previous eras permitted the use of many practices that today are considered dehumanizing. When industry began to deal with masses of machines and products, large numbers of students presented themselves to be taught, and the school "invented" group-based education. In this kind of instructional milieu, the teacher, the knower, played an important role. He was the active planner and doer, the dispenser of knowledge, and the controller of rewards and punishments. He tested and graded, measured his students against the norms for the grade or the normal curve of ability, and endorsed or accelerated or inhibited the progression of each learner through the various levels of learning. In this type of environment, competition and comparison were encouraged; pressure and failure were applied as required; corporal punishment was acceptable as a motivational or disciplinary device; overcrowding, shallow pupil-teacher relationships, and easy anonymity were looked upon as necessary and acceptable parts of the process in many systems.

Also, curriculum tracking and the caste system it nurtured were praised as enlightened administration or excused as necessary evils. However, the inflexible and nonvariable time schedule that caused many of the problems remained unchanged.

The single text approach, with the conformity it encouraged, the frustration it created, and the boredom it engendered, was almost universally the acceptable mode.

Admission to college was looked upon in many districts as the most legitimate and most acceptable postgraduate option.

Conditions Today. The climate in most schools today is not conducive to a perpetuation of these dehumanizing practices, in the same fashion or to the same degree as was true in the past. Although overcrowding and shallow teacher-pupil relationships, for example, may still occur, they are now looked upon as defects to be eliminated, rather than as necessary components of the schooling process.

The trend in this direction appears to favor the following:

1. Expending of great effort to improve communications between the students and the faculty. All teachers are encouraged to engage in group interaction and to seek and listen to student feedback so that course work can be modified.
2. Development of an interest by the teachers in the students as persons. Only by becoming sensitive to the changing moods and pace of students

and by cultivating the ability to respond flexibly can the teacher truly begin to interrelate with the student. Only in this manner can he begin to teach to the individual student level instead of to the grade textbook level.

3. A change from domination of action by an initiating adult to a motivation of action by a catalyst for and guide of the action of students. The humanistic teacher evidences concern and interest not only in what the student does while in the classroom and in the school but while out of school as well. His concern leads him to help each student become more sensitive to the needs and wishes of others.

4. The offering of more options to students, more courses and different schedules, in place of uniform programs for all.

5. Concern for the appropriateness of the program selected by each student, for his potential for meeting with success, and for his need for adapted material to insure success.

6. Insistence that each student be known as a total human being who has the opportunity to interact on an intimate daily basis with some member of the faculty and with his peers.

7. Creation of an environment in which each teacher may utilize his talents and interests. Programs stressing this facet have made great strides in attending to individual differences, and feature differentiated staffing or mini-courses.

8. Introduction of continuous progress provisions in which each student sets a pace that is comfortable for him.

9. Use of noncompetitive systems of reporting pupil progress in which students are graded and moved forward on the basis of their achievements and performances. Comparisons with class norm are no longer used for promotion.

10. Stress upon the element of success and intrinsic satisfaction with learning, as contrasted with heavy use of the fear element and threat of failure. When no student is taxed beyond his capacity to perform and when no results are demanded before the student is capable of producing, a climate of warmth and affection can prevail and will elicit best efforts.

A Final Comment. The task of the new humanities programs has been set by the leaders of the movement: help students to understand themselves so that they will be able to understand their fellow man and be able to live intelligently and happily in a world molded by scientific and technological advances.

The goal of a humane environment in the school is the cultivation of openness of inquiry, where the needs and interests and problems of students are considered and where the differences among individuals are respected. In a climate of this sort the authoritarian mandates of upper level administrators assume a less important role, while rigid schedules, offering minimal options, controlled by unyielding time allotments yield to sensitive in-put.

Teachers in the new programs will be expected to approach their classrooms with zest, to listen well, and to help students interact. As they improve their artistry, it is hoped that teachers will beget in their students a kindred enthusiasm for their fellow man, a thirst for the fullness of life, and a respect for freedom of the mind.

SUGGESTED READING

Beckner, Weldon, and Joe D. Cornett. *The Secondary School Curriculum: Content and Structure*. Scranton, Pa.: Intext Educational Publishers, 1972.

Bruner, J. S. *The Process of Education*. Cambridge, Mass.: Harvard University Press, 1960.

DeCarlo, Julia E., and Constant A. Madon, Eds. *Innovations in Education for the Seventies*. New York: Behavioral Publications, 1973.

Goodlad, John I. *School, Curriculum, and the Individual*. Waltham, Mass.: Ginn/ Blaisdell, 1966.

Heath, Robert W., Ed. *New Curricula*. New York: Harper & Row, Publishers, 1964.

Hillson, Maurie, and Ronald T. Hyman, Eds. *Change and Innovation*. New York: Holt, Rinehart & Winston, Inc., 1972.

Mason, Robert E. *Contemporary Educational Theory*. New York: David McKay Co., Inc., 1972.

Neagley, Ross L., and N. Dean Evans. *Handbook for Effective Curriculum Development*. Englewood Cliffs, N.J.: Prentice-Hall, Inc., 1967.

Saucier, Weems A., Robert L. Wendel, and Richard J. Mueller, Eds. *Toward Humanistic Teaching in High School*. Lexington, Mass.: D. C. Heath & Company, 1975.

Tanner, Daniel. *Secondary Education: Perspectives and Prospects*. New York: Macmillan Publishing Co., Inc., 1972.

Van Til, William, Ed. *Curriculum: Quest for Relevance*. Boston: Houghton Mifflin Company, 1974.

POST TEST

Select the best response to each of the following statements.

1. The structure of a discipline is
   a. a combination of concepts, principles and generalizations about that particular area of knowledge.
   b. the interrelationship of concepts and generalizations to facilitate the discovery and incorporation of additional fact.
   c. the internal connectedness of knowledge in a particular area.
   d. a meaningfulness in an area of knowledge which allows a student to draw implications and relationships from his study.
   e. *b* and *c*.
   f. *a, b, d*.
   g. all of these.

2. The structure of the discipline movement was motivated more by consideration of the needs of the individual student than by the concerns of the nation regarding its competitive position. *True* or *False?*

3. In the discipline movement, students were expected to behave as scholars
   a. to improve the status of scholars already established in the field.
   b. to facilitate the retention of knowledge which is gained within the unity of a discipline.
   c. to help make study in school a more relevant activity.
   d. to achieve needed economies in use of materials, equipment and personnel.
   e. *b* and *c.*
   f. all of these.

4. As compared to the subject-centered curriculum, the discipline-centered curriculum
   a. was designed and arranged by specialists in the various fields working with specialists in education.
   b. featured some new courses but did not change much that had previously been taught.
   c. forced all teachers to design for themselves new approaches to their subject.
   d. was supported mainly by funds from private foundations.
   e. was not hurt by the prepackaging of materials.

5. Two premises upon which new programs in the discipline curriculum were based are that
   a. intellectual pursuits of scholars in a field can be adapted and made appropriate for learners at every level.
   b. scholars in all fields are very much concerned with the way the young learn their discipline.
   c. since the scholar often engages in writing about his discipline, courses in composition need increased importance.
   d. cognitive style of immature learners does not differ from the style of mature learners.

6. "Teacher-proofing" materials consisted of
   a. making each teacher supply the answers to the problems at the end of each chapter.
   b. making each teacher prove the accuracy of the answers supplied by the publisher before teaching the problems in class.
   c. supplying the programs with such intensive and extensive instructions that teachers' mistakes in implementing would be almost eliminated.
   d. insuring input from each teacher involved to prevent teachers' failure to implement.

7. As a consequence of "teacher-proofing"
   a. teachers unable to supply the answers were forced to withdraw from teaching the program.
   b. resentment grew among the teachers because of the lack of opportunity for input to the program.
   c. the mediocre teacher demanded an increase in salary and in status.
   d. districts began to rely more heavily upon professional associations to help teachers supply proof.

8. Five curriculum changes which were effected by the discipline movement are
   a. emphasis upon mastery of skills and processes.
   b. emphasis upon accumulation of information.

c. study in depth of fewer subjects.
d. study in breadth of a number of subjects.
e. increased attention to descriptive subject matter.
f. increased attention to interpretive and theoretical subject matter.
g. guided discovery learning.
h. teacher-directed informing.
i. subject matter selection and textbook writing by education specialists.
j. selection of topics to focus upon made by research scholars.

9. Four emphases of learning by the inquiry and discovery method are
   a. learning how to learn.
   b. student self-teaching by use of questioning skills.
   c. a passive, absorbing process.
   d. interpretation of information rather than replication of facts.
   e. use of teachers as guides, always subject to challenge.

10. Four facets of the discovery and inquiry method are that it
    a. emphasizes intrinsic motivation.
    b. stresses an increase in memory retention.
    c. features student-centered understanding.
    d. tends to minimize group instruction.
    e. stresses an increase of attention to social adjustment.
    f. features more time for students to assimilate and accommodate information.

11. Disadvantages of the discovery method are that it is
    a. time-consuming and inefficient.
    b. students may not learn enough in school to qualify for admission to college.
    c. the ambiguous teacher role regarding divulging of answers is too difficult for most teachers to maintain.
    d. monopolization of discussion time by insightful students is possible.
    e. learning in this fashion is not long lasting.

12. Support for the new humanities programs appears to have resulted because
    a. federal funds were found to support research efforts in this direction.
    b. exclusive attention was being paid to future scientists and mathematicians.
    c. important facets of student personality development were being neglected by minimal exposure to the arts.
    d. compartmentalization and division of knowledge were resulting.
    e. the average student was finding the new subjects too abstract or irrelevant.

13. Write a short paragraph on the catalytic service expected of the new humanities.

_____

_____

_____

_____

_____

_____

14. According to Hurd's predictions, future trends will stress
   a. national responsibility for curriculum development, guided by specialists working with high school teachers
   b. major emphasis upon informational aspects of the disciplines and minimal attention to the processes.
   c. concept formation and systematic thinking.
   d. the personal-social needs of students as the criterion base for choosing course content.
   e. testing on factual information and for "right" answers.
   f. laboratory exercises to demonstrate or verify known information.
   g. education for change and the future.

15. Write a short paragraph on the effect of the urban social upheavals of the summer of 1969.

_____

_____

_____

_____

_____

_____

_____

_____

_____

16. List at least five drawbacks affecting many traditional humanities programs.

_____

_____

_____

_____

_____

_____

17. Three facts about future humanities programs are that
   a. the humanities cannot be taught in linear fashion as can mathematics.
   b. the goal will be to incorporate into daily life the concepts focused upon.
   c. to know about the humanities will suffice for promotion or credit.
   d. sequencing of streams and structuring of courses will be based upon inter-disciplinary concepts.
   e. the humanities, because they are so "arty," will make the curriculum even less relevant than it is at present.
   f. affective learning will be just as important as cognitive learning.

18. Select four true statements which complete the sentence: When the schools began to follow the "factory model,"

    a. group-based instruction became the accepted mode.

    b. the teacher assumed the position of foreman to control rewards and punishments for students.

    c. competition and comparison were resisted in almost all schools.

    d. pressure to achieve and failing students for the year were frowned upon as motivational devices.

    e. corporal punishment was acceptable as a disciplinary technique.

    f. shallow pupil-teacher relationships were discouraged.

    g. tracking and the caste system it nurtured were looked upon as serious weaknesses.

19. Cite seven practices that are moving contemporary schools in the humanistic direction.

_____

_____

_____

_____

_____

_____

_____

Trends in Education for Democratic Living

Martin G. Decker

Middletown, Conn.

module 12

Extreme Instructional Viewpoints / Moderate Instructional Systems

RATIONALE

One of the consistent themes in the history of American public education has been to prepare individuals to function well when they become adults in our democratic society. Educators are expected to provide an education that trains young people to function in a democratic society and are expected to create a school environment that is democratic. Both tasks must be accomplished in such a way that students, their parents, and the society at large are convinced that the school is doing a good job.

During the past ten to fifteen years, the public schools have been more and more criticized, and public school personnel have been asked to be accountable for both the content of what they teach and the way in which they teach. There is widespread criticism which indicates that children are not learning the things which are important for our society.

The broad changes that have occurred in our society and that are evident in the treatment of Black and Spanish-speaking minority groups, American Indians, the poor, and women have made it necessary for the schools to reassess their goals and activities and to accept participation from groups and individuals who had not been given an opportunity to participate previously. Those who make daily decisions about what should be done in the schools find that they have to meet successfully the needs of groups who have had little power in the past. In many cases, the needs expressed are in conflict with one another and often at odds with the ideals and goals of the schools. Therefore, an effective teacher must be aware of the ideals that are held by various groups of people and of the criticisms about the quality of education. It is important that the teacher understand the sources of criticism about education and the way in which this criticism affects the teacher's activities in the school.

Specific Behavioral Objectives

Upon completion of your study of this module, you should be able to do the following:

1. Define "education for democratic living" by using (a) various concepts of of education to define social goals; (b) the behavior of pupils in school to describe goals; and (c) the behavior of teachers in school to describe goals.
2. Describe three basic reasons to support the position that knowledge is the basis for education for democratic living.
3. Describe three basic reasons to support the position that *affective and social education* are necessary for education for democratic living.
4. Describe at least one teaching procedure which has been used to teach (a) knowledge for democratic living; (b) affective development for democratic living; and (c) interpersonal relations for democratic living.
5. Give three reasons why the schools have been slow to adopt the ideas and methods proposed by critics who seek change.

6. Describe a system and its parts which can be used to analyze the purpose and effectiveness of various systems of teaching.
7. Use a system to analyze the purpose and effectiveness of particular systems of teaching and to defend a choice of at least two systems of teaching which seem best suited to a teacher.

MODULE TEXT

Throughout its history, American public education has been oriented toward serving the needs of its society. Since the society defines itself as democratic and education has been seen as preparation for living in that society, school administrators and teachers have always insisted that they have been educating people to live in a democratic society. Although educators have differed in the ways in which they have taught and in what they have taught, there have been broadly consistent patterns within the public schools. One of the predominant outlooks has been that education should prepare a child so that as an adult he will not differ much from any other adult in his society.[1] However much such a definition may sound narrow and undemocratic, it seems very likely that any teacher or administrator who strays too far from it will find himself unemployed.

It is important to remember that the schools have changed little as a result of various reform movements during the past seventy years,[2] and that they have performed in ways which have satisfied most parents of the children they have educated.[3] Theodore Sizer supports this observation by pointing out that if parents and the public had been truly dissatisfied, the schools would have changed in response.[4]

Schools are places where change occurs in ways that support changes occurring in the rest of society. So, instead of creating change, schools generally respond to changes in society after the changes have been made. One problem for schools today is that society is changing so rapidly. Much of the time, changes are not understood well enough so that the schools can react quickly with programs and methods that can be proved effective before more changes occur. Although the schools must respond to changes in society, there is likely to be a lag in their ability to develop curricula and methods adapted to the changes. Policy makers for the schools find it necessary to react cautiously and to move slowly from that which has been effective to new and untested programs. Sizer also points out, as an additional complicating factor, that most of the critics or reformers have come neither from the schools nor from the general public. Instead they have sprung from university settings or have been outsiders to the public school setting.[5] The society and the schools consequently have not always reacted to these critics with

---

[1] Anna Freud, *Psychoanalysis for Parents and Teachers* (Boston: Beacon Press, 1960), p. 45.

[2] Charles Silberman, *Crisis in the Classroom* (New York: Random House, Inc., 1970), pp. 158–159.

[3] Theodore Sizer, *Places of Learning, Places for Joy* (Cambridge, Mass.: Harvard University Press, 1973), p. 1.

[4] Ibid, p. 2.

[5] Ibid.

direct action since the critics have been seen as "far out" and not representative of most people.

Charles Silberman has described four of the conditions which make teaching and learning in school unique.[6]

(1) Education always takes place in groups. Children gather in large numbers in the schools, and teaching is almost invariably done in groups of 15 to 40 students. (2) Students are required to go to school by law and by social pressure. They have no choice. (3) Schooling requires large amounts of time for both the teacher and the student—six or more hours a day, five days a week, thirty-five weeks a year over ten or more years. (4) Schooling almost invariably requires that teachers and other adults make evaluations of the pupil's work and progress.

These four conditions are apparently consistent from society to society, and any changes which occur in the schools must be made in such a way that they can be carried out under these conditions. It is very unlikely that the suggestions of reformers will be accepted by the schools unless they can fit into the framework created by these conditions. As a consequence, Sizer indicates that the substance and process of education has changed very little over the past century.[7]

Extreme Instructional Viewpoints

Needs for Increased Verbal Comprehension and Fluency. As our society has changed from a rural-agricultural society to an urban-technological society during the past 100 years, the needs for people to be verbally sophisticated have increased greatly. For many critics of the school scene, this is the critical issue in preparing children for life in a democratic society. It has been the subject of discussion and the cause of much national concern in the mass media. Vance Packard in the *Reader's Digest,* writes of the "shame" of the schools, because people do not have the reading skills needed for today's living.[8] The need for good reading and language skills is rising all the time, and good skills are a necessity for any person who wishes to succeed. The level of skill for all people, it appears, must now be as high as that which was expected for only a few highly trained people a half-century ago.

Today people must do much more reading, and read at higher levels of difficulty in daily life. Every person must fill out a much greater number of forms to get a job, when on the job, when filing income taxes, and so forth. The estimate of the reading level required for interpreting income tax forms is grade sixteen—the level expected of a college graduate! Just to move around and to protect himself in an urban setting an individual must be more fluent in language use than ever before. He needs to be able to read contracts, loan applications, and the like, and he must engage in much more oral communication in the process of living. Each individual must verbally interact with more people more of the time. In the past, these higher levels of language fluency were thought to be necessary for only

[6] Silberman, op. cit., pp. 121–22.
[7] Sizer, op. cit., p. 31.
[8] Vance Packard, "Are We Becoming a Nation of Illiterates?" *Reader's Digest* **104**:81–85 (April 1974).

the elite of society. Today, however, the poor and minority groups need verbal skills as much, perhaps more than others since they end up filling in more forms and dealing with more people in crisis situations that more affluent people can avoid.

ACCUMULATION OF NEW KNOWLEDGE. The rate at which new knowledge is accumulating is staggering. Since 1940, it has at least doubled every ten years, and estimates are that it now has begun to double every five years. To enter adult life now, a person must know more than did a person in the past. The ability to read and speak well is not adequate. The ability to cope effectively with the demands of a complex society requires that the individual know more facts, develop more concepts, and possess more problem-solving skills than in the past. He must be able to use this knowledge on the job, in running a household, in making purchases, and in participating in an ever more difficult and complex political process.

Another point to consider is that the individual must have different kinds of knowledge than he has needed previously. In the past, a stable, rather unchanging society could provide standards or known "best" ways of coping with living in that society. Today, since change is occurring so rapidly, a much greater load is placed upon the individual to make individual decisions about conditions and choices that have not existed before. The odds are great that a person will have to change careers at least two or three times during his working life, and the careers or jobs available may not have existed a year or two before. New choices and conditions now exist in the use and cost of energy. What kind of energy is the best for heating a house and running appliances? The choice of a car, with sky-rocketing fuel prices and, for that matter, with rapidly rising costs of new and used cars, has become more difficult. In the economics of home management, choices and decisions are more difficult in this era of rising food and appliance costs. The situations in which decisions must be made seem to change on a daily basis, and the conditions that existed to guide one's decisions a short while before have now also changed. The need is for a kind of knowledge that makes it possible for a person to learn and to adapt after he has completed his education. He must know how to identify problems, gather the information necessary to solve the problems, and have a way to evaluate realistically the usefulness of possible solutions. The individual must be able to function much more on his own and deal with a much wider variety of problems. Additionally, he must have a much better idea of how to use the agencies and people available to help him in the society. He has to be able to identify the kind of help he needs, the agency or people who can best help him, and the best way to approach them for help.

People have much more choice about the way in which they wish to live and will probably have more alternatives in the future. Twenty years ago, people had fewer options than exist today, and the predictions are that many more options will exist in the future. The numbers of careers and jobs are much greater, the numbers of leisure-time activities available are greater, geographic mobility is much greater, expression of sexuality is less controlled by society and greater options exist for the individual, and the kinds and numbers of things that an individual can own are much greater. The control which the family and society exerts upon the individual has decreased significantly; much more is left to the individual.

Another point of need results from the change from a rural society to an urban society. Only about ten per cent of our population now lives on farms or in small towns; most people live in cities or in the suburbs surrounding them. This means that even now people must live in the midst of large numbers of people; in addition, our population is expected to reach more than 300 million by the year 2000. One has to live with, meet, get along with many more people than in the past. An important aspect of the situation is that the cities and suburbs are made up of groups of people who come from a great variety of very different backgrounds and who have very different values and ideals. They come from all occupations, wide varieties of ethnic, religious, and racial backgrounds, and approach life in different ways. A person who wishes to live in such a setting (or who must because of the social situation) has to know much more about other groups of people than was true in the past. He must be given knowledge in school that makes it possible for him to get along effectively with a wide assortment of people.

KNOWLEDGE-CENTERED EDUCATION. For the educator, these changes in society mean a pressure to provide students with knowledge about people that was of little or no concern to the schools in the past. Most educators, as a result, have tried to increase the amount and kinds of learning that children get in school.

Most Americans feel that the schools should teach their children the kinds of knowledge that are used by those who have succeeded in society through obtaining power, authority, and financial security.[9] Parents seek the kind of education for their children that makes it possible to read and speak well, to use mathematics to advantage, to influence others, and to obtain good jobs, and positions of influence and power. If the child learns these, then the parents believe that the child is getting a "good" education and that his chances of succeeding as an adult are good. One of the most important aspects of this outlook is that there is an important aggregate of facts and information which must be "passed on" to one generation from another. If the schools do their job, knowledge will be passed on in the same form as it is used by the persons who are currently successful in coping with society. The knowledge gained will help each child to become an adult who has the opportunity to get the best of things from society and to be better off than his parents were.

Therefore, many of the critics of our schools have emphasized the need for more rigorous pursuit of knowledge and have stressed the need to teach more in less time. The three R's are considered of great importance by these critics, and deficiencies in ability to read, to write, and to use arithmetic have been seen as the major fault in the schools. Because of this concern that children learn the "fundamentals," much of the money distributed by the federal government for education has been used to support programs and curriculum development that benefit those groups of people who have had the largest deficiencies in reading and in computation: the "educationally disadvantaged."

No matter what the new program has been, federal funds have been expended to solve a specific problem, but have not been oriented toward reforming the whole school system. Such programs as "the new math" were developed to teach mathematics more effectively, especially so that more people could understand the mathematics needed in a computer-oriented society. The "new" programs in the physical and biological sciences had much the same purpose: to improve

[9] Sizer, op. cit., pp. 39–50.

the levels of knowledge and understanding of science and to provide more scientists.

Most of these programs were greeted as better approaches to the teaching of existing areas of content so that pupils would "learn" them better than before. They have been accepted in the schools quite readily and their use is widespread. Such programs as "Man: A Course of Study" in the social studies, however, have not met the ready acceptance of the other programs, and there is much controversy over the use of this program in particular. Much of the controversy has arisen because the program emphasizes affective and personal education, not factual or socially useful knowledge in the traditional sense.

Needs for Affective and Interpersonal Education. "Man: A Course of Study" centers much of its concern around the need for quality education to provide the kinds of learning that make it possible for people to understand both others and themselves in order to get along with many people who have many different backgrounds and beliefs. Additionally, there is the essential concern that people must "feel good" about themselves if they are to get along effectively with others. At the most extreme, critics with this point of view appear to think that knowledge as it has been offered in the schools is of little or no value, but that, in fact, schools have been terrible places where good feelings about oneself and about others have been destroyed. These critics think that the schools are oppressive, antidemocratic, authoritarian places where some important and basic elements of being human are literally "killed." They feel that independence, creativity, and feelings of self-worth are destroyed by the schools, and they insist that more human conditions must be created if schooling is going to prepare children for a good life in a democratic society. Such critics think that learning should be fun and also think that all children want to learn. They believe that the schools should be primarily concerned with positive mental health and that good mental health is needed before any "real" learning can occur.

These critics are extremely optimistic in their outlook toward children and extremely pessimistic about the way they see children being treated in schools now. They stress that the best way to teach children to live in a democratic society is to make the schools democratic for children and to take away the authority and power now held by adults in the schools. They feel that students must "experience" democratic living in the schools to learn what it is supposed to be, not merely hear it described. The schools should provide a living example of democracy: students should have as much voice as the adults have in deciding rules of conduct, in deciding what should be learned, in deciding how much time should be spent on any one task, and in deciding who should be in any learning group (both teacher and student). The students should be prepared to "participate" in democracy as individuals. The students should be made aware of their own worth; they should be aware of their own capacity to decide what is best for themselves by themselves; and, they should know that they can make good and useful decisions for themselves which benefit society as a whole. People who hold such views believe strongly that many of our social problems arise from a lack of social and personal skills. They believe that children do not learn to interact appropriately with others; that the interactions which pupils have with adults in school are abnormal and are not the kinds of interaction which are useful for adults; and that the students do not learn how to use their own unique skills and personal traits in ways which make them productive adults.

Because of the way children are treated in schools, these critics consider that children lose any belief in their own worth and lose the ability to learn and grow. It is believed that, in too many cases, the children learn that they are inferior as human beings and that they must rely upon other people to make their decisions for them and to judge their worth. The belief is that the schools present the child with an "unreal" living situation and with knowledge which is unimportant. As a result, when children complete their schooling, they are not ready to function in our complex social settings. Two issues are raised: the need for what is done and learned in school to relate directly to what is necessary to live in society, and the need of each individual to be loved and respected if he is to love and respect himself.

One of the arguments put forward for this point of view is that some people who are deemed well educated by virtue of their good grades and advanced degrees have failed to make moral and ethical judgments which take into consideration the needs and welfare of other people and of society as a whole. To illustrate this point, one has only to look at the people involved in the "Watergate" episode which so badly affected our country. All of the people involved in that catastrophic happening were considered well educated, but they certainly did things which had very bad effects upon the whole country. Other observers raise questions about the ability of our producing scientists, of all sorts, to make decisions which really benefit the whole society. The conclusion that they draw is that people who are successful in our educational system appear to emerge from their educational experience as dehumanized, partial people who know all sorts of facts, have knowledge of how to manipulate others through management techniques, but who do not know and respect themselves and others as totally human. Such critics' recommendations for changes within the schools include the following:

1. The schools should operate in a way which gives each child the experience of living in a true democracy.
2. Each child must be known by the adults as a person who is of worth and who is respected.
3. Teachers must give up much of their power and authority and share them with the students.
4. Individuals can learn from one another, no matter how old or experienced the individual is; children and teachers should all be both learners and teachers.
5. The individual student is the one person who knows most about his own needs, capacities, and potentials.
6. True learning is unique and comes from within the individual.
7. Each person must be taught that he is of worth in the same purposeful way that he is taught mathematics and reading.

THE SCHOOL AS A DEMOCRATIC ENVIRONMENT. Current thinking about the schools and about democratic treatment of children can be seen in the attempt to create a "bill of rights" for children. If the student is to learn how to behave in a democratic way, then our institutions, including schools, must provide an experience which is democratic. The four conditions described by Silberman and mentioned earlier in this module, particularly the fact that children are "forced" by law or social pressure to attend school, make it difficult to create a situation in which students can be given an opportunity to experience a real democracy. Students have no choice—they must be in school. Additionally, it is very seldom that a student gets any choice about what school he will attend. So, to begin with, the pupil is in a place spending time doing something he has no choice about.

If a person is really supposed to learn something that will result in changed behavior, certain conditions must exist. Facts and concepts about appropriate behavior must be learned, and then the individual must have an opportunity to practice those concepts. He must be allowed to make mistakes, be given feedback which identifies both the mistake and better ways of behaving, and then be given more chances to behave in appropriate ways. The school should be set up so that each student has ample opportunity to take part in making daily decisions and in establishing the activities and rules by which the schools operate.

The work of John Bremer at the Parkway Program in Philadelphia, and the adaptation of the Parkway ideas in the Shanti School in Hartford, Connecticut, illustrate an application of the democratic approach in American secondary schools. In both Parkway[10] and Shanti[11] the schools are structured in such a way that all people in the schools (teachers, students, administrators) have a real voice in setting policy and regulating day-to-day school life. Students gather in small groups which meet regularly to determine what courses should be offered, to decide who is to teach them, to go into the community to find places where classes can meet, to determine rules of conduct, and to take major responsibility in making sure everyone follows the rules. If rule infractions are made by any person (again, student, teacher, or administrator), the students take responsibility for meting out discipline. Courses offered may include history, mathematics, language, and science, since the students know these are necessary to get into a college. However, other courses such as music, photography, journalism, psychology, and back-packing, may be given by people who are expert in these fields, but not necessarily certified teachers hired by the school system.

Additionally, students in these schools take a major responsibility in selecting teachers, evaluating a teacher's performance, and making recommendations for teacher improvement.

Student involvement in running such schools is extensive. It is important, however, to realize that these schools are not located in traditional school buildings, but are located in facilities that are scattered throughout the whole community in which the student will have to function as an adult. A headquarters must be established; Shanti's is an unused portion of the railroad station, but classes are conducted all over the city. Some are held at the railroad station, others in local colleges, some in the control tower of an airport, others in psychologists' offices, artists' studios, and some in the other three high schools of the city. One of the purposes of this kind of school is to give students direct experiences in identifying the resources available in their city, learning how to obtain use of those resources, an opportunity to have real experiences in dealing

[10] John Bremer and Michael Von Moschzisker, *The School Without Walls* (New York: Holt, Rinehart & Winston, Inc., 1971), pp. 11–27.
[11] Citizens' Committee for Alternative Schools, Hartford, Conn., unpublished working paper.

with the complexities of getting things in the urban environment, and an opportunity to practice verbal and social skills in a real setting.

It is evident that the students in such a school have much more authority and power than do students in most schools. But one of the important parts of learning in these schools is the acceptance by participating students of responsibility for the consequences of the way in which all of the students respond to this use of authority and power.

Although these examples describe schools at the secondary level, many of the same ideas have been tried in the lower grades under the name of *open education*. These open schools operate on the premise that children at all levels of education can be taught in a purposeful way. The only way to do this, however, is to teach the children how to identify problems, to think of possible solutions, to test the solutions with other people, and then to try out the answers or decisions with the full knowledge that pupils have to take the responsibility for the consequences of their decisions.

THE STUDENT AS A WORTHY PERSON. Where open education has been successful, a school and a class atmosphere has been created in which each student is highly regarded by every other person and thinks highly of himself and of every other person. Many schools give very little opportunity for students to feel worthy, and appear to emphasize that the only people of real worth are the adults. As a result, children come to believe that they are not worth much, especially since most of the comments they receive about their efforts and behavior are negative—"You're not trying hard enough," "Your work is sloppy," "You have to do better." A "natural" aspect of teaching in these schools seems to be to give the negative information but to give very little positive feedback to the child. Children (and adults, for that matter) need to receive praise to know they have done a good job, to know they are making progress, and to know that making mistakes is a part of learning.

In addition to the fact that praise is given much less often than negative comments are given, praise, when given, is not always consistent or always appropriate to the behavior. The teacher defines proper behavior, proper learning, and proper expression of that learning, but too often our post-Puritan ethic predisposes all adults to feel that too much praise is worse than none at all. B. F. Skinner[12] writes extensively about this reluctance to give praise, and states that the reason he has become so concerned about applying his theories to the classroom is his observation that so much of the interaction between the teacher and student was either neutral or negative in feeling. He feels that learning without pleasant consequences that are experienced regularly and often is ineffective, if not downright impossible.

Carl R. Rodgers,[13] who has a much different point of view in psychology, also gives much attention to the need for the teacher to assist the child in learning by giving positive, pleasant reports about his learning, behavior, and progress. He points out that this is how a child learns of his own worthiness and develops the capacity to learn and grow more. The only way a child can develop the internal drive to learn more is to have experiences which show him that he can learn and

[12] B. F. Skinner, *The Technology of Teaching* (New York: Appleton-Century-Crofts, 1968), pp. 17–19.

[13] Carl R. Rogers, *On Becoming a Person* (Boston: Houghton Mifflin Company, 1961), pp. 115–123.

that learning is rewarding and productive for him. He further points out that a person who is highly productive and who is willing to exert himself and take the "risks" which exist in learning and growing must be able to accept himself as a worthy person. But, the child can learn that only from the adults and others around him. We learn of our worth and believe we are good only if important people in our lives (teachers, administrators, and parents) interact with us in ways which show that they think we are worthwhile. The problem, as Rogers sees it, is that in most of our schools teachers usually behave in such ways that communicate to children the feeling that they are not worth much. In very personal ways, the pupil learns that he is wrong more often than right, that his feelings are not important enough for the teacher to listen to, and that he must behave in a very narrow range of behaviors if the teacher is to think him worthy. The lack of attention given by most teachers to the students' feelings of joy and elation, anxiety and tension, or fear and sorrow places severe blocks in the path of learning. If the individual student is to feel secure enough to tackle new tasks and try to learn new things, he must be assisted by the teacher and be expected to grow.

Rosenthal and Jacobsen[14] illustrate the results of teacher expectation upon a child's performance in school. They show the relationship between what a teacher expects and the amount a child grows in learning and intellectual capability. The result of teacher expectation is a self-fulfilling prophecy: the teacher expects the child to learn or not to learn and the child performs as the teacher expects.

TEACHERS GIVING UP AUTHORITY. The preceding discussion concerns the need for the teacher to give up much of his authoritarian role. The teacher who wants the student to share and take responsibility in the classroom must give up some large parts of his own authority to the students. Since most of us have been taught in all of our school experience by an authoritarian system, it seems almost "unnatural" for us to teach any other way. We ourselves have little experience in learning in situations in which we have to take responsibility for our own learning, so changing our own behavior as teachers may be difficult. However, Silberman[15] points out that once we do really become less authoritarian, teaching is much more fun, and that most people who have made the change would not go back to their former authoritarian relationship with students. In making the change, the teacher finds himself free of the need to be all-knowing and defensive about how much he knows. He is free to use many more sources of information and learning, and, most importantly, he can let students take over much more responsibility and authority for classroom conduct of learning and behavior without fearing disaster. In fact, he finds that more learning takes place, pupils work harder, and the teacher gets more rewards for his "teaching." He becomes a guide and a helper, not a manipulative enforcer. The amount of learning and the ways in which learning takes place are greater and richer.

ALL INDIVIDUALS AS LEARNERS AND TEACHERS. One important aspect of the idea that the teacher should not be as authoritarian is that all individuals in the classroom (both adults and children) are both learners and teachers. All people have knowledge, information, and skills that can help others to learn, and each

[14] Robert Rosenthal, and Lenore Jacobsen, *Pygmalion in the Classroom* (New York: Holt, Rinehart & Winston, Inc., 1968), Chaps. 1–4.
[15] Silberman, op. cit., pp. 271–272.

person can learn things that are valuable from any other person. The teacher cannot behave as if he stopped learning at the end of college. Instead, he must show in as many ways as possible that he is still learning and growing on a daily basis. He must interact with other teachers, administrators, and other adults, and, most importantly, he must show students that he is learning from and with them. This means that the teacher must value what the student has to offer and let him know that something has been learned. The teacher must behave in such a way that the child knows that his unique background and knowledge are recognized as important and worth sharing and knowing about.

A second part of the "learning" teacher is that he must keep up with new knowledge in his subject matter field and in theories and applications in teaching methodologies and in the psychology of learning. All fields of knowledge have changed significantly over the past twenty years, and changes are occurring at an ever-increasing pace. This writer has time and again come across teachers considered "good" by some who have read nothing about their fields or teaching in general for ten or fifteen years. As a result, they have found themselves out of touch and confused by "new" methods and curricula that have been introduced in their schools. Additionally, although they have received praise for being good teachers at the beginning of their careers, they are finding that neither administrators nor students now think they are doing a good job.

The other side of the coin is that of the student as learner and teacher. If democratic learning situations are to be established, each individual must be given the chance to share the special things he knows with other students. Each child comes to the school with a large store of information and experience that can be used in a meaningful way by having the student share this in helping other children to learn. In some cases, a student can be of more help than an adult, because he is more aware of the difficulties in learning than is the adult.

Herbert Kohl[16] points out that children bring to the classroom many abilities useful for learning and helping others to learn, and that the traditional authoritarian classroom can destroy the child's opportunity to use and develop these abilities. Kohl further points out that in doing what the teacher, alone, defines as learning, "real" learning may be made impossible for the child. The cliché that one learns more when trying to teach others appears to be as true for children as it is for teachers. A child's own knowledge and understanding is of great value in making sense of new things to be learned by the child himself and by other children. If a teacher understands and respects the pupil's ability to "give" in the classroom and then creates a situation in which the child can "give," much more learning will take place. This means that the teacher must keep quiet and listen much more of the time than has been the case in the past.

THE INDIVIDUAL AS A SOURCE OF KNOWLEDGE ABOUT HIMSELF. A great problem for any teacher is the discovering of what a child already knows, how much he can learn in a particular span of time, and whether or not the child has learned what is presented. In the past, people thought that the teacher could be most effective if he learned how to give tests in the classroom, and then used and interpreted standardized tests of achievement and intelligence. Many educators

---

[16] Herbert Kohl, "The Open Classroom, A Practical Guide to a New Way of Teaching" (New York: *New York Review* 1969), pp. 11–13. (A New York Review Book distributed by Vintage Books, NYR 103, February 1971.)

believe, though, that such sources of information as standardized tests are not only misleading, but in reality prevent the teacher from getting to know the child in any real way. The point made is that test scores and grades do not tell much about a child. Therefore, teaching that attempts to get a child to learn on the basis of such scores is doomed to failure. Standardized achievement and intelligence tests are scored in terms of "norms." The children facing a teacher in the classrooms, however, simply do not fit those norms because of differences in family background, in ethnic background, and in social experiences. The way in which this knowledge is put together inside the child is unique for each individual, and the ways in which the child learns best are dependent upon how previous knowledge is "stored" inside. These critics insist that the best way to find out what learning and information a child possesses is to find out from the child by getting to know him very well.

In *36 Children,* Kohl[17] points out that standardized tests can be and are misused in such a way that the children who take them suffer. A child who has been taught how to take tests, no matter what kind, can do better than a child who has not been told the best way to take a test. Additionally, Kohl points out that the tests do not really make sense to most children since they seem to have little to do with what usually happens in school. As a result, many children see them as useless exercises that do not really make sense, or, worse, they find themselves fearing the tests and experience high degrees of anxiety about them. Kohl advocates teaching students to take tests and explaining to children why the tests are given and for what purpose they are used. He believes that this would help the children to do better and to be less afraid of tests.

One of the most undesirable results of use of standardized tests is that the teacher can develop an unrealistically low expectation of the students. Instead of learning from the pupil and setting expectations by that knowledge, the teacher sets his expectations from the test scores, which may give an unrealistically low prediction of how well and how much the child can learn.[18] The biases and inaccuracy of predicting success, which are a part of the tests, can be avoided if the teacher works directly with each student to get the same kinds of information. Most responsible writers indicate that so-called I.Q. test scores have little relationship with ability to learn. They do, however, relate fairly well to a child's ability to get good grades in the schools as they have been operated in the past.

TRUE LEARNING ARISES FROM INSIDE THE INDIVIDUAL. One of the greatest concerns of teachers has been finding ways to motivate the child to learn. This is considered a major responsibility of the teacher, and with twenty-five to forty students sitting in front of him, the teacher has found that task very difficult. Teachers have tried to create motivation by using "stars," grades, or putting a child's work on the bulletin board in the belief that these kinds of things should work. They do work for some students, but unfortunately not for all. Holt[19] feels that interest is the most important single thing that will motivate a child to learn. He thinks that the children should be allowed to select the topics and activities in which they are most interested. Kohl[20] points out that if you remove pressure

[17] Herbert Kohl, *36 Children* (New York: New American Library, 1967), pp. 176–78.
[18] Rosenthal and Jacobsen, op. cit. pp. 1–4.
[19] John Holt, *How Children Learn* (New York: Pitman Publishing Corp., 1969), pp. 185–189.
[20] Kohl, op. cit., p. 109.

in the form of grades or scoring minus points for mistakes, and in public review of work, then, *all* children can learn and will be motivated to learn increasingly more as they gain confidence in their ability to express themselves. Silberman[21] maintains that, in well-run open classrooms, children become interested in doing things which are important to them; and that these are the things which will make it possible for them to act as adults—reading, writing, and using numbers. The children will know what they must know when they become adults and must be allowed to learn these things in their own way. Children will learn things which interest them, and most children are extremely interested in becoming adults and being able to do the things that they see adults do. In these situations, the teacher acts to make it possible for each child to have the books, paper, pencils, and other things which will facilitate learning. The teacher provides a focus on what is needed to become an adult as the one adult most available for children to learn from. If the open situation is to work, however, the teacher has to work harder in preparing materials and in getting to know each child than is the case in the self-contained classroom as it has existed. The more responsibility and freedom the student has, the more work the teacher has to do.

TEACHING EACH INDIVIDUAL THAT HE IS OF WORTH. The final emphasis of all of these points of view is that it is the teacher's job to create activities and situations which encourage the student to believe in his own worth and in his capacity to not only learn, but to learn in his own way. Somehow, the teacher must create a school setting which makes it possible for every child to feel that he is capable and has all those qualities which go together to make a good human being. If a person is expected to get involved in hard learning, he has to believe that he can succeed. Stotland[22] points out that a person will really work at something if he thinks it is important to him and if he believes the chances are good that he can succeed. If the person thinks he cannot achieve a goal, no matter how important that goal is, he will not work at it. Instead, the person will be highly anxious, and high anxiety will cause him to try to escape from the situation or will make it impossible for the individual to make realistic attempts to reach the goal.

If the child is free to learn, the learning goals have to be known to the child and he must know that he has a really good chance to reach them. The best way to make sure that the child can really reach a learning goal is to be very aware of the child's own knowledge of his abilities, rate of learning, and style of learning. The teacher has to help the child be realistic in his knowledge so that this reality will lead the child to feel good about himself and face the challenge of new learning willingly and without fear. For many critics, the child's feeling good about himself and about others is more important than any other kind of learning that can occur in school. He cannot learn the other things he needs to know unless he feels good about himself and about others first!

Moderate Instructional Systems

The positions described in the previous parts of this module are the extreme viewpoints, which contend that we should either stick with what we have now or

---

[21] Silberman, op. cit., pp. 265–322.
[22] Ezra Stotland, *The Psychology of Hope* (San Francisco: Jossey Bass, 1969), pp. 7–13.

change what we are doing completely. As these extremes have been tried in class-rooms and schools, it has become evident that neither extreme provides the answers we seek. There are large numbers of writers and programs in use which take positions between the extremes and stress both kinds of learning described earlier. None of the approaches seems ideal, but they have been tried and can work under the conditions by which most schools operate. Each of the proposed systems puts the teacher in a different position and demands something different from the school, so before going further, we shall discuss a systematic way to analyze systems of instruction so that we can make more sense out of their purposes and uses.

The system discussed here is taken from one described by Joyce and Weil,[23] and it should help you as you try to make your own decisions about what is best for you and for your pupils when you become a teacher.

In the remainder of this module, you will be asked to analyze the various proposals for teaching and learning in the classroom, according to the following factors:

1. What aspects of student learning and the school environment are emphasized most?
   a. What are the goals for the student?
   b. What attributes of the environment are most important for the student in reaching these goals?
2. How does the proposed system work when actually used?
   a. What activities are required?
   b. Are there specific beginnings and ends to activities?
   c. What things must the teacher keep thinking about while doing the activities?
3. What are the general rules the teacher should use to react to the students as they work or study? How should the teacher respond to the things students do?
4. What kinds of authority does the teacher have in his relationship with students?
   a. What are the different things that teachers and students are supposed to do?
   b. What are the desired behaviors and performances that are enforced?
   c. Who starts activity?
5. What kind of and how much training must the teacher have?
6. What are the special results that are supposed to come from the particular plan of instruction?
   a. What are the direct results of instruction?
   b. What are the indirect results of instruction?

Systems of Instruction from Theories in Developmental Psychology. Some very important proposals for teaching have come from theorists in developmental psychology and human development. These scholars place an emphasis upon the ways in which people develop because of biological/physiological growth and learning which occurs as a result of coming into contact with people and things in the environment.

Learning and development are two distinctly different aspects of human growth. Development is considered to occur because there are changes in the person's neurological and physiological structure. Learning is considered to be a result of the individual's interaction with other people and things in the world around him. Learning, however, cannot occur unless the neurological and

[23] Adapted from Bruce Joyce and Marsha Weil, *Models of Teaching* (New York: Prentice-Hall, Inc., 1972), pp. 13–26.

physiological development of the individual has progressed to a point that makes learning possible. The individual must be ready physiologically and neurologically if he is to change through learning.

It is proposed that growth occurs because of *active interaction* of the individual with his surroundings, whether with people or with things. In order to learn, the individual must be able to "get his hands on" the environment and manipulate it in one way or another. The change called learning occurs when he faces a *disequilibrium,* or a situation that does not fit with previously known experiences inside the individual. The person must then change in one of two ways: by *assimilation,* which is by fitting the new experience into the framework that already exists in the individual; or by *accommodation,* which is by changing what is inside a person to "fit" the world outside the individual.

Another concept is that, as development occurs over a period of time, the way one can use his nervous system and intellectual capacity changes in an orderly way. Intellectual capacity changes from being able to deal with very concrete, tangible things in the environment to being able to deal with the environment in abstract ways, using language and generalized rules. One of the necessary components of this development is a child's very active exploration and interaction with people and with things. The final concept in the theory is that development for an individual is uneven across and between the various stages of development. This *decalage* means that children will at times act as if in several stages of intellectual development at once and be using different levels of intellectual development.[24]

Jerome Bruner[25] has a theory which is in many ways similar to Piaget's. However, Bruner believes that a child's active interaction with people and with things is much more important in the school setting and that the teacher can get children to learn more things faster by preparing materials and experiences which increase the child's readiness to learn.

Both of these men place great emphasis upon involving the child in active exploration of the environment and upon the child's ability to learn by finding out important things themselves through discovery learning.

If we use for analysis the Joyce and Weil format, presented on page 285, we develop the following:

1. The student's need to "do" things is very important, and the environment should be set up so that each child can do many different things for short periods of time.
   a. The goals for the student are to do things such as use tools and implements, try out different ideas and ways of working, confront problems and solve them in his own way.
   b. The environment should be full of materials and things from which the child can select to help him solve problems he encounters. The materials and things should be selected so that they will help lead the child in the right direction.
2. When actually used, the system demands that a) children be allowed to

---

[24] Irene Athey and Duane Rubadeau, *Educational Implications of Piaget's Theory* (Waltham, Mass.: Ginn/Blaisdell, 1970), pp. xiv–xxi.

[25] Jerome S. Bruner, *The Process of Education* (New York: Vintage Press, 1960), pp. 38–54.

select their own activities as long as they are related to finding answers to problems important in their learning; b) activities should be in defined sets centered around certain problems; and c) the teacher should be very aware of what questions the student is raising, and think of ways to respond to questions that will lead to learning and understanding.

3. The teacher should remember that the child should keep asking questions and should use the materials to help answer the questions. The teacher should not give answers, but should request the child to find out if the questions and possible answers he has seem right.
4. What kinds of authority exist?
    a. Teachers are supposed to set up the materials and problems so they can be understood and used to answer problems found. They are also supposed to create an atmosphere in which no questions or solutions are wrong but help in learning.
    b. The desired behaviors enforced are questioning, sticking to the task, thinking in one's own way about the question and possible answers.
    c. Activities are started by the teacher when materials are handed out and the task described.
5. The teacher must be very thoroughly trained in the subject matter being studied, must be trained to give direction, to listen carefully, and to avoid being the all-powerful answer giver.
6. The special results should be
    a. direct: the children should find meaning in the activities; the learning should be in their own frame of reference, and in terms of generalizations, not memorized facts.
    b. indirect: the children should have confidence in their ability to think and learn; they also should learn "ways of learning" which they can use in the future.

One criticism of this approach, as it has been used in "Man: A Course of Study," has been made by Richard Jones.[26] Jones feels that the stress upon cognitive learning gives too little attention to the students' feelings and attitudes. Piaget and Bruner feel that this experience of dealing directly with the environment is important not only in developing knowledge, but also because it is the way by which individuals learn to know about and manage their feelings and their affective or emotional life.

Piaget's approach has been used as the basic explanation for the use of open classroom teaching in both England and the United States. Bruner's ideas have been much more widely used at the secondary school level in such programs as the Biological Science Curriculum Study (BSCS), the Physical Science Study Committee (PSSC), and "Man: A Course of Study."

Systems of Instruction from Theories in Cognitive Psychology. Cognitive psychology is probably the most traditional in its outlook toward teaching and learning, and in many ways the people presenting cognitive theories have been most in touch with what has been, and currently is, the most standard method of teaching in the schools. These theories stress the learning of skills and knowledge

---

[26] Richard Jones, *Fantasy and Feeling in Education* (New York: Harper & Row, Publishers, 1968), p. 18.

that have usually been taught in the schools, and give evidence of concern that there is a great deal for children to learn. They stress "efficient" learning of facts, ideas, and concepts. Although there is a major emphasis upon cognitive learning, some theorists do place an emphasis upon the importance of dealing with feelings and the affect as an important support for cognitive learning.

David P. Ausubel states that each individual has a unique internal organization that has great effect upon the way in which he can and does learn.[27] This *cognitive structure* is made up of the person's past learning and experience, as it is different for each person. He points out that if a person is to learn, the new things to be learned must be related to that which already exists in the individual's cognitive structure if it is going to make any sense. New things to be learned must be related to, fitted in with, or attached to something which already exists within the person's cognitive structure. Instruction can be either "rote" or "meaningful." However, things can be learned by either "reception" or "discovery." Ausubel makes the point that either reception or discovery learning can be rote or meaningful.

He describes rote learning as the kind in which the new learning makes no sensible connections with what the individual already knows or what already exists in the cognitive structure. As a result, the new learning cannot be related to anything that the person already knows or hooked into the existing framework of knowledge.

Meaningful material to be learned is essentially the opposite of rote. It makes sense in terms of what is already known; it can be put into the existing system in sensible ways; and there are "hooks" in the cognitive structure which help the child learn.

Ausubel also points out that there are two kinds of meaningfulness with which the teacher must be concerned: logical and psychological. Logical meaningfulness deals with the way the new material is presented to the child to be learned. It must be related to that which is already known or learned and must be related to the general ability of any human beings at the particular age level to learn it. It makes possible the connecting of new things to be learned with ideas and concepts already known.

Psychological meaningfulness is individualistic. It is the individual student's ability to learn something that is logical in meaningfulness and to make it a part of his own unique cognitive structure. Something that is logical in meaning cannot be learned unless it makes sensible connections with what already exists in a particular individual.

The result of this outlook is that the teacher cannot be satisfied that he is doing a good job if his presentation is only organized and logical. It must also fit the psychological structure of each individual; the student must be ready. Additionally, Ausubel stresses the participation of the student in learning. He must be actively involved in the whole process if he is to learn effectively.

An important discussion on the application of cognitive learning theory to classroom teaching is described in the book, *Mastery Learning: Theory and Practice,* edited by James Block.[28] Mastery learning is an attempt to improve the

[27] David P. Ausubel, *Educational Psychology: A Cognitive View* (New York: Holt, Rinehart & Winston, Inc., 1968), pp. 37–41.
[28] James H. Block, ed., *Mastery Learning: Theory and Practice* (New York: Holt, Rinehart & Winston, Inc., 1971), pp. 13–22.

chances of really learning in the classroom and to provide the incentive and opportunity for each student to master the new material at his own pace and in his own style.

Benjamin Bloom, in a chapter of this book, points out that most of the current teaching methods in the schools create an experience of failure for most students—about two thirds of them. This two thirds simply do not achieve the goals which teachers set as desirable. Bloom feels that if mastery learning techniques are used, then 75 per cent of all students can be expected to do as well as the top 20 per cent are now doing, dramatically decreasing the failures. The most important point is that the methods suggested have been used successfully in regular schools with classes of thirty or so children.

In implementing mastery learning, instead of giving each student the same amount of time to learn, as we do in most classrooms, teachers arrange things differently and let each student work at his own pace. It has been shown that learning ability is not related to measured I.Q. or measured scholastic aptitude. Instead, Block proposes that it is related to the amount of time needed to learn. If you give most students enough time, they will be able to master the material and learn it very well. If you do not give the student enough time to learn, however, he will not be able to learn the material well enough. This status of learning is described in the following formula:

Degree of Learning $= f$ (*time actually spent*).

According to this formula, if you give people the time needed, nearly all students can learn as well as only the top students are now learning. To better explain what can happen with different individuals, Block adds some other factors that relate to specific characteristics of the teacher, the child, and the materials to be used which can affect learning.

Degree of Learning $= f$ 1. *Time Allowed* 2. *Perseverance*
3. *Aptitude* 4. *Quality of Instruction*
5. *Ability to Understand Instruction*[29]

The terms *perseverance, aptitude,* and *ability to understand instruction* all relate to the individual. They appear reminiscent of the "psychological meaningfulness" described by Ausubel. How long will the student work at the task? Will he give himself enough time? How fast can he learn? Can he learn in the time he spends with the new material? Can he understand the instructions? Can he read what is given to him? Does he understand the vocabulary the teacher uses? Does the teacher make sense to him?

The *time allowed* and the *quality of instruction* are up to the teacher, however. The quality of instruction is a very important part of the logical meaningfulness.

Block describes six important aspects of mastery learning:[30]

1. Mastery is defined by the particular educational objectives which each student is supposed to achieve;
2. Learning material must be organized into well defined units;

[29] Ibid, pp. 5–9.
[30] Ibid, pp. 2–3.

3. Complete mastery of the material in each unit should be reached before the student goes on to another unit;
4. A diagnostic progress test, which is ungraded, should be given to make sure the student knows how he is doing;
5. On the basis of the diagnostic progress test each student should be shown what he is doing right or wrong; and
6. The amount of time allowed for learning is adapted to each student.

Bloom[31] points out that several important emotional or affective results are achieved by such a system. Interest is increased because the student's confidence in his own ability to cope with learning tasks is increased. For the student, successful learning experiences make it possible for him to use what he has learned to learn more. Since the student has had positive experiences in school through this system, his attitudes will be positive and he will be willing to get involved in more school learning activities. If the student can experience consistent success, his self-concept will be positive and he will feel good about himself. The success must be experienced over extended periods of time, however. If this happens, then the experience the child has in school will lead to sound mental health.

To summarize, we will use the Joyce and Weil format, previously described, to analyze the cognitive models applied to the classroom.

1. The important aspects of learning and of the school environment are
   a. Goals for the student: mastery of particular facts, ideas, and concepts; precise knowledge of what he has to do; and an opportunity to work at his own pace;
   b. Attributes of the environment: a high degree of structure about what to do, plenty of time in which to do it, and a lot of dialogue between teacher and student about the student's progress.
2. How does the system work when used?
   a. The activities required are that the student must study and work at learning, presented in short units; he must stick to the task until finished, and he must check his progress with the teacher.
   b. Activities are centered around specific, rather short-term learning projects with very definite beginnings and ends.
   c. The teacher must be thinking about such things as the goals of learning, encouraging the student to keep working, helping pupils when they get stuck, keeping pupils informed of progress, and making learning a positive, successful experience for the child.
3. As a general rule, the teacher should react and respond to the students in the following ways: she should stress the importance of learning and the student's ability to learn, encourage the student to keep at a task until successful completion, give supportive correction and direction, let the child know that he has finished successfully, and then assign new tasks.
4. What are the kinds of authority teachers and students have? They are just about the same as in the usual classroom.
   a. Teachers are supposed to decide what is to be learned, in what order things are to be learned, and when a student has mastered certain learn-

---

[31] Ibid, pp. 13–22.

ings. The student is expected to work at the tasks assigned by the teacher and keep at the task until he has mastered the material.

   b. The behaviors and performances enforced are learning prescribed things, sticking to a task, and completing assigned work.

   c. The teacher starts students on tasks, but the rate of work may vary; different children may be studying or working at different tasks, and children chose when to stop.

5. What kind of training and how much must the teacher have? Training in the subject matter, since he must break it down into small units; training in how students learn and develop so that learning can be presented at an appropriate level and in an appropriate form; training in setting instructional objectives and in evaluating the achievement of those objectives.

6. What are the results?

   a. Direct results should be an increased level of cognitive learning by all students, an increased interest in learning, better development of self-concept in children, and enthusiasm and respect.

   b. Indirect results should be fewer discipline problems, less competition among students, and less anxiety.

Systems of Instruction from Theories in Social Psychology. A final set of ideas about how teaching and learning should take place has come from people who are concerned about the way in which an individual interacts with other people and the ways in which these interactions affect a person's ability to function in groups of people. These theorists feel that we must include direct teaching of social skills in school as well as the traditional cognitive skills.

Professor Judith Henderson phrases this concern as "preparing children for healthy social-emotional development" and points out that we must educate people as directly and purposefully for this as we do for cognitive reasons.[32] She defines three areas of specific need for social-emotional development:

1. Self/other exploration: a) seeks new experience with diverse people, environments, and ideas; b) seeks new data regarding human feelings, beliefs, and values from the new and diverse experiences.
2. Self/other respect: (a) accepts human behavior by expressing and allowing for the expression of diverse feelings, beliefs, and values; (b) supports human behavior by helping oneself and others pursue personal goals.
3. Self/other responsibility: (a) can describe the predictable effects of one's intended and actual behavior on self and others; (b) takes action to increase constructive intentions and behaviors while decreasing destructive intentions and behaviors for self and others.[33]

To achieve these goals, the teacher must create a large number of activities, make sure the students understand the activities, and ensure that the activities achieve specific goals. These activities should provide situations in which a reality of social interaction can be experienced, but should not create undue anxiety or tension for the students. Field trips, visits from different people, opportunities to

[32] Judith Henderson, "On Doing More Than Complaining About Man's Inhumanity to Man," unpublished (East Lansing, Mich.: Michigan State University), pp. 1–3.
[33] Ibid, p. 4.

do things with children of different socioeconomic and ethnic backgrounds, and provision of opportunities to exercise responsibility must be made a part of the classroom and school experience.

Another way of teaching these things has been proposed by William Glasser, who describes the "Classroom Meeting."[34] This system is oriented toward the individual, but uses group membership and interaction as a way of establishing goals for students, as a way by which goals can be made clear, and as a way to ensure that the students will try to achieve the goals. The basic idea of the approach is that a child cannot feel worthwhile or be worthwhile unless his behavior is acceptable to other people. The six steps in Glasser's method provide that

1. First and most fundamental would be the development of a warm, positive *involvement* within the classroom group, including the teacher.
2. The group must concern itself with *present behavior* rather than emotions.
3. The child must make a *value judgment* on his own behavior, what he is doing now that contributes to his failure.
4. The child must *select a better course of action.*
5. The child after identifying and selecting a better way must make a *commitment* to enact it.
6. Once the value judgment, the selection, and the commitment to behavioral change are made, the teacher who cares exercises *discipline,*[35] accepting no excuse for nonperformance.

The *Classroom Meeting* is demanding for the student, but the demand upon the teacher is also great. It places great emphasis upon a warm, supporting teacher who is also firm and who will carry through on agreements once commitments have been made. The approaches of both Henderson and Glasser demand that we make a purposeful attempt at social education.

There are several other methods for teaching social participation and interaction in the classroom while, at the same time, achieving particular cognitive goals in the standard school subjects. The major difference in these from the other methods, which are moderate approaches to changing process in the schools, is their increased emphasis upon the learning of social skills.

If we use the Joyce and Weil format to analyze these kinds of methods, we find the following:

1. Both the traditional school learnings and social, cooperative skills are emphasized. However, the social skills receive a much greater emphasis than in most other models.
   a. The goals for the student are that he learn specific facts and concepts that are traditional, but that he learn how to work cooperatively with other people and that he learn specific social skills which appear to be of great importance if he is to be a productive, well-functioning adult.
   b. The most important attribute of the environment is that the teacher must be a warm person who listens to and accepts student feelings as stated, but assists the students in placing these feelings within the context of the feelings and needs of the rest of the group.
2. The system works when the following take place:

[34] Joyce and Weil, op. cit., pp. 222–225.
[35] Ibid., pp. 225–226.

a. Required activities are that the student selects tasks in which everyone is involved; that the student must work cooperatively with others in achieving those tasks; that the teacher has an important role in selecting tasks, using an open, warm discussion to assist students as they work together. Also, new social experiences for the students are sought.

b. Activities must have specific beginnings and ends. Activities (whether discussions, field trips, or meeting new people at school) are started at the same time by the group, and the activities are terminated at the same time.

c. The teacher must keep thinking about the following during activities: Does the child know what he is supposed to be doing? Is he interacting with the other students and the teacher appropriately; if not, what should be done? Are the interactions open and honest, but still tactful and considerate of others? Is the teacher being supportive and at the same time providing direction?

3. The general rules that the teacher should use to react to students as they study are these: if there is confusion or conflict, a group discussion will help clarify it; social skill learning can make it easier for the child to learn cognitive materials; cooperation is more important than competition; once commitments are made to do something, the teacher must ensure that they are carried through.

4. The kinds of authority that exist provide the following:

a. The teacher is supposed to decide what goals and activities are important; he is supposed to ensure that children achieve those goals; he is supposed to be warm and concerned, but nevertheless in charge. Students are to be involved in the tasks and activities selected by the teacher, and are to be open in their relationships with students and teacher so that modification and change can be made to provide learning.

b. The desired behaviors and performances to be enforced are that teachers must be able to listen and to be patient, and that children must be able to be patient and to listen, but they are also expected to participate verbally in planning and in activities.

c. Generally, the activities will be started by the teacher.

5. The teacher must be trained in much the same way as has been done in the past as far as knowing his subject matter and being able to break it down into units that children can understand. However, the teacher must be more trained in group management, analyzing and evaluating social skills, and in providing a warm, supportive environment.

6. There are both direct and indirect results of this type of instruction.

a. The direct results are cognitive learnings in mathematics and reading, but also development of knowledge about other people, positive experiences in meeting, talking with and working with other people, and the development of specific skills which make it possible to work comfortably with others.

b. Indirect results should be a better relationship between teacher and students and between student and student; a better feeling by the student of his own self-worth; less fear and anxiety in the student about meeting with and working with different kinds of people.

Summary

Throughout this module we have stressed the things necessary in education if student-products are to be prepared to live productively in a democratic society. Generally, the public schools in America have believed that they were preparing people to live productively in a democratic society. However, during the past twenty years questions have been raised about two major aspects of the outcome of education: ability to use knowledge obtained in school which is based upon the traditional subject matter as a way of coping with a changing society; and the ability to use social skills which have not been taught purposefully in the past.

As a prospective teacher, you must be aware of the needs of children and of the skills they must have as an adult. You must sort out for yourself the things which are important and choose the content and activities of your classroom to achieve the goals you perceive as important. However, whatever you do as a teacher will be open to evaluation by other teachers, administrators, parents and children. If you do not perform in ways which meet with their general approval, the chances are great that you will not be allowed to teach for very long.

The extreme points of view presented were meant to put the more moderate views in a more balanced position, since neither of the extreme views has seemed to make much headway. The process of teaching is becoming more complex and puts a much greater load on the teacher than has ever been the case in the past.

SUGGESTED READING

Athey, Irene J., and Duane O. Rubadeau. *Educational Implications of Piaget's Theory.* Waltham, Mass.: Ginn/Blaisdell, 1970.

Ausubel, David P. *Educational Psychology, A Cognitive View.* New York: Holt, Rinehart & Winston, Inc., 1971.

Block, James H., ed. *Mastery Learning, Theory and Practice.* New York: Holt, Rinehart & Winston, Inc., 1971.

Bremer, John, and Michael Von Moschzisker. *The School Without Walls.* New York: Holt, Rinehart & Winston, Inc., 1971.

Bruner, Jerome S. *The Process of Education.* Cambridge, Mass.: Harvard University Press, 1960.

Freud, Anna. *Psychoanalysis for Parents and Teachers.* Boston: Beacon Press, 1960.

Holt, John. *How Children Learn.* Belmont, Calif.: Pitman Publishing Corp., 1969.

Jones, Richard. *Fantasy and Feeling in Education.* New York: Harper & Row, Publishers, 1968.

Joyce, Bruce, and Marsha Weil. *Models of Teaching.* Englewood Cliffs, N.J.: Prentice-Hall, Inc., 1972.

Kohl, Herbert. *The Open Classroom.* New York: The New York Review, 1969.

———. *36 Children.* New York: Signet/New American Library, 1967.

Packard, Vance, "Are We Becoming a Nation of Illiterates?", *Reader's Digest,* **104**:81–85 (April 1974).

Rogers, Carl R. *On Becoming a Person.* Boston: Houghton Mifflin Company, 1961. Rinehart & Winston, Inc., 1968.

Rosenthal, Robert, and Lenore Jacobsen. *Pygmalion in the Classroom.* New York: Holt, Rinehart & Winston, Inc., 1968.

Silberman, Charles. *Crisis in the Classroom.* New York: Random House, Inc., 1970.

Sizer, Theodore. *Places of Learning, Places for Joy.* Cambridge, Mass.: Harvard University Press, 1973.

Skinner, B. F. *The Technology of Teaching.* New York: Appleton-Century-Crofts, 1968.

Stotland, Ezra. *The Psychology of Hope.* San Francisco: Jossey Bass, 1969.

POST TEST

1. Define "education for democratic living" by describing
    a. the use of education as preparation for adulthood in society.
    b. the things an adult should be able to do as a result of his education.
    c. the way children are expected to behave in school.
    d. the way in which teachers are expected to behave in school.

2. **a.** Give three basic reasons that people use to stress the need for learning facts and ideas in order to be prepared to live in a democratic society.

   b. Give the names of the individuals cited in the module who support the ideas.

   c. Describe the failures of the schools which these individuals have said exist.

   _____

   _____

   _____

   _____

   _____

   _____

   _____

   _____

   _____

   _____

   _____

   _____

   _____

3. **a.** Give three basic reasons that people use to stress the need for learning social skills in order to be prepared to live in a democratic society.

   b. Give the names of the individuals cited in the module who support the ideas.

   c. Describe the failures of the schools which these individuals have said exist.

   _____

   _____

   _____

   _____

   _____

   _____

   _____

   _____

   _____

_____

_____

_____

_____

_____

_____

4. Describe three of the reasons that schools have been slow to adopt the ideas and methods proposed by critics of education.

_____

_____

_____

_____

_____

5. Outline the six parts of the system used to analyze teaching methods outlined in the module.

_____

_____

_____

_____

_____

_____

6. Use the six-part system of analysis to describe
   (a) a system taken from cognitive psychology;
   (b) a system taken from developmental psychology; and
   (c) a system taken from social psychology.

_____

_____

_____

_____

_____

_____

_____

_____

_____

_____

_____

7. Of the systems of teaching described in this module, select one which seems best to you.
   a. Describe the goals of education which you think are most important.
   b. Show how the system you have selected best meets those goals.
   c. Describe the school situation which would make it easiest for you to use your system well.

_____

_____

_____

_____

_____

_____

_____

_____

_____

_____

_____

_____

_____

_____

Post Test Answer Key

Module 1

1. d

2. Vertical organization refers to the route a student follows in progressing from entrance to graduation. Horizontal organization refers to the grouping for instruction at any given point or during any period of time during that progression.

3. c	**4.** d	**5.** c	**6.** d	**7.** e
8. d	**9.** a	**10.** b	**11.** c	**12.** b
13. d	**14.** e	**15.** b	**16.** c	**17.** e
18. c	**19.** d	**20.** c		

Module 2

1. Grouping by I.Q., grouping by achievement, using different types of motivation, using materials that have reading levels of the students being instructed, providing for needs and wants of various racial and cultural groups by having courses for same and extra-curricular activities for same.

2. Some schools use the I.Q. as an indicator of the student's work in relation to his ability. Some also use the I.Q. as an initial criterion for grouping.

3. There are actually five acts for individualizing instruction although only four of the five are asked for: listen, observe, diagnose, prescribe, and evaluate.

4. Individualized strategies include contracts, team teaching, programmed learning, LAP, modular scheduling, tutorial methods, and electronic evaluation.

5. In a school with a continuous program, there are few if any prerequisites. The only ones may be those such as "algebra is necessary before a student can do trigonometry." The continuous program school is characterized by using modular scheduling to accommodate individual student's needs, tutoring, independent study, accessibility of study areas to students during and after school hours, electronic evaluation and record keeping, and much use is made of individual study packets and programmed learning. A truly nongraded school would facilitate a continuous program.

6. A sequential unit is a plan of organizing learning activities so that students will progress from the simple to the complex with the end result being that students will be using higher-level mental processes during and at the end of the unit.

7. Steps for developing a Kleinway sequencing unit:
   a. Select the idea, topic, or area of study.
   b. Determine entry level.
   c. Select recall-level experiences.
   d. Direct students to prepare summaries, lists, and categories.
   e. Develop opportunities for student response.
   f. Provide situations for application of that which has been learned.
   g. Present a large idea, concept, or event for students to analyze into its component parts.
   h. Provide choices of activities for students to demonstrate their ability to synthesize.
   i. Direct students to apply criteria for evaluating tasks.
   j. Diagnose and apply remedial instruction.

8. Modular scheduling is a system of using relatively small time blocks or units to build up a period of time for each learning activity. It provides the flexibility of scheduling teachers and students of twenty-minute to 120-minute periods of activities. Conferences may be scheduled for team taught classes, shops and labs may be given longer periods, and each student may have his own personal program since modular scheduling is done with a computer.

9. Instructional packages usually concentrate on a single concept, include behavioral objectives, allow pupils to progress at their own rate, have many activities and teaching strategies, include enrichment activities, offer self-evaluation by application of criteria, and provide for repetition if mastery of subject matter is desired.

10. A nongraded school is characterized by having no grade designation for subjects and no failure by grade but, rather, individualized progress.

11. Organizations for individualized study or independent study: (a) All independent study sections are scheduled. (b) A definite section for various areas of interest would be scheduled with students selecting the area for investigation. Students are not scheduled to meet with a teacher but select a teacher and consult with the teacher when needed. (c) Students are scheduled for independent study period and are free to consult any person on or off the school campus.

Module 3

1. Interaction analysis is a system of studying the factors of the teaching situation, particularly the verbal behavior of teachers and students, to determine the relationship between and the action among teachers and students.

2. The ten categories are acceptance of feeling, praise or encouragement, accepting ideas, asking questions, lecture, giving directions, criticizing or justifying authority, student response, student initiation, silence or confusion.

3. See pp. 58, 59, 60.

4. Shows that much student talk has been stimulated by the classroom activities.

5. **a.** Fails to meet criteria numbers 1, 2, 3.
   b. Meets all criteria.
   c. Fails to meet criteria numbers 1, 2, 3.

6. Alternative schools to the so-called traditional schools include the open school, vocational schools, technical schools, specialized curriculum schools, school without walls, such as:
   culture oriented—Asian Component in Berkeley, California.
   career education—Milwaukee Vocational School, Milwaukee, Wisconsin.
   basic skills—Berkeley, California.
   special area skills—any college prep high school in any town or city.
   specialized curriculum—Fine Arts High School in New York City.

7. Hair may be regulated only if long hair is a disruptive influence or constitutes a health or safety hazard. List of litigation is in *School and Society,* volume 100, p. 92. For case about hair involving student's rights see *Meyers* v. *Arcata Union High School District* 269 Cal. 2d 549, 75 California Reporter. 68 (1969).

8. Principals can search students' lockers. In *People* v. *Overton,* 249 N.E. (2d) 366 (1969), the court held that principals could search if there was even a suspicion that there might be something illegal in the locker. In the case *In Re Donaldson,* 75 Cal. Rptr. 220 (1969), search was held to be proper if thought that misconduct is related to the contents of the locker.

9. No. *Schwartz* v. *Schuker,* 298 F. Supp. 238. (E. D. N. Y. 1969).

10. The intent of the performance contract law of Arizona is to ensure that each classroom has a competent teacher. It is intended that each teacher be evaluated for what the district determines to be competency and that the teacher meets the standards of recertification.

Module 4

1. Gaming and simulation consists of games to simulate certain phenomena in an effort to learn about the phenomena.

2. Game theory is a mathematical theory which quantitatively determines the play necessary for a contestant to minimize his losses regardless of what play his opponent makes.

3. John von Neumann.

4. A split occurred between game theory and simulation gaming due to the mathematically oriented research associated with the former and the non-mathematical research associated with the latter.

5. Mathematical and nonmathematical.

6. The nonmathematical.

7. Gaming and simulation refer to games that simulate social and business phenomena in an attempt to learn about the phenomena in a qualitative way.

8. The American Management Association.

9. Manual games are less expensive than computer games and they may also be played anytime and place without regard to computer availability.

10. General management games, functional games, industry games, bureaucracy games.

11. Political science, sociology, psychology, anthropology, education.

12. **a.** Instructor participation.
    b. Instructor intervention.
    c. Players' disregard for the rules of the game.
    d. Alienation and apathy.

13. **a.** Simulation gaming may well be looked upon as role playing on the basis that the rules are very nearly the same: the description of the various roles that are to be played is a major aspect of simulation games such as those mentioned in Question 10.
    b. Role playing is a tool of psychology, is generally designed to allow an individual to gain insight into another's point of view, and the roles are generally much less elaborate than the role descriptions of business games.

14. **a.** (Student opinion).
    b. (Student opinion).

15. Simulation gaming is a learning or teaching method wherein games that simulate social and business phenomena are played in an attempt to learn about that phenomena.

16. Programmed instruction may be defined as any form of instruction, textbook, machine, or computer, such that the student may learn by himself, proceeding through sequential tasks to a higher level of proficiency.

17. The behaviorist school of psychology provides the theoretical basis for programmed instruction.

18. B. F. Skinner, a psychologist of the Behaviorist school, was a pioneer in programmed instruction.

19. Homme and Glasser describe the typical programmed text as follows:

> Its external appearance will not differ from an ordinary textbook, but its interior is quite different. Each page consists of *n* (usually four or five) panels; the sequence of the panels is not from the top of the page to the bottom as in a conventional textbook; only one panel is 'read' or responded to before the student turns it. The student begins with the top panel on page 1, responds to it, turns to page 2 to get his answer confirmed on the top panel, goes to the top panel on page 3, responds to it, confirms his answer by turning the page, and so on, to the end of the unit or chapter, where he is instructed to return to page 1 and respond to the second panel on each page, and so on. . . .

20. A linear program in a programmed text consists of a single sequential path wherein the student responds to one question after another, and the path is exactly the same for anyone who participates in the program. Branching, or "intrinsic," programs are flexible. If a student passes a test question, he goes on to the next question; if he misses the question, the program reteaches him and then retests him before he moves on to the next item.

21. Contingencies of reinforcement have been defined by Skinner as the relations that prevail between behavior and the consequences of that behavior.

22. Programmed instruction is often condemned on the grounds that the process of shaping behavior through the impersonal use of machines is a dehumanizing activity.

23. Ideally, the teacher's role under PI changes considerably in that he becomes free to spend more time with individual students. In practice, the teacher's role may retain many of the functions of the traditional teacher.

24. The major constraint is that concerning motivation in that a program by itself quickly exhausts its ability to motivate continued participation.

25. (Student opinion).

26. (Student opinion).

27. Two outstanding advantages of PI are those of remediation and enrichment; programmed texts may be made available to students with a minimum of time expenditure on the part of the teacher.

28. PI has been used extensively in the areas of mathematics and reading.

29. Computer-assisted instruction is a form of programmed instruction that utilizes computers rather than programmed texts and other mechanical teaching machines.

30. The hardware of CAI consists of the computer; the software consists of those programs which have been prepared for the computer.

31. **a.** Record keeper and retriever of information.
    b. Laboratory computing device.
    c. Tutor.
    d. Simulation.

32. Administrative uses of computers represent the most common utilization of the technology in education today.

33. **a.** Mathematics.
    b. Computer related.
    c. Health professions.
    d. Physics.
    e. Foreign languages.
    f. Chemistry.

34. Large numbers of CAI programs are available in those disciplines wherein the practicioners are well schooled in mathematics or computer technology, such as the areas of mathematics, science, and medical technology.

35. Simulation gaming has apparently become an effective teaching tool although there still does not seem to be any conclusive research to substantiate this.

Module 5

1. b	**2.** d	**3.** (3)	**4.** e
5. e	**6.** b, c, e	**7.** a, c, e	**8.** e
9. b	**10.** a	**11.** d	**12.** e
13. e	**14.** c	**15.** e	**16.** d

Module 6

1. c	**2.** b	**3.** d	**4.** a	**5.** a
6. d	**7.** a	**8.** a	**9.** c	**10.** b
11. b	**12.** c	**13.** c	**14.** d	**15.** b
16. a	**17.** d	**18.** c	**19.** b	**20.** d

Module 7

1. b	**2.** d	**3.** b	**4.** a	**5.** d
6. a	**7.** e	**8.** e	**9.** e	**10.** d
11. a	**12.** c	**13.** a	**14.** a	**15.** c

Module 8

1. c	**2.** a	**3.** a	**4.** a	**5.** c
6. b	**7.** e	**8.** c	**9.** a	**10.** b or c
11. a	**12.** b	**13.** c	**14.** d	**15.** e

Module 9

1. a. It informs them about what others are doing.
   b. It gives teachers an opportunity to gain merit.
   c. It predisposes them to change.

2. a. It reminds innovators that success may not follow immediately upon implementation.
   b. It stimulates innovators to work for removal of the impediments to success of innovation.
   c. It reminds innovators not to abandon a project merely because it has been tried before.
   d. It reenforces the necessity for increased effort with older staff members who remember the lack of success with this innovation when it was previously implemented.

3. a. Student interest, morale, and achievement will be improved if they are permitted to pick electives from a broad range of selections that are high in interest values.
   b. Teachers can make more valuable contributions to student schooling if they are permitted to develop courses they want to teach, drawing upon their own areas of interest and specialization.
   c. Grouping for the multielective courses will be of the natural order, based upon interest, not upon grade level or student age.
   d. Teachers serving as course leaders will serve as guidance counselors.

4. a. It keeps departments from overlapping in offerings.
   b. It insures coverage of minimum essentials in each field.
   c. It prevents irrational growth by accretion.
   d. It prevents sacrifice of knowledge to lure of popularity.
   e. It enables students to satisfy the prerequisites for each course.

5. a. Successful teachers will have to confer with students to ascertain their interests in order to prepare a course.
   b. Teachers will have to "sell" potential courses to uncommitted students during advisement period.
   c. Teachers will have to respond to student reaction to course to keep it well patronized.

6. Mini-courses will improve the teaching profession by forcing teachers, who have failed to reach their potential through lack of motivation, to produce. It will also force teachers who are lacking in talent to withdraw from the staff since few will patronize their classes.

7. Natural-order grouping is the type reflective of everyday social life in which people with like interests, regardless of age or social class, gravitate towards each other. It differs from regular school groupings which cluster people in accordance with variables other than interest, e.g. age, aptitude, sex, skill. When natural-order grouping is done in schools, grade, age, and ability designations are ignored and ninth grade boys and girls are clustered with tenth, eleventh, or twelfth grade boys and girls.

8. a. A student knows at the end of seven weeks whether or not he has passed for that unit.
   b. A student who fails a unit may repeat that unit or substitute a new unit for the one he has failed.
   c. A student may change courses after three weeks if he so desires.
   d. A student can avoid the "long corridor of failure."

9. a. Purchases in bulk can produce savings for a school.
   b. Increased and more intensive services can be obtained from the large staff.
   c. Large school budgets can provide for purchase of unusual esoteric equipment.
   d. Larger student population can insure an adequate membership in some programs with limited appeal.
   e. Higher salaries, possible because of larger budget, permit recruitment of staff with increased quality of preparation.

10. a. Administration is too far removed from the students, separated by too many layers.
    b. Anonymity is common.
    c. Staff doesn't get to know the student body.
    d. Bureaucratic provisions replace face-to-face interaction among staff.
    e. Factions and cliques, which introduce conflicts, are formed among larger departments and groups.

11. a. Brings the administration and faculty closer.
    b. Provides large population for esoteric course.
    c. Brings files and records closer to point of use.
    d. Makes all House faculty responsible for all students.
    e. Lets staff participate in educational planning in three levels.
    f. Tends to contribute to growth of esprit de corps.
    g. Makes possible the gains attributed to bigness and also to smallness.

12. In the vertically organized House, students are drawn from each of the grades enrolled in the total institution and represent a cross section of the large school. In the horizontally organized school, each grade is organized into a house and administered as a completely self-contained, self-sufficient school.

13. a. Counselors in each house remain with the same students for three or four years and build understandings.
    b. The ratio of students to counselors is reduced.

  c. More teachers will participate in the guidance function because of the change in atmosphere about the school.

  d. Interaction between counselor and teacher is increased in the house plan.

  e. The proximity of administrators makes it easier (hence, quicker) to process disciplinary cases.

  f. School behavior over-all is improved since student anonymity is eliminated by the reduction in size and change to intimate atmosphere.

14. a. Trauma and confusion of large schools, associated with opening week sessions, are minimized.

  b. Slipping through without really trying or passing becomes more difficult.

  c. School spirit is increased.

  d. There are increased opportunities for students to assume leadership roles.

  e. Faculty members assume more personal responsibility for student progress, behavior, and activities.

  f. The best of two worlds, large and small, becomes possible.

15. a. Features functional variations in period length.

  b. Permits variations in time of meeting.

  c. Permits variation in number of meetings per week.

16. a. It is conducive to correlation of subject matter.

  b. It saves time for learning by eliminating the passing time between periods.

  c. It facilitates group guidance sessions.

  d. It provides opportunities for student-teacher and parent-teacher conferences.

  e. It is easier to schedule field trips, films, and assembly programs.

  f. It puts responsibility for some scheduling in the hands of teachers.

17. a. Stress instruction leading to economic independence.

  b. Emphasize personal fulfillment.

  c. Encourage an appreciation for the dignity of work.

  d. Prepare students for employment upon graduation if they elect to seek it.

  e. Help students prepare themselves to shift careers several times during their lifetime.

  f. Make preparation for making a living a worthy and acceptable goal of education.

  g. Focus on an integration of the values of a work-oriented society into the value structure of each child.

  h. Emphasize the career implications of the content of each subject.

  i. Bring the vocational and the academic components of the school into greater harmony.

  j. Introduce opportunities for practice in career decision making.

18. Primary grades: Awareness of work.

  Introduce students to local workers from various occupations and professions.

  Lower-middle grades, four to six: Awareness building continued.

  Study five basic occupational clusters—industry, commerce, social science, services, arts.

Upper-middle grades, seven to nine: Exploration.

Select eight from the list of twelve clusters of related careers for exploratory study.

High School, ten to twelve: Career prep.

Narrow inquiry to just one of the eight clusters previously explored for an in-depth study.

Module 10

1. f

2. a. Combines best features of self-contained classroom with best features of departmentalized organization.
b. Emphasizes and provides time for field trips.
c. Emphasizes self-understanding.
d. Provides more opportunities for self-direction and places more responsibility for learning on student.
e. Offers expanded number of electives to satisfy exploratory function.

3. a. Ability to stimulate curiosity.
b. Ability to guide inquiry in depth.
c. Capable of responding to student crises of a personal, emotional, or physical nature.
d. Skill in student guidance.
e. Capable and willing to reveal tenderness and interest while supervising.
f. Capable of demonstrating enthusiasm in daily or routine activities.
g. An intellectual interest in a wide variety of scholarly disciplines.
h. An advanced degree of knowledge in at least one discipline.
i. Skillful in teaming with other teachers.

4. Grades six through eight; five to eight; sometimes four to eight.

5. Any five of the following:
a. Continuous progress.
b. Flexible schedules.
c. Independent study.
d. Creative experiences.
e. Auxiliary staffing.
f. Positive and nonthreatening evaluations.
g. Multimedia methods.
h. Team teaching.

6. a. Each individual can learn according to his maturity level.
b. Each individual can learn according to his personal style.
c. Each individual can follow his own interests.
d. Each individual can read at his own reading level.
e. Each individual can learn to understand himself in relationship to others and to his world.
f. Motivation for study can become intrinsic.

    g. Neither the quick nor the slow students are hindered in their study.
    h. Involvement in planning can help insure effort in study.

7. a. Each teacher has a chance to use his individual competencies.
    b. Facilitates the guidance and counseling function.
    c. Makes it possible to resolve teacher-pupil personality conflicts.
    d. Makes it possible to use special teachers to better advantage.
    e. Enables teachers to schedule classes and group students according to teaching goals.

8. a. Each student can be scheduled according to the amount of time needed for his specific learning.
    b. Provides flexibility for large group, small group, and independent study sessions.
    c. Puts scheduling in hands of teachers who know the time requirements necessary for the objectives they have in mind.
    d. Tends to diminish the amounts of compartmentalization found in the subject matter curriculum.
    e. Encourages correlation of teaching goals among teachers.

9. A comprehensive high school is one which offers secondary education for almost all of the children of high school age in a town or school district; provides appropriate education, both academic and vocational, for all young people within a democratic environment. No student is stigmatized because of the sequence he chooses; no student is prohibited from electing courses which meet his needs; no caste results as consequence of programs elected.

10. a. There has been an exodus of students to the suburbs which has removed a large number of the college-bound.
    b. There has been a large influx of students from rural and Southern areas who are not highly motivated to receive or profit from schooling.
    c. There has been an exodus of highly qualified and experienced teachers from the inner city.
    d. In many cases, the defeatist spirit of the ghetto has been permitted to enter and thrive in the school.
    e. Financial difficulties have forced serious cutbacks in many well-established programs.

11. Many students preparing to graduate from the general curriculum programs in 1961 will be forced upon the adult world ill-equipped to find a compatible role to fill. With no training in the technical skills required for employment in a technological era and with no interest in further education as a means of preparing for the learned professions, these high school graduates will probably gravitate in short order toward the incendiary point.

12. (1) e   (2) d   (3) c   (4) b   (5) a

13. The false dichotomy which has emerged in many comprehensive high schools makes technical, vocational, and business education compete with academic education from a position of inferiority. As a consequence, the aims of education are changed and the goals of the comprehensive school are thwarted.

Gifted students who could use the technical courses in preparation for their professions are prohibited from crossing lines. Other students who could profit from technical and business training refuse to elect such courses because of the stigma attached to them.

14. a. Students could be grouped by ability.
   b. Differentiated instruction to meet individual needs could be offered.
   c. Daily class sessions could become more effective because the fast would not be forced to mark time nor the slow to lack understanding.
   d. Capable students would not waste their time in shallow courses.
   e. Slower students could escape from constant failure because of the modification of instruction possible.

15. Many educators opposed the track system because of the havoc that it perpetrated upon the comprehensive school. The most immediate and dramatic consequence was the segregation of students along color and social class lines. White, middle- and upper-middle-class college-oriented students gravitated toward the upper tracks and black, lower-middle and lower-class students found themselves in the lower tracks. Courses for the latter group were watered down to a severe degree and left students poorly prepared to take their place as participating citizens upon graduation.

16. Your answer should reflect your recognition of the difference between "tracking" as it was and "phasing" as it can be.

Module 11

1. g   **2.** f   **3.** e   **4.** a   **5.** a and d   **6.** c   **7.** b   **8.** a, c, f, g, j
9. a, b, d, e   **10.** a, c, d, j   **11.** a, b, c, d   **12.** b, c, d, e

13. The new humanities program is expected to "unfreeze the school" by moving many of the activities outside of the four walls of the school. As a consequence, the role of the student will change. Instead of passive listener to teacher lectures, the student will be expected to question and discuss and become an active inquirer into issues that are vital to mankind's survival.

14. a, c, g

15. The aggressive, destructive, and violent positions taken by recent products of the high school and by some youths still enrolled in school caused most educational thinkers to reexamine the school programs which were turning out such products. Leading spokesmen for the schools began stressing an increased concern for human values, for human interests, for cultivation of feelings of self-worth and self-identity as a way to eliminate the root causes of dissatisfaction.

16. (Any five of the following.)
   a. They are designed for and offered only to seniors or upper-level students.
   b. They consist mostly of single course offerings.
   c. They focus primarily upon literature and art.

    d. They rely upon tests for recall to demonstrate mastery, as much as do other courses.

    e. Very few have integrated the behavioral sciences into the philosophy, art, music, and literature programs as interdisciplinary efforts.

    f. Few have made provisions for multigrade efforts.

    g. Few have chosen the problem-solving route, preferring instead the fact-accumulating method.

17. a, b, f.

18. a, b, e, f.

19. Any seven of the following:

    a. Efforts of faculty to improve communication between students and faculty.

    b. Growth of interest and desire of faculty to know and utilize strengths and weaknesses of each student.

    c. Change from domination of action by initiating adult to catalytic and guidance role.

    d. Replacement of limited uniform programs with multicourse, multioption, multischeduled programs.

    e. Concern and provision for different modes of learning.

    f. Willingness to adapt programs to provide for individual differences.

    g. Provisions for using differing individual strengths of different teachers.

    h. Introduction of continuous progress opportunities.

    i. Elimination of noncompetitive systems of reporting.

    j. Abandoning the fear and failure system of motivation.

Module 12

1. a. Education is preparation for living in society and ours is democratic.

    b. To be verbally sophisticated; possess good reading and language skills; fill out forms; read contracts; verbally interact with large numbers of people; must know more now than in past; has to use knowledge for more sophisticated problem solving and continued learning; must make more personal decisions; must be able to live in the middle of large numbers of diverse people.

    c. Four conditions outlined by Silberman: schooling is in groups; is required; requires time; requires evaluation. Students should read and speak well, use mathematics, emulate people who have made it in society; follow proper form, understand other people and themselves; feel good about themselves and others; be independent; enjoy learning.

    d. Teachers should ensure that learning occurs; provide varieties of experiences for students; show concern and respect for the individual student; give direct experience in democratic living; give knowledge about democratic living; give children as much authority as possible; teachers should "learn" with the children.

2. a. Need for more verbal sophistication; need for more complex use of mathematics; more things to be learned and known; different kinds of knowledge needed; must know more to decide among the many new jobs and careers; must know more to handle the tasks of daily living; must be able to make more complex decisions more often; must be able to handle a more complex urban-technological society in general.

   b. Silberman: reforms really have not worked; Sizer: parents and children want cognitive skills, have not felt they are getting them; Packard: too many young people cannot read and use language.

   c. Children have not learned the skills needed, too many cannot read well, too many have found school a hateful place, they cannot perform on the job; cannot get and keep jobs.

3. **a.** Any of the seven reasons given in outline on page 278, and discussed more completely up through the middle of page 284.

   b. *Bremer:* more authority and power to students; an opportunity to select and make decisions about all matters concerning the school program.
   Skinner: not enough positive reward or attention given to students.
   Rogers: not enough positive pleasant reward; discourage children from stretching themselves and taking risks. Do not let children learn of their own worth.
   Rosenthal and Jacobsen: do not expect enough, thus children perform at lower levels because the teachers expect them to do poorly.

   c. A negative, failure-oriented system; too much authority; teachers stop learning; teachers really do not get to know and trust children.

4. The conditions have remained constant in four aspects: groups, requirement to attend, evaluation, and time. Most Americans feel the schools have done a good job. Schools can change only to meet the needs of society; schools are not the places to initiate change.

5. Your outline should include all of the parts included in the outline on page 285.

6. Your responses should include the general responses found in:
   a. Cognitive psychology: pp. 287–291.
   b. Developmental psychology: pp. 285–287.
   c. Social psychology: pp. 291–293.

7. Your responses will have to be discussed with other students or your instructor. They should include:
   a. Attainment of cognitive skills in language, mathematics, science; social history; self-development; development of self-worth. You should also point out which of the goals are most important, next in importance and so on.
   b. Show how the system you have chosen meets those goals in theory and in practice, as indicated in the analysis on page 285.
   c. Describe the type of school situation which would be best for you concerning the authority relationships between administrators, teachers, students; reliance on certain types of evaluation; the ways in which you could use your time.